THE 850 BLUEPRINT

THE COMPLETE GUIDE TO REPAIRING CREDIT AND ACHIEVING THE ULTIMATE BORROWING POWER

GARRY JORDAN

Printed in the United States of America.

TABLE OF CONTENTS

CHAPTER 1

THE CREDIT FOUNDATION

What Is Credit And Why It Matters

Credit is far more than just a number on a report, it's the financial reputation that follows you throughout your adult life. At its core, credit represents your demonstrated ability to borrow money and pay it back according to agreed-upon terms. This simple concept has evolved into a complex system that influences nearly every major financial decision you'll make.

Your credit profile serves as a proxy for trustworthiness in the eyes of lenders, landlords, employers, and even insurance companies. It's a shorthand way for these entities to assess risk without having to personally know you or conduct extensive background checks. Understanding this fundamental truth is the first step toward mastering your financial future.

The modern credit system operates on the principle of shared information. When you apply for credit, make payments, or default on obligations, this information flows through an intricate network of data collection and reporting systems. Your credit report becomes a living document that tells the story of your financial behavior over time.

The History Of Credit Reporting In America

The credit reporting system didn't emerge overnight. Its roots trace back to the 1800s when local merchants would share information about customers who failed to pay their debts. These informal networks evolved into regional credit bureaus that collected and distributed information about borrowers within specific geographic areas.

The transformation into our modern system began in the 1960s with the advent of computer technology. The three major credit bureaus, Experian, Equifax, and TransUnion, emerged as dominant forces, each developing sophisticated systems to collect, store, and distribute credit information on a national scale.

The Fair Credit Reporting Act of 1970 marked a watershed moment in credit history. This landmark legislation established consumer rights and created the regulatory framework that still governs credit reporting today. It recognized that credit reports had become too powerful to operate without oversight and consumer protection.

The introduction of credit scores in the 1980s, particularly the FICO score created by Fair Isaac Corporation, revolutionized lending decisions. Instead of manually reviewing credit reports, lenders could now use mathematical models to quickly assess risk and make lending decisions. This automation enabled the massive expansion of consumer credit that characterizes today's economy.

How Credit Impacts Every Aspect Of Your Life

Credit's influence extends far beyond traditional lending. Understanding these impacts is crucial for appreciating why credit repair and optimization matter so much in modern life.

***Housing and Real Estate*:** Your credit score directly affects your ability to rent apartments, secure mortgages, and even determine the interest rates you'll pay. A difference of just 50 points in your credit score can mean tens of thousands of dollars in additional interest payments over the life of a mortgage. Landlords routinely check credit reports to assess whether prospective tenants are likely to pay rent on time.

Employment Opportunities: Many employers, particularly in financial services, government, and positions requiring security clearances, review credit reports as part of their hiring process. Poor credit can disqualify you from certain jobs or promotions, especially those involving financial responsibility or access to sensitive information.

Insurance Premiums: Most insurance companies use credit-based insurance scores to set premiums for auto, homeowner's, and other types of coverage.

Studies have shown correlations between credit behavior and insurance claims, leading insurers to charge higher premiums to those with poor credit histories.

Utility and Service Deposits: Utility companies, cell phone providers, and other service companies often require security deposits from customers with poor credit. These deposits tie up your money and represent an additional cost of having damaged credit.

Business and Entrepreneurship: Personal credit often determines your ability to start a business, secure business loans, or even rent commercial space. Many business credit cards and loans require personal guarantees, making your individual credit history a crucial factor in business success.

The True Cost Of Bad Credit

The financial impact of poor credit extends far beyond higher interest rates. When you calculate the true cost of bad credit over a lifetime, the numbers are staggering and serve as powerful motivation for credit repair efforts.

Interest Rate Penalties: The most obvious cost comes in the form of higher interest rates on loans and credit cards. A person with excellent credit might qualify for a mortgage at 3.5% interest, while someone with poor credit might pay 6% or higher. On a $300,000 mortgage, this difference translates to approximately $150,000 in additional interest payments over the life of the loan.

Limited Access to Credit: Poor credit doesn't just make borrowing expensive, it can make it impossible. This limitation forces people into predatory lending situations, including payday loans, title loans, and other high-cost alternatives that can trap borrowers in cycles of debt.

Opportunity Costs: Bad credit creates opportunity costs that are difficult to quantify but enormous in impact. You might miss out on a dream home because you can't qualify for a mortgage, or you might be unable to start a business because you can't access capital. These missed opportunities can alter the trajectory of your entire life.

Deposit Requirements: Poor credit often requires substantial deposits for utilities, cell phones, and apartment rentals. These deposits represent money that could otherwise be invested or saved, creating an additional burden on those who can least afford it.

Employment Limitations: In competitive job markets, poor credit can be the deciding factor that costs you a position. The income difference between jobs can be substantial, and being passed over for credit-related reasons can have long-lasting career implications.

Common Credit Myths Debunked

Misinformation about credit is widespread and can lead to costly mistakes. Addressing these myths is essential for developing an accurate understanding of how credit really works.

Myth: Checking your credit hurts your score. This persistent myth prevents many people from monitoring their credit regularly. In reality, checking your own credit report results in a "soft inquiry" that has no impact on your credit score. You should check your credit reports from all three bureaus at least annually, and more frequently if you're actively working on credit repair.

Myth: Carrying a balance improves your credit score. This costly misconception leads people to pay unnecessary interest charges. Credit scoring models don't distinguish between accounts that carry balances and those that are paid in full each month. What matters is having active accounts that report payment history, not whether you pay interest.

Myth: Closing old accounts improves your credit. Many people believe that closing unused credit cards will improve their credit scores. In reality, closing accounts can hurt your score by reducing your available credit and potentially shortening your credit history. Old accounts in good standing should generally be kept open.

Myth: You only have one credit score. Consumers often speak of "their" credit score as if it's a single number, but you actually have dozens of different credit scores. Different scoring models, different versions of the same model, and different data sources all produce different scores. Understanding this multiplicity is crucial for interpreting score variations.

Myth: Credit repair companies can remove accurate information. While credit repair companies can help dispute inaccurate information, they cannot legally remove accurate negative information from your credit report. Be wary of any company that promises to remove accurate information or guarantees specific results.

The Psychology Of Credit And Financial Behavior

Understanding the psychological aspects of credit and debt is crucial for long-term success in credit repair and financial management. Our relationship with money and credit is often deeply emotional and influenced by factors beyond pure logic.

The Pain of Payment: Research shows that people experience physical discomfort when spending money, particularly when using cash. Credit cards reduce this "pain of payment," making it easier to overspend. Understanding this psychological tendency can help you develop strategies to maintain awareness of your spending even when using credit.

Present Bias and Future Discounting: Humans naturally place more value on immediate rewards than future benefits. This tendency, known as present bias, can lead to decisions that prioritize short-term gratification over long-term financial health. Credit repair requires developing the ability to make decisions based on long-term benefits rather than immediate desires.

The Debt Trap Mentality: Once people fall behind on their financial obligations, they often develop a fatalistic attitude that makes the situation worse. This "debt trap mentality" can lead to avoidance behaviors, such as not opening bills or checking credit reports, which only compound the problems.

Social and Cultural Factors: Your family background, cultural context, and social environment all influence your relationship with credit and debt. Understanding these influences can help you identify and overcome limiting beliefs about money and credit.

The Role of Financial Education: Many credit problems stem from simple lack of knowledge about how credit works. The complexity of the credit system, combined with inadequate financial education in schools, leaves many consumers vulnerable to making costly mistakes.

Developing a healthy relationship with credit requires acknowledging these psychological factors and developing strategies to work with, rather than against, your natural tendencies. This might include automating payments to overcome procrastination, setting up alerts to maintain awareness of balances, or working with a financial counselor to address deeper psychological barriers to financial success.

The foundation of successful credit repair lies in understanding that credit is not just about numbers and algorithms, it's about human behavior, legal rights, and the complex systems that govern financial relationships in our society. With this foundation in place, you're ready to begin the journey toward credit restoration and optimization.

As we move forward in this guide, we'll build upon these fundamental concepts to develop a comprehensive understanding of the credit system and the strategies needed to achieve and maintain excellent credit. The path to an 850 credit score begins with mastering these foundational principles and applying them consistently over time.

CHAPTER 2

THE CREDIT REPORTING ECOSYSTEM

The Three Major Credit Bureaus: Experian, Equifax, And Transunion

The American credit reporting system is dominated by three major credit bureaus, each operating as a private, for-profit company that collects, stores, and sells consumer credit information. Understanding how these bureaus function, their similarities and differences, and their role in the broader financial ecosystem is essential for anyone seeking to optimize their credit profile.

Experian is the largest of the three bureaus globally, though its market share in the United States is roughly equal to its competitors. Founded in 1996 through the merger of TRW Information Systems and Experian UK, the company has built its reputation on innovation and consumer-facing services. Experian has been particularly aggressive in developing direct-to-consumer products, including credit monitoring services and the Experian Boost program, which allows consumers to add utility and phone payments to their credit reports.

Experian's database contains credit information on more than 220 million Americans, making it one of the most comprehensive repositories of consumer financial data in the world. The company generates revenue through multiple channels: selling credit reports to lenders, providing risk management services to businesses, and offering consumer products directly to individuals seeking to monitor or improve their credit.

Equifax, established in 1899, is the oldest of the three major bureaus. Originally founded as the Retail Credit Company, it evolved from a small Atlanta-based firm into a multinational corporation. Equifax has faced significant challenges in recent years, most notably the massive data breach in 2017 that exposed the personal information of 147 million Americans. This incident highlighted the enormous responsibility these companies have as custodians of sensitive financial data.

Despite these challenges, Equifax continues to play a central role in the credit reporting ecosystem. The company has invested heavily in security improvements and has focused on developing advanced analytics and machine learning capabilities to better serve both lenders and consumers. Equifax maintains credit files on approximately 200 million Americans and serves thousands of lenders, employers, and other entities that rely on credit information for decision-making.

TransUnion rounds out the trio of major credit bureaus. Founded in 1968, TransUnion has positioned itself as the most technology-forward of the three bureaus. The company has made significant investments in artificial intelligence and data analytics, developing sophisticated fraud detection systems and alternative credit scoring models that consider non-traditional data sources.

TransUnion has been particularly innovative in the areas of identity verification and fraud prevention. The company's TrueIdentity platform offers comprehensive identity monitoring services, while its alternative credit scoring models help lenders evaluate consumers with limited traditional credit histories. TransUnion maintains files on approximately 200 million Americans and serves clients in more than 30 countries worldwide.

How Credit Bureaus Collect And Store Data

The credit reporting system operates on a massive scale, processing billions of data points each month. Understanding how this data collection and storage process works is crucial for anyone seeking to influence their credit profile through strategic actions or dispute procedures.

Data Collection Networks: Credit bureaus don't actively seek out information about consumers. Instead, they rely on a vast network of data furnishers, banks, credit card companies, mortgage lenders, auto lenders, collection agencies, and other entities, to voluntarily report information about their customers' accounts and payment behavior.

This voluntary reporting system creates both opportunities and challenges. While most major lenders report to all three bureaus, smaller creditors might report to only one or two bureaus, or might not report at all. This explains why your credit reports from different bureaus often contain different information and why your scores can vary significantly between bureaus.

Data Processing and Validation: When credit information arrives at a bureau, it undergoes an automated processing system that attempts to match the data to existing consumer files. This matching process relies on personal identifiers such as Social Security numbers, names, addresses, and dates of birth. The automated systems are sophisticated but not perfect, which can lead to mixed files, where information from different consumers gets combined into a single report.

The bureaus process enormous volumes of data daily. Experian alone processes more than 3 billion pieces of information each month, updating approximately 30 million consumer files daily. This massive scale necessitates automated systems, but it also means that errors can be perpetuated across multiple systems before being detected and corrected.

Data Storage and Maintenance: Credit bureaus maintain their databases using sophisticated computer systems designed to handle massive amounts of data while providing rapid access to information. Each bureau has developed its own proprietary systems and database structures, which explains why identical information might be formatted differently across bureaus.

The storage systems are designed with redundancy and security in mind, given the sensitive nature of the information and the regulatory requirements governing credit reporting. However, the sheer volume of data and the complexity of the matching algorithms mean that maintaining accuracy across all files is an ongoing challenge.

Update Cycles and Timing: Most creditors report information to the credit bureaus on a monthly basis, typically providing updates within a few days of the statement closing date. However, there's no universal standard for when creditors must report, and some may report more or less frequently.

Understanding these update cycles is crucial for credit optimization strategies. If you're trying to improve your credit score for a specific purpose, such as a mortgage application, knowing when your creditors report and how long it takes for updates to appear on your credit report can help you time your actions for maximum impact.

The Role Of Data Furnishers

Data furnishers are the entities that provide information to credit bureaus, and they play a crucial role in determining what appears on your credit report. Understanding their responsibilities, motivations, and limitations is essential for effective credit management and dispute strategies.

Primary Data Furnishers: The most significant data furnishers are traditional creditors: banks, credit card companies, mortgage lenders, auto lenders, and retail creditors. These entities typically report comprehensive information about their customers' accounts, including account opening dates, credit limits, payment history, and current balances.

Most major creditors report to all three bureaus, but this isn't required by law. The decision to report to credit bureaus is purely voluntary, and creditors make this choice based on their own business considerations. Some creditors view reporting as a service to the broader financial community, while others see it primarily as a tool for their own risk management.

Collection Agencies: Collection agencies represent a significant category of data furnishers, and their reporting practices can have devastating effects on credit scores. When an account is charged off or sold to a collection agency, the original creditor typically reports the charge-off, while the collection agency reports the collection account. This can result in the same debt appearing twice on your credit report, amplifying the negative impact.

Collection agencies often purchase debts for pennies on the dollar, and their business model depends on collecting as much as possible from as many debtors as possible. This economic incentive can lead to aggressive reporting practices and sometimes to the reporting of inaccurate information.

Alternative Data Sources: A growing category of data furnishers includes companies that report non-traditional credit information. Rent reporting services, utility companies, and even subscription services are beginning to report payment information to credit bureaus. These alternative data sources can be particularly valuable for consumers with limited traditional credit histories.

Reporting Standards and Practices: While there are legal requirements governing the accuracy of information reported to credit bureaus, there's significant variation in how different furnishers interpret and implement these requirements. Some furnishers have sophisticated systems that ensure accurate and timely reporting, while others rely on manual processes that are more prone to errors.

The Fair Credit Reporting Act requires furnishers to follow reasonable procedures to ensure the accuracy of information they report, but it doesn't specify exactly what these procedures should be. This ambiguity has led to ongoing debates about data furnisher responsibilities and has created opportunities for consumer advocates to challenge reporting practices in court.

Credit Reporting Agencies Vs. Credit Scoring Companies

The distinction between credit reporting agencies and credit scoring companies is often misunderstood but is crucial for understanding how the credit system works and how to navigate it effectively.

Credit Reporting Agencies: The three major credit bureaus are credit reporting agencies, they collect, store, and distribute credit information but don't create the algorithms used to generate credit scores. While each bureau does offer its own credit scoring models, these represent just a small fraction of the scoring models used in the marketplace.

Credit reporting agencies are heavily regulated under the Fair Credit Reporting Act, which governs everything from how they collect information to how they respond to disputes. These regulations create specific rights for consumers and establish clear procedures for challenging inaccurate information.

Credit Scoring Companies: Companies like Fair Isaac Corporation (FICO) and VantageScore are credit scoring companies that develop mathematical models to analyze the information in credit reports and generate credit scores. These companies don't maintain credit files or interact directly with consumers in most cases, they license their scoring models to lenders, who then use these models to evaluate credit applications.

FICO, the most widely used credit scoring company, has developed numerous versions of its scoring model, each optimized for different types of lending decisions. FICO Score 8 is the most commonly used version for general lending, while FICO Score 9 incorporates some improvements in how it handles medical debt and collections. Industry-specific versions, such as FICO

Auto Score and FICO Bankcard Score, are tailored for specific types of lending.

The Scoring Process: When a lender wants to evaluate a credit application, they typically purchase a credit report from one or more bureaus along with a credit score generated using a specific scoring model. The scoring model analyzes the information in the credit report and generates a numerical score that represents the likelihood that the consumer will become delinquent on a new credit obligation.

This separation between data collection and scoring means that the same credit report can generate different scores depending on which scoring model is used. A consumer might have a FICO Score 8 of 720, a FICO Score 9 of 735, and a VantageScore 3.0 of 710, all generated from the same credit report data.

The Business Model Behind Credit Reporting

Understanding the business model of credit reporting helps explain many of the system's characteristics and can inform your strategies for working within the system effectively.

Revenue Streams: Credit bureaus generate revenue through multiple channels, with the largest being the sale of credit reports and scores to lenders. Every time you apply for credit, the lender typically purchases your credit report and score from one or more bureaus. With millions of credit applications processed monthly, this represents a substantial revenue stream.

Additional revenue comes from identity verification services, fraud prevention tools, marketing services, and direct-to-consumer products such as credit monitoring. The bureaus have increasingly focused on developing higher-margin services that go beyond basic credit reporting.

Customer Relationships: While consumers are the subjects of credit reports, they are not the primary customers of credit bureaus. Lenders, employers, landlords, and other entities that make decisions based on credit information are the primary customers. This relationship dynamic is crucial to understand because it influences how the bureaus prioritize different aspects of their business.

The bureaus do offer consumer-facing services, but these represent a smaller portion of their revenue compared to their B2B services. This business model alignment means that the bureaus' primary incentive is to serve the needs of lenders and other commercial customers rather than consumers.

Competitive Dynamics: The three major bureaus compete with each other for clients, which can benefit consumers through improved services and innovation. However, the high barriers to entry in the credit reporting industry mean that new competitors rarely emerge to challenge the established players.

This competitive environment has led to innovation in areas such as alternative credit scoring, fraud detection, and consumer services. Each bureau tries to differentiate itself by developing proprietary technologies and services that provide unique value to their commercial customers.

Regulatory Environment: The credit reporting industry operates under extensive regulatory oversight, with the Fair Credit Reporting Act serving as the primary federal law governing their operations. The Consumer Financial Protection Bureau (CFPB) has increased its oversight of the industry in recent years, focusing on accuracy, consumer rights, and data security.

State laws also play a role in regulating credit reporting, with some states having more restrictive laws than federal requirements. The regulatory environment continues to evolve, with ongoing discussions about issues such as data security, consumer rights, and the use of alternative data in credit decisions.

Understanding the credit reporting ecosystem provides the foundation for effective credit management and repair strategies. By understanding how the system works, who the players are, and what motivates their actions, you can make informed decisions about how to interact with the system to achieve your credit goals.

The next chapter will dive deeper into the specific mechanisms of credit scores and reports, building on this ecosystem understanding to provide the detailed knowledge needed for effective credit optimization strategies.

CHAPTER 3

CREDIT SCORES AND REPORTS DECODED

FICO Vs. Vantagescore Models

The credit scoring landscape is dominated by two primary scoring systems: FICO and VantageScore. Understanding the differences between these models, their various iterations, and their respective market positions is crucial for anyone serious about credit optimization. While both systems analyze the same credit report data, they weigh different factors differently and can produce significantly different scores for the same consumer.

FICO: The Industry Standard

Fair Isaac Corporation's FICO score remains the gold standard in credit scoring, used in approximately 90% of lending decisions in the United States. The dominance of FICO in the marketplace means that when most people refer to their "credit score," they're referring to some version of their FICO score, even though they may not realize it.

FICO's market dominance stems from its early entry into the credit scoring market and its continuous innovation over more than three decades. The company has refined its algorithms through extensive analysis of lending outcomes, creating models that accurately predict the likelihood of future delinquency. This predictive accuracy has made FICO scores invaluable to lenders, who rely on them to make quick, consistent credit decisions.

The basic FICO score ranges from 300 to 850, with higher scores indicating lower credit risk. However, this simple range masks the complexity of the underlying algorithm, which considers dozens of variables and their interactions to produce a final score. The algorithm is proprietary and closely guarded, though FICO has revealed the general factors and their approximate weights.

FICO scores are updated regularly as new information appears on credit reports. Unlike credit reports, which typically update monthly when creditors report new information, FICO scores can change whenever the underlying credit report data changes. This means your FICO score could theoretically change daily, though significant changes usually occur only when major new information is reported.

The scoring algorithm considers both positive and negative information, but negative information generally has a more significant impact on scores. A single missed payment can cause a score drop of 50 to 100 points, while building positive credit history is a gradual process that unfolds over months and years. This asymmetry means that credit damage happens quickly, but credit repair takes time and patience.

VantageScore: The Challenger

VantageScore was created in 2006 as a joint venture between the three major credit bureaus: Experian, Equifax, and TransUnion. The stated goal was to create a more consistent scoring model that would produce more similar scores across all three bureaus, addressing one of the persistent complaints about the credit scoring system.

VantageScore uses the same 300 to 850 range as FICO, but the internal algorithms and factor weights are different. VantageScore tends to be more sensitive to recent credit activity and may produce higher scores for consumers with limited credit histories. The model also handles certain types of negative information differently, particularly medical collections and paid collections.

One of VantageScore's key innovations is its ability to score consumers with limited credit histories. While FICO typically requires at least six months of credit history to generate a score, VantageScore can often produce scores for consumers with as little as one month of credit history. This makes VantageScore particularly useful for young consumers, recent immigrants, and others who are new to the credit system.

Despite these advantages, VantageScore has struggled to gain significant market share in lending decisions. Most lenders continue to use FICO scores for their primary credit decisions, though some use VantageScore for secondary purposes such as account management or marketing. The consumer credit monitoring industry has embraced VantageScore more enthusiastically, with many free credit monitoring services providing VantageScore rather than FICO scores.

The limited adoption of VantageScore in actual lending decisions creates a potential disconnect for consumers. A consumer might monitor their VantageScore and see improvements, only to find that lenders using FICO scores view their creditworthiness differently. This highlights the importance of understanding which scoring model your lender uses when making credit decisions.

Key Differences in Scoring Philosophy

The differences between FICO and VantageScore go beyond simple algorithm variations. They represent different philosophies about how credit risk should be assessed and what factors should be given the most weight.

FICO places heavy emphasis on payment history and amounts owed, with these two factors accounting for 65% of the total score. This reflects FICO's belief that past payment behavior is the best predictor of future payment behavior, and that high utilization rates indicate financial stress that could lead to future payment problems.

VantageScore takes a more nuanced approach, considering factors such as the trend in credit utilization and the recency of credit activity. The model is designed to be more dynamic, responding more quickly to changes in credit behavior. This can benefit consumers who are actively working to improve their credit, as positive changes may be reflected more quickly in VantageScore than in FICO scores.

The treatment of paid collections illustrates another key difference between the models. FICO Score 9 and VantageScore 3.0 and 4.0 ignore paid collections entirely, while earlier versions of both models continued to factor them into scores. However, since many lenders still use older versions of FICO (particularly FICO Score 8), paid collections may still impact your score with some lenders even though they don't affect newer scoring models.

Different Types Of FICO Scores

The FICO scoring system is far more complex than most consumers realize. Rather than a single score, FICO offers dozens of different scoring models, each optimized for specific types of lending decisions. Understanding these variations is crucial for interpreting score differences and understanding why your score might vary depending on where you check it or what type of credit you're applying for.

Base FICO Scores

Base FICO scores are the general-purpose scoring models used for a wide variety of credit decisions. These are the scores most consumers think of when they refer to their "FICO score," though even within this category, there are multiple versions with different characteristics.

FICO Score 8, introduced in 2009, is currently the most widely used base FICO score. This version refined the treatment of isolated late payments and small-balance collections, making it somewhat more forgiving than earlier versions for consumers with otherwise good credit. FICO Score 8 also increased the penalty for high credit utilization rates, reflecting research showing that consumers who max out their credit cards are at higher risk of default.

FICO Score 9, released in 2014, introduced several consumer-friendly changes. Most notably, it ignores paid collections entirely and reduces the impact of medical collections. The model also handles rental history more favorably when it appears on credit reports. However, adoption of FICO Score 9 has been slower than expected, with many lenders continuing to use FICO Score 8 for their primary credit decisions.

FICO Score 10 and 10T represent the newest generation of base FICO scores, introduced in 2020. These models incorporate trended data, looking at how credit utilization and other factors have changed over time rather than just considering current levels. FICO Score 10T is particularly sophisticated, considering up to 24 months of historical data to identify trends in credit behavior.

The newer models are generally more sensitive to both positive and negative changes in credit behavior. Consumers who are improving their credit management may see faster score improvements, while those who are developing credit problems may see faster score declines. This increased sensitivity makes the newer models more predictive but also more volatile.

Industry-Specific FICO Scores

In addition to base scores, FICO offers industry-specific scoring models optimized for particular types of lending. These models use modified algorithms that emphasize the factors most relevant to specific types of credit decisions.

FICO Auto Scores are optimized for auto lending decisions and typically range from 250 to 900. These models place greater emphasis on previous auto loan payment history and may be more forgiving of other types of credit problems. The extended range allows for finer distinctions between consumers at both the high and low ends of the credit spectrum.

Auto lenders use these specialized scores because they provide more accurate risk assessment for auto loans specifically. A consumer with a poor general credit score might still qualify for an auto loan if their auto-specific score is higher, perhaps because they've always made car payments on time even when struggling with other obligations.

FICO Bankcard Scores, also ranging from 250 to 900, are designed specifically for credit card lending decisions. These models emphasize factors most relevant to revolving credit performance, such as credit utilization rates and payment history on existing credit cards. The models may be more sensitive to high utilization rates and more forgiving of installment loan problems.

Mortgage lenders often use older versions of FICO scores, particularly FICO Scores 2, 4, and 5, depending on which credit bureau's report they're using. This practice stems from regulations and industry standards that have been slow to adopt newer scoring models. The continued use of these older models means that mortgage applicants may be evaluated using scoring algorithms that are decades old and may not reflect the most current understanding of credit risk.

Commercial and Small Business FICO Scores

FICO also offers scoring models designed for small business lending, which consider both personal and business credit information. These models recognize that small business lending often involves personal guarantees and that the creditworthiness of the business owner is closely tied to the business's ability to repay loans.

The FICO Small Business Scoring Service (SBSS) combines personal credit information with business credit data and other business-related factors to produce a comprehensive risk assessment. This approach provides lenders with a more complete picture of small business credit risk than would be available from either personal or business credit information alone.

Understanding that different types of lenders may use different scoring models helps explain why you might be approved for one type of credit while being denied for another, even though both lenders claim to use "FICO scores." The specific version and type of FICO score can make a significant difference in lending decisions.

Score Ranges And What They Mean

Credit scores are often treated as simple numbers, but understanding what different score ranges actually mean in terms of lending outcomes and consumer opportunities is crucial for setting realistic expectations and priorities in your credit improvement journey.

The 300-850 Scale Breakdown

While both FICO and VantageScore use the 300-850 range, the distribution of consumers across this range is not uniform. Understanding where most people fall and what different ranges typically mean to lenders provides crucial context for interpreting your own scores.

Scores in the 300-579 range are considered "Poor" or "Very Poor" by most standards. Only about 16% of consumers have scores in this range, and they typically face significant challenges in obtaining traditional credit. Consumers in this range often have recent bankruptcies, foreclosures, or multiple serious delinquencies on their credit reports.

Lenders view consumers in this score range as high-risk, and those who do offer credit typically charge very high interest rates and require substantial down payments or security deposits. Credit cards for consumers in this range often come with high fees, low credit limits, and unfavorable terms. However, secured credit cards and credit-builder loans can provide pathways for consumers to begin rebuilding their credit.

The 580-669 range is typically classified as "Fair" credit. About 18% of consumers fall into this category, and while they face more challenges than higher-scoring consumers, they have significantly more options than those with poor credit. Consumers in this range may qualify for some conventional loans, though typically at higher interest rates.

FHA mortgages are available to consumers with scores as low as 580 (with a 3.5% down payment), making homeownership possible for many consumers in this range. Auto loans are generally available, though at subprime rates. Credit cards are accessible, but terms are still unfavorable compared to those offered to consumers with good credit.

Scores in the 670-739 range are considered "Good" credit, encompassing about 21% of consumers. This is where lending opportunities begin to open up significantly, and consumers start to see more favorable terms and rates. Most conventional loans are available to consumers in this range, though the best rates may still be reserved for those with higher scores.

Consumers with good credit typically qualify for rewards credit cards, though they may not receive the highest credit limits or best rewards rates. Auto loans are readily available at reasonable rates, and mortgage options are plentiful. However, there's still room for improvement, and moving from good to excellent credit can result in meaningful financial benefits.

Excellent Credit: The 740+ Territory

Scores of 740 and above are generally considered "Very Good" to "Excellent," with about 45% of consumers falling into this category. This is where the best lending terms become available, and consumers have access to premium credit products with the most favorable rates and terms.

The 740-799 range represents "Very Good" credit and opens the door to most premium credit products. Consumers in this range typically qualify for the best mortgage rates, premium rewards credit cards, and favorable terms on auto loans and other credit products. The difference in borrowing costs between this range and lower ranges can be substantial over time.

Scores of 800 and above are considered "Exceptional" and represent roughly 21% of consumers. While the practical benefits of scores above 740 are limited, exceptional scores do provide some advantages and serve as a buffer against future credit damage. Consumers with exceptional scores often receive pre-approved offers for the best credit products and may have more negotiating power with lenders.

The Myth of the Perfect 850 Score

While 850 represents the highest possible FICO score, actually achieving and maintaining this perfect score is extremely rare and provides no practical benefits over scores in the 760-800 range. Less than 1% of consumers have perfect 850 scores, and the requirements for achieving this score are so stringent that it's often more a matter of luck and timing than superior credit management.

To achieve an 850 score, you typically need a perfect payment history going back many years, very low credit utilization (often below 5%), a mix of different types of accounts, older accounts, and no recent credit inquiries. Even consumers with excellent credit habits may never reach 850 simply because of the precision required in all these factors.

More importantly, there are no lending benefits to having an 850 score versus a score in the 760-800 range. Lenders typically offer their best rates and terms to anyone with a score above 740 or 760, meaning that the difference between a 760 and 850 score is purely psychological rather than financial.

Industry-Specific Score Interpretations

Different industries may interpret the same score ranges differently based on their risk tolerance and business models. Auto lenders, for example, are generally more willing to lend to consumers with lower scores because the vehicle serves as collateral. Credit card companies, dealing with unsecured debt, may be more conservative in their underwriting standards.

Understanding these industry differences is important when applying for credit. A score that qualifies you for an excellent rate on an auto loan might not be sufficient for the best credit card offers. Similarly, mortgage lenders often have different standards and may focus on different aspects of your credit profile beyond just your score.

Factors That Influence Your Credit Score

Understanding the specific factors that influence credit scores and their relative importance is essential for developing effective credit improvement strategies. While the exact algorithms are proprietary, both FICO and VantageScore have revealed the general categories of factors and their approximate weights.

Payment History: The Foundation of Credit Scoring

Payment history is the single most important factor in credit scoring, typically accounting for 35% of your FICO score and having similar importance in VantageScore models. This factor looks at whether you've made payments on time across all your accounts, how late any payments were, how recently late payments occurred, and how many accounts show late payments.

The impact of late payments depends on several factors: how late the payment was (30, 60, 90, or 120+ days), how recently it occurred, and how many late payments appear on your report. A single 30-day late payment on an otherwise perfect credit report might cause a score drop of 50-100 points, while multiple recent late payments can be devastating to your score.

Different types of accounts carry different weights in payment history calculations. Mortgage payments are typically weighted more heavily than credit card payments, reflecting both the larger dollar amounts involved and the secured nature of mortgage debt. However, this doesn't mean credit card payment history is unimportant, consistent on-time payments across all accounts is crucial for maintaining high scores.

The recency of payment problems matters significantly. A late payment from five years ago has much less impact than one from last month. This time-based decay means that even consumers with past payment problems can see their scores improve as negative information ages, provided they maintain perfect payment history going forward.

Charge-offs, collections, and other severe delinquencies have major impacts on payment history. These items can cause score drops of 100-150 points and continue to impact scores for the full seven years they remain on credit reports. However, their impact does diminish over time, and the presence of recent positive payment history can help offset older negative information.

Amounts Owed: The Utilization Factor

The amount owed category, which accounts for about 30% of your FICO score, primarily focuses on credit utilization, how much you owe relative to your available credit limits. This factor is crucial because it can be influenced quickly, making it a powerful tool for rapid score improvement.

Credit utilization is calculated both on individual accounts and across all accounts combined. Having high utilization on even one account can hurt your score, even if your overall utilization is low. Conversely, having zero utilization across all accounts can also have a slight negative impact, as it suggests you're not actively using credit.

The optimal utilization range appears to be between 1% and 9% of available credit limits. Consumers with the highest scores typically have utilization in this range, with many having overall utilization below 5%. However, the relationship between utilization and scores is not linear, moving from 30% to 20% utilization has a bigger impact than moving from 20% to 10%.

Recent research has shown that credit scoring models also consider utilization trends over time. Rapidly increasing utilization may be viewed as a sign of financial distress, while steadily decreasing utilization suggests improving financial health. This trend analysis is particularly prominent in newer scoring models like FICO Score 10T.

The timing of utilization reporting can be manipulated for score improvement. Since most creditors report balances on statement closing dates, paying down balances before the statement closes can result in lower reported utilization and higher scores. This technique, known as "balance manipulation" or "statement date optimization," can produce significant short-term score improvements.

Length of Credit History: Time as an Asset

Credit history length accounts for about 15% of your FICO score and considers several time-related factors: the age of your oldest account, the age of your newest account, and the average age of all accounts. This factor rewards consumers for maintaining long-term relationships with creditors and penalizes those who frequently open new accounts.

The age of your oldest account serves as an anchor for your credit history. Closing your oldest account can significantly reduce your average account age and hurt your score, which is why financial experts generally recommend keeping old accounts open even if you don't use them regularly.

Average account age is calculated across all open accounts, meaning that opening new accounts dilutes this average and can temporarily hurt your score. This effect is most pronounced for consumers with limited credit histories, where a single new account can dramatically reduce the average account age.

The impact of credit history length becomes more significant as scores increase. For consumers with excellent credit, account age can be the difference between a good score and an exceptional score. This factor also provides stability to scores over time, consumers with long credit histories typically experience less score volatility than those with newer credit profiles.

Credit Mix: Diversity in Lending Types

Credit mix accounts for about 10% of your FICO score and examines the variety of account types in your credit profile. Scoring models favor consumers who have successfully managed different types of credit, including revolving accounts (credit cards), installment loans (auto loans, mortgages), and other specialized accounts.

Having a diverse credit mix demonstrates to lenders that you can handle different types of credit obligations with different payment structures and terms. A consumer who has only credit cards may be viewed as having less comprehensive credit experience than one who has managed credit cards, an auto loan, and a mortgage.

However, credit mix should never be the primary focus of credit building efforts. Opening accounts you don't need simply to improve credit mix can backfire by increasing your debt load, generating hard inquiries, and reducing your average account age. Credit mix improvement should happen naturally as you take on different types of credit for legitimate financial reasons.

The impact of credit mix varies depending on the rest of your credit profile. For consumers with limited credit histories, having diverse account types can provide a meaningful score boost. For consumers with extensive credit histories, the impact of credit mix is typically minimal.

New Credit: The Double-Edged Sword

New credit activity accounts for about 10% of your FICO score and includes both recent credit inquiries and recently opened accounts. This factor attempts to identify consumers who may be experiencing financial distress and seeking credit from multiple sources.

Hard inquiries occur when lenders check your credit in response to a credit application. These inquiries typically cause small, temporary score drops of 5-10 points and remain on your credit report for two years, though they only impact your score for the first 12 months. Multiple inquiries for the same type of credit (auto loans, mortgages) within a focused time period are typically counted as a single inquiry for scoring purposes.

The impact of inquiries depends on your overall credit profile. Consumers with extensive credit histories and high scores typically see minimal impact from new inquiries, while those with limited credit histories may see larger score drops. This factor recognizes that opening new credit is riskier for consumers who don't have a long track record of managing credit successfully.

Recently opened accounts also factor into the new credit category. Opening multiple accounts in a short period can significantly impact your score, both through the new credit factor and by reducing your average account age. This is why credit experts recommend spacing out credit applications and only applying for credit you actually need.

The new credit factor also considers how long it's been since you last opened an account. Consumers who haven't opened new accounts recently may actually benefit from opening a new account, as it demonstrates ongoing credit activity and can help maintain an active credit profile.

Understanding these five factors and their relative importance provides the foundation for all effective credit improvement strategies. By focusing your efforts on the factors with the greatest impact, payment history and amounts owed, you can achieve the most significant score improvements in the shortest time.

How To Read And Interpret Your Credit Report

Your credit report contains the raw data that forms the basis of your credit scores, but reading and interpreting this document requires understanding its structure, terminology, and the significance of different types of information.

Mastering credit report analysis is essential for identifying errors, understanding score factors, and developing effective improvement strategies.

Credit Report Structure and Sections

Credit reports are organized into several distinct sections, each containing different types of information about your financial history. Understanding the purpose and contents of each section helps you navigate the report efficiently and identify potential issues.

The personal information section appears at the top of your report and includes your name, current and previous addresses, Social Security number, date of birth, and employment information. This section doesn't directly impact your credit scores, but errors here can indicate identity theft or file mixing issues that could affect other parts of your report.

Variations in how your name appears (nicknames, middle initials, etc.) are normal and usually don't indicate problems. However, completely different names or Social Security numbers suggest serious file mixing issues that require immediate attention. Similarly, addresses you've never lived at or employers you've never worked for may indicate fraud or file errors.

The account information section forms the heart of your credit report and contains detailed information about each of your credit accounts. This section is divided into different categories based on the status and type of accounts: open accounts, closed accounts, and accounts with negative payment history.

Each account listing includes the creditor name, account number (usually partially masked for security), account type, date opened, payment terms, credit limit or original loan amount, current balance, payment status, and payment history. Understanding how to interpret each of these fields is crucial for identifying errors and understanding their impact on your scores.

The public records section contains information about bankruptcies, tax liens, civil judgments, and other legal matters that could affect your creditworthiness. Most public records have significant negative impacts on credit scores and remain on reports for seven to ten years, depending on the type of record.

The inquiries section lists entities that have accessed your credit report, divided into hard inquiries (which can affect your scores) and soft inquiries (which don't affect scores). Understanding the difference between these types of inquiries and recognizing unauthorized inquiries is important for protecting your credit and identity.

Account Status Codes and Their Meanings

Credit reports use standardized codes to describe the status of each account, and understanding these codes is essential for interpreting your report accurately. These codes provide detailed information about your payment history and current account standing.

Current account status codes indicate whether accounts are current, past due, or charged off. "Current" or "Pays as Agreed" indicates that payments are up to date. Past due codes specify how many days behind payments are: 30, 60, 90, or 120+ days past due. These codes directly correlate with the severity of score impact.

Charge-off status indicates that the creditor has written off the debt as uncollectible, typically after 120-180 days of non-payment. Charge-offs have severe negative impacts on credit scores and remain on reports for seven years from the original delinquency date. Understanding that charge-offs can continue to accrue interest and remain legally collectable is important for managing these situations.

Collection status appears when accounts have been transferred to collection agencies or sold to debt buyers. Collection accounts can appear in addition to the original account, meaning the same debt might show up twice on your report with different impacts on your score.

Closed account codes indicate why accounts were closed: closed by consumer, closed by creditor, or closed due to credit grantor decision. Accounts closed by the creditor, especially due to delinquency, are viewed more negatively than accounts closed by the consumer in good standing.

Payment History Interpretation

The payment history section of each account provides a month-by-month record of your payment performance, typically showing the most recent 24 months of history. This information is crucial for understanding score impacts and identifying patterns in your credit behavior.

Payment history is typically displayed using a grid format with symbols representing different payment statuses. "OK" or checkmarks indicate on-time payments, while numbers (30, 60, 90, 120) indicate how many days late payments were. Other symbols might indicate missed payments, charge-offs, or other negative events.

The pattern and recency of payment problems matter as much as their existence. A single isolated late payment followed by months of on-time payments has less impact than multiple recent late payments. Recent payment problems weigh much more heavily in score calculations than older issues.

Seasonal patterns in payment history can indicate specific financial challenges. For example, late payments every December might suggest holiday spending issues, while late payments during summer months might indicate seasonal employment challenges. Identifying these patterns can help develop strategies to prevent future payment problems.

Understanding Credit Limits and Balances

The relationship between reported balances and credit limits directly impacts your credit utilization ratios, making accurate interpretation of this information crucial for score optimization.

Credit limits represent the maximum amount you're authorized to borrow on revolving accounts. For installment loans, this field might show the original loan amount. High credit limits generally benefit your scores by reducing utilization ratios, assuming you maintain low balances.

Reported balances reflect what you owed when the creditor last reported to the credit bureau, typically on your statement closing date. These balances might differ from your current actual balances, which can be confusing when analyzing your report.

Utilization calculations are based on reported balances and credit limits, not your current balances. This means that paying off your balance after the statement closes won't immediately improve your utilization ratio. Understanding this timing difference is crucial for effective utilization management.

Zero balances on all accounts can actually hurt your scores slightly, as it suggests you're not actively using credit. Maintaining small balances on a few accounts while keeping overall utilization low typically produces the highest scores.

Identifying and Documenting Errors

Credit report errors are surprisingly common, with studies showing that significant errors appear on a substantial percentage of credit reports. Developing systematic approaches to identifying and documenting these errors is essential for maintaining accurate credit information.

Common errors include accounts that don't belong to you, incorrect payment history, wrong balances or credit limits, accounts listed as open when they're closed, and incorrect personal information. Each type of error requires different dispute strategies and documentation.

When reviewing your report, compare the information against your own records. Keep detailed records of all your credit accounts, including statements, payment confirmations, and correspondence with creditors. These records provide the documentation needed to dispute inaccurate information effectively.

Pay particular attention to accounts you don't recognize, as these could indicate identity theft or file mixing errors. Similarly, payment history that doesn't match your records might indicate reporting errors by creditors or processing errors by credit bureaus.

Document all errors systematically, noting the specific inaccurate information, the correct information, and any supporting documentation you have. This documentation forms the basis of effective dispute letters and helps ensure that disputes are resolved accurately.

Understanding how to read and interpret credit reports provides the foundation for all credit improvement activities. Whether you're disputing errors, negotiating with creditors, or developing score improvement strategies, accurate interpretation of your credit report is the first step toward achieving your credit goals.

The complexity of credit reports means that thorough analysis takes time and attention to detail, but this investment pays dividends in more effective credit management and faster achievement of your credit objectives. In the next chapter, we'll explore how credit damage occurs and the various paths that lead to credit problems, building on this foundation of report analysis to understand prevention and early intervention strategies.

CHAPTER 4

THE ROAD TO CREDIT DESTRUCTION

Common Paths To Credit Damage

Understanding how credit damage occurs is essential for both prevention and repair. Credit problems rarely happen overnight, they typically develop through a series of decisions and circumstances that compound over time. By examining the most common paths to credit destruction, we can identify warning signs early and develop strategies to prevent or mitigate damage before it becomes severe.

The Gradual Slide: Lifestyle Inflation and Overspending

One of the most common paths to credit damage begins innocuously with lifestyle inflation, the tendency to increase spending as income rises. This pattern often starts during positive life changes such as promotions, new jobs, or career advancement. What begins as justified increases in standard of living can gradually evolve into unsustainable spending patterns that outpace income growth.

The process typically unfolds over months or years. Initial purchases seem reasonable and affordable based on current income and available credit. Credit cards provide easy access to additional purchasing power, and minimum payment requirements make debt accumulation seem manageable. The psychological distance between spending and payment consequences allows debt to accumulate gradually without triggering immediate concern.

As balances grow, an increasing portion of income goes toward debt service rather than discretionary spending. This reduction in available cash flow creates pressure to use credit for expenses that were previously paid in cash.

The cycle accelerates as credit becomes necessary for maintaining established lifestyle levels, leading to utilization rates that negatively impact credit scores.

The tipping point often comes when unexpected expenses or income disruptions occur. Without adequate emergency savings, often depleted by lifestyle inflation, consumers must rely entirely on credit to handle financial surprises. This reliance can push utilization rates above sustainable levels and create payment difficulties that begin the transition from credit use to credit abuse.

Credit score deterioration in this scenario typically follows a predictable pattern. Utilization increases gradually, causing steady score declines. As financial stress mounts, payment timing becomes erratic, leading to occasional late payments that accelerate score damage. Eventually, some accounts may be charged off or sent to collections, causing severe score damage that takes years to repair.

The Medical Debt Trap

Medical emergencies represent one of the most devastating and unpredictable paths to credit destruction. Unlike other forms of debt, medical debt often occurs suddenly, in large amounts, and without the consumer's choice or control. The complexity of medical billing, insurance coverage disputes, and collection practices makes medical debt particularly challenging to manage.

The medical debt cycle often begins with an unexpected health emergency that generates substantial bills. Even consumers with health insurance may face significant out-of-pocket costs due to deductibles, copayments, or coverage limitations. Emergency situations rarely allow for price shopping or cost comparison, leaving consumers vulnerable to bills that far exceed their financial capacity.

Medical billing complexity compounds the problem. Bills may arrive weeks or months after treatment, making it difficult to budget for expenses. Multiple providers, hospitals, physicians, laboratories, and specialists, often bill separately for the same treatment episode, creating confusion about total costs and payment obligations. Insurance processing delays can postpone final bill amounts for months, making financial planning nearly impossible.

When medical bills exceed available resources, consumers face limited options. Payment plans may be available, but they often require immediate commitment to monthly payments that strain already tight budgets. Failure to arrange payment plans quickly can result in accounts being sent to collection agencies, which typically report negative information to credit bureaus immediately upon assignment.

Medical collections can devastate credit scores rapidly. Unlike other forms of debt that typically go through several stages of delinquency before collection assignment, medical debt often moves directly from unpaid status to collection agency assignment. This acceleration means that consumers may experience severe credit damage before they've had adequate opportunity to address the underlying financial situation.

The impact of medical collections on credit scores has been partially mitigated by recent changes to credit scoring models and reporting practices. FICO Score 9 and VantageScore models give less weight to medical collections than other types of collections. Additionally, the credit bureaus have implemented policies requiring medical collections to be on credit reports for 180 days before they impact scores, providing consumers with time to resolve insurance disputes or arrange payments.

However, many lenders still use older scoring models that treat medical collections the same as other collection accounts. This means that medical debt can still cause significant credit damage, particularly for consumers seeking mortgages or other major loans that rely on older scoring models.

Divorce and Family Financial Disruption

Divorce represents one of the most complex and emotionally challenging paths to credit destruction. The financial implications of divorce extend far beyond the immediate costs of legal proceedings, encompassing fundamental changes to income, expenses, assets, and debt obligations that can overwhelm even financially sophisticated consumers.

The divorce process typically begins with increased expenses at a time when household resources are being divided. Legal fees, temporary housing costs, and duplicate household expenses strain budgets that were previously adequate for combined household income. These immediate pressures often force reliance on credit cards to maintain basic living standards during the transition period.

Joint account management becomes particularly challenging during divorce proceedings. Both spouses typically remain legally responsible for joint debts regardless of how the divorce decree allocates responsibility. This continued liability means that one spouse's financial difficulties or vindictive behavior can damage both parties' credit profiles. Charges made by either spouse to joint accounts become the responsibility of both parties, creating potential for credit damage beyond either party's direct control.

Asset division often requires liquidating investments or retirement accounts to buy out one spouse's interest in jointly owned property. These liquidations can trigger tax consequences and penalties that further strain finances. Simultaneously, each spouse must establish independent housing, often requiring deposits, utility connections, and household purchases that compete with debt service obligations for limited resources.

Income disruption is common during and after divorce. One or both spouses may need to change jobs, reduce working hours to handle divorce proceedings and childcare, or accept lower-paying positions due to relocation or other constraints. Child support and alimony obligations, while legally mandated, may be irregular or insufficient, creating ongoing financial uncertainty.

The combination of increased expenses, reduced income, and legal liability for joint debts creates a perfect storm for credit problems. Many divorced individuals find themselves unable to maintain payments on all obligations, leading to strategic decisions about which debts to prioritize. These decisions often result in some accounts becoming delinquent, with corresponding credit score damage.

Recovery from divorce-related credit damage is often complicated by ongoing financial obligations and limited income. Child support and alimony obligations reduce available income for debt service, while the need to maintain separate households increases basic living expenses. These constraints can make credit recovery a slow, multi-year process that requires careful prioritization and planning.

Employment Loss and Income Disruption

Job loss represents another major pathway to credit destruction, particularly in an economy where many households live paycheck to paycheck with limited emergency savings. Unlike other financial disruptions that may develop gradually, employment loss creates immediate income disruption that can quickly overwhelm existing credit obligations.

The immediate impact of job loss varies significantly based on the individual's financial preparation and the circumstances of employment termination. Workers who lose jobs due to company layoffs may receive severance packages and continued benefits that provide temporary financial cushioning. However, workers terminated for cause or those whose employers close suddenly may face immediate income cutoffs with no transition period.

Unemployment benefits, while helpful, typically replace only a fraction of previous income and may take weeks or months to begin. The application process can be complex and time-consuming, particularly for workers with non-traditional employment arrangements or those who worked in multiple states. Even when benefits are approved, the reduced income level often cannot support existing debt obligations that were based on full employment income.

The psychological impact of job loss often compounds financial challenges. Depression, anxiety, and loss of self-esteem can impair decision-making and motivation just when clear thinking and aggressive action are most needed. Some individuals retreat from financial responsibilities, avoiding creditor communications and failing to take proactive steps to minimize damage.

Credit card balances often increase rapidly during unemployment periods as individuals use available credit to maintain basic living expenses. This increase occurs at precisely the time when payment capacity is most constrained, creating a dangerous combination of rising balances and reduced payment ability. The resulting utilization increases cause immediate credit score damage, even before any payments are missed.

The duration of unemployment significantly affects the severity of credit damage. Short-term unemployment may result only in temporarily elevated credit utilization that can be corrected once employment resumes. Extended unemployment periods often lead to missed payments, charge-offs, and collections that create lasting credit damage requiring years to repair.

Industry-specific employment disruptions, such as those affecting manufacturing, retail, or hospitality sectors during economic downturns, can affect entire communities simultaneously. These widespread disruptions can overwhelm local support services and create additional challenges for affected workers seeking new employment or financial assistance.

Business Failure and Entrepreneurial Risks

Small business ownership carries inherent credit risks that many entrepreneurs underestimate. The failure rate for new businesses is substantial, and business failure often translates directly into personal credit damage due to personal guarantees and the blending of business and personal finances that characterizes many small enterprises.

Business credit applications typically require personal guarantees from business owners, particularly for new or small businesses without established credit histories. These guarantees make business owners personally liable for business debts, meaning that business failure can result in personal credit damage even if the business failure was due to market conditions rather than mismanagement.

Cash flow challenges are endemic in small business operations, particularly during startup phases or seasonal fluctuations. Many business owners use personal credit cards to bridge cash flow gaps, believing that business revenue will allow rapid repayment. When business projections prove overly optimistic, these personal advances can become unmanageable personal debt obligations.

The interconnection between business and personal finances creates unique vulnerabilities. Business owners often pledge personal assets as collateral for business loans, and business cash flow problems can quickly affect personal financial obligations. Similarly, personal financial problems can impact business operations by limiting access to credit or requiring business resources to address personal obligations.

Business failure rarely occurs suddenly. Most businesses experience declining revenues, increasing expenses, or cash flow problems over extended periods before ultimately closing. During these declining phases, business owners often make increasingly desperate attempts to save their enterprises, including using personal credit to fund business operations or deferring personal obligations to preserve business cash flow.

The decision of when to close a failing business versus continuing to invest resources in turnaround efforts creates particularly challenging dilemmas. Continuing to operate a failing business can result in accumulating additional debt and deeper financial problems. However, closing prematurely might waste recoverable investments and destroy potential future income streams.

Recovery from business-related credit damage is often complicated by ongoing legal and financial obligations related to the failed enterprise. Lease obligations, supplier debts, and employee claims can continue for months or years after business closure. These ongoing obligations compete with personal credit repair efforts for limited financial resources.

Life Events That Impact Credit

Certain life events carry inherent risks for credit damage, regardless of how well-prepared or financially sophisticated individuals may be. Understanding these risks allows for proactive planning and mitigation strategies that can minimize credit impact even when challenging circumstances cannot be avoided entirely.

Death of a Spouse or Family Member

The death of a spouse or close family member creates both immediate financial pressures and long-term financial restructuring challenges that can significantly impact credit profiles. The combination of emotional grief and complex financial decisions creates particular vulnerability for credit management mistakes.

Immediate expenses associated with death, funeral costs, medical bills, legal fees, often exceed available liquid assets and require credit financing. These expenses typically cannot be postponed or reduced, creating forced borrowing at a time when income may be disrupted and decision-making capacity is impaired by grief.

Joint account management becomes immediately complex when one spouse dies. Surviving spouses may lose access to accounts that were primarily in the deceased spouse's name, even if they were previously authorized users. Simultaneously, they become solely responsible for joint debts that may have been manageable with dual incomes but become burdensome on single incomes.

Social Security and pension benefits may be reduced or eliminated upon a spouse's death, creating permanent income reductions that require corresponding adjustments to debt obligations and living expenses. These adjustments often take months to implement fully, during which time existing credit obligations continue at their original levels.

Estate settlement processes can freeze access to assets for months or years, particularly when estates are complex or contested. During these periods, surviving family members may need to rely on credit to maintain basic living expenses while waiting for estate assets to become available. This forced reliance on credit can quickly lead to unsustainable debt levels.

Life insurance proceeds, when available, may provide temporary financial relief but often come with tax consequences or restrictions on use that limit their effectiveness for immediate credit management. Additionally, life insurance coverage is often inadequate to replace the full economic contribution of the deceased, particularly when that contribution included both income and household management services.

The emotional impact of grief significantly affects financial decision-making capacity. Depression, anxiety, and cognitive disruption associated with loss can impair judgment and motivation just when clear thinking and proactive financial management are most crucial. Many surviving spouses report making financial decisions during grief periods that they later regret and that created lasting financial problems.

Military Deployment and Service-Related Disruptions

Military service creates unique credit challenges that civilian financial advisors often underestimate. Deployments, permanent change of station moves, and the transition to civilian life all carry specific risks for credit damage that require specialized knowledge and planning.

Deployment financial management challenges stem from the combination of changed spending patterns, limited financial oversight capability, and family separation stress. Service members often experience increased income during deployments due to combat pay exclusions and family separation allowances, but they may simultaneously face increased expenses from family support obligations and deployment-related costs.

Spouse financial management during deployments creates particular vulnerabilities. Spouses left to manage household finances during extended deployments may lack experience with credit management or may face unexpected expenses that exceed deployment budgets. Communication challenges and time zone differences can delay financial decision-making and problem resolution.

Permanent change of station moves occur frequently in military careers and create substantial one-time expenses that can strain even well-managed budgets. Moving expenses, security deposits, utility connections, and housing-related costs often occur simultaneously with income disruptions related to travel time and administrative processing delays.

Military housing privatization has created new credit vulnerabilities for service families. Private military housing companies increasingly use credit checks for housing assignments and may report rent payment information to credit bureaus. Late rent payments or housing-related charges can now impact credit scores in ways that were not possible under traditional military housing systems.

The transition to civilian employment creates unique credit challenges as veterans adapt to different pay schedules, benefit structures, and financial management requirements. Veterans may face delays in accessing education benefits, challenges obtaining civilian employment at military salary levels, or difficulties qualifying for civilian credit without traditional employment histories.

The Servicemembers Civil Relief Act provides important protections for military borrowers, including interest rate reductions and foreclosure protections, but these benefits require active application and management. Many service members are unaware of available protections or fail to apply for them promptly when eligible.

Natural Disasters and Emergency Situations

Natural disasters create sudden, large-scale financial disruptions that can overwhelm even well-prepared households. Unlike other financial challenges that develop gradually, disasters create immediate needs for housing, transportation, and basic necessities that must be addressed regardless of available resources.

Property damage represents the most obvious financial impact of natural disasters. Even households with adequate insurance coverage often face significant out-of-pocket costs due to deductibles, coverage limitations, or disputes over covered damages. Insurance claim processing can take months or years, during which time households must finance repairs or alternative housing using credit.

Income disruption often accompanies natural disasters as businesses close or reduce operations in affected areas. Service sector employees, in particular, may face extended unemployment periods as damaged businesses rebuild. Even businesses that reopen quickly may operate with reduced hours or staffing levels that decrease employee income.

Evacuation and temporary housing costs can quickly exhaust available resources. Hotel costs, restaurant meals, and other evacuation expenses typically exceed normal budget allocations and must be financed using available credit. Extended evacuation periods, which may last weeks or months for major disasters, can create unsustainable credit utilization levels.

Infrastructure damage affecting utilities, transportation, and communications can disrupt normal financial management routines. Online banking access, automatic payments, and routine credit monitoring may be interrupted just when financial vigilance is most important. These disruptions can lead to missed payments or financial oversights that damage credit scores.

The psychological impact of disaster trauma affects financial decision-making capacity similarly to other traumatic events. Stress, depression, and cognitive disruption can impair judgment and delay necessary financial actions. Many disaster victims report difficulty focusing on financial tasks or making decisions about insurance claims and recovery planning.

Federal disaster assistance, while helpful, often comes with restrictions and delays that limit its effectiveness for immediate credit protection. FEMA assistance may not be available for all types of losses or may require extensive documentation that takes time to compile. Small Business Administration disaster loans provide additional resources but must be repaid and may not cover all disaster-related expenses.

Identity Theft and Financial Fraud

Identity theft represents a unique path to credit damage because it occurs without the victim's knowledge or consent. Unlike other forms of credit damage that result from financial decisions or circumstances, identity theft damage can occur even when victims are managing their finances responsibly.

The scope of identity theft continues to expand as financial transactions become increasingly digital. Traditional forms of identity theft focused on credit card fraud or bank account access, but modern identity theft can encompass tax fraud, benefits fraud, employment fraud, and medical fraud, each with different implications for credit damage.

Credit-related identity theft typically involves unauthorized account openings or unauthorized charges to existing accounts. New account fraud can be particularly damaging because victims may not discover the fraud until months after accounts are opened and subsequent payment defaults have been reported to credit bureaus.

Detection of identity theft often occurs accidentally during routine credit monitoring or when applying for new credit. By the time fraud is discovered, significant damage may have already occurred, and the resolution process can take months or years to complete fully.

The dispute process for identity theft differs from normal credit disputes and requires additional documentation and persistence. Victims must file police reports, complete identity theft affidavits, and provide detailed documentation to each creditor and credit bureau separately. The burden of proof often falls on victims to demonstrate that accounts or charges are fraudulent.

Credit freezes and fraud alerts provide important protection tools, but they can also create inconvenience for legitimate credit activities. Balancing security measures with credit accessibility requires ongoing attention and planning, particularly for consumers who need regular access to credit for business or personal reasons.

Recovery from identity theft often takes longer than recovery from other forms of credit damage because the resolution process is complex and involves multiple parties. Even after fraudulent accounts are removed from credit reports, the experience often leaves victims with heightened anxiety about future fraud and more conservative credit management approaches.

The Domino Effect Of Missed Payments

Understanding how missed payments cascade into broader credit problems is crucial for both prevention and early intervention. What begins as a single missed payment can trigger a series of consequences that compound over time, making recovery increasingly difficult with each missed payment cycle.

The First Missed Payment: Crossing the Threshold

The transition from perfect payment history to missed payment status represents a critical threshold in credit management. This first missed payment often occurs during temporary financial stress and may seem manageable in isolation, but it begins a process that can quickly escalate beyond the original problem.

Most creditors provide a grace period between the due date and the late payment reporting date, typically 30 days from the original due date. During this period, late fees and penalty interest rates may apply, but no negative information is reported to credit bureaus. This grace period provides crucial time for consumers to bring accounts current without credit score damage.

However, the financial impact of late fees and penalty rates can create additional strain on already tight budgets. A $39 late fee on a credit card with a $500 balance represents a significant percentage of the outstanding debt and reduces available credit for other expenses. Penalty interest rates, often 29.99% or higher, can dramatically increase future payment requirements.

The psychological impact of the first missed payment can be as significant as the financial impact. Many consumers experience shame, anxiety, and loss of control when they miss their first payment after years of perfect payment history. These emotional responses can lead to avoidance behaviors that compound the original problem.

Creditor communication patterns often change after the first missed payment. Automated payment reminders, phone calls, and written notices increase in frequency and urgency. While these communications are intended to encourage payment, they can create additional stress and may contribute to avoidance behaviors in some consumers.

The first missed payment also represents a breach of the original credit agreement terms, which may trigger additional fees, rate increases, or changes to account terms. These consequences can make the account more expensive and difficult to manage going forward, even if payments resume immediately.

The 30-Day Late Payment: Credit Score Impact Begins

When an account reaches 30 days past due, most creditors report this delinquency to credit bureaus, triggering immediate and significant credit score damage. This first reported late payment typically causes score drops of

50-100 points, depending on the consumer's previous credit profile and overall score level.

The impact of a 30-day late payment is particularly severe for consumers with previously excellent credit. A consumer with an 800 credit score may see a larger point drop than a consumer with a 650 score, reflecting the scoring models' emphasis on consistency and reliability at higher score levels.

The reported late payment immediately affects credit utilization calculations by reducing available credit on that account. Many creditors automatically reduce credit limits when payments become late, further impacting utilization ratios and credit scores. This reduction can trigger overlimit fees if balances exceed the new, lower credit limits.

Other creditors may respond to the reported late payment by reducing credit limits on their accounts, even if those accounts are current. This phenomenon, known as "universal default," means that a late payment on one account can trigger adverse actions across multiple credit relationships.

The 30-day late payment also affects account management options. Many creditors restrict online account access, automatic payment enrollment, or other convenience features for accounts that become delinquent. These restrictions can make it more difficult to manage the account going forward and may contribute to additional payment problems.

Collection activity typically intensifies once accounts reach 30 days past due. Phone calls become more frequent, written notices become more urgent, and creditors may begin discussing workout arrangements or payment plans. While these options can be helpful, they often require immediate decisions and commitments that stressed consumers may not be prepared to make.

The 60-Day Threshold: Escalating Consequences

Accounts that reach 60 days past due face significantly more severe consequences than those at 30 days. The additional score damage from a 60-day late payment compounds the damage from the original 30-day late, creating cumulative effects that can push scores into poor credit ranges.

Many creditors implement automatic account restrictions at 60 days past due, including suspension of charging privileges and acceleration of payment demands. These restrictions can force consumers to find alternative funding sources for essential expenses, often leading to problems with other accounts or reliance on expensive alternative credit sources.

The legal framework around debt collection becomes more aggressive at 60 days past due. Creditors may begin formal collection procedures, including demand letters from attorneys and threats of legal action. While actual lawsuits are rare for unsecured debts under $5,000, the threat of legal action creates additional stress and urgency.

Account closure often occurs at or before the 60-day mark, particularly for credit cards and other revolving credit accounts. Once accounts are closed due to delinquency, the available credit from those accounts is lost permanently, reducing total available credit and potentially increasing utilization ratios on remaining accounts.

The 60-day late payment also triggers more aggressive cross-selling of debt management services by creditors and third parties. Debt settlement companies, credit counseling agencies, and other service providers often target consumers with 60-day late payments, offering services that may or may not be appropriate for the specific situation.

Internal collection efforts typically escalate at 60 days, with specialized collection departments taking over account management from customer service representatives. These specialized collectors have different training, different authority levels, and different performance incentives that may result in more aggressive collection tactics.

The 90-Day Mark: Approaching Charge-Off

At 90 days past due, accounts approach the charge-off threshold used by most creditors for unsecured debts. The combination of three consecutive missed payments creates severe credit score damage that can reduce scores by 150+ points from their original levels.

Creditor communication at 90 days often includes final demand notices and clear statements about impending charge-off or collection assignment. These communications typically offer last-chance settlement opportunities or payment arrangements that require immediate response and often demand substantial lump-sum payments.

The 90-day threshold represents the point where most creditors begin serious consideration of legal action for larger debts. While the economics of lawsuit filing often favor creditors only for debts above certain dollar thresholds, the threat of legal action becomes more credible and immediate.

Account terms often change dramatically at 90 days, with interest rates increasing to maximum levels and various fees being assessed. The combination of penalty rates, late fees, and over-limit fees can cause balances to grow rapidly even without additional purchases, making eventual resolution more expensive.

Credit limit reductions typically become more severe at 90 days, often reducing limits to current balance levels or below. These reductions can trigger over-limit fees and make it impossible to use remaining available credit, forcing consumers to find alternative funding sources for essential expenses.

The psychological impact of reaching 90 days past due often includes feelings of hopelessness and inevitability about charge-off. These feelings can lead to complete avoidance of creditor communications and abandonment of efforts to resolve the situation, making charge-off and its consequences more likely.

Charge-Off: The Point of No Return

Charge-off represents the point where creditors write off debts as uncollectible for accounting purposes, typically occurring at 120-180 days past due depending on the type of debt and creditor policies. However, charge-off does not eliminate the debt or end collection efforts, it merely changes the approach to collecting the debt.

The credit score impact of charge-off is severe and long-lasting. Charge-offs typically cause score drops of 100-150 points and remain on credit reports for seven years from the original delinquency date. The impact diminishes over time but continues to affect scores throughout the reporting period.

Charged-off accounts often continue to accrue interest and fees even after charge-off, causing balances to grow significantly over time. A $5,000 credit card debt that is charged off may grow to $8,000 or more over the seven-year reporting period due to continued interest and collection fees.

Collection assignment typically occurs immediately after charge-off, either to internal collection departments with expanded authority or to external collection agencies. These collection efforts are often more aggressive than pre-charge-off efforts and may include threats of legal action, wage garnishment, or asset seizure.

The charge-off also triggers tax consequences for both creditors and consumers. Creditors may issue 1099-C forms for forgiven debt, creating potential tax liability for consumers even if they never receive any benefit from the debt forgiveness. Understanding and planning for these tax consequences is important for complete financial recovery.

Recovery options after charge-off become more limited and expensive. Settlement negotiations often require lump-sum payments of 40-60% of the original balance, and creditors may be less willing to remove charge-off notation from credit reports even after payment. These limitations make early intervention before charge-off far preferable to post-charge-off resolution attempts.

How Collections Escalate

The collection process follows predictable patterns that become increasingly aggressive and intrusive over time. Understanding this escalation helps consumers recognize where they are in the process and what options remain available before more severe consequences occur.

Internal Collections: The First Phase

Internal collection efforts begin immediately when accounts become past due and intensify as delinquency periods extend. These efforts are typically handled by customer service representatives or specialized collection departments within the original creditor's organization.

Initial collection contacts focus on payment reminders and assume that missed payments result from oversight or temporary cash flow problems. Automated phone calls, text messages, and emails remind consumers of past due amounts and encourage immediate payment. These early contacts are typically non-threatening and may offer simple solutions such as payment extensions or due date changes.

As delinquency extends beyond 30 days, collection contacts become more frequent and urgent. Live collector calls replace automated messages, and collectors begin exploring the reasons for non-payment and discussing potential solutions. These conversations often include offers for payment arrangements, hardship programs, or temporary account modifications.

Internal collectors typically have authority to offer various workout arrangements without supervisory approval. These arrangements might include payment plans, interest rate reductions, fee waivers, or temporary payment suspensions. However, the specific options available vary significantly between creditors and may change based on the consumer's payment history and current financial situation.

Documentation of collection contacts becomes important during this phase. Federal and state laws require collectors to maintain records of their communications with consumers, but consumers should also maintain their own records of all collection contacts, including dates, times, collector names, and details of any agreements or arrangements discussed.

The tone and approach of internal collection efforts often depend on the consumer's response to initial contacts. Consumers who are responsive, honest about their financial situation, and willing to work toward resolution typically receive more patient and flexible treatment than those who avoid contact or are uncooperative.

External Collection Assignment: Escalating Pressure

When internal collection efforts fail to produce payment or satisfactory arrangements, creditors typically assign accounts to external collection agencies. This assignment usually occurs between 90-180 days past due, depending on the creditor's policies and the specific circumstances of each account.

Collection agencies operate under different business models and regulatory frameworks than original creditors. Most agencies work on contingency fee arrangements, earning 25-50% of amounts collected. This compensation structure creates strong incentives for aggressive collection tactics and may result in treatment that differs significantly from internal collection approaches.

The transition to external collection is often marked by a change in communication style and frequency. Collection agency representatives may be more aggressive, less patient, and more focused on immediate payment than internal collectors. The personal relationship between consumer and creditor is effectively severed, replaced by a purely adversarial collection relationship.

Legal leverage increases significantly once accounts are assigned to collection agencies. Many collection agencies are affiliated with law firms or have easy access to legal services, making threats of legal action more credible. However, actual lawsuit filing depends on factors such as debt amount, consumer assets, and local legal costs.

Verification rights become crucial when accounts are assigned to collection agencies. The Fair Debt Collection Practices Act provides consumers with rights to request verification of debt details, but these rights must be exercised promptly and properly to be effective. Failure to request verification within the required timeframes may limit future dispute options.

Collection agency reporting practices often differ from original creditor practices. Collection agencies typically report collection accounts as separate entries on credit reports, meaning that the same debt may appear twice, once as a charge-off from the original creditor and once as a collection account from the agency. This double reporting amplifies the negative credit impact.

Legal Action Threats and Implementation

The threat of legal action represents a significant escalation in collection efforts and typically occurs when other collection methods have failed and the debt amount justifies the costs of litigation. Understanding when legal threats are credible and what legal action actually entails helps consumers make informed decisions about response strategies.

The economics of debt collection lawsuits favor creditors primarily for larger debts or when they can obtain default judgments efficiently. Most collection attorneys prefer cases with balances above $1,000-$2,000, though this threshold varies based on local court costs and the likelihood of successful collection.

Pre-litigation demand letters often precede actual lawsuit filing by several weeks or months. These letters typically come from attorneys representing the creditor or collection agency and demand payment within a specified timeframe to avoid legal action. While many of these letters are form letters sent to multiple consumers, they should be taken seriously as indicators of potential legal action.

The decision to file a lawsuit depends on multiple factors beyond just the debt amount. Creditors consider the consumer's apparent ability to pay, the strength of their documentation, the age of the debt, and the likelihood of successful collection through other means. Consumers with substantial assets or steady income are more likely to face lawsuits than those who appear judgment-proof.

Actual lawsuit filing triggers additional consumer rights and options. Consumers have the right to respond to lawsuits, challenge the creditor's claims, and raise various legal defenses. However, exercising these rights typically requires legal knowledge or attorney assistance that may be expensive relative to the debt amount.

Default judgments occur when consumers fail to respond to lawsuits within required timeframes. These judgments give creditors additional collection tools, including wage garnishment, bank account levies, and liens on real property. Default judgment rates in debt collection cases are extremely high, often exceeding 90% in some jurisdictions.

Post-Judgment Collection: Maximum Leverage

Judgments provide creditors with powerful collection tools that can make debt avoidance much more difficult. Understanding these tools and their limitations helps consumers develop appropriate response strategies and protection measures.

Wage garnishment represents the most common post-judgment collection tool and can result in automatic deduction of 25% of disposable income (after taxes and mandatory deductions) until the judgment is satisfied. Garnishment orders are typically sent directly to employers, creating potential workplace embarrassment and complications.

Bank account levies allow judgment creditors to freeze and seize funds in consumer bank accounts. These levies can occur without advance warning and may affect accounts at multiple banks if creditors conduct asset searches. Essential funds such as Social Security benefits have some legal protections, but these protections require active assertion by consumers.

Real property liens attach judgments to real estate owned by consumers, making it difficult to sell or refinance property without satisfying the judgment. These liens can remain in effect for many years and may accrue additional interest and fees over time.

Asset discovery procedures allow judgment creditors to compel consumers to disclose information about their income, assets, and financial accounts. Failure to comply with these discovery orders can result in contempt of court charges and additional legal consequences.

Judgment renewal procedures vary by state but typically allow creditors to extend judgment enforceability for additional periods, sometimes indefinitely. This means that judgments can remain collectible long after the original debt was incurred, particularly if consumers fail to address them promptly.

Protection planning becomes crucial once judgments are obtained. Consumers may need to consider asset protection strategies, exemption planning, or bankruptcy options to protect essential assets and income from collection efforts. However, these strategies are most effective when implemented before judgments are obtained rather than afterward.

Understanding the collection escalation process provides crucial context for developing effective response strategies at each stage. Early intervention is almost always more effective and less costly than waiting for collection efforts to escalate to their maximum levels. The next chapter will explore prevention strategies and early intervention techniques that can help consumers avoid or minimize collection consequences.

CHAPTER 5

PREVENTION AND EARLY INTERVENTION

Warning Signs Of Credit Trouble

Recognizing the early warning signs of credit trouble is essential for preventing minor financial difficulties from escalating into major credit damage. Most credit problems develop gradually over time, providing multiple opportunities for intervention before serious damage occurs. Understanding these warning signs and taking prompt action can save years of credit repair efforts and thousands of dollars in additional costs.

Increasing Credit Utilization Patterns

One of the earliest and most reliable indicators of developing credit problems is a gradual increase in credit utilization across multiple accounts. This pattern often begins innocuously, with consumers using slightly more of their available credit each month to cover temporary expenses or lifestyle increases. However, when this pattern persists over several months, it typically indicates that expenses are outpacing income or that financial discipline is deteriorating.

The progression of utilization problems typically follows a predictable pattern. Initial increases may be barely noticeable, rising from 10% to 15% utilization over several months. However, as financial pressure mounts, the rate of increase often accelerates. Consumers may find themselves reaching 30%, then 50%, and eventually approaching their credit limits across multiple accounts.

This escalation occurs because credit becomes increasingly necessary for basic expenses as more of the consumer's income goes toward debt service rather than discretionary spending. As minimum payments consume larger portions of available income, consumers must rely on credit for expenses they previously paid in cash. This creates a dangerous cycle where credit use becomes necessary rather than optional.

The psychological aspect of increasing utilization is particularly insidious. Small increases feel manageable and temporary, leading consumers to delay taking corrective action. By the time utilization reaches problematic levels, the required behavioral changes and financial adjustments may seem overwhelming, leading to paralysis rather than action.

Credit card statement analysis reveals utilization trends that may not be apparent from month to month casual observation. Comparing utilization percentages across several months can reveal concerning patterns even when absolute dollar amounts seem reasonable. This analysis should include both individual card utilization and overall utilization across all accounts.

Balance transfer activity often accompanies increasing utilization, as consumers attempt to manage growing debt loads by moving balances to accounts with lower interest rates or promotional offers. While balance transfers can be legitimate debt management tools, frequent transfers or transfers that merely shift debt without reducing total amounts may indicate developing credit problems.

Minimum payment increases provide another early warning signal, particularly when they outpace income growth. Credit card companies typically set minimum payments at 2% to 4% of outstanding balances, meaning that growing balances automatically increase minimum payment requirements. When minimum payments across all accounts begin consuming more than 10% to 15% of gross income, serious financial stress is likely developing.

Cash Flow Deterioration Indicators

Changes in cash flow patterns often precede credit problems by several months, providing opportunities for early intervention if recognized and addressed promptly. These changes may be subtle initially but typically accelerate over time as financial pressure increases.

The frequency of account balance checking often increases as consumers become more concerned about their financial position. Consumers who previously checked account balances weekly or monthly may begin checking daily or multiple times per day as they become uncertain about their available funds. This behavioral change often indicates growing anxiety about cash flow adequacy.

Increased reliance on overdraft protection or insufficient funds fees suggests that cash flow timing has become problematic. Even consumers with adequate overall income may experience cash flow timing issues when debt service payments consume larger portions of their paychecks, leaving insufficient funds for unexpected expenses or timing mismatches between income and expenses.

Payment timing becomes increasingly strategic as cash flow tightens. Consumers may begin timing payments more carefully, waiting until payday to make payments or spreading payments throughout the month rather than paying all bills when they arrive. While strategic payment timing can be a legitimate cash flow management technique, it often indicates that cash flow margins have become uncomfortably thin.

Emergency fund depletion represents a critical warning sign that financial resilience is deteriorating. Consumers who previously maintained emergency savings of three to six months of expenses may find themselves gradually depleting these reserves to cover current expenses or unexpected costs. Once emergency savings are depleted, any financial shock can precipitate immediate credit problems.

Side income seeking behavior often increases as consumers recognize that their primary income is insufficient to support their current lifestyle and debt obligations. This might include taking part time jobs, selling personal possessions, or exploring gig economy opportunities. While additional income can help address financial problems, the need to seek additional income often indicates underlying budget imbalances.

Investment liquidation or retirement account borrowing represents more serious indicators of financial stress. Consumers who begin liquidating investments or borrowing from retirement accounts to meet current expenses are typically experiencing significant financial pressure that requires immediate attention and intervention.

Behavioral and Emotional Warning Signs

The psychological aspects of developing financial problems often manifest before the financial indicators become severe. Recognizing these behavioral and emotional changes can provide early warning of credit trouble and opportunities for intervention before serious damage occurs.

Financial avoidance behaviors typically increase as financial stress develops. This might include delaying opening bills, avoiding budget reviews, or postponing financial planning activities. While these avoidance behaviors are natural responses to stress, they often prevent consumers from taking timely action to address developing problems.

Sleep disruption and anxiety related to finances often accompany developing credit problems. Consumers may find themselves lying awake at night worrying about bills, calculating payment scenarios, or feeling overwhelmed by their financial situation. These stress responses can impair decision making capacity just when clear thinking is most needed.

Relationship stress related to money typically increases as financial problems develop. Couples may find themselves arguing more frequently about spending decisions, bill paying responsibilities, or financial priorities. These relationship stresses can compound financial problems by creating additional emotional burdens and potentially leading to poor financial decisions made in anger or frustration.

Impulse control deterioration may seem counterintuitive but often accompanies developing financial stress. Some consumers respond to financial pressure by making impulsive purchases that provide temporary emotional relief but worsen their financial situation. This might include emotional shopping, dining out more frequently, or making luxury purchases they cannot afford.

Social withdrawal from activities that require spending money represents another behavioral indicator of financial stress. Consumers may begin declining social invitations, avoiding restaurants or entertainment venues, or making excuses to avoid activities that require spending. While reducing discretionary spending can be an appropriate response to financial pressure, social withdrawal can also indicate shame or embarrassment about financial circumstances.

Work performance changes may occur as financial stress affects concentration and focus. Consumers experiencing serious financial pressure may find it difficult to concentrate at work, may be distracted by financial concerns, or may need to take time off to deal with creditor calls or financial meetings. These work performance issues can potentially threaten job security just when stable income is most crucial.

Creditor Communication Pattern Changes

Changes in communication patterns with creditors often provide early warning of developing payment problems and opportunities for proactive intervention before accounts become seriously delinquent.

Automated payment failures begin occurring more frequently as cash flow becomes unpredictable. Consumers who previously relied on automatic payments may find that their accounts lack sufficient funds when payments are processed, resulting in insufficient funds fees and potential late payment charges. These automated payment failures often indicate that cash flow timing has become problematic.

Payment timing strategies become more sophisticated as consumers work to manage tight cash flows. This might include timing payments to occur immediately after payday, spreading payments throughout the month, or making partial payments to avoid late fees while preserving cash flow for other obligations. While these strategies can be effective short term cash flow management techniques, they often indicate that financial margins have become uncomfortably thin.

Customer service inquiry frequency typically increases as consumers become more concerned about their account status, available credit, or payment options. Consumers may begin calling more frequently to check balances, inquire about due dates, or explore payment arrangement options. This increased inquiry activity often indicates growing financial anxiety even before serious payment problems develop.

Request for account modifications such as due date changes, credit limit increases, or payment arrangement discussions often precede actual payment problems. Consumers who recognize developing financial pressure may proactively contact creditors to explore options before missing payments. These proactive contacts can be opportunities for early intervention that prevents more serious problems.

Promotional offer acceptance patterns may change as consumers become more sensitive to interest rates and fees. Consumers experiencing financial pressure may become more likely to accept balance transfer offers, promotional interest rates, or credit limit increases as they attempt to manage growing debt loads or reduce borrowing costs.

Late payment fee assessments, even if accounts remain current, often indicate that payment timing has become problematic. Consumers may make payments a few days late to preserve cash flow for other obligations, resulting in late fees even though payments are made before the account becomes officially delinquent.

Emergency Action Plans

Developing and implementing emergency action plans when financial trouble first appears can prevent minor problems from escalating into major credit damage. These plans should be specific, actionable, and designed to preserve credit while addressing underlying financial issues.

Immediate Financial Triage Procedures

When financial trouble first appears, immediate triage procedures help prioritize actions and resources to minimize damage while creating time for longer term solutions. This triage approach focuses on protecting the most critical obligations while buying time to address root causes.

The first step in financial triage involves categorizing all obligations by their potential consequences and legal protections. Secured debts such as mortgages and auto loans typically receive priority because default can result in loss of essential assets. Utility bills and other essential services also receive high priority because disconnection can affect health, safety, and employment.

Credit card debts and other unsecured obligations typically receive lower priority in emergency triage, though this prioritization may change based on specific circumstances. Credit cards that are essential for business purposes or that represent the consumer's only remaining available credit may receive higher priority than cards that are maxed out or rarely used.

Cash flow analysis becomes critical during emergency triage. This involves calculating minimum required payments for all priority obligations and comparing these requirements to available income. Any shortfall indicates the amount that must be generated through income increases, expense reductions, or temporary arrangements with creditors.

Asset liquidation consideration should focus on non essential assets that can be converted to cash quickly without significant tax consequences or penalties. This might include selling luxury items, unused vehicles, or recreational equipment. However, retirement account liquidation should generally be avoided due to tax consequences and penalties unless no other options exist.

Emergency fund utilization requires careful consideration of how much to use immediately versus preserving reserves for ongoing emergencies. Using all emergency funds to catch up on bills may provide temporary relief but leave the consumer vulnerable to future financial shocks that could create even worse problems.

Income acceleration strategies might include requesting advance payments from employers, collecting outstanding loans from friends or family, or engaging in short term income generating activities. However, these strategies should focus on legitimate opportunities that don't create additional financial obligations or legal problems.

Creditor Communication Strategies

Proactive communication with creditors before missing payments often yields better results than reactive communication after problems have developed. Effective communication strategies focus on demonstrating good faith, providing realistic proposals, and documenting all agreements.

The timing of creditor contact is crucial for achieving favorable outcomes. Contacting creditors before missing payments demonstrates good faith and often results in more favorable treatment than waiting until accounts become delinquent. Most creditors prefer to work with consumers who are proactive about addressing financial difficulties rather than those who avoid communication.

Preparation for creditor conversations should include gathering relevant financial information, calculating realistic payment proposals, and identifying specific requested accommodations. Creditors respond more favorably to consumers who have clearly thought through their situation and can present realistic proposals rather than vague requests for help.

Documentation of all creditor communications becomes essential for protecting consumer rights and ensuring that agreed upon arrangements are honored. This documentation should include dates, times, representative names, details of discussions, and confirmation of any agreements reached. Email follow up communications can provide additional documentation of verbal agreements.

Hardship program exploration should begin as soon as financial difficulty appears rather than waiting until payments are missed. Many creditors offer formal hardship programs that provide temporary payment reductions, interest rate modifications, or other accommodations for consumers experiencing financial difficulties. These programs often have qualification criteria and waiting periods that make early application advantageous.

Payment arrangement negotiations should focus on realistic proposals that address the consumer's financial constraints while providing creditors with reasonable assurance of payment. Overly optimistic payment arrangements that cannot be maintained often result in worse treatment from creditors than more conservative proposals that can be honored consistently.

Written confirmation of arrangements protects both consumers and creditors by ensuring clear understanding of agreed upon terms. Consumers should request written confirmation of any payment arrangements, hardship program enrollments, or account modifications. This documentation prevents misunderstandings and provides evidence if disputes arise later.

Resource Mobilization Techniques

When financial emergencies arise, quickly mobilizing available resources can provide the funds needed to prevent credit damage while longer term solutions are developed. Effective resource mobilization requires understanding all available options and their associated costs and risks.

Family and friend assistance often provides the most accessible source of emergency funds, but these arrangements require careful consideration of relationship impacts and clear agreement terms. Loans from family or friends should be documented with written agreements that specify repayment terms, interest rates if any, and consequences for non payment. These arrangements work best when they're treated as seriously as commercial loans.

Credit line utilization requires strategic thinking about which sources of credit to use and in what order. Home equity lines of credit typically offer the lowest interest rates but put homes at risk. Credit cards provide immediate access but often carry higher interest rates. Personal loans may offer fixed payment terms but require application processes that take time.

Asset liquidation strategies should focus on non essential assets that can be converted to cash quickly with minimal transaction costs. Online marketplaces, consignment shops, and precious metals dealers can provide relatively quick asset conversion, though consumers should research fair market values to avoid accepting below market prices due to urgency.

Insurance policy loans or cash value withdrawals can provide emergency funds for consumers with whole life or universal life insurance policies. These loans typically don't require credit checks or lengthy application processes, but they do reduce death benefits and may have tax implications if policies lapse.

Retirement account loans allow borrowing against 401k or similar employer sponsored retirement plans without tax consequences if repaid according to plan terms. However, these loans typically must be repaid immediately if employment terminates, creating additional risks that must be considered carefully.

Side income acceleration might include increasing hours at current employment, taking temporary or part time work, or monetizing skills through freelance or gig economy opportunities. While additional income takes time to develop, starting these efforts early can provide ongoing financial relief beyond the immediate emergency.

Expense Reduction Implementation

Rapid expense reduction often provides the most sustainable solution to financial emergencies because it addresses ongoing cash flow problems rather than providing one time financial relief. Effective expense reduction requires systematic analysis of all spending categories and implementation of immediate changes.

Housing cost reduction represents the largest potential source of expense reduction for most consumers but also requires the longest implementation time. Options might include downsizing, taking in roommates, refinancing mortgages, or negotiating rent reductions. While these changes take time to implement, beginning the process early can provide significant long term relief.

Transportation cost reduction can often be implemented relatively quickly through changes in commuting patterns, vehicle usage, or vehicle ownership. This might include using public transportation, carpooling, selling expensive vehicles, or moving closer to work. Transportation represents the second largest expense category for most consumers, making it a priority for reduction efforts.

Food and dining cost reduction can be implemented immediately through changes in shopping patterns, meal planning, and dining habits. Eliminating restaurant dining, shopping with lists and coupons, buying generic brands, and cooking at home can reduce food expenses by 30% to 50% or more for many consumers.

Entertainment and discretionary spending elimination provides immediate cash flow relief, though the amounts involved may be relatively small for consumers who were already managing their money carefully. Canceling subscriptions, avoiding entertainment venues, and eliminating impulse purchases can free up funds for essential obligations.

Insurance cost reduction through increased deductibles, coverage reduction, or provider changes can provide ongoing monthly savings, though consumers must balance cost savings against coverage adequacy. Shopping for insurance annually can often yield significant savings without coverage reduction.

Utility cost reduction through conservation measures, plan changes, or service modifications can provide ongoing monthly savings. This might include adjusting thermostats, using energy efficient appliances, switching to cheaper phone plans, or eliminating premium cable services.

Communicating With Creditors Before Default

Effective communication with creditors before payment problems develop can prevent minor financial difficulties from escalating into major credit damage. Understanding creditor perspectives, motivations, and procedures enables consumers to approach these conversations strategically and achieve better outcomes.

Understanding Creditor Perspectives and Motivations

Creditors approach workout negotiations from business perspectives focused on maximizing recovery while minimizing costs and risks. Understanding these business motivations helps consumers present proposals that align with creditor interests and increase the likelihood of favorable outcomes.

Recovery maximization represents the primary creditor motivation in workout situations. Creditors typically prefer receiving reduced payments over extended periods rather than receiving nothing through charge off and collection processes. This preference creates opportunities for consumers to negotiate payment arrangements that provide creditors with reasonable assurance of payment while reducing consumer payment burdens.

Cost minimization drives many creditor decisions about workout arrangements and collection activities. Collection efforts, legal proceedings, and account management all involve costs that reduce net recovery amounts. Creditors often prefer workout arrangements that avoid these costs, particularly when dealing with smaller balance accounts where collection costs might exceed potential recovery amounts.

Regulatory compliance considerations influence creditor willingness to negotiate and the types of arrangements they can offer. Bank regulators scrutinize loan modification and workout practices, encouraging creditors to work with borrowers experiencing financial difficulties while ensuring that arrangements are realistic and appropriate.

Risk assessment affects creditor evaluation of proposed arrangements and their willingness to provide various types of accommodations. Creditors prefer arrangements with borrowers who demonstrate stable income, realistic payment proposals, and commitment to honoring agreements. Consumers who can present their situations clearly and propose realistic solutions typically receive more favorable treatment.

Portfolio management objectives may influence individual account decisions based on overall portfolio performance and regulatory requirements. Creditors managing large numbers of accounts often have guidelines and procedures that limit individual account representative discretion but also provide standardized programs that can benefit qualified consumers.

Public relations considerations increasingly influence creditor approaches to borrower relations, particularly for large financial institutions that face public scrutiny. Many creditors have formal hardship programs and borrower assistance policies designed to demonstrate responsible lending practices and community commitment.

Hardship Program Navigation

Most major creditors offer formal hardship programs designed to help borrowers experiencing temporary financial difficulties. Understanding these programs, their qualification criteria, and application processes can provide access to accommodations that prevent credit damage during financial emergencies.

Program eligibility criteria typically focus on demonstrating legitimate financial hardship that is temporary in nature and likely to improve within a reasonable timeframe. Common qualifying hardships include job loss, medical emergencies, divorce, natural disasters, and other documented financial disruptions beyond the borrower's control.

Documentation requirements for hardship programs usually include proof of hardship such as termination letters, medical bills, or divorce decrees, along with financial information demonstrating current income and expenses. Gathering this documentation before contacting creditors can expedite application processing and demonstrate seriousness about seeking assistance.

Available accommodation types vary significantly between creditors and programs but commonly include temporary payment reductions, interest rate modifications, payment deferrals, and term extensions. Some programs allow combination approaches that might include several types of accommodations to create manageable payment arrangements.

Application procedures for hardship programs typically involve initial phone contact with specialized customer service representatives, completion of hardship applications, and submission of required documentation. Some creditors offer online application processes that can expedite processing and provide written documentation of requests.

Program duration limitations are common features of hardship programs, with most offering accommodations for three to twelve months. Understanding these time limitations helps consumers plan for eventual return to regular payment schedules and develop strategies for addressing underlying financial problems during the accommodation period.

Performance requirements during hardship programs typically include making all modified payments on time, avoiding additional charges or advances, and providing updated financial information when requested. Failure to meet these requirements usually results in program termination and return to original payment terms.

Program completion planning should begin when entering hardship programs, focusing on how financial circumstances will improve sufficiently to resume regular payments when accommodations end. This planning might include job search activities, expense reduction implementation, or income enhancement strategies.

Negotiation Tactics and Strategies

Successful creditor negotiations require preparation, realistic proposals, and understanding of common creditor concerns and limitations. Effective negotiation tactics focus on creating win win solutions that provide creditors with reasonable payment assurance while reducing consumer payment burdens.

Preparation for negotiations should include complete financial analysis, calculation of realistic payment capacity, research of creditor policies and programs, and development of specific proposals with alternative options. Well prepared consumers typically achieve better outcomes than those who approach negotiations without clear objectives or realistic proposals.

Proposal development should focus on what the consumer can realistically afford rather than what they would prefer to pay. Creditors respond more favorably to conservative proposals that can be honored consistently than optimistic proposals that may result in future payment problems. Proposals should address payment amounts, timing, and duration while providing creditors with reasonable assurance of performance.

Alternative scenario planning helps negotiations by providing options when initial proposals are rejected. This might include developing proposals with different payment amounts, timing arrangements, or accommodation types that can be presented if first proposals are declined. Having alternatives demonstrates flexibility and commitment to finding workable solutions.

Documentation of agreements becomes crucial for protecting both parties and ensuring that negotiated arrangements are implemented correctly. Consumers should request written confirmation of any agreements and should follow up verbal agreements with email or written summaries that confirm understanding of terms.

Representative identification helps ensure consistency in negotiations and follow up communications. Consumers should request names and direct contact information for representatives they work with and should document these contacts for future reference. Working with the same representative when possible often yields better results than starting over with new representatives.

Escalation procedures should be understood before beginning negotiations, as initial representatives may have limited authority to approve certain types of arrangements. Understanding when and how to escalate requests to supervisors or specialized departments can help consumers access accommodations that aren't available at initial contact levels.

Timing considerations affect negotiation outcomes, as creditors may be more willing to negotiate at certain times of month, quarter, or year based on their internal reporting and collection objectives. Understanding these timing factors can help consumers approach negotiations when creditors are most motivated to reach agreements.

Written Agreement Documentation

Documenting negotiated agreements protects consumers from misunderstandings, ensures proper implementation of arrangements, and provides evidence if disputes arise later. Effective documentation practices require attention to detail and follow through to confirm that agreements are implemented correctly.

Agreement confirmation should be requested in writing whenever possible, either through email or formal letters that specify all terms of negotiated arrangements. This confirmation should include payment amounts, due dates, duration of arrangements, and any other relevant terms or conditions.

Key terms documentation should capture all important aspects of agreements including payment amounts, timing, duration, interest rate modifications, fee waivers, and credit reporting impacts. Missing or ambiguous terms often lead to disputes later when arrangements are implemented or when circumstances change.

Implementation verification requires monitoring accounts after agreements are reached to ensure that negotiated terms are implemented correctly. This might include checking that payment amounts are correct, that promised fee waivers are applied, or that credit reporting modifications are made as agreed.

Performance tracking helps ensure that consumers honor their parts of agreements and provides documentation of compliance if disputes arise. This might include maintaining records of payments made, dates payments were submitted, and confirmation of receipt by creditors.

Modification procedures should be established for situations where agreed upon arrangements need to be changed due to changing circumstances. Understanding how to request modifications and who to contact can prevent arrangements from failing when minor adjustments are needed.

Dispute resolution procedures should be understood in case disagreements arise about agreement terms or implementation. This might include understanding internal creditor dispute procedures, relevant regulatory agencies, or legal options if agreements are not honored.

Follow up communication requirements may be specified in agreements, such as periodic financial updates or contact before arrangement expiration dates. Understanding and fulfilling these requirements helps maintain good relationships with creditors and may facilitate future accommodations if needed.

Hardship Programs And Options

Financial institutions offer various hardship programs designed to help borrowers navigate temporary financial difficulties without defaulting on their obligations. Understanding the range of available programs, their qualification criteria, and their potential impacts helps consumers access appropriate assistance before credit damage occurs.

Types of Available Hardship Programs

Payment modification programs represent the most common type of hardship assistance and typically involve temporary reductions in monthly payment amounts to levels that struggling borrowers can manage. These modifications might include reducing payments to interest only, reducing payments to amounts less than interest charges, or temporarily suspending payments entirely.

Interest rate reduction programs provide temporary or permanent reductions in interest rates charged on existing balances, reducing the cost of carrying debt and making payments more manageable. These programs are particularly valuable for consumers with higher rate debt who are experiencing temporary income reductions but expect their financial situation to improve.

Term extension programs allow borrowers to extend repayment periods for installment loans, reducing monthly payment amounts by spreading payments over longer periods. While these extensions increase total interest costs over the life of loans, they can provide crucial payment relief during temporary financial hardships.

Principal forbearance programs allow temporary suspension or reduction of principal payments while maintaining interest payments, providing payment relief while preserving the creditor's interest in the outstanding debt. These programs are commonly used for mortgage loans during temporary financial hardships.

Fee waiver programs eliminate or reduce various account fees such as late payment fees, over limit fees, or annual fees for consumers experiencing financial hardships. While fee waivers may seem minor compared to other accommodations, they can provide meaningful relief for consumers struggling with tight budgets.

Debt consolidation programs offered by creditors may allow combining multiple accounts into single payment arrangements with reduced interest rates or extended terms. These programs can simplify payment management while reducing overall payment requirements for consumers with multiple accounts with the same creditor.

Skip payment programs allow borrowers to skip one or more payments without penalty, with skipped payments typically added to the end of loan terms. These programs provide immediate payment relief but extend repayment periods and increase total interest costs.

Qualification Criteria and Application Processes

Hardship qualification typically requires demonstrating legitimate financial hardship that is temporary in nature and beyond the borrower's reasonable control. Acceptable hardships commonly include job loss, medical emergencies, natural disasters, divorce, death in family, military deployment, and other documented financial disruptions.

Documentation requirements vary between programs and creditors but typically include proof of hardship such as termination letters, medical bills, insurance claims, or legal documents, along with current financial statements showing income, expenses, and other debt obligations. Complete and accurate documentation expedites application processing and demonstrates seriousness about seeking assistance.

Income verification requirements help creditors assess borrowers' ability to meet modified payment arrangements and determine appropriate accommodation levels. This verification might include recent pay stubs, tax returns, unemployment benefit statements, or other documentation of current income sources.

Asset disclosure requirements help creditors understand borrowers' complete financial situations and ability to address financial difficulties through asset liquidation. While having assets doesn't automatically disqualify borrowers from hardship programs, creditors may consider asset levels when determining appropriate accommodation types and durations.

Credit history review may influence qualification decisions, with creditors considering previous payment performance, account management history, and overall creditworthiness when evaluating hardship applications. Borrowers with good previous payment histories typically receive more favorable consideration than those with previous payment problems.

Application timing affects program availability and effectiveness, with early application generally preferred over waiting until payments are missed. Many programs have waiting periods or processing times that make early application essential for avoiding payment problems during application processing.

Approval timeframes vary significantly between creditors and programs, ranging from immediate phone approvals for simple accommodations to several weeks for complex modifications requiring documentation review and approval processes. Understanding expected timeframes helps borrowers plan appropriate interim payment strategies.

Program Benefits and Limitations

Temporary payment relief represents the primary benefit of hardship programs, providing immediate reduction in payment obligations that can help borrowers navigate financial emergencies without defaulting on their obligations. This relief can be crucial for maintaining housing, transportation, and other essential services during financial crises.

Credit protection benefits vary between programs, with some providing formal protection against negative credit reporting while others merely prevent additional damage that would occur through default and collection processes. Understanding credit reporting impacts helps borrowers evaluate program benefits accurately.

Interest savings can be significant for programs that reduce interest rates or suspend interest accrual, though these savings must be balanced against potential term extensions that might increase total interest costs over time. Calculating total cost impacts helps borrowers make informed decisions about program participation.

Administrative simplification benefits help borrowers manage multiple obligations more effectively by consolidating payments, reducing payment frequency, or eliminating various account management requirements during hardship periods. These benefits can be particularly valuable for borrowers dealing with multiple financial obligations simultaneously.

Program duration limitations typically range from three to twelve months, with most programs designed to address temporary rather than permanent financial problems. Understanding duration limitations helps borrowers develop plans for transitioning back to regular payment schedules when programs end.

Qualification restrictions may limit program availability to borrowers who meet specific criteria or exclude borrowers who have previously participated in hardship programs within certain timeframes. These restrictions emphasize the temporary nature of hardship assistance and encourage borrowers to use programs judiciously.

Future credit implications may include notation of hardship program participation on credit reports or in creditor files, potentially affecting future credit decisions even when programs are completed successfully. Understanding these implications helps borrowers weigh program benefits against potential future consequences.

Exit strategy requirements may specify conditions that must be met for successful program completion, such as resuming regular payments, providing updated financial information, or maintaining account performance standards. Planning for program completion from the beginning increases the likelihood of successful transition back to regular payment schedules.

Building Credit Resilience

Credit resilience refers to the ability to maintain good credit standing even when facing financial challenges or unexpected life events. Building this resilience requires developing financial systems, habits, and resources that protect credit during difficult periods and enable rapid recovery when problems do occur.

Emergency Fund Development Strategies

Emergency fund adequacy represents the foundation of credit resilience, providing liquid resources that can address unexpected expenses without forcing reliance on credit. Traditional recommendations call for three to six months of expenses in emergency funds, but individual needs vary based on income stability, family circumstances, and risk tolerance.

Fund accumulation strategies should focus on consistent, automatic contributions that build emergency reserves gradually without creating current financial stress. Starting with small amounts such as $25 or $50 per month can establish saving habits that can be increased as financial circumstances improve. Automatic transfers to dedicated savings accounts help ensure consistent contributions without requiring ongoing decision making.

Account structure considerations help protect emergency funds from casual spending while maintaining accessibility during genuine emergencies. High yield savings accounts, money market accounts, or certificates of deposit with penalty structures that discourage casual withdrawals can provide growth while preserving accessibility for true emergencies.

Funding source diversification might include combining traditional savings with other resources such as Roth IRA contributions that can be withdrawn penalty free, cash value life insurance policies, or other accessible assets that can supplement emergency funds when needed. This diversification provides additional layers of protection while maximizing growth potential.

Usage criteria establishment helps distinguish between genuine emergencies that justify fund usage and financial wants that should be addressed through budget adjustments or additional income. Clear criteria prevent emergency fund depletion for non emergency purposes while ensuring that funds are available when truly needed.

Replenishment planning should begin immediately after emergency fund usage, with specific plans for restoring fund levels through increased savings rates, reduced expenses, or additional income. Rapid replenishment prevents multiple emergencies from creating cumulative damage to financial stability.

Growth strategies for larger emergency funds might include laddered certificates of deposit, Treasury bills, or other low risk investments that provide higher returns than traditional savings accounts while maintaining reasonable accessibility. However, growth strategies should never compromise the primary objectives of capital preservation and liquidity.

Multiple Income Source Development

Income diversification provides crucial protection against employment disruptions that represent one of the most common causes of credit problems. Developing multiple income sources requires planning, skill development, and ongoing maintenance but provides significant security benefits.

Primary skill monetization involves identifying skills from primary employment that can be marketed independently through consulting, freelancing, or part time work. Professional skills such as writing, design, programming, or business analysis often translate well into side income opportunities that can provide additional financial security.

Passive income development focuses on creating income streams that require minimal ongoing time investment once established. This might include rental property income, dividend investing, peer to peer lending, or digital product sales. While passive income typically requires significant upfront investment or effort, it can provide ongoing financial security with minimal time requirements.

Gig economy participation provides flexible income opportunities that can be scaled up during financial difficulties or scaled down during stable periods. Ride sharing, food delivery, task services, and other gig opportunities provide immediate income potential that can supplement primary employment or replace income during employment transitions.

Investment income generation through dividend paying stocks, bonds, or real estate investment trusts can provide ongoing income supplements that grow over time through reinvestment and principal appreciation. While investment income requires capital accumulation, it provides long term financial security that enhances overall credit resilience.

Business development opportunities might include starting small businesses based on personal skills, interests, or market opportunities. While business ownership carries risks, successful small businesses can provide significant additional income and long term financial security that enhances credit resilience substantially.

Skill development planning should focus on building marketable skills that can generate income during employment disruptions or economic downturns. This might include technical skills, certifications, or licenses that increase employability and income potential across multiple industries or economic conditions.

Network building activities help create relationships and opportunities that can provide income during difficult periods or career transitions. Professional networks, industry associations, and community involvement can provide access to opportunities that might not be available through traditional job search methods.

Credit Monitoring and Early Warning Systems

Proactive credit monitoring provides early detection of changes that might indicate developing problems or identity theft, enabling rapid response before serious damage occurs. Effective monitoring systems combine automated alerts with regular manual reviews of credit reports and scores.

Credit report monitoring services provide automated alerts when new accounts are opened, payment problems are reported, or other significant changes occur on credit reports. Many services offer monitoring of all three major credit bureaus, providing comprehensive coverage of credit activity.

Score tracking systems monitor changes in credit scores across different scoring models and bureaus, providing early warning of developing problems or confirmation of improvement efforts. Understanding normal score fluctuations helps distinguish between routine variations and significant changes that require attention.

Account monitoring procedures involve regular review of all credit accounts for unauthorized activity, billing errors, or changes in terms that might affect credit standing. Monthly statement reviews and online account monitoring help detect problems early when they're easier to resolve.

Identity theft protection services provide monitoring of personal information usage beyond traditional credit monitoring, including monitoring of Social Security number usage, public records, and other identity theft indicators. Comprehensive identity protection can prevent credit damage from fraudulent activity.

Alert system optimization involves configuring monitoring services to provide appropriate levels of notification without creating alert fatigue that reduces responsiveness to genuine problems. Balancing comprehensive monitoring with manageable alert volumes helps ensure that important notifications receive appropriate attention.

Response protocol development establishes clear procedures for responding to different types of credit monitoring alerts, ensuring rapid and appropriate responses to potential problems. Having predetermined response plans reduces reaction time and improves outcomes when problems are detected.

Documentation systems help maintain records of credit monitoring activities, alert responses, and resolution efforts that can be valuable for dispute procedures or legal proceedings if identity theft or other problems occur. Systematic documentation provides evidence and chronology that support consumer rights protection efforts.

Building credit resilience requires ongoing attention and investment but provides crucial protection against the financial shocks that can destroy credit standing rapidly. The investment in resilience building pays dividends through avoided credit damage, reduced financial stress, and improved ability to take advantage of opportunities that require good credit. In the next chapter, we will explore the legal framework that governs credit reporting and provides consumer rights and protections.

CHAPTER 6

THE FAIR CREDIT REPORTING ACT (FCRA)

The Fair Credit Reporting Act stands as the cornerstone of consumer credit protection in America, enacted in 1970 and significantly amended multiple times to address evolving credit practices. Understanding FCRA is absolutely critical for anyone serious about credit repair, as it provides the legal framework that governs how your credit information is collected, reported, and used.

FCRA establishes your fundamental rights regarding credit reporting and creates binding obligations for credit reporting agencies, furnishers of information, and users of credit reports. The law recognizes that credit reporting affects your ability to obtain employment, insurance, housing, and credit itself, making accuracy and fairness paramount concerns.

The Act's primary purpose is ensuring credit reporting agencies maintain reasonable procedures to ensure maximum possible accuracy of credit information. This doesn't mean perfect accuracy, the law uses "reasonable" standards, but it does mean credit bureaus must investigate disputes and correct verified errors. Understanding this distinction is crucial because many consumers expect perfection when the law only requires reasonableness.

FCRA also recognizes your right to access your credit information and dispute inaccurate items. Before FCRA, credit reports were secretive documents you couldn't access. The law opened this black box, requiring credit bureaus to provide you with your credit report and the information used to compile it.

The Act establishes specific timeframes for various credit reporting activities. Most negative information must be removed after seven years, while bankruptcies remain for ten years. However, these aren't automatic processes, items often remain longer unless you actively monitor and dispute them.

FCRA creates different rules for different types of credit report users. Employers must get your written consent before accessing your credit report and follow specific procedures if taking adverse action based on credit information. Insurance companies have different requirements than lenders, and background check companies operate under their own set of FCRA rules.

Understanding FCRA's structure helps you leverage its protections effectively. The law operates on the principle that accurate credit information benefits everyone, creditors get better risk assessment tools, and consumers get fair treatment based on accurate data. When this system breaks down through inaccurate reporting, FCRA provides mechanisms for correction and compensation for violations.

FCRA's evolution reflects changing credit practices and technology. The original 1970 Act focused on basic accuracy and access rights. The 1996 amendments addressed the growth of credit reporting beyond traditional lending, adding employment protections and identity theft provisions. The 2003 FACT Act amendments responded to identity theft concerns and strengthened consumer rights significantly.

Modern FCRA interpretation by courts and regulators continues evolving. Recent decisions have clarified furnisher obligations, dispute procedures, and damages for violations. Staying current with FCRA developments helps you understand your rights and leverage new protections as they emerge.

The Act's scope extends beyond the three major credit bureaus to specialty reporting agencies that track checking account history, rental payments, insurance claims, and employment backgrounds. These companies must also comply with FCRA, though many consumers don't realize these specialized reports exist or how to access them.

FCRA distinguishes between consumer reporting agencies and furnishers of information. Credit bureaus are consumer reporting agencies that compile and maintain credit files. Furnishers are the banks, collection agencies, and other entities that provide information to credit bureaus. Each has different obligations under FCRA, and understanding these distinctions helps you determine where to direct your disputes and complaints.

The law also recognizes that credit reports serve legitimate business needs while protecting consumer privacy. Permissible purposes for accessing credit reports include credit transactions, employment screening, insurance underwriting, and legitimate business needs involving consumer transactions. However, these purposes must be genuine – using credit reports for unauthorized purposes violates FCRA and can result in significant penalties.

FCRA's remedial scheme includes both individual lawsuit rights and regulatory enforcement. You can sue for willful or negligent violations, seeking actual damages, statutory damages, and attorney fees. Federal regulators also enforce FCRA through investigations, consent orders, and penalties against violating companies.

The Act's preemption provisions limit state law regulation of credit reporting in some areas while preserving state rights in others. This creates a complex legal landscape where federal and state laws interact, sometimes providing additional protections beyond basic FCRA requirements.

Understanding FCRA's penalties helps you evaluate potential violations. Negligent violations can result in actual damages and attorney fees. Willful violations add statutory damages of $100 to $1,000 per violation, plus punitive damages in egregious cases. These penalty structures make FCRA violations costly for companies, encouraging compliance.

Your rights under FCRA begin with access to your credit information. You're entitled to one free credit report annually from each major credit bureau through annualcreditreport.com, the only authorized source for free reports under federal law. Additional free reports are available after adverse actions, if you're unemployed and job searching, receiving public assistance, or are identity theft victims.

Beyond annual free reports, you can purchase additional credit reports directly from bureaus or through authorized resellers. However, be cautious of "free" credit report offers that require credit card information or enroll you in monitoring services, these aren't the federally mandated free reports and often involve recurring charges.

When requesting credit reports, you can obtain them online, by phone, or by mail. Online access provides immediate results but requires answering identity verification questions that may be difficult if your credit file contains errors or outdated information. Phone and mail requests take longer but avoid online verification issues.

Your credit report must include all information in your file, the sources of information, and identification of everyone who accessed your report recently. This includes creditors who obtained reports for existing account management, potential creditors who accessed reports for preapproved offers, employers who obtained reports for screening, and insurance companies checking for rate determinations.

FCRA requires disclosure of credit scores when you purchase credit reports, but not for free annual reports. Many credit bureaus offer scores separately or as part of paid monitoring services. Understanding that different scoring models exist helps you interpret score variations between sources, your mortgage lender might use a different score version than your credit card company.

The law mandates that credit reports be understandable to consumers. Technical codes must be explained, and reports must include instructions for disputing inaccurate information. However, credit report format varies significantly between bureaus, making comparison challenging without understanding each bureau's presentation style.

Your access rights extend beyond traditional credit reports to specialty consumer reports covering areas like check writing history, rental screening, employment background, and insurance claims. These reports require separate requests to different companies, and many consumers remain unaware of their existence despite their potential impact on creditworthiness assessments.

FCRA also provides access to information about who has accessed your credit reports. Recent inquiry lists help you identify unauthorized access and monitor legitimate usage patterns. Understanding inquiry categories helps you distinguish between "hard" inquiries that affect credit scores and "soft" inquiries used for account monitoring and preapproved offers.

The dispute process represents FCRA's most powerful consumer protection mechanism. When you identify inaccurate information on your credit report, the law requires credit bureaus to investigate and correct or remove unverified items within thirty days of receiving your dispute. This investigation requirement forms the foundation of most credit repair strategies.

FCRA's dispute requirements are specific and enforceable. Credit bureaus must provide free dispute mechanisms, investigate disputes within reasonable timeframes, and notify furnishers of disputed information. The investigation must be reasonable under the circumstances, though courts interpret "reasonable" differently depending on the dispute's complexity and available evidence.

Understanding what makes an effective dispute is crucial for success. Simply claiming information is "not mine" or "inaccurate" rarely succeeds without supporting explanation. Effective disputes identify specific inaccuracies, provide supporting documentation when available, and clearly explain why the information is incorrect or incomplete.

The thirty-day investigation timeline begins when the credit bureau receives your complete dispute, not when you mail it. Incomplete disputes lacking sufficient information to investigate may be rejected without investigation. This makes clear, detailed dispute letters more effective than vague complaints or form letters.

During investigations, credit bureaus must notify furnishers of disputed information and request verification. Furnishers must investigate their records and report results to credit bureaus. If furnishers cannot verify disputed information or find errors in their reporting, they must request correction or removal from your credit file.

Credit bureaus must provide written results of dispute investigations, including copies of corrected credit reports if changes were made. If investigations result in no changes, credit bureaus must explain why and inform you of your right to add a consumer statement to your file explaining your position on disputed items.

The law prohibits credit bureaus from putting disputed information back on your credit report unless the furnisher certifies the information as accurate and notifies you of the reinsertion. This prevents "yo-yo" reporting where negative items disappear and reappear without proper verification.

FCRA violations in dispute handling are common and actionable. Bureaus that fail to investigate, investigate unreasonably, or violate procedural requirements may be liable for damages. Understanding these violation patterns helps you identify when legal action might be appropriate.

Your dispute rights extend beyond initial investigations to re-disputes when new information becomes available or when investigations appear inadequate. However, credit bureaus can treat repeat disputes as frivolous unless you provide new supporting information or identify specific investigation deficiencies.

Furnisher obligations under FCRA create additional dispute avenues beyond credit bureau procedures. The 2003 FACT Act amendments established direct dispute rights with furnishers when you provide copies of credit bureau dispute results showing continued reporting of disputed information. This creates a two-step dispute process that can be more effective than credit bureau disputes alone.

When disputing directly with furnishers, they must investigate and respond within thirty days, similar to credit bureau requirements. However, furnisher investigations often prove more thorough since they have direct access to account records and transaction history. This can result in corrections that credit bureau investigations might miss.

Furnisher obligations extend beyond responding to disputes to initial reporting accuracy. They must have reasonable procedures to ensure information accuracy and must investigate and correct errors discovered through internal processes. They cannot report information known to be inaccurate, and they must update credit bureaus when account information changes.

The law requires furnishers to provide specific information when reporting negative items, including account numbers, account types, payment history, and current status. Missing required information can make negative items vulnerable to dispute challenges, especially when credit bureaus cannot verify incomplete data with furnishers.

Understanding furnisher categories helps target disputes effectively. Original creditors, collection agencies, and debt buyers have different record-keeping practices and verification capabilities. Collection agencies often lack complete account histories, making their reporting more vulnerable to successful disputes than original creditor reporting.

FCRA's furnisher provisions include special rules for debt collectors. When consumers dispute debts with collection agencies, they must investigate and cease collection efforts until verification is complete. This links FCRA disputes with Fair Debt Collection Practices Act protections, creating additional leverage in dispute situations.

Medical debt reporting receives special treatment under FCRA amendments requiring 180-day waiting periods before initial reporting and automatic removal when insurance payments satisfy debts. These provisions recognize medical debt's unique characteristics and provide additional protection beyond standard reporting rules.

Furnisher violations can result in both regulatory enforcement and private lawsuits. Companies that willfully disregard accuracy requirements face significant penalties, making furnisher compliance increasingly important as enforcement actions become more common.

The relationship between credit bureau and furnisher obligations creates overlapping responsibilities that benefit consumers. When either party fails to meet FCRA requirements, violations may occur regardless of the other party's compliance, providing multiple avenues for addressing reporting errors.

FCRA's permissible purpose requirements govern who can access your credit reports and when. These restrictions protect your privacy while allowing legitimate business access for specific purposes defined by law. Understanding permissible purposes helps you identify unauthorized credit report access and protect against identity theft.

Credit transactions represent the most common permissible purpose, including applications for credit cards, loans, mortgages, and other credit products. However, this purpose requires genuine credit-granting intent, pulling reports for general background checks without specific credit applications violates FCRA.

Employment purposes require written consumer consent and must follow specific adverse action procedures. Employers cannot obtain credit reports without your knowledge and must provide specific notices if taking adverse employment actions based on credit information. These protections recognize that employment credit checks can perpetuate discrimination and economic disadvantage.

Insurance purposes allow access for underwriting and rating decisions but restrict use to legitimate business needs. Insurance companies cannot use credit information for discriminatory purposes prohibited by other laws, and some states impose additional restrictions on insurance credit reporting.

Legitimate business need provisions allow access for account management, collection activities, and business transactions involving consumers. However, these purposes must be genuine and specific, general curiosity or harassment purposes violate FCRA's access restrictions.

Court orders and government investigations provide additional permissible purposes but require proper legal procedures. Law enforcement access requires appropriate warrants or subpoenas, and government agencies must follow specific protocols for accessing consumer credit information.

The written instructions permissible purpose allows access when consumers specifically authorize credit report access in writing. This provision enables consumers to provide credit information to landlords, attorneys, and other parties who don't otherwise qualify for access.

Child support enforcement agencies have special access rights under FCRA, allowing them to obtain credit reports for locating parents and enforcing support obligations. These provisions recognize the government's interest in child support collection while maintaining basic privacy protections.

Unauthorized credit report access violations carry significant penalties, including actual damages, statutory damages up to $1,000 per violation, and attorney fees. Identity thieves who obtain credit reports face additional criminal penalties under federal and state laws.

Recent court decisions have clarified permissible purpose requirements, particularly regarding debt buyer access and account management activities. Understanding these developments helps you identify potential violations and protect against unauthorized access to your credit information.

Statute of limitations provisions under FCRA establish how long negative information can remain on credit reports. These time limits recognize that old negative information loses predictive value and that consumers deserve opportunities to rehabilitate their credit standing over time.

Most negative information must be removed after seven years from the date of first delinquency that led to the negative status. This includes late payments, collections, charge-offs, and most public records. Understanding the seven-year period's calculation helps you determine when items should automatically fall off your reports.

Bankruptcies remain reportable for ten years from filing dates, regardless of discharge timing. This longer period reflects bankruptcy's more significant impact on creditworthiness, though the practical impact often diminishes significantly after three to four years when new credit becomes available.

The seven-year period runs from the original delinquency date, not when accounts were closed, sent to collection, or sold to debt buyers. This prevents negative information from being refreshed through collection activities or account transfers, protecting consumers from indefinite reporting of old debts.

Paid collection accounts and satisfied judgments must still be removed after seven years, contrary to common misconceptions that paying extends reporting periods. Payment may improve credit scores while negative items remain reportable, but it doesn't extend reporting timeframes under federal law.

Tax liens previously remained on credit reports until paid plus seven additional years, but all three major bureaus voluntarily removed tax liens from credit reports in 2017. However, liens may still appear on specialty background reports and public records databases.

Criminal convictions face different rules than credit-related negative information. Convictions may be reported indefinitely for certain high-paying positions or financial industry employment, though many states impose their own restrictions on background check reporting periods.

Positive account information can remain on credit reports indefinitely, encouraging consumers to maintain good credit relationships over time. Closed accounts with positive payment history typically remain for ten years, providing ongoing credit score benefits even after account closure.

Student loans have special provisions allowing rehabilitation to remove default reporting after successful rehabilitation program completion. This provides student loan borrowers with opportunities to repair credit damage that other debt types don't offer.

Medical debt reporting faces additional restrictions beyond standard statute of limitations, including 180-day waiting periods and automatic removal requirements when insurance payments satisfy debts. These provisions recognize medical debt's unique characteristics and provide additional consumer protections.

FCRA enforcement mechanisms include both private lawsuit rights and regulatory oversight through multiple federal agencies. Understanding these enforcement options helps you determine appropriate responses to credit reporting violations and maximize potential remedies for FCRA non-compliance.

Private lawsuit rights allow consumers to sue credit bureaus, furnishers, and credit report users for FCRA violations. These lawsuits can seek actual damages, statutory damages, punitive damages, and attorney fees, providing meaningful remedies for violations while encouraging compliance through financial consequences.

Actual damages in FCRA cases include financial losses caused by violations, such as higher interest rates, loan denials, employment rejections, or insurance premium increases. Documenting actual damages requires maintaining records of adverse actions and their financial impact, though proving causation can be challenging.

Statutory damages of $100 to $1,000 per willful violation provide remedies even when actual damages are difficult to prove. Courts consider violation severity, company size, and violation patterns when determining statutory damage amounts within this range.

Punitive damages are available for willful FCRA violations showing reckless disregard for consumer rights. These damages can significantly exceed statutory amounts in cases involving systematic violations or particularly egregious conduct by credit reporting companies.

Attorney fee provisions make FCRA lawsuits viable for consumers who might otherwise lack resources to pursue legal action. Successful FCRA plaintiffs can recover reasonable attorney fees and court costs, encouraging attorneys to accept cases and companies to comply with the law.

Class action lawsuits allow groups of consumers to pursue similar FCRA violations collectively, particularly effective for systematic credit bureau or furnisher violations affecting many consumers. Recent class actions have addressed mixed file problems, dispute handling failures, and furnisher reporting errors.

Regulatory enforcement operates through the Consumer Financial Protection Bureau (CFPB), Federal Trade Commission (FTC), and banking regulators depending on the entity type. These agencies can investigate violations, impose penalties, and require corrective actions through consent orders and enforcement actions.

CFPB supervision covers larger credit bureaus and provides ongoing oversight of credit reporting practices. The Bureau's examination reports often reveal systematic compliance problems and result in significant penalties for widespread violations.

State attorney general enforcement provides additional oversight through state consumer protection laws and concurrent jurisdiction over FCRA violations. State enforcement often focuses on local companies or practices affecting state residents, providing more targeted intervention than federal oversight.

Credit bureau obligations under FCRA extend far beyond basic dispute handling to encompass comprehensive accuracy procedures, consumer notification requirements, and systematic compliance programs. Understanding these obligations helps you evaluate whether credit bureaus are meeting their legal responsibilities and identify potential violations.

Reasonable procedures requirements mandate that credit bureaus maintain systems to ensure maximum possible accuracy of reported information. This includes verifying furnisher identity, maintaining current addresses and contact information, and implementing controls to prevent mixing of consumer files.

Mixed file problems, where information from different consumers appears in single credit files, represent serious FCRA violations that credit bureaus must prevent through reasonable procedures. When mixed files occur, bureaus must investigate thoroughly and implement measures to prevent recurrence.

Consumer notification obligations require credit bureaus to provide clear, accurate information about consumer rights, dispute procedures, and credit report contents. Notifications must be understandable to average consumers and include required disclosures about score availability and interpretation.

Credit bureaus must maintain current contact information for furnishers and establish effective communication procedures for dispute investigations. When furnishers become unreachable or fail to respond to verification requests, bureaus must remove unverified information rather than continuing to report it.

The requirement to follow reasonable procedures applies to both automated systems and manual processes. Credit bureaus cannot rely solely on automated matching without human oversight, particularly for complex disputes or unusual circumstances requiring individual attention.

Reinvestigation procedures must be genuine investigations, not mere confirmation of previous reporting. Credit bureaus must review available evidence, contact furnishers for verification, and make independent determinations about information accuracy based on investigation results.

Consumer statement rights allow you to add explanations to your credit file when disputes result in no changes. While these statements have limited practical impact on credit decisions, they provide a record of your position and may influence manual underwriting decisions.

Security obligations require credit bureaus to protect consumer information from unauthorized access and maintain appropriate safeguards for sensitive data. These requirements have become increasingly important as identity theft and data breaches threaten consumer information.

Accuracy improvement initiatives by credit bureaus often exceed minimum FCRA requirements as companies recognize that accuracy benefits both consumers and credit-granting clients. However, these voluntary programs don't eliminate legal obligations or create additional consumer rights beyond FCRA's baseline requirements.

Furnisher responsibilities under FCRA have expanded significantly since the original Act, particularly following the 2003 FACT Act amendments that established direct dispute rights and accuracy standards for information providers. Understanding these obligations helps you leverage furnisher responsibilities in credit repair efforts.

Initial reporting accuracy requires furnishers to have reasonable policies and procedures to ensure information accuracy before reporting to credit bureaus. This includes verifying account ownership, payment history accuracy, and current account status before initial reporting begins.

Ongoing accuracy maintenance obligates furnishers to update credit bureaus when account information changes, including payment updates, balance changes, and status modifications. Furnishers cannot simply report initial information and ignore subsequent changes that affect credit report accuracy.

Investigation obligations require furnishers to review their records and respond to credit bureau verification requests within reasonable timeframes. These investigations must be genuine reviews of available information, not mere confirmation of previous reporting decisions.

Direct dispute procedures, triggered when consumers provide copies of credit bureau dispute results, require furnishers to conduct independent investigations and respond directly to consumers. These procedures often prove more effective than credit bureau disputes since furnishers have direct access to account records.

Notification requirements mandate that furnishers inform credit bureaus of investigation results, including corrections, account closures, or continued reporting justifications. When furnishers discover errors, they must request corrections from all credit bureaus receiving their reports.

Special obligations for debt collectors include enhanced dispute investigation requirements and restrictions on reporting disputed debts during verification periods. These provisions recognize that collection agencies often lack complete account information and may report based on limited documentation.

Accuracy standards prohibit furnishers from reporting information known to be inaccurate, regardless of whether consumers have disputed the information. This creates proactive obligations to correct errors discovered through internal processes or customer contacts.

Account closure reporting requires furnishers to update credit bureaus when accounts are closed, including identifying whether closure was voluntary or involuntary. Proper closure reporting prevents confusion about account status and ensures accurate credit utilization calculations.

Charge-off and collection reporting must follow specific timing requirements and include accurate balance information. Furnishers cannot report inflated balances or add fees that increase reported debt beyond original amounts without proper disclosure and justification.

Documentation requirements obligate furnishers to maintain records supporting their credit reporting, particularly for disputed items. Adequate documentation becomes crucial during investigations and potential legal proceedings challenging reporting accuracy.

Employment credit reporting under FCRA involves complex procedures designed to balance employer needs for relevant information with employee privacy rights and protection against discrimination. Understanding these procedures helps you navigate employment credit checks and protect your rights during job searches.

Written consent requirements mandate that employers obtain clear, standalone authorization before accessing your credit report for employment purposes. This consent cannot be buried in general employment applications and must specifically address credit report access and potential uses.

Adverse action procedures require specific notices when employers take negative employment actions based on credit information. These notices must include copies of credit reports used, explanation of your dispute rights, and contact information for credit reporting agencies providing the reports.

Pre-adverse action notices must be provided before making final negative employment decisions based on credit reports, giving you opportunities to review report contents and dispute inaccurate information before adverse actions become final. This protects against decisions based on erroneous credit information.

Job relevance standards limit employment credit reporting to positions where credit history relates to job duties. While FCRA doesn't define specific job categories, positions involving financial responsibility, access to confidential information, or fiduciary duties typically justify credit report access.

State law variations provide additional protections beyond federal FCRA requirements in many states. Some states prohibit employment credit reporting for certain positions, require additional disclosures, or establish stricter adverse action procedures than federal law mandates.

Discrimination concerns arise when employment credit reporting disproportionately affects protected groups, potentially violating equal employment opportunity laws. Employers must ensure that credit reporting policies don't perpetuate discrimination based on race, gender, or other protected characteristics.

Background check companies serving employers must comply with FCRA's consumer reporting agency requirements, including accuracy procedures, dispute handling, and consumer rights notifications. These companies often combine credit reports with other background information, creating comprehensive screening reports.

Dispute rights during employment screening allow you to challenge inaccurate credit information that might affect employment decisions. However, dispute investigations may not complete before hiring decisions must be made, making proactive credit monitoring important for job seekers.

Current employee credit monitoring by employers requires ongoing compliance with FCRA procedures, including periodic consent renewal and continued adverse action obligations. Employers cannot use credit reports for general employee surveillance without specific business justifications.

Termination and credit reporting intersects when employment actions might affect credit standing, such as through missed loan payments or financial hardship. Understanding these connections helps you protect both employment and credit standing during career transitions.

Insurance credit reporting operates under specialized FCRA provisions that recognize insurance companies' legitimate needs for credit information while protecting consumers from unfair discrimination. Understanding these provisions helps you navigate insurance credit reporting and protect your rights as an insurance consumer.

Underwriting purposes allow insurance companies to access credit reports for determining coverage eligibility and premium rates for property, casualty, and some life insurance products. However, credit information cannot be the sole factor in coverage decisions and must be combined with traditional underwriting criteria.

Rate determination uses credit scores and report information to predict claim likelihood and set appropriate premiums. Insurance companies argue that credit information correlates with claim frequency and severity, though consumer advocates challenge these correlations and their fairness implications.

State regulatory oversight varies significantly regarding insurance credit reporting, with some states prohibiting or restricting the practice while others allow broad usage. Understanding your state's rules helps you know what protections apply to insurance credit reporting in your jurisdiction.

Adverse action requirements apply when insurance companies take negative actions based on credit information, including coverage denials, non-renewals, or premium increases. These notices must explain credit report usage and provide information about obtaining credit reports used in decisions.

Score disclosure obligations in many states require insurance companies to inform consumers when credit scores significantly affect their rates or coverage. These disclosures help consumers understand credit report impacts and take corrective action if necessary.

Prohibited discrimination factors prevent insurance companies from using credit information as proxies for race, religion, national origin, or other protected characteristics. However, proving discriminatory intent can be challenging when companies claim legitimate business reasons for credit-based decisions.

Medical debt exceptions in insurance credit reporting recognize that medical debt may not predict insurance claims as accurately as other debt types. Some states prohibit considering medical debt in insurance credit decisions or require special treatment of medical collections.

Identity theft protections extend to insurance credit reporting, allowing consumers to request special handling when credit reports contain fraudulent information. Insurance companies must have procedures for addressing identity theft situations without penalizing victims.

Appeals processes for adverse insurance decisions based on credit reports vary by state and company. Understanding available appeals helps you challenge unfair insurance actions and seek reconsideration based on complete or corrected credit information.

Credit improvement timing affects insurance rates differently than lending decisions, with some insurance companies updating credit information more frequently than others. Understanding update timing helps you optimize insurance rate improvements through credit enhancement efforts.

FCRA preemption provisions create a complex relationship between federal and state credit reporting laws, determining which regulations apply to different credit reporting activities. Understanding preemption helps you identify all available protections and avoid conflicts between overlapping legal requirements.

Complete preemption areas prevent states from regulating certain credit reporting aspects, including dispute procedures, information reporting periods, and basic accuracy requirements. These provisions ensure national uniformity in core credit reporting functions while preventing conflicting state requirements.

Partial preemption allows states to provide additional consumer protections beyond FCRA minimums while preventing weaker state standards from undermining federal protections. This creates a floor of federal rights while allowing states to build additional protections above that floor.

State law preservation in areas like identity theft, privacy rights, and defamation allows states to maintain existing protections that complement rather than conflict with FCRA requirements. These preserved areas often provide additional remedies for credit reporting violations.

Banking regulation coordination ensures that federal banking agencies maintain oversight of credit reporting activities by banks and credit unions while preserving CFPB authority over larger credit bureaus and non-bank furnishers. This coordination prevents regulatory gaps and overlapping jurisdiction.

Insurance regulation remains primarily state-based despite FCRA's federal framework, creating complex interactions between federal credit reporting requirements and state insurance laws. Understanding both frameworks is essential for insurance credit reporting issues.

Employment law interactions preserve state and federal equal employment opportunity laws while accommodating FCRA's employment credit reporting provisions. This ensures that credit reporting cannot circumvent existing employment discrimination protections.

Enforcement jurisdiction allows both federal and state authorities to pursue FCRA violations within their respective areas of authority. State attorneys general can enforce FCRA violations while federal agencies maintain primary oversight of systematic credit reporting problems.

Litigation venue rules determine where FCRA lawsuits can be filed, with federal courts typically hearing cases involving pure FCRA claims while state courts may address cases combining FCRA violations with state law claims.

Constitutional considerations underlying FCRA preemption reflect federalism principles and interstate commerce regulation, ensuring that credit reporting regulation remains coherent across state boundaries while preserving legitimate state interests in consumer protection.

Recent court decisions continue clarifying preemption boundaries as credit reporting technology and practices evolve. Staying current with these developments helps you understand the full scope of available protections under both federal and state law.

FCRA damages and remedies provide meaningful compensation for violations while encouraging compliance through financial consequences. Understanding available remedies helps you evaluate potential legal action and negotiate favorable settlements for credit reporting violations.

Actual damages compensate for financial losses caused by FCRA violations, including higher interest rates on loans, denied credit applications, increased insurance premiums, lost employment opportunities, and costs incurred in correcting credit report errors. Documenting these damages requires careful record-keeping and evidence of causation.

Emotional distress damages may be available in some jurisdictions for FCRA violations that cause significant psychological harm beyond financial losses. However, courts vary in recognizing emotional distress claims, and documentation of psychological impact typically requires professional evaluation.

Statutory damages of $100 to $1,000 per willful violation provide compensation even when actual damages are difficult to prove or calculate. Courts consider factors including violation severity, defendant's conduct, and plaintiff's circumstances when determining statutory damage amounts within the prescribed range.

Punitive damages apply to willful FCRA violations involving reckless disregard for consumer rights or malicious conduct. These damages can exceed statutory amounts significantly and serve to punish defendants and deter future violations by the defendant and industry participants.

Attorney fee awards make FCRA litigation accessible to consumers who might otherwise lack resources to pursue legal action. Successful FCRA plaintiffs can recover reasonable attorney fees and court costs, encouraging legal representation and promoting enforcement of consumer rights.

Injunctive relief can require defendants to change their practices, implement compliance procedures, or cease violating activities. This remedy addresses systematic problems and prevents ongoing violations that might affect many consumers beyond individual plaintiffs.

Settlement considerations in FCRA cases often involve combinations of monetary payments, credit report corrections, and procedural changes by defendants. Understanding settlement values helps you evaluate offers and negotiate favorable resolutions without lengthy litigation.

Class action remedies allow groups of consumers to address widespread FCRA violations collectively, particularly effective for systematic credit bureau problems or furnisher reporting errors affecting many people. Recent class actions have resulted in significant settlements and industry practice changes.

Regulatory enforcement through CFPB, FTC, and banking regulators can result in penalties, corrective actions, and systematic changes that benefit all consumers, not just individual complainants. Regulatory actions often address problems that individual lawsuits cannot resolve effectively.

Limitation periods for FCRA lawsuits typically range from two to five years depending on violation types and applicable statutes of limitations. Understanding these deadlines is crucial for preserving legal rights and pursuing timely legal action when violations occur.

Recent FCRA developments reflect evolving credit reporting technology, changing business practices, and enhanced regulatory oversight. Staying current with these developments helps you understand emerging rights and protection as the credit reporting system continues evolving.

CFPB supervisory authority over larger credit bureaus has resulted in detailed examination reports identifying systematic compliance problems and requiring corrective actions. These examinations often reveal widespread issues affecting millions of consumers and result in significant enforcement actions.

Credit bureau modernization initiatives aim to improve dispute handling, enhance accuracy procedures, and provide better consumer interfaces. While these improvements benefit consumers, they don't eliminate legal obligations or create additional rights beyond existing FCRA requirements.

Alternative data reporting expansion includes rent payments, utility bills, and other non-traditional credit information in credit reports. This expansion offers opportunities for consumers with limited credit history while raising new questions about accuracy, privacy, and fair reporting practices.

Medical debt reporting changes include voluntary removal of certain medical collections and enhanced verification requirements for medical debt reporting. These changes recognize medical debt's unique characteristics and provide additional consumer protections beyond standard reporting rules.

Identity theft protections continue expanding through enhanced verification requirements, fraud alert improvements, and security freeze enhancements. These developments respond to increasing identity theft threats while providing consumers with better tools for protection and recovery.

Artificial intelligence and automated decision-making in credit reporting raise new questions about accuracy, fairness, and consumer rights. As credit bureaus increasingly rely on automated systems, understanding how these systems work and their potential biases becomes crucial for effective credit repair.

State law developments provide additional consumer protections beyond federal FCRA requirements, including restrictions on certain types of credit reporting, enhanced dispute rights, and additional remedies for violations. Understanding state law variations helps you identify all available protections.

International credit reporting influences affect American consumers with foreign credit history or international financial connections. Understanding how international information affects U.S. credit reports helps you address cross-border credit issues and leverage positive foreign credit history.

Fintech innovations in credit reporting and scoring create new opportunities and challenges for consumers. Understanding how these innovations work and their potential impacts helps you adapt credit repair strategies to changing credit reporting landscapes.

Legislative proposals for FCRA reform continue emerging in Congress, addressing issues like medical debt reporting, dispute procedures, and credit bureau accountability. While these proposals may not become law, understanding proposed changes helps you anticipate potential future developments in credit reporting regulation.

CHAPTER 7

THE FAIR DEBT COLLECTION PRACTICES ACT (FDCPA)

The Fair Debt Collection Practices Act represents one of the most powerful consumer protection laws in America, specifically designed to eliminate abusive debt collection practices while allowing legitimate debt collection to continue. Enacted in 1977, FDCPA fundamentally changed the debt collection landscape by establishing clear rules about what collectors can and cannot do when attempting to collect debts from consumers.

Understanding FDCPA is crucial for credit repair because debt collection activities often intersect with credit reporting, and many credit repair disputes involve collection accounts. The Act provides leverage in negotiations with collectors and creates opportunities to remove negative items from credit reports when collectors violate the law.

FDCPA applies to third-party debt collectors, collection agencies, debt buyers, and attorneys who regularly collect debts for others. The law generally doesn't cover original creditors collecting their own debts, though this distinction has important exceptions and complications that affect how you approach different types of collection situations.

The Act's core purpose is protecting consumers from harassment, deception, and unfair practices while preserving legitimate debt collection rights. FDCPA recognizes that debt collection serves legitimate business purposes but requires collectors to operate within reasonable boundaries that respect consumer dignity and rights.

FDCPA violations are common in the debt collection industry, partly because many collectors operate with inadequate legal knowledge and partly because some deliberately push legal boundaries to maximize collection results. This creates opportunities for consumers who understand their rights to challenge improper collection practices effectively.

The law creates both defensive and offensive rights for consumers. Defensively, FDCPA protects you from abusive collection practices and provides grounds for stopping improper collection efforts. Offensively, violations create lawsuit rights that can result in damages, attorney fees, and leverage in debt settlement negotiations.

FDCPA intersects with credit reporting through several mechanisms. Collection accounts that appear on credit reports often involve FDCPA-covered collectors, validation rights affect credit reporting accuracy, and FDCPA violations can provide leverage for negotiating removal of negative items from credit reports.

The Act's enforcement mechanism relies heavily on private lawsuits, as consumers can sue for violations and recover damages plus attorney fees. This creates financial incentives for compliance while providing meaningful remedies when violations occur. Understanding these enforcement rights helps you evaluate when legal action might be appropriate.

Recent court decisions have clarified many FDCPA provisions and expanded consumer protections in some areas while limiting them in others. Staying current with legal developments helps you understand the full scope of your rights and leverage them effectively in collection situations.

FDCPA's scope and coverage determine which collectors and collection activities are subject to the law's requirements. Understanding these coverage rules helps you identify when FDCPA protections apply and which collection practices might violate federal law.

Third-party debt collectors represent the primary target of FDCPA coverage, including collection agencies that collect debts for others, debt buyers who purchase debts and collect them, and attorneys who regularly engage in debt collection activities. These entities must comply with all FDCPA requirements regardless of their collection methods or business models.

Original creditors generally remain exempt from FDCPA when collecting their own debts directly. However, this exemption has important limitations – if original creditors use names substantially different from their actual business names during collection, they may become subject to FDCPA as if they were third-party collectors.

The "regularly collects debts" requirement means that entities must engage in debt collection as a substantial part of their business to fall under FDCPA coverage. Occasional collection activities by businesses that don't primarily collect debts may not trigger FDCPA obligations, though state law often provides similar protections.

Consumer debt coverage includes debts incurred primarily for personal, family, or household purposes. Business debts generally don't receive FDCPA protection, though the line between personal and business debt can become blurred when individuals guarantee business obligations or use personal property as collateral.

Collection attorneys face special obligations under FDCPA because they often combine debt collection activities with legal representation. When attorneys send collection letters or initiate collection lawsuits, they must comply with FDCPA requirements in addition to professional responsibility rules governing lawyer conduct.

Debt buyers represent a growing segment of the debt collection industry and face full FDCPA coverage when collecting purchased debts. These entities often lack complete documentation about original debts, creating verification challenges that consumers can leverage in disputes and legal challenges.

Creditor subsidiaries and related entities may qualify as third-party collectors under FDCPA if they operate as separate businesses from original creditors. Complex corporate structures in the financial services industry can create coverage questions that affect consumer rights and protection levels.

State law interactions with FDCPA create overlapping protection systems, with many states providing additional consumer protections beyond federal requirements. Understanding both federal and state coverage helps you identify all available protections and remedies for improper collection practices.

Recent court decisions continue refining FDCPA coverage rules, particularly regarding creditor-related entities, debt buyer obligations, and attorney collection activities. These developments affect the scope of protection available to consumers and the obligations facing different types of collectors.

Prohibited collection practices under FDCPA establish clear boundaries for collector behavior and create actionable violations when collectors exceed these limits. Understanding these prohibitions helps you identify violations and protect yourself from abusive collection tactics.

Harassment and abuse prohibitions prevent collectors from using threats of violence, profane language, repeated phone calls intended to annoy, or publication of debt information to embarrass consumers. These provisions protect basic human dignity during collection processes while allowing legitimate collection communications.

False, deceptive, or misleading representations include threats to take actions that cannot legally be taken, misrepresenting debt amounts or legal status, falsely claiming to be attorneys or government representatives, and threatening legal action without intent to file lawsuits. These prohibitions ensure that collection communications provide accurate information to consumers.

Unfair practices encompass collection fees not authorized by law or original contracts, depositing post-dated checks before their dates, threatening to seize property without legal right to do so, and communicating with consumers regarding debts known to be disputed without disclosing the dispute status.

Communication restrictions limit when, where, and how collectors can contact consumers. Collectors cannot contact consumers at work if they know employers prohibit such contact, cannot call before 8 AM or after 9 PM in the consumer's time zone, and must cease contact when consumers request communication cessation in writing.

Third-party contact limitations prevent collectors from discussing debts with anyone other than consumers, their spouses, or attorneys. When collectors contact third parties to locate consumers, they cannot reveal debt information and must identify themselves only as necessary to obtain location information.

Legal action threats require genuine intent to file lawsuits or take other legal action. Collectors cannot threaten litigation unless they actually intend to sue and have legal authority to file such actions. Empty threats of legal action constitute false representations under FDCPA.

Credit reporting threats and representations must be accurate regarding collectors' intentions and abilities to report debts to credit bureaus. Collectors cannot threaten credit reporting unless they actually intend to report debts, and they must provide accurate information about credit reporting impacts.

Validation notice requirements mandate that collectors provide specific information about debts within five days of initial contact, including debt amounts, creditor names, and consumer rights to dispute debts. Failure to provide proper validation notices creates immediate FDCPA violations.

Documentation requirements, while not explicitly stated in FDCPA, become crucial when collectors make representations about debt validity, amounts, or legal status. Collectors must have adequate documentation to support their claims, though FDCPA doesn't specify exact documentation requirements.

Multiple debt considerations affect how collectors must handle situations where consumers owe multiple debts to the same creditor or collection agency. Collectors must properly allocate payments and cannot manipulate payment applications to maximize collection fees or extend collection periods.

Debt validation rights under FDCPA provide powerful tools for challenging questionable debts and obtaining information about debt origins and amounts. Understanding these rights helps you verify debt legitimacy and challenge collections that lack proper documentation.

The validation notice requirement mandates that collectors provide specific information within five days of initial contact, including the amount of debt, name of current creditor, statement that collectors will assume debt validity unless disputed within thirty days, and notice that collectors will obtain verification if consumers dispute debts within the thirty-day period.

Thirty-day dispute periods begin when consumers receive validation notices, not when collectors first attempt contact. During this period, consumers can dispute debts in writing and require collectors to obtain verification before continuing collection efforts. This creates a pause in collection activities that benefits consumers.

Dispute letter requirements under FDCPA are minimal – any written communication disputing debt validity triggers collectors' verification obligations. However, specific dispute letters that challenge particular aspects of debts often prove more effective than general disputes that simply claim debts are invalid.

Verification obligations require collectors to obtain and provide evidence of debt validity when consumers dispute debts within thirty days of receiving validation notices. The Act doesn't specify exactly what constitutes adequate verification, leading to ongoing litigation about verification standards.

Cease collection requirements mandate that collectors stop collection activities when consumers dispute debts until verification is provided. Collectors who continue collection efforts without providing verification violate FDCPA's dispute procedures and may face liability for improper collection practices.

Original creditor information must be provided if consumers request it and if the debt has been transferred or assigned. This helps consumers identify debt origins and contact original creditors for account information or resolution discussions.

Documentation standards for verification remain somewhat unclear under FDCPA, with courts reaching different conclusions about what constitutes adequate verification. Generally, collectors must provide evidence showing debt validity, amount accuracy, and their authority to collect, though specific requirements vary by jurisdiction.

Multiple debt scenarios require careful attention to validation procedures when consumers owe several debts to the same creditor or collection agency. Each debt typically requires separate validation notices and verification procedures, though collectors sometimes attempt to streamline these processes inappropriately.

Verification timing requirements mandate that collectors provide verification before resuming collection activities, but FDCPA doesn't specify exact timeframes for verification responses. Reasonable periods typically range from several weeks to a few months depending on debt complexity and required documentation.

Credit reporting implications of debt validation create intersections between FDCPA and FCRA protections. When collectors report unverified debts to credit bureaus or continue reporting disputed debts without verification, they may violate both FDCPA validation requirements and FCRA accuracy standards.

Communication restrictions under FDCPA establish detailed rules about when, where, and how debt collectors can contact consumers. These restrictions protect consumer privacy and prevent harassment while allowing legitimate collection communications to proceed.

Time restrictions prohibit collection calls before 8 AM or after 9 PM in the consumer's time zone. This protection recognizes that collection calls at inappropriate hours constitute harassment and interfere with family life and rest. Collectors must determine consumers' time zones and adjust calling schedules accordingly.

Workplace contact limitations prevent collectors from calling consumers at work when collectors know or should know that employers prohibit such calls. Consumers can inform collectors that workplace contact is prohibited, after which collectors must cease work-related contact attempts.

Cease communication rights allow consumers to stop most collector communications by sending written requests for communication cessation. Once collectors receive such requests, they can only contact consumers to acknowledge cessation requests or notify consumers of specific actions like lawsuit filings.

Third-party contact restrictions prevent collectors from discussing debts with anyone other than consumers, their spouses, or attorneys representing consumers. When collectors contact third parties for location information, they cannot reveal debt-related information and must limit discussions to obtaining contact information.

Location information guidelines limit third-party contacts to situations where collectors need to find consumers who have moved or changed contact information. Collectors cannot contact third parties repeatedly or use location services as pretexts for harassment or embarrassment.

Attorney representation notifications require consumers to inform collectors when they have attorney representation for debt matters. Once collectors receive such notifications, they must direct future communications to attorneys rather than consumers directly, unless attorneys fail to respond within reasonable periods.

Convenient time and place standards require collectors to respect consumers' reasonable requests about communication timing and methods. While FDCPA establishes basic time restrictions, consumers can request additional limitations based on work schedules, family circumstances, or other legitimate considerations.

Electronic communication rules address email, text messaging, and social media contact by debt collectors. While FDCPA predated these technologies, courts and regulators have applied the Act's principles to electronic communications, generally requiring consumer consent for electronic contact methods.

Voice mail and answering machine messages must comply with FDCPA's third-party contact restrictions since other household members might hear recorded messages. Collectors must be careful not to reveal debt information in messages that others might access.

Multiple contact attempts per day may constitute harassment under FDCPA, though the Act doesn't specify exact limits on contact frequency. Courts consider factors like total number of calls, timing patterns, and consumer responses when evaluating whether contact frequency violates harassment prohibitions.

False, deceptive, and misleading practices represent some of the most common FDCPA violations, as collectors often make inaccurate statements about debt amounts, legal consequences, or their authority to take specific actions. Understanding these prohibitions helps you identify violations and challenge improper collection tactics.

Legal action threats require genuine intent and authority to file lawsuits or take other legal action. Collectors cannot threaten litigation unless they actually intend to sue and have legal grounds for such actions. Empty threats designed to pressure payment constitute false representations under FDCPA.

Amount misrepresentations include inflated debt balances, unauthorized fees, and incorrect interest calculations. Collectors must be able to document debt amounts and explain how balances were calculated, including principal amounts, interest charges, and any collection fees or costs.

Attorney misrepresentations occur when collectors falsely claim to be attorneys, suggest attorney involvement when none exists, or use attorney letterheads without actual attorney review. These violations often involve collection agencies using attorney names or legal terminology to create impressions of legal action.

Government agency impersonation involves collectors falsely claiming to represent courts, law enforcement, or government agencies. These violations typically occur when collectors attempt to create urgency or fear by suggesting government consequences for unpaid debts.

Credit reporting misrepresentations include false statements about reporting intentions, inaccurate descriptions of credit impact, or threats to report information that collectors cannot legally report. Collectors must accurately describe their credit reporting practices and cannot threaten reporting as leverage without genuine intent.

Document misrepresentations involve collectors sending communications that appear to be legal documents when they are not, such as "summons" or "warrant" notices that are actually collection letters. These practices deceive consumers about legal status and potential consequences.

Debt validation misrepresentations occur when collectors provide inaccurate information about debt origins, amounts, or validation procedures. Collectors must provide accurate validation notices and cannot misrepresent consumers' rights or obligations during validation processes.

Settlement authority misrepresentations happen when collectors claim settlement authority they don't possess or misrepresent settlement terms and consequences. Collectors must accurately describe their authority to accept payments and any conditions attached to settlement agreements.

Time-barred debt misrepresentations involve collectors threatening legal action on debts beyond statute of limitations periods or failing to disclose that debts are too old for lawsuits. While collectors can still attempt collection of time-barred debts, they cannot threaten impossible legal action.

Identity and purpose misrepresentations include collectors failing to identify themselves as debt collectors or misrepresenting the purpose of their communications. FDCPA requires clear identification of collector status and debt collection purposes in initial communications.

Unfair practices under FDCPA encompass collection tactics that, while not necessarily false or harassing, are deemed fundamentally unfair to consumers. These prohibitions address collection practices that violate basic fairness principles even when technically legal under other laws.

Unauthorized fee collection represents one of the most common unfair practices, as collectors often attempt to charge fees not authorized by original debt agreements or applicable law. Consumers should scrutinize all fees and demand documentation showing fee authorization before paying disputed amounts.

Post-dated check threats involve collectors threatening to deposit post-dated checks before their dates or using post-dated checks as leverage for additional collection pressure. Collectors who accept post-dated checks must honor the dates unless consumers agree to earlier processing.

Property seizure threats without legal authority constitute unfair practices when collectors threaten to take property they cannot legally seize. Most consumer debts don't create security interests in property, making seizure threats inappropriate and potentially illegal.

Payment application manipulation occurs when collectors improperly allocate payments among multiple debts to maximize collection fees or extend collection periods. Consumers who owe multiple debts to the same collector should specify payment applications in writing to prevent manipulation.

Communication timing manipulation involves collectors using unusual communication methods or timing to pressure consumers unfairly. While FDCPA allows contact within specified hours, collectors cannot use timing strategically to cause maximum disruption or embarrassment.

Legal process abuse includes filing lawsuits in inappropriate venues, seeking improper remedies, or using legal procedures primarily for harassment rather than legitimate collection purposes. Collectors must use legal processes appropriately and cannot manipulate court procedures for collection advantages.

Third-party embarrassment tactics involve collectors attempting to embarrass consumers through third-party contacts or public disclosure of debt information. These practices violate both unfairness prohibitions and third-party contact restrictions under FDCPA.

Economic coercion beyond legitimate collection pressure may constitute unfair practices when collectors use threats or tactics designed to coerce payment through means other than normal collection procedures. This includes threats affecting employment, housing, or other essential services.

Documentation withholding when collectors refuse to provide reasonable documentation about debt validity, amounts, or their collection authority may constitute unfair practices. While FDCPA doesn't require extensive documentation, collectors must provide reasonable verification when requested.

Settlement manipulation involves collectors misrepresenting settlement terms, changing agreed-upon terms without notice, or using settlement discussions to gather information for increased collection pressure. Consumers should document settlement discussions and confirm agreements in writing.

Multiple debt confusion occurs when collectors deliberately obscure which payments apply to which debts or combine multiple debts inappropriately to confuse consumers about their obligations. Clear communication about debt identification and payment applications helps prevent these problems.

FDCPA enforcement and remedies provide meaningful consequences for violations while creating financial incentives for compliance. Understanding these enforcement mechanisms helps you evaluate potential legal action and negotiate favorable settlements when violations occur.

Private lawsuit rights allow consumers to sue debt collectors for FDCPA violations in federal or state court within one year of violations. These lawsuits can seek actual damages, statutory damages, and attorney fees, making legal action viable even for consumers with limited financial resources.

Actual damages in FDCPA cases include financial losses caused by violations, such as costs incurred due to illegal collection practices, lost wages from harassment at work, or expenses related to changing phone numbers or addresses to avoid improper contact. Documentation of these damages strengthens potential legal claims.

Statutory damages up to $1,000 per lawsuit (not per violation) provide compensation even when actual damages are difficult to prove. Courts consider factors like violation severity, collector's conduct patterns, and consumer circumstances when determining statutory damage amounts within this limit.

Attorney fee provisions make FDCPA litigation accessible to consumers who might otherwise lack resources for legal action. Successful FDCPA plaintiffs can recover reasonable attorney fees and court costs, encouraging legal representation and promoting law enforcement through private actions.

Class action lawsuits allow groups of consumers to address systematic FDCPA violations collectively, particularly effective when collectors use standardized practices that violate the law across many cases. Recent class actions have addressed automated calling systems, form letter violations, and widespread documentation problems.

Settlement considerations in FDCPA cases often involve combinations of monetary payments, debt forgiveness, and agreement to cease collection efforts. Understanding settlement values helps you evaluate offers and negotiate favorable resolutions that address both FDCPA violations and underlying debt obligations.

State attorney general enforcement provides additional oversight through state consumer protection laws and concurrent jurisdiction over FDCPA violations. State enforcement often focuses on systematic violations affecting state residents and can result in significant penalties and industry practice changes.

Federal Trade Commission oversight includes investigation of systematic FDCPA violations and enforcement actions against major debt collection companies. FTC enforcement typically addresses industry-wide problems rather than individual consumer complaints but can result in substantial penalties and corrective actions.

Consumer Financial Protection Bureau supervision covers larger debt collection companies and provides ongoing oversight of collection practices. CFPB examinations often reveal systematic compliance problems and result in enforcement actions that benefit all affected consumers.

Bankruptcy considerations affect FDCPA enforcement when consumers file bankruptcy during or after collection activities. Bankruptcy discharge eliminates most debt collection obligations but doesn't prevent FDCPA lawsuits for violations that occurred before discharge.

Credit reporting connections create additional leverage when FDCPA violations involve inaccurate credit reporting or threats of credit damage. Combining FDCPA claims with FCRA violations can increase settlement values and provide multiple legal theories for challenging improper collection practices.

Debt validation strategies under FDCPA create powerful tools for challenging questionable collection efforts and obtaining essential information about debt origins and legitimacy. Effective validation requests can stop collection efforts, identify documentation problems, and create leverage for favorable debt resolutions.

Strategic timing of validation requests maximizes their effectiveness and legal protection. Sending validation letters immediately upon receiving collection notices preserves the full thirty-day dispute period and demonstrates prompt action to challenge questionable debts.

Comprehensive validation letters should request specific information about debt origins, current ownership, payment history, and collector authority. While FDCPA requires minimal verification, detailed requests often reveal documentation problems that strengthen your position in dispute negotiations.

Documentation analysis helps you evaluate verification responses and identify potential weaknesses in collectors' claims. Adequate verification typically includes account statements, assignment documentation, and proof of collector authority, though exact requirements vary by jurisdiction.

Original creditor contact information must be provided when requested, allowing you to verify debt legitimacy directly with original creditors and potentially negotiate better resolution terms than collection agencies might offer.

Chain of title documentation becomes crucial when debts have been sold multiple times, as collectors must prove legal authority to collect through complete assignment chains. Missing links in ownership documentation can invalidate collection efforts.

Account statements and payment histories help verify debt accuracy and identify potential errors in balance calculations, payment applications, or fee additions. Collectors who cannot provide adequate account documentation may lack sufficient proof for continued collection efforts.

Verification inadequacy creates opportunities to challenge continued collection efforts when collectors provide insufficient documentation in response to validation requests. Inadequate verification responses may violate FDCPA's dispute procedures and provide grounds for legal action.

Credit bureau challenges often complement validation strategies when collectors report unverified debts to credit bureaus or continue reporting disputed debts without adequate verification. Combining FDCPA validation rights with FCRA dispute procedures maximizes pressure for accurate reporting.

Statute of limitations considerations affect validation strategies when debts may be too old for legal collection. While collectors can attempt collection of time-barred debts, they cannot threaten legal action, and validation requests may reveal debt ages that affect collection viability.

Settlement leverage increases when validation reveals documentation problems or FDCPA violations during validation processes. Weak documentation positions often motivate collectors to accept lower settlement amounts rather than risk legal challenges to their collection authority.

Follow-up procedures become necessary when collectors fail to respond adequately to validation requests or continue collection efforts without providing verification. Documenting these failures creates evidence for potential FDCPA violations and strengthens positions in dispute negotiations.

Cease and desist letters provide powerful tools for stopping unwanted collection communications while preserving your legal rights under FDCPA. Understanding how to use these letters effectively helps you control collection contact while avoiding unintended consequences.

Written communication requirements mandate that cease and desist requests be made in writing to trigger FDCPA protections. Verbal requests don't create binding obligations for collectors, though they may influence collector behavior in practice.

Comprehensive cessation requests should specify all forms of communication you want stopped, including telephone calls, letters, emails, text messages, and third-party contacts. Specific requests prevent collectors from switching to alternative communication methods not explicitly mentioned.

Limited cessation options allow you to stop some types of contact while permitting others, such as requesting cessation of phone calls while allowing written communications. This flexibility helps you control collection contact without completely stopping communication.

Legal consequences of cessation include collectors' rights to notify you of specific actions like lawsuit filings or account closures. FDCPA permits limited contact after cessation requests to provide legally required notices or inform you of definitive collection actions.

Credit reporting implications of cessation requests should be considered, as stopping communication doesn't prevent collectors from reporting debts to credit bureaus. You may need to address credit reporting separately through dispute procedures or settlement negotiations.

Collection continuation despite cessation may violate FDCPA, as collectors who ignore proper cessation requests face liability for improper communication. However, cessation doesn't stop collection efforts entirely – collectors can still file lawsuits or pursue other legal remedies.

Strategic considerations include timing cessation requests to maximize advantage while preserving opportunities for favorable debt resolution. Early cessation may prevent you from receiving settlement offers, while delayed cessation may subject you to continued unwanted contact.

Documentation requirements include keeping copies of cessation letters and using certified mail to prove delivery. Proper documentation helps establish FDCPA violations if collectors continue improper contact after receiving cessation requests.

Multiple collector situations require separate cessation letters to each collecting entity, as cessation requests don't transfer between different collection agencies or debt buyers who may acquire debts subsequently.

Revocation possibilities allow you to resume communication with collectors if circumstances change or if you want to explore settlement opportunities. Revocation should be made in writing to ensure clarity about your intentions.

Attorney involvement may influence cessation letter effectiveness, as some collectors respect attorney correspondence more than consumer letters. However, attorney representation isn't required for effective cessation requests under FDCPA.

Settlement negotiations become more complex after cessation requests, as collectors cannot initiate contact to discuss settlement options. You may need to initiate settlement discussions or temporarily revoke cessation to explore resolution opportunities.

Credit reporting intersections between FDCPA and FCRA create powerful leverage for challenging both improper collection practices and inaccurate credit reporting. Understanding these connections helps you maximize protection under both laws and achieve better results in credit repair efforts.

Dual violations often occur when collectors engage in improper collection practices while simultaneously reporting inaccurate information to credit bureaus. These situations provide multiple legal theories for challenging collector behavior and may increase settlement values in dispute negotiations.

Verification requirements under both laws create overlapping obligations for collectors who report to credit bureaus. FDCPA validation requirements may exceed FCRA verification standards, providing additional tools for challenging questionable debt reporting.

Credit reporting threats must be accurate under FDCPA, preventing collectors from making false statements about reporting intentions or credit impact. Collectors cannot threaten credit reporting unless they actually intend to report debts and must accurately describe reporting consequences.

Dispute timing coordination between FDCPA validation and FCRA disputes can maximize pressure on collectors and credit bureaus to resolve reporting errors. Strategic timing of both types of disputes often produces better results than pursuing them separately.

Documentation standards for credit reporting should meet both FDCPA validation requirements and FCRA accuracy standards. Collectors who cannot satisfy either standard may lack sufficient documentation to continue both collection efforts and credit reporting.

Pay-for-delete negotiations often involve both FDCPA considerations and credit reporting agreements. Collectors who violate FDCPA during collection efforts may be more willing to agree to credit report removal as part of settlement agreements.

Time-barred debt reporting creates complex intersections between collection laws and credit reporting rules. While collectors may continue attempting collection of old debts under some circumstances, credit reporting of time-barred debts may violate FCRA's reporting period limitations.

Identity theft implications affect both collection efforts and credit reporting when disputed debts result from identity theft. FDCPA validation requirements and FCRA identity theft protections work together to help identity theft victims challenge fraudulent accounts.

Multiple collector reporting situations arise when debts are sold between collection agencies, potentially resulting in duplicate credit reporting or conflicting information from different sources. Both FDCPA and FCRA provide tools for addressing these problems.

Settlement documentation should address both collection cessation and credit reporting removal when negotiating resolutions that involve both FDCPA violations and credit repair goals. Comprehensive settlement agreements protect against future collection efforts and credit reporting problems.

Legal action coordination allows consumers to pursue both FDCPA and FCRA claims in single lawsuits when collectors violate both laws. Combined legal actions often provide stronger positions and better settlement leverage than separate proceedings.

Regulatory oversight from CFPB and other agencies addresses both debt collection practices and credit reporting accuracy, providing administrative complaint options when collectors violate multiple consumer protection laws simultaneously.

Working with debt collection attorneys requires understanding their dual roles as both debt collectors subject to FDCPA and legal professionals bound by attorney ethics rules. This combination creates unique opportunities and challenges when collection attorneys become involved in debt collection efforts.

Attorney collector obligations include full compliance with FDCPA requirements when collecting debts, regardless of their status as licensed attorneys. Attorney collection letters must include validation notices, communications must comply with contact restrictions, and attorney collectors cannot engage in prohibited practices.

Legal document misrepresentation by attorney collectors often involves using attorney letterheads or legal terminology to create false impressions of legal action when no litigation is planned. These practices violate both FDCPA prohibitions against false representations and attorney professional responsibility rules.

Litigation threat evaluation becomes crucial when attorney collectors threaten legal action, as attorneys should not threaten litigation unless they have genuine intent to sue and adequate documentation to support lawsuits. Empty litigation threats by attorneys may violate both FDCPA and professional ethics standards.

Professional responsibility rules create additional obligations for attorney collectors beyond FDCPA requirements, including duties to provide competent representation, maintain client confidentiality, and avoid conflicts of interest. These rules may provide additional grounds for challenging improper attorney collection practices.

Settlement authority clarity becomes important when dealing with attorney collectors, as attorneys may have different settlement authority than non-attorney collectors. Understanding attorney authority helps ensure that settlement agreements are enforceable and properly documented.

Court filing requirements mandate that attorney collectors who file lawsuits must have adequate documentation and legal grounds for litigation. Attorneys who file frivolous lawsuits or fail to investigate debt validity before litigation may face both FDCPA liability and professional discipline.

Response strategies to attorney collection letters should consider both FDCPA rights and the possibility of actual litigation. While attorney involvement may indicate serious collection intent, it doesn't eliminate your validation rights or other FDCPA protections.

Bar complaint options provide additional enforcement mechanisms when attorney collectors violate professional responsibility rules in addition to FDCPA requirements. State bar associations can investigate attorney misconduct and impose professional discipline separate from FDCPA remedies.

Fee shifting considerations in litigation with attorney collectors may affect settlement calculations, as attorney fee awards in FDCPA cases can be substantial when attorney collectors violate the law. This creates additional leverage in settlement negotiations.

Documentation preservation becomes crucial when dealing with attorney collectors, as litigation becomes more likely and proper documentation of FDCPA violations strengthens potential legal claims against attorney collectors who violate the law.

Judgment enforcement limitations apply even when attorney collectors obtain court judgments, as consumer protection laws limit collection methods and exempt certain property from collection. Understanding these limitations helps you protect assets even after adverse court decisions.

Multiple representation issues may arise when attorney collectors represent multiple creditors or collection agencies, potentially creating conflicts of interest that affect collection effectiveness and provide additional grounds for challenging collection efforts.

State law variations in debt collection regulation create additional consumer protections beyond federal FDCPA requirements, with many states providing stronger protections, shorter limitation periods, or additional remedies for collection violations. Understanding state law helps you identify all available protections.

Enhanced communication restrictions in some states limit collection contact more strictly than FDCPA, including prohibitions on workplace contact regardless of employer policies, stricter time restrictions, or broader third-party contact limitations. These variations often provide additional protection in states with strong consumer protection traditions.

Licensing requirements for debt collectors exist in many states, creating regulatory oversight and disciplinary mechanisms beyond federal enforcement. State licensing violations may provide additional grounds for challenging collection efforts and may affect collectors' legal authority to operate.

Statute of limitations variations affect collection lawsuit timeframes and threat evaluation, with states establishing different limitation periods for different debt types. Understanding your state's limitation periods helps you evaluate litigation threats and identify time-barred debt situations.

Interest and fee limitations in state law may restrict collectors' ability to add collection costs or interest beyond amounts authorized by original agreements or state law. These limitations can help you challenge inflated debt amounts and negotiate better settlement terms.

Garnishment restrictions vary significantly between states, with some states providing broader exemptions or stricter procedural requirements than federal law mandates. Understanding garnishment protections helps you evaluate collection risks and protect assets from collection efforts.

Notice requirements in some states exceed FDCPA validation notice standards, requiring additional disclosures or different notice timing. Enhanced state notice requirements may provide additional grounds for challenging collection efforts that comply with federal law but violate state requirements.

Attorney regulation through state bar associations creates additional oversight of attorney collectors beyond FDCPA enforcement. State disciplinary mechanisms can address attorney collection violations and may provide remedies not available under federal debt collection law.

Small claims court limitations in many states restrict collection lawsuit venues or procedures, potentially affecting where collectors can sue and what remedies they can seek. Understanding small claims rules helps you evaluate litigation risks and defense strategies.

Consumer protection law overlaps create multiple legal theories for challenging improper collection practices when state consumer protection laws provide broader coverage or different remedies than FDCPA. These overlapping protections often strengthen legal positions against violating collectors.

Regulatory enforcement through state attorneys general offices provides additional complaint mechanisms and enforcement options beyond federal oversight. State enforcement often focuses on local collection agencies or practices affecting state residents specifically.

Preemption limitations prevent federal law from overriding stronger state consumer protections, ensuring that FDCPA creates minimum standards while allowing states to provide additional protections. Understanding preemption helps you identify the full scope of available legal protection.

Identity theft and FDCPA intersections create special considerations when collection efforts involve fraudulent accounts or identity theft situations. Understanding these connections helps identity theft victims challenge collection efforts effectively while protecting their rights under multiple consumer protection laws.

Identity theft disputes with collectors require specific documentation and procedures to establish that debts result from identity theft rather than legitimate consumer obligations. Collectors must investigate identity theft claims and cannot continue collection efforts on verified fraudulent accounts.

Documentation requirements for identity theft claims typically include police reports, identity theft affidavits, and evidence supporting claims that accounts were opened fraudulently. Comprehensive documentation strengthens identity theft claims and may expedite resolution of collection disputes.

Credit reporting implications of identity theft extend to collection accounts, as fraudulent collection accounts must be removed from credit reports when identity theft is verified. FDCPA validation rights complement FCRA identity theft protections in challenging fraudulent collection efforts.

Collector investigation obligations require legitimate investigation of identity theft claims rather than mere continuation of collection efforts. Collectors who ignore credible identity theft evidence may violate FDCPA requirements for accurate debt information.

Burden of proof considerations in identity theft cases generally require collectors to verify debt legitimacy rather than requiring consumers to prove fraud. However, credible identity theft evidence strengthens consumer positions and may shift investigation burdens more clearly to collectors.

Criminal activity reporting may be necessary when collection efforts involve clear identity theft or fraud. While this doesn't directly affect FDCPA obligations, criminal complaints may provide additional evidence supporting identity theft claims in collection disputes.

Legal remedies for collection efforts on fraudulent debts may include both FDCPA violations and state law claims for wrongful collection attempts. Identity theft victims may have stronger legal positions than consumers disputing legitimate debts.

Prevention strategies include monitoring credit reports for unauthorized accounts, promptly disputing suspicious collection efforts, and maintaining documentation of identity theft reports and resolution efforts. Early intervention often prevents collection problems from escalating.

Resolution coordination between identity theft reports, credit bureau disputes, and collector communications helps ensure comprehensive resolution of fraud-related collection problems. Systematic approaches often produce better results than addressing each issue separately.

Ongoing monitoring remains necessary even after resolving identity theft collection issues, as fraudulent accounts may reappear or new collection efforts may arise from the same underlying identity theft incidents.

Law enforcement involvement may strengthen identity theft claims with collectors, as police reports and criminal investigations provide official documentation of fraud that collectors typically cannot ignore or challenge effectively.

Recovery rights for damages caused by collection efforts on fraudulent accounts may include both identity theft remedies and FDCPA damages when collectors violate the law during collection of fraudulent debts.

Bankruptcy and debt collection intersections create complex legal situations where FDCPA protections interact with bankruptcy law's automatic stay provisions and discharge protections. Understanding these interactions helps consumers navigate collection efforts before, during, and after bankruptcy proceedings.

Automatic stay protections immediately halt most collection efforts when consumers file bankruptcy, creating broader protection than FDCPA cessation rights. However, FDCPA violations that occur before bankruptcy filing remain actionable even after bankruptcy discharge.

Pre-bankruptcy collection activities may violate FDCPA even when bankruptcy eventually discharges underlying debts. Collectors cannot escape FDCPA liability by arguing that bankruptcy eliminates the relevance of their collection violations, as FDCPA damage claims survive bankruptcy and remain collectible by consumers.

Post-discharge collection efforts on discharged debts violate both bankruptcy law and potentially FDCPA when collectors attempt to collect debts eliminated by bankruptcy discharge. These violations often carry enhanced penalties and may justify significant damage awards.

Reaffirmation considerations affect FDCPA protections when consumers consider reaffirming debts during bankruptcy proceedings. Collectors cannot use FDCPA violations or threats to pressure consumers into reaffirmation agreements, and such pressure may invalidate reaffirmation attempts.

Payment plan modifications may be necessary when FDCPA violations affect consumers' ability to maintain bankruptcy payment plans. Courts may consider collection violations when evaluating payment plan modifications or hardship discharge requests.

Asset exemption protection works alongside FDCPA to protect consumer property from collection efforts both before and after bankruptcy. Understanding exemption laws helps consumers protect assets while pursuing FDCPA claims for collection violations.

Trustee involvement in bankruptcy cases may affect FDCPA claim pursuit, as some FDCPA claims become bankruptcy estate property while others remain with individual consumers. Consulting bankruptcy attorneys helps determine how to preserve FDCPA claims during bankruptcy proceedings.

Creditor meeting protections prevent collectors from using required bankruptcy meetings as opportunities for collection pressure or FDCPA violations. Collectors who are also creditors must respect bankruptcy procedures and cannot circumvent automatic stay protections.

Discharge violation remedies include both bankruptcy court sanctions and potential FDCPA damages when collectors violate discharge orders through continued collection efforts. These overlapping protections often provide strong remedies for post-bankruptcy collection violations.

Timeline considerations affect both bankruptcy filing strategies and FDCPA claim pursuit, as consumers must balance immediate collection pressure against long-term financial recovery goals. Strategic timing can maximize benefits under both laws.

Attorney coordination becomes crucial when pursuing both bankruptcy protection and FDCPA claims, as specialized knowledge in both areas helps ensure optimal outcomes and prevents conflicts between different legal strategies.

Credit reporting after bankruptcy intersects with FDCPA when collectors continue reporting discharged debts or make inaccurate representations about post-bankruptcy debt status. These situations may violate both bankruptcy law and credit reporting requirements.

Technological developments in debt collection create new applications of FDCPA principles to modern communication methods and collection practices. Understanding how traditional FDCPA rules apply to new technologies helps you protect your rights in an evolving collection environment.

Automated calling systems used by collectors must comply with FDCPA communication restrictions, including time limitations, frequency restrictions, and cessation requirements. Automated systems cannot excuse collectors from FDCPA compliance obligations, and technological convenience doesn't override consumer protection requirements.

Text messaging and email collection efforts fall under FDCPA jurisdiction when used by covered collectors, requiring compliance with communication restrictions and validation notice requirements. Collectors must obtain proper consent for electronic communications and respect cessation requests across all communication channels.

Social media collection activities by debt collectors raise significant FDCPA concerns, particularly regarding third-party contact restrictions and public disclosure prohibitions. Collectors cannot use social media to embarrass consumers or reveal debt information to unauthorized parties.

Voice recognition technology and caller ID spoofing present new challenges for FDCPA compliance, as collectors must accurately identify themselves and cannot use technology to deceive consumers about communication origins or purposes.

Data analytics and consumer profiling by collectors must comply with FDCPA fairness requirements and cannot be used to circumvent communication restrictions or engage in harassment through targeted contact timing or methods.

Mobile payment demands and electronic fund transfer threats require careful evaluation under FDCPA unfair practice prohibitions, particularly when collectors use technology to pressure immediate payments or circumvent normal payment processing protections.

Credit reporting automation by collectors must maintain FDCPA accuracy standards even when using automated systems for reporting disputed or unverified debts. Technology cannot excuse collectors from investigation obligations or validation requirements.

Artificial intelligence applications in debt collection must comply with FDCPA requirements for accurate representations and cannot be programmed to make false or misleading statements about debt amounts, legal consequences, or collector authority.

Digital document delivery for validation notices and legal communications must meet FDCPA notice requirements and ensure consumer receipt. Electronic delivery cannot diminish consumer rights or collector obligations under traditional notice provisions.

Online dispute processing systems offered by collectors must provide meaningful dispute resolution opportunities equivalent to traditional validation procedures. Technological dispute systems cannot limit consumer rights or circumvent FDCPA protection requirements.

Cybersecurity considerations affect collector obligations to protect consumer information and prevent unauthorized disclosure of debt information through electronic systems. Data breaches may create additional FDCPA violations when they result in unauthorized third-party disclosure.

Regulatory adaptation to technological changes continues evolving as agencies interpret FDCPA requirements in light of new collection technologies and practices. Staying current with regulatory guidance helps you understand how established rights apply to new collection methods.

Settlement negotiations with debt collectors require understanding how FDCPA violations affect negotiation dynamics and settlement values. FDCPA violations often create leverage that can result in better settlement terms or complete debt elimination beyond what financial circumstances alone might justify.

Violation documentation should be comprehensive and well-organized before entering settlement negotiations, as specific FDCPA violations carry different settlement values and some violations are easier to prove than others. Strong documentation strengthens negotiation positions significantly.

Settlement timing considerations include balancing immediate resolution benefits against potential legal action values. FDCPA lawsuits can result in substantial damages and attorney fees, but settlement offers provide immediate resolution without litigation risks and expenses.

Comprehensive settlement agreements should address both debt resolution and FDCPA violation releases, ensuring that settlements provide complete resolution of all issues between consumers and collectors. Incomplete settlements may leave unresolved claims that complicate future interactions.

Credit reporting provisions in settlements often prove crucial for consumers seeking credit repair benefits from settlement agreements. Collectors may agree to credit report removal or correction as part of settlements that address both debt obligations and FDCPA violations.

Payment terms in FDCPA settlements should be clearly documented and realistic for consumer circumstances. Collectors may accept reduced payments or extended payment terms when FDCPA violations strengthen consumer negotiation positions.

Release scope limitations help consumers preserve certain claims while settling others, particularly important when multiple collectors are involved or when violations occurred over extended periods. Careful release drafting protects against overly broad claim releases.

Attorney involvement in settlement negotiations often improves outcomes, as collectors may take settlement discussions more seriously when consumers are represented by attorneys familiar with FDCPA litigation values and procedures.

Tax implications of debt settlement should be considered, as forgiven debt amounts may create taxable income for consumers. However, FDCPA violation settlements typically don't create taxable income since they compensate for damages rather than debt forgiveness.

Documentation preservation remains important even after settlement completion, as settlement agreements may need enforcement if collectors fail to comply with settlement terms. Maintaining complete records protects against future collection attempts on settled debts.

Multiple collector coordination becomes necessary when debts have been sold or assigned multiple times, requiring resolution with current collectors while protecting against claims by previous collectors. Comprehensive settlements should address chain of title issues.

Enforcement mechanisms for settlement agreements vary depending on agreement terms and applicable law. Understanding enforcement options helps ensure that collectors comply with settlement terms and provides remedies when they don't.

Future collection prevention through settlement agreements helps protect consumers against renewed collection efforts by the same collectors or subsequent debt buyers. Effective settlements should include provisions preventing future collection on settled debts.

Consumer Financial Protection Bureau (CFPB) oversight of debt collection has significantly enhanced FDCPA enforcement through examination authority, regulatory guidance, and systematic enforcement actions against major debt collection companies. Understanding CFPB involvement helps consumers leverage federal oversight in debt collection disputes.

Examination authority over larger debt collectors provides ongoing oversight of collection practices and often reveals systematic compliance problems affecting thousands of consumers. CFPB examination reports frequently identify widespread FDCPA violations and result in significant enforcement actions.

Consumer complaint systems through CFPB provide accessible mechanisms for reporting debt collection violations and obtaining assistance with collection disputes. CFPB complaint data also influences regulatory priorities and enforcement actions against problematic collectors.

Regulatory guidance from CFPB clarifies FDCPA requirements and addresses emerging issues in debt collection practices. This guidance helps consumers understand their rights and provides collectors with compliance expectations in evolving technological and business environments.

Enforcement actions by CFPB against major debt collection companies often result in significant penalties, consumer redress, and industry practice changes that benefit all consumers. These actions demonstrate federal commitment to FDCPA enforcement and deter violations industry-wide.

Industry-wide initiatives by CFPB address systematic problems in debt collection through coordinated enforcement, regulatory guidance, and stakeholder engagement. These initiatives often result in improved industry practices and enhanced consumer protections.

Coordination with state regulators enhances enforcement effectiveness by combining federal oversight with state regulatory authority and local knowledge. This coordination helps address regional collection problems and ensures comprehensive regulatory coverage.

Data collection and analysis by CFPB helps identify industry trends, emerging problems, and enforcement priorities in debt collection. Consumer complaint data and examination findings inform regulatory policy and enforcement strategy development.

Public reporting by CFPB about debt collection violations and enforcement actions provides transparency about industry problems and regulatory responses. This information helps consumers understand common violations and protection strategies.

Policy development through CFPB rulemaking may enhance debt collection regulation beyond current FDCPA requirements. Proposed and final rules provide insights into future regulatory directions and potential changes in consumer protection standards.

International coordination on debt collection issues helps address cross-border collection activities and ensures consistent consumer protection standards. This coordination becomes increasingly important as collection operations globalize.

Educational initiatives by CFPB help consumers understand their debt collection rights and provide resources for addressing collection problems. These resources complement legal protections with practical guidance for exercising consumer rights effectively.

Technological innovation oversight by CFPB addresses how new collection technologies and practices comply with existing consumer protection requirements. This oversight helps ensure that technological advances don't undermine established consumer protections.

Advanced FDCPA strategies combine technical legal knowledge with practical negotiation skills to maximize consumer protection and achieve optimal outcomes in debt collection situations. These strategies require understanding both letter-of-the-law compliance and strategic application of FDCPA rights.

Statute of limitations leverage involves understanding how time-barred debts affect collection practices and FDCPA obligations. While collectors can attempt collection of old debts, they cannot threaten legal action on time-barred debts, creating violation opportunities and settlement leverage.

Multiple debt management requires strategic coordination when consumers owe several debts to the same collector or related entities. Collectors must handle each debt separately for validation purposes, but payment allocation and settlement negotiations may involve multiple debts simultaneously.

Successor liability issues arise when collection agencies merge, sell portfolios, or transfer collection rights to other entities. FDCPA obligations typically transfer with collection rights, and successor collectors remain liable for predecessor violations in many circumstances.

Documentation trail analysis helps identify weaknesses in collectors' authority to collect specific debts. Missing assignments, incomplete account transfers, or inadequate documentation often create leverage for challenging collection authority and negotiating favorable resolutions.

Regulatory complaint coordination combines FDCPA rights with regulatory oversight to maximize pressure on violating collectors. Strategic timing of complaints to CFPB, state regulators, and attorney general offices can enhance negotiation positions.

Class action participation opportunities may arise when consumers experience violations similar to those affecting many other consumers. Understanding class action procedures and deadlines helps consumers participate in or opt out of class actions strategically.

Expert witness utilization in complex FDCPA cases helps establish violation patterns, damage calculations, and industry standard practices. Expert testimony often proves crucial in cases involving sophisticated collection operations or novel legal issues.

Discovery strategies in FDCPA litigation help uncover systematic violations, inadequate procedures, and documentation problems that strengthen consumer positions. Effective discovery often reveals violations beyond those initially apparent to consumers.

Appeal considerations in FDCPA cases require understanding how trial court decisions affect industry practices and future consumer rights. Strategic appeal decisions can establish favorable precedents or preserve important legal principles.

Legislative advocacy opportunities allow consumers to support FDCPA improvements and enhanced consumer protections. Understanding legislative processes helps consumers participate effectively in policy development that affects debt collection regulation.

Industry monitoring helps consumers stay current with collection industry practices, regulatory developments, and emerging violation patterns. This knowledge helps consumers anticipate problems and adapt protection strategies to changing industry practices.

Professional network development with consumer attorneys, financial counselors, and consumer advocates provides resources for addressing complex debt collection situations. These professional relationships often prove valuable when consumers face sophisticated collection operations or unusual circumstances.

Future developments in debt collection regulation and FDCPA interpretation continue evolving as technology advances, industry practices change, and regulatory priorities shift. Understanding emerging trends helps consumers anticipate changes and adapt protection strategies accordingly.

Regulatory modernization efforts by CFPB and other agencies aim to address technological developments and changing business models in debt collection. These efforts may result in enhanced consumer protections and clarified regulatory requirements for emerging collection practices.

Court decision trends in FDCPA interpretation continue refining consumer rights and collector obligations through case law development. Recent decisions have addressed issues like automated calling systems, electronic communications, and verification standards that affect consumer protection levels.

Industry consolidation in debt collection creates larger, more sophisticated collection operations that may have better compliance systems but also greater capacity for systematic violations. Understanding how consolidation affects consumer protection helps adapt dispute strategies.

Technology integration in collection practices raises new questions about FDCPA compliance and consumer rights. Artificial intelligence, automated decision-making, and digital communication platforms require applying traditional legal principles to new technological contexts.

International debt collection activities affect American consumers through cross-border collection efforts and global debt trading markets. Understanding how FDCPA applies to international collection activities helps protect consumers from foreign collection operations.

Alternative dispute resolution mechanisms may become more prevalent in debt collection, potentially providing faster and less expensive resolution options than traditional litigation. However, consumers should ensure that alternative procedures don't diminish FDCPA rights.

Consumer education initiatives by regulators, consumer advocates, and industry organizations aim to improve understanding of debt collection rights and procedures. Enhanced consumer knowledge often improves compliance and reduces violations through informed consumer responses.

Data privacy considerations increasingly affect debt collection practices as privacy regulations expand and consumer awareness grows. The intersection of debt collection and data privacy may create new protection opportunities for consumers.

Credit reporting integration with debt collection continues evolving as credit bureaus and collection agencies develop closer business relationships. Understanding these relationships helps consumers leverage credit reporting leverage in collection disputes.

Legislative proposals for FDCPA reform periodically emerge in Congress, addressing issues like damages, coverage, and technological adaptations. While these proposals may not become law, they indicate potential future directions in debt collection regulation.

Economic factors affecting debt collection include unemployment rates, consumer debt levels, and financial market conditions that influence collection volumes and practices. Understanding economic contexts helps predict collection industry behavior and regulatory responses.

Global regulatory coordination on consumer protection issues may influence American debt collection regulation through international best practices and regulatory harmonization efforts. This coordination potentially enhances consumer protection through improved regulatory standards and enforcement cooperation.

CHAPTER 8

ADDITIONAL CONSUMER PROTECTION LAWS

Beyond the Fair Credit Reporting Act and Fair Debt Collection Practices Act, a comprehensive framework of federal consumer protection laws governs credit-related activities and provides additional tools for credit repair and consumer protection. Understanding these laws helps you leverage multiple legal protections simultaneously and address credit problems from various angles that may not be covered by FCRA or FDCPA alone.

The Fair Credit Billing Act (FCBA) provides specific protections for credit card billing disputes and error resolution procedures. While primarily focused on billing accuracy, FCBA intersects with credit reporting when billing disputes affect credit report information or when creditors report disputed amounts inaccurately during dispute resolution periods.

The Truth in Lending Act (TILA) requires extensive disclosures about credit terms and provides remedies for lending violations that can affect credit reporting and debt collection. TILA violations often create leverage in credit repair situations, particularly when original lending violations affect subsequent collection or reporting activities.

The Equal Credit Opportunity Act (ECOA) prohibits discrimination in credit decisions and establishes notification requirements for adverse credit actions. ECOA intersects with credit repair when discrimination affects credit report information or when creditors fail to provide required adverse action notices that might trigger additional consumer rights.

The Credit CARD Act of 2009 enhanced consumer protections for credit card accounts and established new requirements for rate increases, fee limitations, and account management practices. These protections often affect credit reporting and provide leverage when credit card companies violate the Act's requirements.

State consumer protection laws vary significantly but often provide broader protections than federal laws, including enhanced disclosure requirements, stricter lending limitations, and additional remedies for consumer protection violations. Understanding state law variations helps identify all available protections and remedies.

Bankruptcy law intersects with credit repair through discharge protections, automatic stay provisions, and requirements for accurate post-bankruptcy credit reporting. While bankruptcy isn't primarily a consumer protection law, its provisions create important rights that affect credit repair strategies and creditor behavior.

The Electronic Fund Transfer Act (EFTA) and Regulation E govern electronic payment systems and provide error resolution procedures that may affect credit reporting when electronic payment disputes involve credit accounts or when payment errors affect credit standing.

The Home Ownership and Equity Protection Act (HOEPA) provides enhanced protections for high-cost mortgages and establishes requirements that affect mortgage-related credit reporting and debt collection activities.

Understanding how these laws interact with FCRA and FDCPA creates opportunities to leverage multiple legal protections simultaneously, often resulting in stronger positions for credit repair and debt resolution than relying on single legal theories.

Recent regulatory developments continue expanding consumer protections through enhanced enforcement, regulatory guidance, and coordination between different consumer protection agencies, creating an evolving landscape of consumer rights that affects credit repair strategies.

The Fair Credit Billing Act establishes detailed procedures for resolving billing disputes on open-end credit accounts, primarily credit cards, and creates specific obligations for creditors during dispute resolution periods. Understanding FCBA helps you address billing errors that may affect credit reporting and provides leverage when creditors violate billing dispute procedures.

Billing error definitions under FCBA include charges for goods or services not accepted or not delivered as agreed, mathematical errors in account statements, charges for amounts different from agreed prices, charges for goods or services not provided to consumers or their authorized users, and failure to credit payments or returns properly.

Written dispute requirements mandate that billing error claims be made in writing within sixty days of receiving statements containing alleged errors. Verbal complaints don't trigger FCBA protections, making written dispute letters essential for preserving your rights under the Act.

Creditor investigation obligations require acknowledgment of billing disputes within thirty days and resolution within two billing cycles (not exceeding ninety days). During investigations, creditors cannot report disputed amounts as delinquent to credit bureaus or take collection action on disputed amounts.

Credit reporting restrictions during FCBA disputes prohibit creditors from reporting disputed amounts as delinquent while investigations are pending. Creditors may report that amounts are disputed but cannot damage credit ratings based on disputed charges until disputes are resolved.

Resolution procedures require creditors to either correct billing errors or explain why they believe charges are correct. If creditors find errors, they must correct accounts and credit any finance charges on disputed amounts. If creditors find no errors, they must provide written explanations.

Interest and penalty protections prevent creditors from charging interest or penalties on disputed amounts while disputes are pending. These protections prevent billing errors from snowballing during investigation periods and protect consumers from additional charges on disputed items.

Documentation requirements obligate creditors to provide evidence supporting disputed charges when consumers request it. Creditors must provide copies of receipts, statements, or other documentation showing that disputed charges are accurate and properly applied to consumer accounts.

Collection restrictions during billing disputes prevent creditors from pursuing collection activities on disputed amounts until disputes are resolved. Creditors cannot threaten adverse credit reporting or demand immediate payment of disputed amounts during investigation periods.

Violation remedies under FCBA include actual damages, penalties up to fifty dollars, and attorney fees for creditors who fail to comply with billing dispute procedures. While penalties are modest, FCBA violations often create leverage for broader dispute resolution.

Credit card specific applications of FCBA address unauthorized charges, billing error corrections, and dispute procedures that are particularly relevant for credit card accounts. Understanding these applications helps you address credit card problems that may affect credit reports.

Integration with other laws creates opportunities to combine FCBA claims with FCRA disputes when billing errors affect credit reporting, or with FDCPA claims when collection activities violate billing dispute protections.

The Truth in Lending Act requires comprehensive disclosure of credit terms and provides remedies for lending violations that can significantly affect credit repair strategies. TILA violations often create leverage in credit disputes and may affect the validity of underlying debt obligations that appear on credit reports.

Disclosure requirements under TILA mandate specific information about credit costs, including annual percentage rates (APR), finance charges, payment schedules, and total payment amounts. Inadequate disclosures can invalidate debt obligations or provide grounds for challenging collection and reporting activities.

Annual Percentage Rate (APR) calculations must follow specific TILA requirements, and errors in APR disclosure can result in significant violations. APR errors often affect the total cost of credit and may provide grounds for challenging debt amounts reported to credit bureaus.

Right of rescission for certain transactions, particularly home equity loans and refinancing, allows consumers to cancel credit transactions within three days of closing. Violations of rescission rights can void debt obligations and provide powerful leverage in credit disputes.

High-cost mortgage protections under HOEPA establish enhanced disclosure requirements and substantive protections for loans that exceed cost thresholds. HOEPA violations can provide strong defenses against foreclosure and collection activities on high-cost loans.

Damage remedies for TILA violations include actual damages, statutory damages, and attorney fees. In some cases, TILA violations can result in complete debt forgiveness or significant reductions in debt amounts, providing powerful tools for credit repair.

Statute of limitations for TILA claims generally allows one year for disclosure violations and three years for rescission claims. Understanding these deadlines helps determine whether TILA claims remain viable for challenging credit obligations.

Credit card specific TILA requirements include enhanced disclosures for credit card terms, limitations on interest rate increases, and restrictions on penalty fees. The Credit CARD Act significantly enhanced these protections with additional requirements for credit card issuers.

Mortgage lending protections under TILA have expanded significantly through Dodd-Frank Act amendments, including ability-to-repay requirements, qualified mortgage standards, and enhanced disclosure requirements that affect mortgage-related credit issues.

Predatory lending connections often involve TILA violations combined with other deceptive practices. Understanding how TILA fits into broader predatory lending patterns helps identify comprehensive legal strategies for addressing complex credit problems.

Documentation preservation becomes crucial for TILA claims, as consumers must demonstrate what disclosures were provided and what violations occurred. Maintaining loan documentation helps preserve TILA claims that might affect credit repair strategies.

Integration with credit repair strategies allows consumers to leverage TILA violations in negotiations with creditors, debt collectors, and credit bureaus. TILA violations often provide stronger negotiation positions than credit reporting disputes alone.

The Equal Credit Opportunity Act prohibits discrimination in credit decisions based on race, color, religion, national origin, sex, marital status, age, or receipt of public assistance. ECOA intersects with credit repair when discrimination affects credit decisions or when creditors fail to comply with notification requirements.

Prohibited discrimination factors extend beyond obvious categories to include subtle forms of discrimination that may affect credit decisions. Understanding prohibited factors helps identify potential ECOA violations in credit denials, rate increases, or account management decisions.

Adverse action notice requirements mandate that creditors provide specific notifications when taking negative actions based on credit reports or other factors. These notices must include specific reasons for adverse actions and information about consumer rights to obtain credit reports.

Credit report-based adverse actions trigger specific ECOA notice requirements that complement FCRA adverse action provisions. Creditors must provide detailed explanations of adverse actions and cannot use vague or generic reasons when credit reports influence their decisions.

Spousal signature restrictions prevent creditors from requiring spousal signatures or guarantees except in specific circumstances. Violations of these restrictions may invalidate debt obligations or provide leverage in credit disputes involving married consumers.

Age discrimination protections prevent creditors from discriminating against older consumers or treating age as a negative factor in credit decisions. These protections are particularly important for older consumers facing credit problems or seeking credit repair assistance.

Public assistance discrimination prohibitions prevent creditors from considering receipt of public benefits as negative factors in credit decisions. Consumers receiving disability benefits, unemployment compensation, or other assistance maintain full credit rights under ECOA.

Credit scoring discrimination occurs when credit scoring models have disparate impacts on protected groups. While credit scoring is generally permitted, scoring systems that systematically discriminate may violate ECOA requirements.

Enforcement mechanisms for ECOA include private lawsuits, regulatory enforcement, and class action procedures. Successful ECOA plaintiffs can recover actual damages, punitive damages up to $10,000, and attorney fees for willful violations.

Documentation requirements for ECOA claims include evidence of discriminatory treatment, comparative analysis of similarly situated consumers, and records of creditor decision-making processes. Building strong ECOA cases requires careful documentation of discrimination evidence.

Regulatory oversight through CFPB and other agencies provides administrative enforcement mechanisms for ECOA violations. Regulatory complaints may result in investigations, enforcement actions, and industry-wide compliance improvements.

Integration with credit repair strategies allows consumers to challenge discriminatory credit decisions that affect credit reports, negotiate removals of accounts involving ECOA violations, and leverage discrimination claims in broader credit repair efforts.

The Credit CARD Act of 2009 established comprehensive consumer protections for credit card accounts, including restrictions on interest rate increases, fee limitations, and enhanced disclosure requirements. Understanding these protections helps identify violations that may affect credit reporting and provide leverage in credit card disputes.

Interest rate increase restrictions prevent credit card companies from increasing rates on existing balances except in specific circumstances, including promotional rate expirations, variable rate changes, and payment defaults. Violations of these restrictions may provide grounds for challenging reported debt amounts.

Notice requirements for rate increases mandate forty-five days advance notice before implementing rate increases and must include specific information about consumer rights to reject increases and pay off balances under existing terms.

Payment allocation rules require credit card companies to apply payments above minimum amounts to highest-rate balances first, preventing manipulation of payment applications to maximize interest charges. Violations may affect reported balance accuracy and provide leverage in disputes.

Fee limitations restrict many types of credit card fees, including limitations on over-limit fees, penalty fee amounts, and restrictions on fees during the first year after account opening. Excessive fees may result in inflated balances reported to credit bureaus.

Young consumer protections establish enhanced requirements for credit cards issued to consumers under twenty-one, including income verification and co-signer requirements. Violations may affect account validity and reporting accuracy for young consumer accounts.

Gift card protections establish requirements for gift card expiration dates and fee disclosures that may affect credit card-related gift card programs. While not directly related to credit reporting, these protections demonstrate the Act's comprehensive approach to credit card regulation.

Disclosure enhancements require improved clarity in credit card terms, fee disclosures, and periodic statement information. Enhanced disclosures help consumers understand their rights and identify potential violations that might affect credit reporting.

Promotional rate protections establish minimum time periods for promotional rates and restrict changes to promotional terms. Violations may affect interest calculations and debt amounts that appear on credit reports.

Due date and payment timing rules require consistent due dates and provide minimum time periods for payment processing. Violations may affect late payment reporting and credit score calculations based on payment history.

Opt-in requirements for over-limit fees prevent automatic enrollment in over-limit programs and require specific consumer consent for over-limit transactions. Violations may result in unauthorized fees that affect reported account balances.

Enforcement mechanisms include regulatory oversight through CFPB, state attorney general enforcement, and private lawsuit rights for some violations. Understanding enforcement options helps consumers address Credit CARD Act violations effectively.

Integration with credit repair involves challenging credit card accounts that violate the Act's requirements, negotiating removal of accounts with violations, and leveraging violations in broader credit repair strategies.

State consumer protection laws provide varying levels of additional protection beyond federal requirements, with many states offering enhanced disclosure requirements, stricter lending limitations, and broader remedies for consumer protection violations. Understanding state law variations helps identify all available protections and maximize credit repair opportunities.

Disclosure requirements in many states exceed federal minimums, requiring additional information about credit terms, fees, and consumer rights. Enhanced state disclosures may provide grounds for challenging credit agreements that comply with federal law but violate state requirements.

Interest rate limitations vary significantly between states, with some states imposing strict usury limits while others allow unlimited rates. Understanding rate limitations helps identify violations that may affect debt validity and credit reporting accuracy.

Fee restrictions in state law often limit various types of charges that federal law permits, including application fees, processing charges, and penalty assessments. State fee violations may provide leverage for challenging reported debt amounts and negotiating account corrections.

Licensing requirements for lenders and servicers create regulatory oversight mechanisms that may provide additional consumer protections and complaint procedures. Unlicensed lender violations may affect debt validity and credit reporting authority.

Cooling-off periods and rescission rights in some states provide broader cancellation rights than federal law requires, particularly for certain types of high-cost loans or home improvement contracts. Extended rescission rights may affect debt validity and collection authority.

Debt collection regulations at the state level often provide enhanced protections beyond FDCPA, including stricter communication restrictions, enhanced validation requirements, and broader prohibition categories. Understanding state debt collection law helps maximize protection against collection violations.

Credit repair regulation varies by state, with some states requiring licensing, bonding, or specific contract terms for credit repair services. Understanding state credit repair laws helps consumers work with legitimate service providers and avoid scams.

Banking regulation differences between states affect credit products and consumer protections available to state residents. State banking laws may provide additional grounds for challenging credit decisions or account management practices.

Attorney general enforcement provides state-level oversight of consumer protection violations and may offer complaint procedures, investigation services, and enforcement actions against violating businesses. State enforcement often addresses local problems that federal agencies might not prioritize.

Class action law variations between states affect consumer rights to participate in group litigation against violating creditors or service providers. Understanding state class action rules helps consumers evaluate litigation options and protection strategies.

Preemption analysis determines which state laws apply to federally regulated institutions and which areas remain subject to state regulation. Understanding preemption helps identify all applicable protections and avoid conflicts between federal and state requirements.

Bankruptcy law provides powerful consumer protections through discharge procedures, automatic stay provisions, and requirements for accurate post-bankruptcy credit reporting. While bankruptcy isn't primarily consumer protection legislation, its provisions create important rights that significantly affect credit repair strategies and creditor behavior.

Chapter 7 discharge eliminates most consumer debts and provides fresh start opportunities that creditors and credit bureaus must respect. Post-discharge collection attempts and inaccurate credit reporting of discharged debts violate bankruptcy law and may provide grounds for sanctions and damages.

Chapter 13 payment plans allow consumers to reorganize debts while maintaining property and provide discharge protection after successful plan completion. Credit reporting during Chapter 13 cases must accurately reflect plan status and cannot show delinquencies for payments made according to confirmed plans.

Automatic stay protections immediately halt most collection and credit reporting activities when consumers file bankruptcy, providing broader protection than other consumer protection laws. Stay violations can result in sanctions, damages, and attorney fee awards.

Discharge violations occur when creditors attempt collection or credit reporting on discharged debts. These violations often provide strong grounds for sanctions and may result in significant damage awards, particularly when violations are willful or systematic.

Reaffirmation agreement protections prevent creditors from pressuring consumers into reaffirming discharged debts through deceptive practices or inadequate disclosures. Invalid reaffirmation agreements may affect post-bankruptcy credit reporting and collection authority.

Credit reporting accuracy requirements mandate that bankruptcy-related information be reported correctly, including discharge dates, case status, and individual debt discharge status. Inaccurate bankruptcy reporting provides grounds for FCRA disputes and potential legal action.

Exemption protections preserve certain consumer property from creditor collection both before and after bankruptcy. Understanding exemptions helps consumers protect assets while pursuing credit repair strategies that may involve legal action against creditors.

Preference payment recovery by bankruptcy trustees may affect credit reporting when payments made before bankruptcy are recovered from creditors. Consumers should understand how preference actions might affect their credit reports and post-bankruptcy financial planning.

Student loan considerations in bankruptcy involve complex rules about discharge ability and credit reporting requirements. While most student loans survive bankruptcy, certain circumstances may allow discharge, and credit reporting must accurately reflect post-bankruptcy status.

Tax debt treatment in bankruptcy varies depending on debt types and timing, with some tax debts dischargeable under specific circumstances. Accurate credit reporting of tax-related debt requires understanding complex bankruptcy and tax law interactions.

Credit rebuilding strategies after bankruptcy benefit from understanding how bankruptcy affects credit scores, lending decisions, and available credit products. Strategic post-bankruptcy credit management can accelerate credit score recovery and improve financial opportunities.

The Electronic Fund Transfer Act and Regulation E govern electronic payment systems and establish error resolution procedures that may affect credit reporting when electronic payment disputes involve credit accounts or when payment processing errors affect credit standing.

Electronic payment error resolution procedures provide specific timelines and requirements for investigating disputed electronic transactions. When payment errors affect credit accounts, these procedures may influence credit reporting accuracy and provide leverage in credit disputes.

Unauthorized transaction protections limit consumer liability for unauthorized electronic payments and require financial institutions to investigate and resolve unauthorized transaction claims. These protections may affect credit reporting when unauthorized payments impact account status.

Preauthorized payment rights allow consumers to stop automatic payments and revoke authorization for recurring electronic transfers. Understanding these rights helps consumers control automatic payments that might affect credit accounts and credit reporting.

Error resolution timelines under Regulation E require financial institutions to investigate electronic payment disputes within specific timeframes and provide provisional credit during investigations. These protections may affect credit account balances and reporting during dispute periods.

Documentation requirements for electronic payment disputes mandate specific procedures for notifying financial institutions of errors and disputes. Proper documentation helps preserve consumer rights and may affect credit reporting accuracy when disputes involve credit accounts.

Liability limitations for unauthorized electronic transfers protect consumers from excessive liability when electronic payment systems are compromised. These protections may affect debt amounts and credit reporting when unauthorized transactions occur on credit accounts.

Disclosure requirements for electronic payment services mandate specific information about fees, rights, and procedures. Inadequate disclosures may provide grounds for challenging electronic payment arrangements that affect credit accounts.

Debit card protections under Regulation E provide error resolution and liability protection that may affect credit reporting when debit card disputes involve overdraft credit or linked credit accounts. Understanding these protections helps consumers navigate complex payment disputes.

ATM and point-of-sale transaction protections establish specific requirements for electronic payment processing and error resolution. These protections may affect credit reporting when electronic payment errors impact credit account status or balances.

International transaction considerations under EFTA address cross-border electronic payments and error resolution procedures. Understanding international payment protections helps consumers address payment disputes that might affect credit accounts.

Integration with credit repair strategies allows consumers to leverage electronic payment protections when addressing credit account disputes, particularly when payment processing errors contribute to credit reporting inaccuracies or account management problems.

The Home Ownership and Equity Protection Act provides enhanced protections for high-cost mortgages and establishes requirements that significantly affect mortgage-related credit reporting and debt collection activities. Understanding HOEPA helps consumers address predatory lending situations that may affect credit reports.

High-cost mortgage definitions under HOEPA establish rate and fee thresholds that trigger enhanced protections. Loans exceeding these thresholds face additional disclosure requirements, substantive restrictions, and enhanced consumer rights that may affect credit reporting.

Enhanced disclosure requirements for HOEPA loans mandate additional information about loan terms, costs, and risks beyond standard TILA disclosures. Inadequate HOEPA disclosures may provide grounds for challenging loan validity and related credit reporting.

Prohibited practices for high-cost mortgages include restrictions on balloon payments, negative amortization, prepayment penalties, and other features that may harm consumers. Violations may affect loan validity and provide leverage in credit disputes.

Assignee liability provisions hold loan purchasers responsible for HOEPA violations by original lenders, creating ongoing accountability for predatory lending practices. These provisions may affect debt collection and credit reporting by secondary market participants.

Refinancing restrictions prevent lenders from repeatedly refinancing loans without tangible consumer benefits. Violations may affect loan validity and provide grounds for challenging collection and credit reporting activities.

Counseling requirements mandate pre-loan counseling for certain high-cost mortgages. Violations of counseling requirements may affect loan validity and provide consumer defenses against collection and foreclosure activities.

Damage remedies for HOEPA violations include statutory damages, actual damages, and attorney fees. In some cases, violations may result in loan rescission or significant damage awards that affect debt amounts and credit reporting.

Foreclosure protections under HOEPA provide enhanced notice requirements and procedural protections that may affect foreclosure-related credit reporting. Understanding these protections helps consumers challenge inaccurate foreclosure reporting.

Integration with other laws allows consumers to combine HOEPA claims with TILA, FCRA, and state law claims when addressing predatory lending situations. Multiple legal theories often provide stronger positions than single law approaches.

Documentation preservation becomes crucial for HOEPA claims, as consumers must demonstrate loan terms, disclosure adequacy, and violation circumstances. Maintaining loan documentation helps preserve claims that might affect credit repair strategies.

Credit repair applications of HOEPA involve challenging mortgage-related credit reporting when loans violate the Act's requirements, negotiating removal of accounts with violations, and leveraging violations in foreclosure defense and debt collection challenges.

Consumer protection law enforcement operates through multiple agencies with overlapping jurisdiction, creating comprehensive oversight systems that consumers can leverage when addressing credit-related problems. Understanding enforcement mechanisms helps consumers access appropriate assistance and maximize protection under various laws.

Consumer Financial Protection Bureau (CFPB) supervision covers most major financial institutions and provides ongoing oversight of consumer protection compliance. CFPB examinations often reveal systematic violations and result in enforcement actions that benefit all affected consumers.

Federal Trade Commission (FTC) enforcement focuses on deceptive practices, privacy violations, and competition issues that affect consumer protection. FTC actions often address industry-wide problems and result in significant penalties and corrective measures.

Banking regulator oversight through OCC, FDIC, and Federal Reserve provides specialized supervision of banking activities and consumer protection compliance. Banking regulator enforcement often addresses institution-specific problems and may provide complaint resolution assistance.

State attorney general enforcement provides local oversight and may offer investigation services, mediation programs, and enforcement actions against businesses operating in specific states. State enforcement often addresses problems that federal agencies might not prioritize.

Coordination between agencies prevents enforcement gaps and ensures comprehensive coverage of consumer protection violations. Inter-agency coordination often results in more effective enforcement and better consumer outcomes than individual agency actions.

Consumer complaint systems provide accessible mechanisms for reporting violations and obtaining assistance with consumer protection issues. Understanding how to use complaint systems effectively helps consumers access regulatory assistance and influence enforcement priorities.

Private enforcement through consumer lawsuits provides individual remedies and creates compliance incentives through potential liability. Understanding private enforcement rights helps consumers evaluate legal action options and negotiate favorable settlements.

Class action mechanisms allow groups of consumers to address systematic violations collectively, often providing more effective remedies than individual actions. Understanding class action procedures helps consumers participate effectively in group litigation.

Regulatory guidance clarifies legal requirements and provides compliance expectations for businesses and consumer rights information for consumers. Staying current with regulatory guidance helps consumers understand evolving protection standards.

Industry initiatives often result from regulatory pressure and provide enhanced consumer protections beyond minimum legal requirements. Understanding industry initiatives helps consumers access additional protections and services.

Legislative advocacy by consumer organizations, regulatory agencies, and industry groups continues shaping consumer protection law through proposed legislation and regulatory reforms. Understanding legislative processes helps consumers participate in policy development.

International coordination addresses cross-border consumer protection issues and ensures consistent protection standards. International cooperation becomes increasingly important as financial services globalize and affect consumers across national boundaries.

Privacy laws increasingly intersect with credit reporting and consumer protection as data privacy regulations expand and consumer awareness grows. Understanding privacy law connections helps consumers leverage additional protections and address comprehensive data protection issues.

Gramm-Leach-Bliley Act (GLBA) privacy provisions require financial institutions to provide privacy notices and protect consumer information. GLBA violations may provide additional grounds for challenging credit reporting and collection activities that involve improper information sharing.

Fair Credit Reporting Act privacy protections establish permissible purpose requirements and restrict credit report access to authorized users. Understanding FCRA privacy provisions helps consumers identify unauthorized access and protect against identity theft.

State privacy laws vary significantly but often provide broader protections than federal requirements, including restrictions on information collection, sharing limitations, and enhanced disclosure requirements. Understanding state privacy laws helps identify all available protections.

Identity theft protection laws establish procedures for addressing fraud and unauthorized account opening. These laws often provide enhanced rights beyond standard credit reporting protections and may offer additional remedies for identity theft victims.

Data breach notification laws require businesses to notify consumers when personal information is compromised. Understanding notification requirements helps consumers respond effectively to data breaches that might affect credit information.

Social security number protection laws restrict collection and use of social security numbers by businesses and government agencies. Violations may provide additional grounds for challenging improper collection and credit reporting practices.

Medical privacy protections under HIPAA restrict disclosure of medical information that might affect credit reporting. Understanding medical privacy rights helps consumers address medical debt reporting and collection issues.

Children's privacy protections under COPPA restrict collection of information from minors and may affect credit reporting involving young consumers. Understanding children's privacy rights helps protect minor's credit information and prevent identity theft.

Electronic privacy protections address digital communications, online data collection, and electronic surveillance that may affect consumer financial information. Understanding electronic privacy helps consumers protect financial data in digital environments.

International privacy considerations affect consumers with foreign financial connections or international data transfers. Understanding international privacy law helps consumers address cross-border credit and data protection issues.

Enforcement mechanisms for privacy violations include regulatory oversight, private lawsuits, and criminal penalties for some violations. Understanding enforcement options helps consumers address privacy violations that affect credit information.

Integration with credit repair strategies allows consumers to leverage privacy violations when addressing credit reporting problems, particularly when unauthorized information sharing or data breaches contribute to credit reporting inaccuracies.

Predatory lending practices often involve multiple consumer protection law violations and require comprehensive legal strategies that combine various consumer protection theories. Understanding how different laws interact in predatory lending situations helps consumers develop effective responses to complex credit problems.

High-cost lending characteristics include excessive interest rates, high fees, unnecessary insurance products, and loan terms that benefit lenders rather than consumers. Identifying these characteristics helps consumers recognize predatory lending and understand available legal protections.

Deceptive practice patterns in predatory lending often involve misrepresentations about loan terms, hidden fees, bait-and-switch tactics, and pressure tactics that violate multiple consumer protection laws simultaneously.

Vulnerable population targeting by predatory lenders often focuses on elderly consumers, minority communities, and financially distressed individuals. Understanding targeting patterns helps identify discrimination claims and enhanced protection opportunities.

Equity stripping practices involve structuring loans to extract home equity rather than benefit consumers, often through unnecessary refinancing, excessive fees, and loan terms that make default likely.

Loan flipping involves repeated refinancing that generates fees for lenders while providing no consumer benefit. Understanding flipping patterns helps identify TILA violations and provides grounds for challenging loan validity.

Mandatory arbitration clauses in predatory loans may limit consumer rights to pursue legal remedies. Understanding arbitration law helps consumers evaluate enforcement options and challenge unconscionable arbitration agreements.

Regulatory response to predatory lending includes enhanced oversight, new regulatory requirements, and enforcement actions against predatory lenders. Understanding regulatory initiatives helps consumers access protection and assistance programs.

Documentation analysis in predatory lending cases requires examining loan terms, disclosure adequacy, and compliance with multiple consumer protection laws. Comprehensive documentation review often reveals violation patterns that strengthen consumer positions.

Legal strategy development for predatory lending involves combining multiple legal theories, including TILA, HOEPA, ECOA, and state law claims. Coordinated legal strategies often provide stronger positions than single-law approaches.

Settlement considerations in predatory lending cases may involve loan modifications, principal reductions, fee refunds, and credit reporting corrections. Understanding settlement options helps consumers negotiate comprehensive resolutions.

Prevention education helps consumers recognize predatory lending practices and avoid problematic loans. Understanding warning signs and protective strategies helps consumers make informed credit decisions.

Recovery assistance programs provide counseling, legal aid, and financial assistance for predatory lending victims. Understanding available resources helps consumers access assistance and support during recovery processes.

Consumer protection law compliance creates ongoing obligations for creditors, servicers, and other financial service providers that consumers can monitor and leverage when violations occur. Understanding compliance requirements helps consumers identify violations and exercise their rights effectively.

Compliance management systems required by regulators establish policies, procedures, and monitoring mechanisms that financial institutions must maintain. Understanding compliance requirements helps consumers evaluate whether institutions are meeting their obligations.

Training requirements for financial service employees ensure understanding of consumer protection obligations. Inadequate training may contribute to violations and provide grounds for challenging institutional practices and individual employee actions.

Record keeping obligations require financial institutions to maintain documentation supporting their consumer protection compliance. Understanding record keeping requirements helps consumers request relevant documentation and identify potential violations.

Audit requirements mandate regular review of consumer protection compliance by internal and external auditors. Audit findings may reveal systematic violations and provide evidence for consumer protection claims.

Regulatory examination procedures provide ongoing oversight of financial institution compliance and often result in examination reports that identify violations and required corrective actions. Understanding examination processes helps consumers access regulatory assistance.

Corrective action requirements mandate that financial institutions address identified violations and implement measures to prevent recurrence. Understanding corrective action procedures helps consumers monitor institutional improvements and ensure violation resolution.

Consumer complaint handling requirements establish procedures for receiving, investigating, and responding to consumer complaints. Understanding complaint procedures helps consumers use institutional complaint processes effectively.

Board oversight responsibilities require financial institution boards to monitor consumer protection compliance and ensure adequate resources for compliance programs. Understanding board responsibilities helps consumers evaluate institutional commitment to compliance.

Vendor management obligations require financial institutions to ensure that service providers comply with consumer protection requirements. Understanding vendor management helps consumers address violations by third-party service providers.

Technology compliance considerations address how financial institutions must ensure that automated systems and digital processes comply with consumer protection requirements. Understanding technology compliance helps consumers address violations involving electronic systems.

Enforcement coordination between regulatory agencies ensures comprehensive oversight and consistent enforcement of consumer protection requirements. Understanding enforcement coordination helps consumers access appropriate regulatory assistance.

Continuous improvement expectations require financial institutions to regularly assess and enhance their consumer protection programs. Understanding improvement expectations helps consumers evaluate institutional progress and identify ongoing concerns.

International consumer protection considerations affect American consumers through cross-border financial services, international debt collection, and global data sharing arrangements. Understanding international aspects helps consumers protect their rights in an increasingly globalized financial system.

Cross-border credit reporting involves information sharing between American credit bureaus and international credit reporting systems. Understanding international reporting helps consumers with foreign credit history leverage positive information and address negative reporting across borders.

International debt collection activities affecting American consumers require compliance with American consumer protection laws regardless of collector location. Understanding jurisdictional issues helps consumers enforce their rights against foreign collectors.

Treaty obligations and international agreements may provide additional consumer protections beyond domestic law, particularly regarding data privacy and cross-border enforcement. Understanding international agreements helps consumers access enhanced protections.

Regulatory cooperation between American agencies and foreign regulators addresses cross-border consumer protection issues and enforcement coordination. Understanding regulatory cooperation helps consumers access international assistance when needed.

Conflict of laws issues arise when consumer transactions involve multiple jurisdictions with different legal requirements. Understanding choice of law principles helps consumers determine which protections apply to international transactions.

Currency and exchange rate considerations may affect debt amounts and payment obligations in international consumer transactions. Understanding currency issues helps consumers address disputes involving foreign exchange calculations.

Language and cultural barriers may affect consumer understanding of international financial services and protection rights. Understanding cultural considerations helps consumers navigate international financial services effectively.

Enforcement challenges in international consumer protection include jurisdiction limitations, service of process difficulties, and judgment enforcement problems. Understanding enforcement challenges helps consumers evaluate realistic remedies for international violations.

Documentation requirements for international consumer protection claims may involve translation services, authentication procedures, and foreign legal standards. Understanding documentation requirements helps consumers build effective international cases.

Alternative dispute resolution mechanisms may provide more effective remedies than traditional litigation for international consumer protection disputes. Understanding international arbitration and mediation helps consumers access appropriate dispute resolution.

Technology and digitalization continue expanding international consumer protection issues as online financial services cross traditional boundaries. Understanding technological impacts helps consumers protect themselves in digital international marketplaces.

Future developments in international consumer protection include enhanced cooperation agreements, standardized protection principles, and improved enforcement mechanisms. Understanding emerging trends helps consumers anticipate changes and access evolving protections.

Integration strategies for multiple consumer protection laws maximize consumer leverage by combining various legal theories and enforcement mechanisms to address complex credit problems comprehensively. Understanding integration helps consumers develop effective strategies that address all aspects of their credit situations.

Legal theory coordination involves identifying all applicable consumer protection laws and developing strategies that leverage multiple legal theories simultaneously. Coordinated approaches often provide stronger positions than single-law strategies and may result in better outcomes.

Evidence development for multiple claims requires systematic documentation that supports various legal theories while avoiding conflicts between different law requirements. Comprehensive evidence development strengthens all claims and provides flexibility in litigation strategy.

Settlement negotiation leverage increases significantly when consumers can demonstrate multiple legal violations across different consumer protection laws. Understanding how violations interact helps consumers negotiate favorable comprehensive settlements.

Regulatory complaint coordination involves filing complaints with appropriate agencies while ensuring consistency across different regulatory systems. Strategic complaint filing maximizes regulatory assistance and avoids conflicting agency actions.

Attorney selection considerations include finding legal representation with expertise across multiple consumer protection areas rather than specialists in single laws. Comprehensive legal expertise often produces better results in complex cases.

Timing coordination ensures that various legal actions and administrative procedures are pursued in optimal sequence to maximize effectiveness and avoid procedural conflicts. Strategic timing helps consumers maintain momentum while preserving all available rights.

Documentation organization becomes crucial when pursuing multiple legal theories that may have different evidence requirements and procedural standards. Systematic documentation helps consumers present coherent cases across multiple legal frameworks.

Cost-benefit analysis for comprehensive strategies considers the potential benefits of pursuing multiple claims against the costs and complexity of coordinated legal action. Understanding cost-benefit helps consumers make informed decisions about strategy scope.

Enforcement priority assessment helps consumers focus resources on the most promising legal theories while maintaining other options. Understanding enforcement priorities helps optimize limited resources for maximum impact.

Outcome coordination ensures that resolutions in one legal area don't negatively affect prospects in other areas. Comprehensive planning helps consumers achieve optimal overall outcomes rather than piecemeal solutions.

Long-term strategy development considers how immediate actions affect future opportunities and rights under various consumer protection laws. Strategic planning helps consumers maintain flexibility while pursuing immediate relief.

Success measurement for integrated strategies requires evaluating outcomes across multiple objectives rather than single-law success criteria. Comprehensive evaluation helps consumers assess overall strategy effectiveness and plan future actions accordingly.

CHAPTER 9

MASTERING CREDIT DISPUTES

Credit disputes represent the cornerstone of effective credit repair, providing the legal mechanism through which consumers can challenge inaccurate, incomplete, or unverifiable information on their credit reports. Under the Fair Credit Reporting Act, you have the absolute right to dispute any information you believe is incorrect, and credit bureaus have binding legal obligations to investigate these disputes thoroughly and fairly.

The dispute process is far more nuanced than simply claiming something is "not mine" or "inaccurate." Effective disputes require strategic thinking, proper documentation, clear communication, and understanding of the legal standards that govern credit bureau investigations. When executed properly, disputes can result in removal of negative items, correction of inaccurate information, and significant improvements to credit scores.

Understanding when to dispute versus when not to dispute is crucial for success. Disputing accurate negative information is not only ineffective but can actually harm your position by creating a paper trail of unsuccessful disputes. Credit bureaus may label repeated unsuccessful disputes as "frivolous," making future legitimate disputes more difficult. The key is identifying genuine inaccuracies, incomplete information, or unverifiable items that violate FCRA standards.

The legal foundation for disputes rests on FCRA's requirement that credit reporting agencies maintain "reasonable procedures to assure maximum possible accuracy" of reported information. This doesn't mean perfect accuracy – the law uses the term "reasonable" – but it does mean that credit bureaus must investigate disputes and remove information they cannot verify as accurate.

Credit bureaus must complete investigations within thirty days of receiving complete disputes, though this timeline can be extended to forty-five days if you provide additional relevant information during the investigation period.

Understanding these timelines helps you plan dispute strategies and follow up appropriately when bureaus fail to meet their deadlines.

The investigation process requires credit bureaus to contact furnishers of disputed information and request verification. If furnishers cannot verify the information or find errors in their reporting, they must request correction or removal from your credit files. This creates a chain of accountability that you can leverage when pursuing disputes.

Modern credit repair often involves multiple rounds of disputes using different strategies and approaches. What fails in one dispute round may succeed in subsequent attempts using different dispute angles, additional documentation, or alternative dispute methods. Persistence and strategic variation often produce results where single disputes fail.

Digital versus traditional dispute methods each offer advantages and disadvantages. Online dispute systems provide convenience and speed but often limit your ability to provide detailed explanations and supporting documentation. Written disputes sent by mail provide more control and documentation but take longer to process.

The anatomy of effective disputes involves several key components that distinguish successful challenges from ineffective form letters. Understanding these components helps you craft disputes that credit bureaus take seriously and investigate thoroughly rather than dismissing with generic responses.

Clear identification of disputed items must be specific and unambiguous. Rather than disputing "collections" generally, effective disputes identify specific accounts by creditor name, account number, and reported information. Vague disputes often result in bureaus claiming they cannot identify what you're disputing, leading to delayed investigations or outright rejections.

Specific dispute reasons should articulate exactly what is wrong with the reported information. Common dispute reasons include wrong dates, incorrect amounts, accounts that don't belong to you, duplicate reporting, outdated information that should have been removed, and accounts with incorrect status reporting. Each reason requires different evidence and argumentation strategies.

Supporting documentation strengthens disputes significantly when relevant documentation is available. This might include payment records showing accounts were paid as agreed, letters from creditors acknowledging errors, police reports for identity theft situations, or divorce decrees showing responsibility for debts. However, documentation should support your dispute rather than overwhelming the investigation.

Professional presentation through well-written, organized dispute letters demonstrates seriousness and competence. Credit bureau personnel are more likely to conduct thorough investigations when disputes appear professionally prepared rather than hastily written or emotionally charged. Clear, business-like communication gets better results than angry or threatening language.

Strategic timing of disputes can affect investigation quality and outcomes. Disputes submitted during holiday periods or peak dispute seasons may receive less attention than those submitted during normal business periods. Additionally, spacing multiple disputes over time often produces better results than submitting numerous disputes simultaneously.

Evidence organization helps investigators understand your position quickly and encourages thorough investigation. Presenting evidence logically with clear explanations of how it supports your dispute makes investigations easier and more likely to result in favorable outcomes.

Legal language and FCRA references demonstrate knowledge of your rights and credit bureau obligations. While disputes don't need to cite specific FCRA sections, references to accuracy requirements, investigation obligations, and maximum possible accuracy standards remind bureaus of their legal duties.

Follow-up strategies ensure that disputes receive proper attention and investigations are completed within required timeframes. Systematic follow-up on overdue investigations, inadequate responses, or incomplete corrections often resolves problems that initial disputes alone cannot address.

Escalation procedures become necessary when standard dispute processes fail to produce fair results. Understanding how to escalate disputes to supervisory personnel, regulatory agencies, or legal action helps ensure that legitimate disputes ultimately receive proper resolution.

Types of disputable items encompass virtually any information appearing on credit reports that you believe is inaccurate, incomplete, or unverifiable. FCRA provides broad dispute rights that extend beyond obviously incorrect information to include subtle inaccuracies and reporting violations that many consumers overlook.

Personal identifying information errors include incorrect names, addresses, social security numbers, employment information, or date of birth. These errors might seem minor but can indicate file mixing problems or identity theft situations that require immediate attention. Correcting personal information helps prevent future errors and protects against fraud.

Account information disputes address errors in account details such as opening dates, credit limits, balances, payment history, and account status. Even small errors in account information can affect credit scores and should be disputed when identified. Incorrect account details often indicate broader data quality problems.

Payment history inaccuracies represent some of the most impactful disputable items since payment history comprises the largest component of credit score calculations. Disputes might address late payments that were actually on time, missed payments on accounts that were current, or payment history for accounts you never opened.

Balance reporting errors can significantly affect credit utilization calculations and credit scores. Disputable balance issues include incorrect current balances, failure to update paid-off accounts to zero balances, or reporting balances on closed accounts. Accurate balance reporting is crucial for optimal credit scores.

Date-related disputes address incorrect reporting dates for various account activities including opening dates, closing dates, last activity dates, and date of first delinquency. Incorrect dates can affect how long negative information remains on credit reports and may violate FCRA's reporting period limitations.

Duplicate account reporting occurs when the same debt appears multiple times on credit reports, often happening when accounts are sold between collection agencies or reported by both original creditors and collectors. Duplicate reporting artificially inflates negative information and should be disputed aggressively.

Status reporting errors include accounts showing as open when they're closed, closed accounts showing as open, or incorrect status designations such as charge-offs reported as collections. Accurate status reporting helps potential creditors understand your true credit obligations and payment history.

Inquiry disputes can address unauthorized credit inquiries, inquiries resulting from identity theft, or inquiries that remain on reports longer than permitted time periods. While inquiry impact decreases over time, removing unauthorized inquiries can provide immediate credit score benefits.

Public record disputes address incorrect bankruptcy information, tax liens that were paid or never existed, judgments that were satisfied or incorrectly reported, and other public record data that affects credit reports. Public record errors often have severe credit impacts and require aggressive dispute strategies.

Mixed file disputes address situations where information from other consumers appears on your credit reports, often due to similar names, addresses, or social security numbers. Mixed files require special attention since they may indicate systematic credit bureau problems that affect multiple aspects of your credit reports.

Dispute letter construction requires balancing professionalism with assertiveness while clearly communicating your position and supporting evidence. Effective dispute letters follow proven formats that credit bureau personnel recognize and process efficiently, while including specific details that distinguish your disputes from generic form letters.

Header information should include your complete contact information, date, and specific credit bureau address for disputes. Using certified mail provides proof of delivery and demonstrates the seriousness of your dispute. Include your full name exactly as it appears on your credit report to avoid processing delays.

Account identification must be precise and complete to ensure investigators can locate disputed items quickly. Include creditor names, account numbers, dates of service, and any reference numbers from your credit report. Unclear account identification often results in delayed investigations or claims that disputed items cannot be located.

Dispute statement clarity requires explaining exactly what is wrong with reported information without unnecessary emotional language or irrelevant details. Focus on factual inaccuracies rather than complaints about creditor behavior or personal circumstances that led to account problems.

Legal basis references can strengthen disputes by citing relevant FCRA requirements, though extensive legal citations aren't necessary for effective disputes. Simple references to accuracy requirements and investigation obligations remind bureaus of their legal duties without appearing overly legalistic.

Evidence references should mention supporting documentation without overwhelming the dispute letter. Indicate what evidence you're providing and how it supports your position, but let the evidence speak for itself rather than providing lengthy explanations in the dispute letter.

Resolution requests should be specific about what action you want the credit bureau to take. Whether seeking deletion, correction, or updating of information, clear resolution requests help ensure that successful investigations result in appropriate corrections to your credit files.

Timeline references can be helpful when disputes involve time-sensitive issues such as reporting period violations or urgent credit decisions. However, avoid threatening language about timelines and instead reference FCRA's investigation requirements professionally.

Professional tone throughout dispute letters helps ensure serious consideration of your disputes. Avoid emotional language, threats, or personal attacks that might prejudice investigators against your position. Business-like communication produces better results than confrontational approaches.

Contact information should include multiple ways for bureaus to reach you if they need additional information during investigations. Providing phone numbers and email addresses in addition to mailing addresses can expedite investigation processes when bureaus need clarification.

Signature and date complete dispute letters with handwritten signatures that match your identification documents. Some bureaus may question electronic signatures or photocopied signatures, potentially delaying dispute processing.

Investigation standards under FCRA require credit bureaus to conduct "reasonable" investigations of consumer disputes, though the law doesn't define exactly what constitutes reasonable investigation procedures. Understanding these standards helps you evaluate whether bureaus are meeting their obligations and identify potential violations when investigations are inadequate.

Reasonable investigation requirements mandate that credit bureaus contact furnishers of disputed information and request verification of accuracy. The investigation must be appropriate to the circumstances of the dispute, considering the complexity of issues raised and available evidence supporting the dispute.

Furnisher contact obligations require credit bureaus to notify furnishers of disputed information and request verification within reasonable timeframes. If furnishers cannot verify information or find errors in their records, they must report these findings to credit bureaus for appropriate action.

Documentation review standards vary depending on the nature of disputes and available evidence. Credit bureaus must consider evidence provided by consumers, though they're not required to accept consumer evidence over furnisher verification. However, strong consumer evidence may require more thorough investigations.

Timeline compliance mandates that investigations be completed within thirty days of receiving complete disputes, though this period may be extended to forty-five days if consumers provide additional relevant information during investigations. Failure to meet these deadlines violates FCRA requirements.

Verification standards require furnishers to check their records and confirm the accuracy of disputed information. If furnishers cannot verify information as accurate and complete, they should report this to credit bureaus rather than simply confirming previous reporting without actual verification.

Investigation scope must address all aspects of consumer disputes rather than cherry-picking elements that are easy to verify while ignoring more complex dispute components. Partial investigations that fail to address complete disputes may violate FCRA's reasonable investigation requirements.

Evidence evaluation procedures should consider both consumer evidence and furnisher responses in making investigation determinations. Credit bureaus cannot simply defer to furnisher responses without considering contrary evidence provided by consumers.

Systematic investigation procedures help ensure consistent and thorough dispute handling across different personnel and time periods. Credit bureaus should have policies and procedures that promote reasonable investigations rather than perfunctory reviews designed to minimize work.

Reinvestigation requirements apply when consumers provide new evidence or identify specific inadequacies in previous investigations. Credit bureaus cannot treat legitimate reinvestigation requests as frivolous simply because previous disputes were unsuccessful.

Quality control measures should ensure that investigation procedures are followed consistently and that personnel conducting investigations have adequate training and resources. Poor quality control often leads to inadequate investigations and FCRA violations.

Results communication must clearly explain investigation findings and any actions taken based on investigation results. Vague or confusing results notifications may violate FCRA's requirement for clear communication about investigation outcomes.

Method of Verification (MOV) requests represent an advanced dispute strategy that challenges credit bureaus to prove they actually conducted proper investigations of disputed items. Under FCRA, you have the right to know what method bureaus used to verify disputed information, and inadequate verification methods may provide grounds for challenging investigation results.

MOV request procedures involve sending written requests to credit bureaus asking them to provide specific information about how they verified disputed information. These requests should be made after receiving dispute results and should reference specific disputed items and investigation outcomes.

Verification method types that credit bureaus might use include contacting furnishers by automated systems, manual review of furnisher records, electronic verification systems, or telephone verification procedures. Understanding different verification methods helps evaluate their adequacy for specific dispute circumstances.

Inadequate verification indicators include automated confirmations without human review, verification requests that lack specific dispute details, furnisher responses that don't address actual dispute issues, or verification processes that couldn't reasonably confirm disputed information accuracy.

Documentation requirements for MOV requests include copies of original disputes, credit bureau responses, and specific questions about verification procedures used. Clear documentation helps credit bureaus understand what verification information you're seeking and demonstrates the seriousness of your request.

Response evaluation involves analyzing credit bureau MOV responses to determine whether verification methods were adequate for the circumstances. Inadequate verification methods may provide grounds for challenging investigation results and demanding reinvestigation with proper procedures.

Legal standards for verification adequacy vary by jurisdiction, but generally require that verification methods be appropriate to the complexity and nature of disputed information. Simple automated confirmations may be adequate for straightforward disputes but insufficient for complex accuracy challenges.

Follow-up procedures become necessary when credit bureaus fail to respond to MOV requests, provide inadequate verification information, or reveal verification procedures that appear insufficient for proper investigation. Systematic follow-up often produces better responses than single requests.

Evidence development through MOV requests helps build cases for potential legal action when credit bureaus fail to conduct adequate investigations. Documentation of inadequate verification procedures strengthens FCRA violation claims and provides leverage in settlement negotiations.

Strategic timing of MOV requests should allow adequate time for investigation completion while preserving legal deadlines for challenging inadequate investigations. Understanding timing requirements helps maximize the effectiveness of MOV strategies.

Integration with other dispute strategies allows MOV requests to complement traditional dispute approaches and provide additional pressure for proper investigation procedures. Combined strategies often produce better results than relying solely on standard dispute methods.

Regulatory oversight of verification procedures continues evolving as agencies scrutinize credit bureau investigation practices and establish guidelines for adequate verification methods. Understanding regulatory developments helps consumers leverage emerging standards in MOV requests.

Direct disputes with furnishers create alternative avenues for challenging inaccurate credit reporting that often prove more effective than credit bureau disputes alone. The FACT Act amendments to FCRA established specific rights to dispute information directly with the companies that provide information to credit bureaus.

Furnisher dispute rights arise when credit bureau disputes result in no changes but you believe the information remains inaccurate. You can then dispute directly with the furnisher by providing a copy of the credit bureau's investigation results along with your dispute of the continued reporting.

Timing requirements for furnisher disputes mandate that you provide notice of disputes within specific timeframes, typically triggered by receiving credit bureau investigation results. Understanding these timing requirements helps preserve your rights to pursue furnisher disputes effectively.

Investigation obligations for furnishers mirror credit bureau requirements but often prove more thorough since furnishers have direct access to account records and transaction history. Furnishers must investigate disputed information and correct or delete inaccurate reporting.

Documentation advantages in furnisher disputes include the possibility that furnishers may have more complete records than credit bureaus and better ability to research account history. This can result in corrections that credit bureau investigations might miss due to limited access to detailed account information.

Response requirements mandate that furnishers respond to legitimate disputes and provide results of their investigations. Furnishers who fail to respond or investigate properly may violate FCRA's furnisher provisions and face potential liability.

Evidence presentation to furnishers can be more detailed and comprehensive than credit bureau disputes since furnishers often have more time and resources for investigation than credit bureau personnel handling thousands of disputes simultaneously.

Leverage opportunities with furnishers may include their desire to avoid regulatory scrutiny, legal liability, or customer relations problems. Furnishers may be more willing to make corrections when approached directly rather than through credit bureau intermediaries.

Industry variations affect furnisher dispute effectiveness, with original creditors often having better records and more authority to make corrections than collection agencies or debt buyers who may lack complete account documentation.

Resolution tracking becomes important when pursuing furnisher disputes since results must be communicated to all credit bureaus receiving reports from the furnisher. Successful furnisher disputes should result in corrections across all three major credit bureaus.

Follow-up procedures with furnishers should include verification that corrections have been implemented across all credit reporting systems and that future reporting reflects investigation results. Systematic follow-up ensures that dispute resolutions are implemented completely.

Integration with credit bureau disputes allows consumers to pursue both avenues simultaneously or sequentially, maximizing pressure for accurate reporting and increasing the likelihood of successful dispute resolution.

Dispute documentation and record keeping form the foundation of effective credit repair strategies and provide essential evidence for potential legal action when credit bureaus fail to meet their FCRA obligations. Systematic documentation helps track dispute progress, identify patterns, and build cases for escalation when necessary.

Baseline documentation should include copies of credit reports from all three bureaus before beginning dispute activities, providing clear evidence of what information existed prior to your dispute efforts. This establishes the starting point for measuring dispute effectiveness and proves the existence of disputed items.

Dispute correspondence copies must be maintained for all communications with credit bureaus, including original dispute letters, follow-up correspondence, and any additional information provided during investigation periods. Complete correspondence files demonstrate your compliance with dispute procedures.

Certified mail receipts provide proof of delivery for dispute letters and establish timeline compliance for credit bureau investigation obligations. Maintaining delivery receipts helps prove that bureaus received disputes and must investigate within required timeframes.

Credit bureau responses should be preserved completely, including investigation results, updated credit reports, and any explanatory letters. These responses provide evidence of bureau actions and may reveal investigation inadequacies that support escalation efforts.

Supporting evidence compilation includes maintaining copies of all documentation provided to support disputes, such as payment records, account statements, correspondence with creditors, or identity theft reports. Organized evidence files facilitate future dispute efforts and legal action if necessary.

Progress tracking through systematic logging of dispute activities, response dates, and resolution outcomes helps identify effective strategies and patterns in bureau responses. Detailed logs also help ensure that follow-up actions are taken timely and appropriately.

Timeline documentation proves compliance with procedural requirements and identifies bureau violations when investigations exceed permitted timeframes. Accurate timeline records are crucial for potential FCRA violation claims.

Communication logs should record all telephone contacts with credit bureaus, including dates, personnel names, reference numbers, and conversation summaries. Phone communication often supplements written disputes and provides additional evidence of bureau interactions.

Result verification involves maintaining updated credit reports that show the outcomes of dispute efforts and provide evidence of successful corrections or continued inaccuracies. Regular credit report monitoring helps track long-term dispute effectiveness.

Electronic organization of dispute files facilitates easy access to documentation and enables efficient management of ongoing dispute activities. Digital filing systems should include backup procedures to prevent loss of important documentation.

Legal preparation through systematic documentation creates the foundation for potential FCRA violation claims when credit bureaus fail to meet their obligations. Well-organized files significantly improve the effectiveness of legal action when disputes alone are insufficient.

Privacy protection for sensitive documentation ensures that personal financial information is secured while remaining accessible for dispute activities. Secure document storage protects against identity theft while preserving essential dispute evidence.

Online versus mail dispute strategies each offer distinct advantages and disadvantages that affect dispute effectiveness, timeline control, and documentation quality. Understanding these differences helps you choose optimal dispute methods for specific situations and maximize the likelihood of successful outcomes.

Online dispute advantages include immediate submission, faster processing times, automatic confirmation of receipt, and convenient tracking of investigation progress. Credit bureau websites provide user-friendly interfaces that make dispute submission accessible and efficient for many consumers.

Online dispute limitations often include restricted explanation space that limits your ability to provide detailed dispute reasoning, automatic categorization that may not accurately reflect your specific dispute issues, and limited documentation upload capabilities that prevent submission of supporting evidence.

Mail dispute benefits include unlimited space for detailed explanations, ability to include comprehensive supporting documentation, professional presentation through well-crafted letters, and certified mail proof of delivery that establishes legal compliance timelines.

Mail dispute disadvantages involve longer processing times, potential postal delays that affect investigation timelines, higher costs for certified mailing, and less convenient tracking of dispute progress compared to online systems.

Hybrid strategies combine online and mail approaches to maximize advantages while minimizing limitations. This might involve initial online disputes for speed followed by mail disputes with detailed documentation, or mail disputes supplemented by online status monitoring.

Documentation considerations differ significantly between online and mail disputes, with online systems typically providing electronic confirmations while mail disputes create paper trails with certified mail receipts and physical correspondence files.

Dispute complexity affects optimal method selection, with simple disputes often suitable for online submission while complex disputes requiring detailed explanation and extensive documentation benefiting from mail submission methods.

Bureau preferences vary among the three major credit bureaus, with some offering more robust online dispute systems while others provide better mail dispute processing. Understanding bureau-specific strengths helps optimize dispute method selection.

Legal protection considerations favor mail disputes in many situations since certified mail provides stronger proof of compliance with FCRA requirements and mail disputes create more comprehensive documentation for potential legal action.

Time sensitivity factors may favor online disputes when quick resolution is crucial, such as pending mortgage applications or urgent credit decisions. However, mail disputes often produce better long-term results despite longer initial processing times.

Follow-up procedures differ between online and mail disputes, with online systems providing digital tracking while mail disputes require more active follow-up to monitor compliance with investigation timelines and ensure proper resolution.

Strategic sequencing involves using different dispute methods in optimal sequence to maximize effectiveness, such as starting with online disputes for immediate action followed by detailed mail disputes for comprehensive resolution.

Timing strategies for credit disputes can significantly affect investigation quality, processing efficiency, and ultimate success rates. Understanding optimal timing helps maximize dispute effectiveness while avoiding periods when credit bureaus may provide less attention to dispute investigations.

Business cycle considerations recognize that credit bureaus experience varying workloads throughout the year that affect investigation quality. Understanding these patterns helps time disputes for periods when investigators may have more time and resources for thorough reviews.

Holiday impact on dispute processing includes potential delays during major holiday periods when credit bureau staffing may be reduced and investigation timelines extended. Planning dispute activities around holiday schedules helps ensure timely processing.

Quarterly patterns in credit bureau operations may affect dispute handling quality as bureaus manage reporting cycles, regulatory deadlines, and business priorities. Understanding quarterly patterns helps optimize dispute timing for better results.

Regulatory examination periods when credit bureaus face increased scrutiny from federal agencies may result in more careful dispute handling as bureaus work to demonstrate compliance with FCRA requirements during examination periods.

Dispute volume considerations recognize that individual dispute effectiveness may be reduced during periods when credit bureaus receive high volumes of disputes. Strategic timing during lower-volume periods may result in more thorough investigations.

Personal timing factors include coordinating disputes with credit monitoring schedules, planned credit applications, and major financial decisions that might be affected by credit report changes. Personal timeline coordination helps maximize dispute benefits.

Sequential dispute planning involves spacing multiple disputes over time to avoid overwhelming credit bureau systems and ensure adequate attention for each dispute issue. Systematic sequencing often produces better results than simultaneous mass disputes.

Urgency assessment helps determine when expedited dispute procedures might be necessary despite potential timing disadvantages. Understanding urgency factors helps balance optimal timing with immediate needs.

Follow-up timing ensures that dispute progress is monitored appropriately and that investigation deadlines are enforced effectively. Systematic follow-up scheduling helps maintain pressure for timely resolution.

Appeal timing becomes crucial when initial disputes are unsuccessful and appeals or reinvestigations are necessary. Understanding appeal deadlines and optimal timing helps preserve rights for continued dispute efforts.

Legal action timing considers limitation periods for FCRA violation claims and optimal coordination between dispute efforts and potential legal action. Strategic timing helps preserve legal options while maximizing dispute effectiveness.

Long-term planning recognizes that credit repair is often a multi-month or multi-year process requiring sustained effort and strategic timing throughout the improvement period. Comprehensive timing strategies help maintain momentum while optimizing resource allocation.

Common dispute mistakes can significantly reduce the effectiveness of credit repair efforts and may actually harm your position by creating negative precedents or triggering adverse reactions from credit bureaus. Understanding these mistakes helps avoid counterproductive strategies and focus efforts on approaches that produce positive results.

Vague dispute language represents one of the most common errors, with consumers simply stating that information is "wrong" or "not mine" without providing specific details about what is inaccurate. Credit bureaus often respond to vague disputes with generic denials rather than conducting thorough investigations.

Emotional dispute content including angry language, personal attacks on creditors, or emotional explanations of financial difficulties rarely produces positive results and may prejudice investigators against your position. Professional, factual disputes get better results than emotional appeals.

Overwhelming documentation by including excessive paperwork without clear organization or relevance can actually hinder investigations by making it difficult for investigators to understand your key points. Strategic documentation selection proves more effective than comprehensive file dumps.

Identical form letters copied from credit repair companies or internet sources are easily recognized by credit bureau personnel and often receive perfunctory attention rather than thorough investigation. Personalized disputes tailored to specific circumstances produce better results.

Simultaneous mass disputes targeting numerous items at once can trigger credit bureau suspicions about credit repair company involvement and may result in reduced attention to individual dispute items. Strategic sequencing often works better than overwhelming assault approaches.

Frivolous dispute claims targeting accurate negative information waste resources and may cause credit bureaus to label future disputes as frivolous. Focus on legitimate inaccuracies rather than attempting to remove accurate negative items.

Inadequate follow-up allows credit bureaus to ignore investigation deadlines or provide inadequate responses without consequences. Systematic follow-up ensures that disputes receive proper attention and investigation deadlines are enforced.

Legal threats without merit can backfire by prompting credit bureaus to refer matters to legal departments that may be less willing to make corrections than customer service departments. Reserve legal threats for situations where actual violations exist.

Duplicate disputes across multiple bureaus using identical language can trigger coordination between bureaus that reduces investigation effectiveness. Tailored disputes for each bureau considering their specific reporting often work better.

Impatience leading to premature escalation before investigation deadlines expire wastes escalation opportunities and may reduce credibility when legitimate escalation becomes necessary. Understanding proper timing helps preserve escalation effectiveness.

Insufficient documentation backup when claims require supporting evidence weakens dispute credibility and may result in rejections that could have been avoided with proper evidence presentation.

Identity confusion by disputing items without clearly identifying yourself or disputed accounts can cause processing delays and may result in disputes being rejected for inadequate identification rather than being investigated on their merits.

Advanced dispute techniques go beyond basic dispute letter submission to leverage sophisticated strategies that address complex credit reporting problems and maximize the likelihood of successful outcomes. These techniques require deeper understanding of FCRA requirements and credit bureau operations.

Procedural violation challenges focus on credit bureau failures to comply with FCRA investigation procedures rather than simply disputing information accuracy. These challenges can succeed even when disputed information is technically accurate if bureaus failed to investigate properly.

Estoppel by silence arguments contend that credit bureau failure to respond adequately to disputes constitutes admission that disputed information cannot be verified. While not universally accepted, these arguments can provide leverage in negotiations and legal proceedings.

Cascading dispute strategies involve disputing related information in sequence to create cumulative pressure for resolution. For example, disputing account details before disputing the account itself can reveal investigation inadequacies that strengthen subsequent challenges.

Evidence timing manipulation involves providing additional evidence at strategic points during investigations to extend investigation periods or trigger reinvestigation requirements. This can give you more time to develop stronger cases for dispute resolution.

Verification gap exploitation identifies and challenges situations where credit bureaus cannot obtain adequate verification from furnishers due to record-keeping problems, business closures, or ownership changes. These gaps often provide successful dispute opportunities.

Technical compliance challenges address credit bureau failures to meet technical FCRA requirements such as proper notice timing, investigation deadlines, or result communication standards. Technical violations can provide grounds for successful challenges regardless of information accuracy.

Cross-bureau coordination involves leveraging differences in how the three major credit bureaus handle identical disputes to create pressure for consistent resolution across all bureaus. Inconsistent bureau responses often reveal investigation inadequacies.

Systematic approach documentation creates comprehensive records of credit bureau non-compliance patterns that strengthen legal positions and provide evidence for regulatory complaints. Documented patterns of violations are more compelling than isolated incidents.

Expert consultation involves working with attorneys or credit repair professionals who have experience with advanced dispute techniques and can provide guidance on complex situations that exceed typical consumer knowledge.

Industry knowledge leverage involves understanding credit bureau operations, furnisher practices, and regulatory oversight patterns to identify optimal dispute strategies for specific circumstances and types of disputed information.

Regulatory pressure coordination combines dispute activities with strategic regulatory complaints to maximize pressure for proper investigation and resolution. Coordinated pressure often produces better results than disputes alone.

Legal action integration coordinates dispute activities with potential legal action to preserve rights while maximizing opportunities for favorable resolution. Strategic integration helps avoid conflicts between dispute and litigation strategies.

Dispute escalation procedures provide structured approaches for addressing inadequate credit bureau responses and ensuring that legitimate disputes ultimately receive proper resolution. Understanding escalation helps you persist effectively when initial disputes fail to produce satisfactory results.

Internal escalation within credit bureaus starts with requesting supervisory review of dispute handling when initial investigations appear inadequate or when investigation deadlines are missed. Most bureaus have internal escalation procedures for disputing consumers who request management attention.

Escalation triggers include missed investigation deadlines, clearly inadequate investigation procedures, failure to address all components of disputes, inconsistent responses to similar disputes, or obvious errors in investigation results. Understanding triggers helps determine when escalation is appropriate.

Documentation requirements for effective escalation include complete records of original disputes, bureau responses, evidence of procedural violations, and clear explanations of why initial investigations were inadequate. Well-documented escalation requests receive more serious attention.

Supervisory contact procedures vary among credit bureaus but typically involve written requests for management review that reference specific disputes and investigation inadequacies. Professional escalation requests that cite specific FCRA requirements often produce better results.

Regulatory escalation through CFPB complaints provides federal oversight when credit bureaus fail to resolve disputes properly through internal procedures. CFPB complaints can result in bureau contact and resolution assistance that internal escalation cannot achieve.

State attorney general involvement may provide additional escalation options in states with active consumer protection programs. State escalation can be particularly effective for consumers facing systematic problems with credit bureaus.

Legal escalation through attorney consultation or legal action represents the ultimate escalation when other procedures fail to produce fair resolution. Understanding when legal escalation is appropriate helps preserve legal rights while maximizing other resolution opportunities.

Executive escalation involves contacting credit bureau executive offices when systematic problems affect dispute handling. Executive contact should be reserved for serious procedural violations or patterns of non-compliance that indicate systematic bureau problems.

Media escalation through consumer reporters or regulatory oversight publicity can provide additional pressure for resolution when credit bureaus fail to respond to other escalation efforts. Media attention often motivates prompt resolution of consumer complaints.

Industry escalation through trade association complaints or industry ombudsman programs may provide alternative resolution mechanisms when standard escalation procedures fail. Understanding industry resources helps access all available escalation options.

Timing considerations for escalation include allowing adequate time for initial dispute resolution while preserving deadlines for legal action or regulatory complaints. Strategic escalation timing helps maintain pressure without premature escalation that wastes opportunities.

Persistence strategies for effective escalation require sustained effort over time while maintaining professional communication and clear documentation. Systematic persistence often produces results where single escalation attempts fail.

Results evaluation and follow-up procedures ensure that successful disputes produce lasting corrections and that unsuccessful disputes receive appropriate further attention. Systematic evaluation helps maximize the benefits of dispute activities while identifying areas requiring additional work.

Initial response analysis involves carefully reviewing credit bureau investigation results to determine whether disputes were successful, partially successful, or unsuccessful. Understanding response categories helps determine appropriate next steps for each disputed item.

Correction verification requires obtaining updated credit reports to confirm that successful disputes resulted in actual corrections across all credit reporting systems. Credit bureaus sometimes report successful disputes without implementing actual corrections.

Score impact assessment helps determine whether dispute successes translated into credit score improvements and identifies additional opportunities for score enhancement through further dispute activities or other credit repair strategies.

Reinvestigation planning for unsuccessful disputes involves analyzing investigation responses to identify potential grounds for challenging investigation adequacy or providing additional evidence for renewed dispute efforts.

Cross-bureau consistency checking ensures that dispute resolutions are implemented consistently across all three major credit bureaus. Inconsistent implementation often requires additional dispute efforts to achieve complete resolution.

Long-term monitoring involves systematic tracking of disputed items to ensure that corrections remain in place and that removed items don't reappear on future credit reports. Ongoing monitoring helps maintain dispute benefits over time.

Documentation updates should reflect dispute outcomes and provide organized records for future dispute activities. Updated documentation helps track progress and provides foundation for additional dispute efforts when necessary.

Strategy refinement based on dispute results helps improve future dispute effectiveness by identifying successful approaches and avoiding strategies that proved ineffective. Learning from results helps optimize ongoing credit repair efforts.

Regulatory reporting of bureau non-compliance may be appropriate when dispute results reveal systematic violations or procedural failures. Regulatory reports help improve industry practices while potentially providing individual assistance with dispute problems.

Legal evaluation involves assessing whether unsuccessful disputes or inadequate investigations provide grounds for potential FCRA violation claims. Understanding legal options helps preserve rights while continuing other resolution efforts.

Success celebration and motivation maintenance helps sustain long-term credit repair efforts by recognizing achievements and maintaining momentum through challenging periods. Credit repair requires sustained effort that benefits from positive reinforcement.

Planning integration ensures that dispute results are incorporated into broader credit repair strategies and that future activities build on dispute successes while addressing remaining challenges. Integrated planning helps maximize overall credit improvement effectiveness.

Future dispute planning and strategy development help maintain momentum in credit repair efforts while adapting approaches based on experience and changing circumstances. Systematic planning ensures that dispute activities contribute to long-term credit improvement goals rather than producing scattered short-term results.

Pipeline management involves maintaining a systematic approach to dispute activities that addresses current problems while preparing for future dispute opportunities. Effective pipeline management prevents gaps in dispute activities while avoiding overwhelming approaches.

Priority assessment helps focus dispute efforts on items that will produce the greatest credit improvement benefits. Understanding priority factors helps allocate limited time and resources to disputes with the highest potential impact.

Timing coordination ensures that dispute activities are scheduled to support major financial goals such as mortgage applications or credit card approvals. Strategic timing helps maximize the benefits of credit improvements for important financial decisions.

Resource allocation involves balancing time, effort, and potential costs across different dispute strategies and approaches. Understanding resource requirements helps maintain sustainable dispute activities over extended periods.

Technology integration includes using credit monitoring services, dispute tracking software, and electronic organization systems to improve dispute efficiency and effectiveness. Technology tools can significantly enhance dispute management capabilities.

Professional assistance evaluation helps determine when consulting attorneys, credit repair companies, or other professionals might enhance dispute effectiveness. Understanding when professional help is beneficial helps optimize resource allocation.

Industry development monitoring involves staying current with changes in credit bureau procedures, regulatory requirements, and legal developments that affect dispute strategies. Ongoing education helps adapt approaches to changing circumstances.

Performance measurement through systematic tracking of dispute outcomes, score improvements, and goal achievement helps evaluate overall strategy effectiveness and identify areas requiring adjustment. Regular performance review helps optimize dispute approaches.

Motivation maintenance strategies help sustain long-term dispute efforts through challenging periods when progress seems slow or setbacks occur. Credit repair requires persistence that benefits from systematic motivation support.

Goal integration ensures that dispute activities support broader financial goals and credit improvement objectives. Understanding how disputes fit into overall financial planning helps maintain focus and direction.

Exit strategy planning involves determining when dispute activities have achieved their objectives and when to transition to maintenance monitoring rather than active dispute efforts. Understanding completion criteria helps avoid unnecessary continued disputing.

Legacy planning considers how dispute successes can be maintained over time and how dispute experience can benefit future credit management decisions. Long-term perspective helps maximize the lasting benefits of dispute activities while avoiding behaviors that might recreate credit problems.

CHAPTER 10

ADVANCED DISPUTE STRATEGIES

Advanced dispute strategies represent sophisticated approaches that go beyond basic credit report challenges to leverage complex legal principles, procedural requirements, and industry practices. These strategies require deeper understanding of FCRA mechanics, credit bureau operations, and the intricate relationships between credit reporting agencies, furnishers, and regulatory oversight bodies.

The evolution from basic to advanced dispute techniques reflects the credit repair industry's maturation and the increasing sophistication of both credit bureau defense mechanisms and consumer advocacy approaches. As credit bureaus have implemented automated systems and standardized responses to handle millions of disputes annually, effective credit repair has required more nuanced strategies that address system weaknesses and procedural vulnerabilities.

Advanced strategies often succeed where basic disputes fail because they target the operational and legal frameworks underlying credit reporting rather than simply claiming information is inaccurate. These approaches recognize that credit reporting operates within complex regulatory and business environments that create multiple pressure points for achieving favorable outcomes.

Understanding the distinction between disputing information accuracy and challenging reporting procedures is crucial for advanced strategy success. While basic disputes focus on whether reported information is correct, advanced strategies often challenge whether credit bureaus and furnishers are following proper procedures, meeting legal obligations, or maintaining adequate systems for ensuring accuracy.

The legal foundation for advanced strategies rests on FCRA's comprehensive regulatory framework that establishes specific procedural requirements, timeline obligations, and accuracy standards. Violations of these requirements can provide grounds for successful challenges even when disputed information might be technically accurate under narrow interpretation.

Procedural compliance failures by credit bureaus create opportunities for advanced dispute strategies that leverage institutional weaknesses rather than relying solely on information accuracy arguments. These failures often occur because credit bureaus prioritize efficiency over thoroughness in their dispute handling processes.

Advanced strategies require systematic documentation and strategic patience since they often involve multiple rounds of interaction with credit bureaus and furnishers. Success frequently depends on building cumulative cases that demonstrate patterns of non-compliance rather than isolated incidents.

The intersection of advanced dispute strategies with potential legal action creates additional leverage since documented procedural violations can support FCRA damage claims. This creates incentives for credit bureaus to resolve advanced disputes favorably rather than risk legal exposure.

Industry knowledge becomes crucial for advanced strategies since effective approaches often exploit gaps between regulatory requirements and industry practices, or leverage competitive pressures and regulatory oversight to achieve favorable outcomes.

Risk assessment is essential because advanced strategies can sometimes trigger enhanced scrutiny from credit bureaus or prompt defensive responses that make future dispute efforts more difficult. Understanding these risks helps deploy advanced techniques strategically rather than routinely.

Method of Verification (MOV) challenges represent one of the most powerful advanced dispute strategies, targeting the adequacy and appropriateness of procedures credit bureaus use to verify disputed information. These challenges can succeed even when disputed information is accurate if verification procedures fail to meet FCRA's reasonableness standards.

The legal basis for MOV challenges stems from FCRA's requirement that credit bureaus maintain "reasonable procedures" for investigating disputes and ensuring maximum possible accuracy. When verification methods are inadequate for the complexity or nature of disputed information, investigations may violate FCRA regardless of ultimate accuracy.

Common verification inadequacies include automated confirmations without human review, verification requests that fail to communicate specific dispute issues to furnishers, investigations that don't address all components of consumer disputes, and verification procedures that couldn't reasonably confirm disputed information accuracy given available evidence.

MOV request procedures involve sending written demands to credit bureaus requiring detailed disclosure of verification methods used for specific disputes. These requests should reference particular disputed items, investigation dates, and specific questions about verification procedures employed during investigations.

Documentation requirements for effective MOV challenges include copies of original disputes, credit bureau responses, specific questions about verification methods, and any evidence that suggests verification procedures were inadequate. Comprehensive documentation strengthens MOV challenges and provides evidence for potential legal action.

Timing considerations for MOV requests should allow credit bureaus adequate opportunity to respond while preserving deadlines for legal action or regulatory complaints. Strategic timing helps maximize MOV effectiveness while maintaining other enforcement options.

Response evaluation involves analyzing credit bureau MOV responses to identify verification inadequacies that violate FCRA standards. Common inadequacies include reliance on automated systems for complex disputes, failure to communicate dispute specifics to furnishers, or verification procedures that couldn't reasonably address dispute issues.

Escalation strategies for inadequate MOV responses include regulatory complaints, supervisory escalation within credit bureaus, and potential legal action for investigation violations. Documented MOV inadequacies often provide strong grounds for FCRA violation claims.

Evidence development through MOV challenges helps build comprehensive cases for advanced dispute strategies by documenting systematic failures in credit bureau investigation procedures. This evidence can support broader challenges to credit bureau operations and provide leverage for favorable resolutions.

Integration with other strategies allows MOV challenges to complement traditional dispute approaches and provide additional pressure for proper investigation procedures. Combined approaches often produce better results than relying solely on MOV techniques.

Follow-up procedures ensure that MOV challenges receive proper attention and that verification inadequacies are addressed appropriately. Systematic follow-up often produces better responses than single MOV requests.

Regulatory implications of MOV challenges include potential CFPB oversight when systematic verification problems are identified. Regulatory attention can result in broader industry improvements while providing individual assistance with specific MOV issues.

Procedural violation strategies target credit bureau failures to comply with specific FCRA procedural requirements rather than focusing primarily on information accuracy. These strategies can achieve favorable outcomes even when disputed information is technically correct if credit bureaus fail to follow proper procedures during investigation processes.

Investigation timeline violations occur when credit bureaus exceed the thirty-day investigation period without proper justification or consumer consent for extensions. Timeline violations create immediate FCRA non-compliance that can support successful challenges regardless of information accuracy.

Inadequate notice procedures involve credit bureau failures to provide proper dispute acknowledgments, investigation result notifications, or required disclosures about consumer rights. Notice violations can invalidate investigation results and require reinvestigation with proper procedures.

Incomplete investigation responses that fail to address all components of consumer disputes violate FCRA's requirement for thorough investigation of dispute issues. Partial investigations often provide grounds for challenging entire investigation processes.

Communication failures between credit bureaus and furnishers during investigations can violate FCRA requirements for adequate verification procedures. When bureaus fail to communicate dispute specifics to furnishers, resulting investigations may be inadequate regardless of furnisher responses.

Documentation preservation failures by credit bureaus can violate regulatory requirements and make it impossible to verify that adequate investigations were conducted. Poor documentation practices often provide grounds for challenging investigation adequacy.

Reinvestigation violations occur when credit bureaus treat legitimate reinvestigation requests as frivolous or fail to conduct proper reinvestigations when consumers provide new evidence or identify specific investigation inadequacies.

System failure implications arise when credit bureau computer systems, automated processes, or operational procedures fail to meet FCRA requirements for reasonable investigation procedures. Systematic failures often affect multiple consumers and provide grounds for broader challenges.

Quality control inadequacies in credit bureau dispute handling processes can violate FCRA requirements for reasonable procedures. Poor quality control often results in inconsistent investigation outcomes and procedural violations.

Training deficiencies among credit bureau personnel handling disputes can contribute to procedural violations and inadequate investigations. Understanding training requirements helps identify systemic problems that affect investigation quality.

Regulatory oversight of procedural compliance provides external pressure for credit bureau adherence to FCRA requirements. Leveraging regulatory attention can enhance the effectiveness of procedural violation strategies.

Evidence development for procedural challenges requires systematic documentation of credit bureau failures to meet specific FCRA requirements. Comprehensive evidence helps support successful procedural challenges and potential legal action.

Strategic application of procedural challenges involves identifying the most promising procedural violations for specific circumstances and disputes. Targeted procedural challenges often prove more effective than broad challenges that attempt to address multiple procedural issues simultaneously.

Estoppel by silence arguments contend that credit bureau failures to respond adequately to disputes or provide proper verification constitutes implicit admission that disputed information cannot be verified as accurate. While not universally accepted by courts, these arguments can provide leverage in settlement negotiations and some legal proceedings.

Legal theory foundation for estoppel arguments rests on the principle that parties who fail to respond to specific allegations may be deemed to have admitted those allegations under certain circumstances. Applied to credit disputes, this theory suggests that inadequate bureau responses constitute admissions of verification inadequacy.

Application requirements for effective estoppel arguments include clear, specific disputes that identify particular inaccuracies, adequate opportunity for credit bureaus to respond, and bureau failures to address dispute specifics adequately. Vague disputes or adequate bureau responses typically prevent successful estoppel arguments.

Documentation standards for estoppel strategies require comprehensive records demonstrating specific dispute allegations, bureau response inadequacies, and clear patterns of non-responsive behavior. Strong documentation helps establish the foundational elements necessary for estoppel arguments.

Timing considerations affect estoppel argument effectiveness since bureaus must have adequate opportunity to respond before silence can be interpreted as admission. Understanding timing requirements helps structure disputes to support potential estoppel arguments.

Jurisdictional variations in estoppel recognition affect the viability of these arguments in different courts and legal contexts. Understanding local legal standards helps evaluate whether estoppel arguments are likely to succeed in specific jurisdictions.

Strategic limitations of estoppel arguments include their novelty in credit reporting contexts and varying judicial acceptance of the theory. These limitations suggest that estoppel arguments work best as components of broader legal strategies rather than standalone approaches.

Settlement leverage from estoppel arguments can be significant even when courts might not fully accept the legal theory. The possibility of novel legal arguments often motivates credit bureaus to settle disputes rather than risk adverse legal precedents.

Evidence requirements for estoppel arguments include demonstrating specific opportunities for bureau response, clear dispute allegations that required response, and patterns of inadequate responses that suggest inability to verify disputed information.

Integration with other strategies allows estoppel arguments to complement traditional dispute approaches and provide additional theoretical foundations for challenging credit bureau non-compliance. Combined approaches often prove more effective than relying solely on estoppel theories.

Regulatory considerations for estoppel strategies include potential CFPB interest in systematic bureau failures to respond adequately to disputes. Regulatory attention can provide additional pressure for favorable resolutions beyond traditional estoppel arguments.

Professional consultation becomes particularly important for estoppel strategies since these approaches involve novel legal theories that benefit from experienced legal guidance. Understanding when professional assistance is necessary helps optimize estoppel argument effectiveness.

Cascading dispute strategies involve sequencing related disputes to create cumulative pressure for resolution while building comprehensive cases for challenging complex credit reporting problems. These strategies recognize that individual disputes often address components of broader reporting inaccuracies that require systematic approaches.

Sequential targeting begins with disputing peripheral issues before addressing core problems, creating opportunities to identify investigation inadequacies and procedural violations that strengthen subsequent challenges. This approach often reveals systematic problems in credit bureau or furnisher procedures.

Relationship mapping involves identifying connections between different disputed items, such as accounts from the same creditor, similar timing issues, or related procedural problems. Understanding these relationships helps structure cascade sequences for maximum effectiveness.

Evidence development through cascading allows each dispute to contribute information that strengthens subsequent challenges. Early disputes often reveal documentation problems or procedural inadequacies that provide ammunition for more complex later disputes.

Timing coordination ensures that cascade elements are spaced appropriately to allow adequate investigation time while maintaining momentum toward resolution. Strategic timing helps prevent bureaus from treating cascaded disputes as frivolous repetition.

Documentation integration across cascade elements creates comprehensive records that demonstrate patterns of credit bureau non-compliance or furnisher reporting problems. Integrated documentation often provides stronger evidence than isolated dispute records.

Pressure escalation through cascading creates cumulative stress on credit bureau and furnisher systems while demonstrating persistent attention to resolution. This pressure often motivates favorable outcomes that individual disputes might not achieve.

Investigation fatigue can work in favor of consumers when cascading strategies expose systematic inadequacies in credit bureau investigation procedures. Bureaus may become more willing to resolve disputes favorably rather than continue inadequate investigation cycles.

Strategic patience becomes crucial for cascading success since these approaches require sustained effort over extended periods. Understanding the long-term nature of cascading helps maintain motivation during challenging phases.

Complexity management involves organizing cascade elements to avoid overwhelming credit bureau systems while maintaining systematic pressure for resolution. Balanced complexity helps optimize cascade effectiveness without triggering defensive responses.

Resource allocation for cascading strategies requires careful planning since these approaches involve multiple dispute rounds with associated time and effort investments. Understanding resource requirements helps maintain sustainable cascade activities.

Success measurement for cascading involves evaluating cumulative outcomes rather than individual dispute results. Comprehensive evaluation helps optimize cascade strategies and identify successful approaches for future applications.

Risk mitigation in cascading includes avoiding patterns that might trigger frivolous dispute designations or other adverse credit bureau responses. Strategic risk management helps maintain cascade effectiveness while preserving consumer rights.

Verification gap exploitation strategies identify and leverage situations where credit bureaus cannot obtain adequate verification from furnishers due to record-keeping problems, business changes, or communication failures. These gaps often provide successful dispute opportunities even when original information was accurate.

Common verification gaps include furnisher business closure so, corporate mergers or acquisitions that disrupt record-keeping systems, employee turnover that affects institutional knowledge, and technology changes that make historical records difficult to access.

Gap identification techniques involve researching furnisher business histories, monitoring industry changes that affect record-keeping, and analyzing patterns in credit bureau responses that suggest verification difficulties. Systematic gap identification helps target disputes strategically.

Documentation research for gap exploitation includes investigating furnisher business status, ownership changes, regulatory actions, and other factors that might affect their ability to maintain adequate records for verification purposes.

Timing advantages in gap exploitation recognize that verification difficulties often worsen over time as records become less accessible and personnel changes reduce institutional knowledge. Strategic timing helps maximize gap exploitation effectiveness.

Evidence development for gap strategies involves documenting furnisher changes, communication failures, or other factors that prevent adequate verification. Strong evidence helps support arguments that verification gaps make continued reporting inappropriate.

Legal theories supporting gap exploitation include FCRA requirements for reasonable verification procedures and furnisher obligations to maintain adequate records. When gaps prevent reasonable verification, continued reporting may violate accuracy standards.

Strategic communication about verification gaps should clearly explain why gaps prevent adequate verification without appearing to encourage removal of accurate information. Professional communication helps ensure that gap arguments receive serious consideration.

Integration with other strategies allows gap exploitation to complement traditional dispute approaches and provide additional pressure for favorable resolution. Combined strategies often prove more effective than relying solely on gap exploitation.

Follow-up procedures for gap strategies include monitoring furnisher status changes and verification responses to identify additional gap opportunities. Systematic follow-up helps maximize gap exploitation effectiveness over time.

Regulatory implications of verification gaps include potential CFPB interest in systematic problems that prevent adequate verification procedures. Regulatory attention can provide additional pressure for industry improvements while assisting individual consumers.

Industry monitoring helps identify emerging verification gaps as business conditions change and new gap opportunities develop. Understanding industry trends helps anticipate future gap exploitation opportunities.

Ethical considerations for gap exploitation include focusing on legitimate verification inadequacies rather than attempting to create artificial gaps through deceptive practices. Ethical gap exploitation maintains credibility while achieving legitimate objectives.

Technical compliance challenges focus on credit bureau failures to meet specific technical requirements under FCRA, such as proper notice timing, investigation deadlines, result communication standards, and documentation preservation obligations. These challenges can succeed regardless of information accuracy when bureaus fail to meet technical requirements.

Notice requirement violations include failures to provide proper dispute acknowledgments within required timeframes, inadequate investigation result notifications, or missing disclosures about consumer rights during dispute processes. Technical notice violations can invalidate investigation results.

Timeline compliance failures occur when credit bureaus exceed investigation deadlines without proper justification or consumer consent for extensions. These violations create immediate grounds for challenging investigation adequacy regardless of ultimate findings.

Communication standard violations involve credit bureau failures to provide clear, understandable results notifications or inadequate explanations of investigation findings. Poor communication can violate FCRA requirements for meaningful consumer notification.

Documentation preservation violations occur when credit bureaus fail to maintain adequate records of dispute investigations, making it impossible to verify that proper procedures were followed. Poor documentation practices often provide grounds for compliance challenges.

System requirement failures involve credit bureau computer systems or operational procedures that don't meet FCRA standards for reasonable investigation procedures. Systematic compliance failures often affect multiple consumers and provide grounds for broader challenges.

Quality assurance violations occur when credit bureaus lack adequate quality control procedures to ensure FCRA compliance. Poor quality assurance often results in systematic compliance failures that provide grounds for technical challenges.

Regulatory standard violations involve credit bureau failures to meet specific requirements established by CFPB or other regulatory agencies. These violations often provide additional grounds for challenging bureau operations beyond basic FCRA requirements.

Evidence development for technical challenges requires systematic documentation of specific compliance failures with clear references to violated requirements. Precise evidence helps establish technical violation claims effectively.

Legal precedent research helps identify successful technical compliance challenges and understand how courts interpret specific FCRA technical requirements. Understanding precedent helps structure effective technical challenges.

Strategic application of technical challenges involves identifying the most promising compliance violations for specific circumstances. Targeted technical challenges often prove more effective than broad challenges addressing multiple compliance issues.

Integration with accuracy disputes allows technical compliance challenges to complement traditional dispute approaches and provide additional grounds for favorable resolution. Combined approaches often achieve better results than single-strategy efforts.

Escalation procedures for technical violations include regulatory complaints, supervisory escalation within credit bureaus, and potential legal action for systematic compliance failures. Technical violations often provide strong grounds for escalation efforts.

Cross-bureau coordination strategies leverage differences in how the three major credit bureaus handle identical disputes to create pressure for consistent resolution and identify investigation inadequacies. These strategies recognize that bureau inconsistencies often reveal systematic problems in dispute handling procedures.

Inconsistency identification involves comparing bureau responses to identical disputes to identify differences in investigation outcomes, verification procedures, or result explanations. Significant inconsistencies often indicate inadequate investigation procedures by one or more bureaus.

Documentation coordination requires submitting identical or substantially similar disputes to all three bureaus while maintaining comprehensive records of each bureau's response. Systematic documentation helps identify patterns and inconsistencies across bureaus.

Analysis procedures for cross-bureau results involve comparing investigation timelines, verification methods, evidence evaluation, and ultimate outcomes to identify differences that suggest investigation inadequacies. Thorough analysis helps identify the most promising inconsistencies for challenge.

Leverage development from inconsistencies involves using differences in bureau responses to challenge inadequate investigations and pressure for consistent resolution across all bureaus. Inconsistencies often provide compelling evidence of investigation problems.

Strategic communication about inconsistencies should clearly explain how different bureau responses to identical disputes demonstrate investigation inadequacies without appearing to encourage uniformly negative responses. Professional communication helps ensure serious consideration.

Follow-up coordination ensures that successful resolutions with one bureau are communicated to other bureaus for consistent implementation. Cross-bureau follow-up helps achieve comprehensive resolution rather than partial success.

Evidence preservation across bureaus requires maintaining comprehensive records from all three bureaus to document inconsistencies and support challenges to inadequate investigations. Complete evidence helps strengthen cross-bureau coordination strategies.

Timing considerations for cross-bureau strategies include coordinating dispute submission timing to enable meaningful comparison while avoiding appearance of mass dispute activities. Strategic timing helps optimize cross-bureau effectiveness.

Regulatory implications of bureau inconsistencies include potential CFPB interest in systematic differences that suggest investigation inadequacies. Regulatory attention can provide additional pressure for improved investigation procedures.

Integration with other strategies allows cross-bureau coordination to complement various dispute approaches and provide additional evidence for challenging investigation adequacy. Combined strategies often achieve better results than single approaches.

Quality assessment through cross-bureau comparison helps evaluate overall dispute effectiveness and identify bureaus with superior or inferior investigation procedures. Understanding quality differences helps optimize future dispute strategies.

Industry implications of cross-bureau coordination include potential pressure for industry standardization of investigation procedures and quality standards. Successful coordination can contribute to broader improvements in dispute handling practices.

Systematic approach documentation creates comprehensive records of credit bureau non-compliance patterns that strengthen legal positions and provide evidence for regulatory complaints. These approaches recognize that documented patterns of violations are more compelling than isolated incidents.

Documentation framework establishment involves creating systematic procedures for recording all interactions with credit bureaus, including dispute submissions, investigation responses, timeline compliance, and procedural adherence. Comprehensive frameworks help ensure complete record-keeping.

Pattern identification through systematic documentation helps reveal recurring problems in credit bureau operations such as timeline violations, inadequate investigation procedures, or communication failures. Understanding patterns helps identify systemic problems rather than isolated incidents.

Evidence organization procedures ensure that systematic documentation is accessible and presentable for legal action or regulatory complaints. Well-organized evidence significantly improves the effectiveness of escalation efforts.

Timeline tracking across multiple disputes helps identify credit bureau compliance patterns and violations of investigation deadlines. Systematic timeline documentation often reveals persistent compliance problems.

Quality analysis through systematic documentation involves evaluating investigation quality patterns across different dispute types, time periods, and bureau personnel. Quality analysis helps identify systematic investigation inadequacies.

Regulatory presentation of systematic documentation provides compelling evidence for CFPB complaints and other regulatory interventions. Organized systematic evidence often receives more serious regulatory attention than individual complaint documentation.

Legal preparation through systematic documentation creates strong foundations for potential FCRA violation claims by demonstrating patterns of non-compliance rather than isolated incidents. Systematic evidence significantly strengthens legal positions.

Strategic patience for systematic approaches requires sustained documentation efforts over extended periods to build compelling cases. Understanding the long-term nature helps maintain motivation during documentation phases.

Technology integration in systematic documentation includes using software tools, spreadsheets, and electronic organization systems to manage comprehensive records effectively. Technology tools can significantly improve documentation efficiency.

Update procedures ensure that systematic documentation remains current and includes all relevant interactions with credit bureaus. Regular updates help maintain comprehensive records while preventing information gaps.

Analysis procedures for systematic documentation involve regular review of accumulated evidence to identify emerging patterns and develop strategic responses. Systematic analysis helps optimize ongoing dispute activities based on documented experience.

Presentation strategies for systematic evidence involve organizing documentation for maximum impact in legal proceedings, regulatory complaints, or settlement negotiations. Effective presentation helps ensure that systematic evidence receives appropriate consideration.

Expert consultation and professional assistance become increasingly valuable for advanced dispute strategies that involve complex legal theories, sophisticated documentation requirements, and potential legal action. Understanding when and how to seek professional help optimizes advanced strategy effectiveness.

Attorney consultation timing involves understanding when legal expertise becomes necessary for advanced dispute strategies, potential FCRA violation claims, or complex credit reporting problems that exceed typical consumer knowledge. Strategic timing helps optimize professional assistance benefits.

Credit repair professional evaluation includes assessing legitimate credit repair companies that offer advanced dispute services while avoiding fraudulent operations that make unrealistic promises. Understanding professional credentials helps identify qualified assistance providers.

Cost-benefit analysis for professional assistance involves weighing potential benefits against costs while considering the complexity of credit situations and available alternatives. Strategic cost analysis helps optimize resource allocation for professional services.

Credential verification procedures help ensure that professional assistance providers have appropriate qualifications, licensing, and experience for specific credit repair needs. Proper verification helps avoid fraudulent or incompetent service providers.

Service scope definition involves clearly understanding what professional assistance providers will and won't do, including specific strategies, timeline expectations, and success criteria. Clear scope understanding helps ensure appropriate service selection.

Quality indicators for professional services include track records, client references, transparent pricing, realistic timeline estimates, and ethical business practices. Understanding quality indicators helps identify superior service providers.

Collaboration strategies with professional assistance involve maintaining active participation in credit repair efforts while leveraging professional expertise effectively. Effective collaboration helps optimize professional assistance benefits.

Documentation coordination with professionals includes providing complete records while understanding how professional assistance affects evidence development and legal strategy. Proper coordination helps ensure that professional assistance enhances rather than compromises consumer positions.

Legal strategy integration involves understanding how professional assistance affects potential legal action and ensuring that professional services support rather than conflict with legal objectives. Strategic integration helps optimize overall outcomes.

Independence maintenance involves retaining control over major decisions while benefiting from professional expertise and assistance. Understanding independence helps ensure that professional assistance serves consumer interests effectively.

Performance monitoring for professional services includes tracking progress, evaluating effectiveness, and ensuring that professional assistance produces promised results. Systematic monitoring helps optimize professional assistance benefits.

Exit strategy planning involves understanding how to conclude professional assistance relationships while maintaining progress and preserving consumer rights. Proper exit planning helps ensure smooth transitions when professional assistance is no longer needed.

Regulatory pressure coordination combines advanced dispute activities with strategic regulatory complaints to maximize pressure for proper investigation and resolution. This coordination recognizes that regulatory oversight can provide additional leverage beyond traditional dispute mechanisms.

CFPB complaint integration involves timing regulatory complaints strategically with dispute activities to provide maximum pressure for fair resolution while avoiding conflicts between different enforcement mechanisms. Strategic integration often produces better results than pursuing either approach alone.

Complaint documentation standards require comprehensive records that demonstrate systematic problems or clear violations rather than isolated incidents. Strong documentation significantly improves regulatory complaint effectiveness and potential for favorable intervention.

Agency coordination procedures involve understanding which agencies have jurisdiction over specific credit reporting problems and coordinating complaints appropriately. Proper coordination helps ensure that complaints reach appropriate regulatory personnel.

Timeline coordination between disputes and regulatory complaints ensures that both mechanisms support each other rather than creating conflicts. Strategic timing helps maximize pressure while preserving all available remedies.

Evidence development for regulatory complaints involves organizing systematic documentation to demonstrate patterns of non-compliance or systematic problems affecting multiple consumers. Comprehensive evidence helps regulatory agencies understand the scope of problems.

Follow-up procedures for regulatory complaints include monitoring agency responses, providing additional information when requested, and coordinating agency actions with ongoing dispute activities. Systematic follow-up helps optimize regulatory assistance effectiveness.

Escalation pathways within regulatory agencies provide additional options when initial complaints don't produce satisfactory responses. Understanding escalation procedures helps maximize regulatory assistance potential.

Industry impact considerations recognize that successful regulatory complaints can result in broader industry improvements that benefit all consumers while providing individual assistance. Understanding broader impacts helps evaluate regulatory complaint strategies.

Privacy considerations for regulatory complaints include understanding what information agencies may share and how complaints might affect future interactions with credit bureaus. Proper privacy understanding helps make informed decisions about regulatory complaints.

Strategic communication with regulatory agencies involves providing clear, factual information that helps agencies understand problems without appearing to encourage inappropriate regulatory intervention. Professional communication helps ensure serious agency consideration.

Resolution coordination ensures that regulatory interventions support rather than conflict with other resolution efforts. Strategic coordination helps achieve optimal outcomes through combined pressure mechanisms.

Long-term monitoring of regulatory responses helps evaluate agency effectiveness and identify successful regulatory strategies for future use. Understanding agency patterns helps optimize future regulatory coordination efforts.

Legal action integration coordinates advanced dispute activities with potential FCRA violation claims to preserve legal rights while maximizing opportunities for favorable resolution without litigation. This integration requires understanding how dispute activities affect legal strategy and evidence development.

Statute of limitations preservation involves understanding deadlines for FCRA violation claims and coordinating dispute activities to preserve legal rights while pursuing other resolution mechanisms. Proper timeline management helps maintain all available options.

Evidence development for potential legal action requires systematic documentation that would support FCRA violation claims while pursuing dispute resolution. Comprehensive evidence development helps strengthen legal positions regardless of ultimate resolution methods.

Legal theory coordination involves understanding how different dispute strategies affect potential legal claims and ensuring that dispute activities support rather than undermine legal positions. Strategic coordination helps optimize overall effectiveness.

Settlement leverage from potential legal action often motivates credit bureaus to resolve disputes favorably rather than risk litigation exposure. Understanding legal leverage helps enhance dispute negotiation effectiveness.

Attorney consultation timing involves understanding when legal consultation becomes necessary while continuing dispute activities. Strategic consultation helps optimize legal assistance benefits without premature escalation.

Documentation preservation for legal action requires maintaining comprehensive records that would support litigation while pursuing other resolution mechanisms. Proper preservation helps ensure that legal options remain viable.

Risk assessment for legal action involves evaluating potential benefits against costs and risks while understanding how legal action affects other resolution strategies. Strategic assessment helps make informed decisions about legal escalation.

Cost-benefit analysis for litigation includes understanding potential damages, attorney fees, and litigation costs while evaluating alternatives. Comprehensive analysis helps determine when legal action is appropriate.

Strategic patience for legal preparation involves understanding that strong legal positions often require systematic evidence development over time. Long-term perspective helps optimize legal strategy effectiveness.

Alternative resolution consideration includes understanding how potential legal action affects settlement negotiations and other resolution mechanisms. Strategic consideration helps optimize overall resolution outcomes.

Professional relationship management involves coordinating between dispute activities and legal representation to ensure consistent strategy implementation. Effective coordination helps optimize combined approaches.

Outcome optimization through legal integration involves leveraging potential legal action to enhance other resolution mechanisms while preserving options for actual litigation when necessary. Strategic integration helps achieve optimal results through combined pressure.

Industry knowledge leverage involves understanding credit bureau operations, furnisher practices, regulatory oversight patterns, and industry trends to identify optimal dispute strategies and pressure points for specific circumstances. Deep industry knowledge often provides advantages that generic dispute approaches cannot achieve.

Credit bureau operational understanding includes knowledge of internal procedures, personnel structures, technology systems, and business pressures that affect dispute handling quality. Understanding operations helps identify strategic opportunities for successful disputes.

Furnisher practice analysis involves understanding how different types of creditors and collection agencies maintain records, handle disputes, and interact with credit bureaus. Industry-specific knowledge helps tailor dispute strategies for maximum effectiveness.

Regulatory cycle awareness includes understanding examination schedules, enforcement priorities, and regulatory pressure patterns that affect credit bureau behavior. Strategic awareness helps time activities for maximum regulatory leverage.

Technology system knowledge involves understanding credit bureau computer systems, automated procedures, and data processing limitations that affect dispute handling. Technical knowledge helps identify system vulnerabilities for strategic exploitation.

Personnel pattern recognition includes understanding credit bureau staffing, training levels, and personnel turnover that affect dispute investigation quality. Understanding personnel factors helps optimize dispute presentation for specific circumstances.

Business pressure awareness involves understanding credit bureau revenue sources, competitive pressures, and regulatory costs that affect their willingness to resolve disputes favorably. Business understanding helps leverage appropriate pressure points.

Industry trend monitoring includes staying current with regulatory developments, technology changes, and business practice evolution that affect dispute strategies. Ongoing monitoring helps adapt strategies to changing circumstances.

Competitive intelligence gathering involves understanding differences between credit bureaus in procedures, technology, and personnel that affect dispute outcomes. Competitive knowledge helps optimize bureau-specific strategies.

Regulatory relationship understanding includes knowledge of agency oversight patterns, enforcement priorities, and regulatory pressure mechanisms that affect credit bureau behavior. Regulatory understanding helps leverage oversight effectively.

Professional network development includes relationships with consumer attorneys, industry professionals, and regulatory personnel that provide insights into effective strategies. Professional networks often provide valuable strategic intelligence.

Documentation standards in industry practice help understand what types of evidence and presentation methods are most effective with specific credit bureaus or furnishers. Understanding standards helps optimize dispute effectiveness.

Strategic timing based on industry knowledge involves understanding optimal periods for dispute activities based on regulatory cycles, business patterns, and operational factors. Strategic timing helps maximize dispute effectiveness through industry awareness.

Technology integration in advanced dispute strategies includes leveraging software tools, electronic monitoring systems, and digital organization methods to enhance dispute effectiveness and management efficiency. Strategic technology use can significantly improve advanced dispute outcomes.

Dispute tracking software helps manage multiple dispute activities, deadlines, and follow-up requirements systematically. Comprehensive tracking prevents missed opportunities and helps maintain systematic pressure on credit bureaus.

Credit monitoring integration provides real-time updates on credit report changes and helps identify new dispute opportunities or verify dispute outcomes. Strategic monitoring helps optimize dispute timing and effectiveness.

Electronic organization systems help manage comprehensive documentation, evidence files, and correspondence records efficiently. Digital organization significantly improves access to information and evidence presentation quality.

Communication automation tools can help manage routine correspondence and follow-up activities while maintaining personal attention for complex strategic decisions. Strategic automation helps optimize resource allocation for advanced strategies.

Research database access provides information about furnisher business status, regulatory actions, and industry changes that affect dispute strategies. Comprehensive research helps identify strategic opportunities and verification gaps.

Document management systems help organize evidence, correspondence, and strategic documentation for easy access and presentation. Professional document management improves dispute effectiveness and legal preparation.

Timeline management software helps track investigation deadlines, follow-up requirements, and strategic timing considerations across multiple disputes. Systematic timeline management helps ensure optimal strategy coordination.

Analytics tools help evaluate dispute effectiveness patterns, identify successful strategies, and optimize future activities based on historical data. Strategic analytics help improve dispute outcomes through data-driven decisions.

Backup and security systems protect comprehensive dispute documentation and evidence files from loss or unauthorized access. Proper security helps preserve essential evidence while maintaining privacy protection.

Integration coordination ensures that different technology tools work together effectively rather than creating conflicts or duplicated efforts. Strategic integration helps optimize overall technology benefits.

Training and adaptation procedures help ensure effective use of technology tools while avoiding over-reliance on automated systems for strategic decisions. Balanced technology use helps optimize benefits while maintaining strategic flexibility.

Future technology planning involves staying current with emerging tools and capabilities that might enhance dispute effectiveness. Forward-thinking technology planning helps maintain competitive advantages in dispute strategies.

Risk management for advanced dispute strategies involves understanding potential adverse consequences and implementing safeguards to protect consumer interests while pursuing sophisticated approaches. Strategic risk management helps optimize advanced strategy benefits while minimizing potential negative outcomes.

Frivolous dispute designation risks arise when credit bureaus determine that dispute activities are repetitive, abusive, or lacking legitimate basis. Understanding these risks helps structure advanced strategies to avoid triggering adverse bureau responses.

Escalation backlash potential includes increased bureau scrutiny, defensive responses, or reduced willingness to consider future disputes favorably. Risk assessment helps balance aggressive strategies with long-term relationship management.

Legal exposure considerations include understanding how advanced strategies might affect potential legal action or create evidence that could be used against consumer interests. Strategic legal risk management helps preserve favorable legal positions.

Documentation vulnerability involves ensuring that comprehensive evidence development doesn't inadvertently create damaging admissions or undermine consumer positions. Careful documentation helps maintain strategic advantages.

Privacy protection considerations include securing sensitive financial information while maintaining accessibility for dispute activities. Proper privacy protection helps prevent identity theft while preserving dispute effectiveness.

Regulatory attention risks include potential agency scrutiny when advanced strategies are highly visible or appear to challenge regulatory authority. Understanding regulatory risks helps structure strategies appropriately.

Professional relationship effects involve ensuring that advanced strategies don't damage relationships with attorneys, credit repair professionals, or other assistance providers. Strategic relationship management helps maintain professional support.

Financial cost management includes understanding resource requirements for advanced strategies and ensuring sustainable approaches that don't exceed available resources. Cost management helps maintain long-term strategy viability.

Time investment optimization involves balancing advanced strategy benefits against time requirements to ensure efficient resource allocation. Strategic time management helps optimize overall outcomes.

Credit score impact considerations include understanding how advanced dispute activities might temporarily affect credit scores during dispute periods. Score impact awareness helps manage timing for important financial decisions.

Alternative strategy preservation involves maintaining options for different approaches when advanced strategies encounter obstacles or prove ineffective. Strategic flexibility helps ensure continued progress toward resolution.

Exit strategy planning includes understanding how to conclude advanced activities gracefully while preserving gains and maintaining future options. Proper exit planning helps optimize long-term outcomes regardless of immediate results.

Performance measurement for advanced dispute strategies requires sophisticated evaluation methods that assess cumulative outcomes, strategic effectiveness, and long-term benefits rather than simple dispute win-loss ratios. Comprehensive measurement helps optimize strategy selection and resource allocation.

Outcome tracking systems should monitor multiple success indicators including credit score improvements, negative item removals, account corrections, and overall credit profile enhancement. Comprehensive tracking provides complete pictures of strategy effectiveness.

Timeline analysis helps evaluate strategy efficiency by measuring time requirements for different approaches and identifying optimal sequencing for complex dispute activities. Efficiency analysis helps optimize resource allocation and planning.

Cost-effectiveness evaluation includes measuring resource investments against achieved outcomes to identify the most efficient strategies for specific circumstances. Strategic evaluation helps optimize approach selection and resource management.

Quality assessment procedures evaluate the durability and completeness of achieved outcomes rather than simply counting immediate successes. Quality evaluation helps ensure that strategy outcomes provide lasting benefits.

Comparative analysis between different strategies helps identify optimal approaches for specific circumstances and types of credit problems. Strategic comparison helps refine strategy selection and improve future effectiveness.

Benchmark establishment provides standards for evaluating strategy performance and identifying areas requiring improvement or adjustment. Strategic benchmarks help maintain consistent performance evaluation.

Progress monitoring systems track ongoing strategy effectiveness and identify emerging opportunities or problems requiring attention. Systematic monitoring helps maintain strategy momentum and optimize ongoing activities.

Success criteria definition involves establishing clear objectives and measurement standards for different strategy components. Clear criteria help evaluate strategy effectiveness and make informed adjustment decisions.

Documentation analysis helps evaluate evidence quality, strategy implementation effectiveness, and compliance with procedural requirements. Comprehensive analysis helps identify improvement opportunities and optimize future activities.

Learning integration involves incorporating strategy experience into future planning and approach refinement. Strategic learning helps continuously improve dispute effectiveness through experience-based optimization.

Adaptation procedures help modify strategies based on performance results, changing circumstances, and emerging opportunities. Strategic adaptation helps maintain effectiveness as conditions change.

Reporting systems provide clear summaries of strategy performance for personal planning and professional consultation purposes. Effective reporting helps optimize strategy communication and decision-making support.

Advanced strategy integration involves combining multiple sophisticated approaches into coherent overall credit repair plans that leverage synergies between different techniques while avoiding conflicts or redundancies. Strategic integration often produces better results than pursuing individual advanced strategies separately.

Strategy compatibility assessment involves evaluating how different advanced techniques interact and ensuring that combined approaches support rather than undermine each other. Compatibility evaluation helps optimize integrated strategy effectiveness.

Sequencing optimization involves determining optimal timing and coordination for different strategy components to maximize cumulative effectiveness. Strategic sequencing helps ensure that strategy elements build on each other productively.

Resource allocation across multiple strategies requires balancing time, effort, and costs among different approaches while maintaining sustainable overall activity levels. Strategic allocation helps optimize integrated approach effectiveness.

Coordination procedures ensure that different strategy components are implemented consistently and support overall objectives rather than creating conflicts. Effective coordination helps maximize integrated strategy benefits.

Communication integration involves maintaining consistent messaging and presentation across different strategy components to avoid confusion or contradictory positions. Integrated communication helps ensure coherent overall approaches.

Documentation coordination ensures that evidence development for different strategies supports overall objectives while avoiding conflicts or inconsistencies. Coordinated documentation helps strengthen overall positions.

Timeline management for integrated strategies involves coordinating deadlines, follow-up requirements, and strategic timing across multiple advanced approaches. Comprehensive timeline management helps ensure that integrated strategies maintain momentum while meeting all procedural requirements.

Risk management for integrated approaches requires understanding how combined strategies affect overall risk profiles and implementing safeguards that protect against cumulative adverse consequences. Integrated risk management helps optimize benefits while minimizing potential negative outcomes.

Performance evaluation for integrated strategies involves assessing overall effectiveness rather than individual component success to understand true strategic value. Comprehensive evaluation helps optimize integrated approach selection and refinement.

Adaptation procedures for integrated strategies include modifying combined approaches based on partial results, changing circumstances, and emerging opportunities. Strategic adaptation helps maintain integrated approach effectiveness over time.

Professional coordination involves managing relationships with attorneys, credit repair professionals, and other assistance providers across multiple strategy components. Effective coordination helps optimize professional assistance benefits for integrated approaches.

Success measurement for integrated strategies requires sophisticated evaluation methods that assess synergistic effects and cumulative outcomes rather than simple component addition. Advanced measurement helps understand true integrated strategy value.

Long-term strategic planning for advanced dispute activities involves developing comprehensive approaches that address current credit problems while building foundations for sustained credit improvement and ongoing credit management excellence. Strategic planning helps ensure that advanced dispute investments produce lasting benefits.

Goal hierarchy establishment involves prioritizing different credit improvement objectives and understanding how advanced dispute strategies support broader financial goals. Clear hierarchies help optimize strategy selection and resource allocation for maximum long-term benefit.

Timeline development for long-term strategies requires understanding typical dispute resolution periods, credit score improvement timelines, and major financial milestone requirements. Comprehensive timeline planning helps coordinate dispute activities with important financial decisions.

Resource sustainability assessment involves evaluating long-term capacity for advanced dispute activities and ensuring that strategic approaches remain viable over extended periods. Sustainability planning helps maintain consistent progress toward credit improvement goals.

Milestone identification helps establish intermediate objectives and measurement points for evaluating long-term strategy progress. Clear milestones help maintain motivation and provide opportunities for strategy adjustment based on progress.

Adaptation planning involves understanding how strategies may need to change as credit profiles improve and different types of credit problems become priorities. Forward-thinking adaptation helps maintain strategy relevance throughout improvement processes.

Maintenance strategy development includes planning for ongoing credit monitoring and protection activities after major dispute objectives are achieved. Maintenance planning helps preserve dispute gains and prevent future credit problems.

Professional relationship development involves building long-term connections with attorneys, credit professionals, and financial advisors who can provide ongoing assistance. Strategic relationship building helps ensure continued access to professional expertise.

Education investment includes ongoing learning about credit laws, industry practices, and emerging strategies that might enhance long-term credit management effectiveness. Continuous education helps maintain strategic advantages and adaptation capabilities.

Technology evolution planning involves staying current with emerging tools and capabilities that might enhance long-term credit management and dispute effectiveness. Technology planning helps maintain competitive advantages in credit improvement.

Financial integration ensures that credit improvement strategies support broader financial planning objectives and coordinate with other wealth-building activities. Integrated planning helps optimize overall financial outcomes through credit improvement.

Legacy planning involves understanding how current credit improvement efforts affect long-term financial opportunities and ensuring that strategies support lasting financial success. Legacy perspective helps optimize strategic decision-making for maximum long-term benefit.

Exit strategy development includes planning for transition from active dispute activities to maintenance monitoring and ongoing credit management. Strategic exit planning helps optimize the transition to sustained credit excellence.

Advanced dispute psychology involves understanding the human factors that affect credit bureau personnel, furnisher representatives, and regulatory officials to optimize communication effectiveness and strategic positioning. Psychological understanding can significantly enhance advanced strategy outcomes.

Authority relationship dynamics include understanding how credit bureau personnel respond to different types of communication, presentation styles, and strategic approaches. Professional relationship management helps optimize dispute reception and investigation quality.

Credibility establishment involves presenting disputes and communications in ways that demonstrate competence, seriousness, and legitimate basis for concerns. Strong credibility helps ensure that advanced strategies receive appropriate attention and consideration.

Pressure point identification includes understanding what factors motivate credit bureaus and furnishers to resolve disputes favorably rather than pursuing prolonged conflicts. Strategic pressure application helps optimize resolution outcomes.

Negotiation psychology involves understanding how to present advanced strategies and evidence to maximize persuasive impact while maintaining professional relationships. Effective psychological positioning helps achieve favorable outcomes through enhanced communication.

Resistance pattern recognition includes understanding common defensive responses from credit bureaus and furnishers to develop strategies that overcome resistance effectively. Pattern recognition helps anticipate obstacles and develop counter-strategies.

Communication optimization involves adapting presentation styles, documentation methods, and strategic approaches to match recipient preferences and institutional cultures. Optimized communication helps ensure that advanced strategies receive favorable consideration.

Motivation alignment includes understanding what outcomes benefit both consumers and credit industry participants to identify win-win resolution opportunities. Aligned motivation helps achieve sustainable resolutions that satisfy multiple parties.

Escalation psychology involves understanding how to escalate disputes effectively while maintaining relationships and credibility for future interactions. Strategic escalation helps achieve resolution while preserving ongoing effectiveness.

Professional presentation involves demonstrating competence and seriousness through high-quality documentation, clear communication, and systematic approach implementation. Professional presentation helps ensure that advanced strategies receive appropriate attention.

Persistence optimization includes understanding how to maintain consistent pressure for resolution while avoiding appearance of harassment or frivolous activity. Strategic persistence helps achieve resolution through sustained professional effort.

Relationship maintenance involves preserving working relationships with credit industry personnel while pursuing aggressive strategies for favorable outcomes. Effective relationship management helps ensure continued access and effectiveness.

Strategic patience includes understanding when to wait for optimal timing versus when to accelerate activities based on psychological factors and institutional dynamics. Patient strategy implementation often produces better outcomes than rushed approaches.

Regulatory environment navigation involves understanding the complex oversight landscape that governs credit reporting and leveraging regulatory dynamics to enhance advanced dispute strategy effectiveness. Strategic regulatory navigation can provide significant advantages in dispute resolution.

Agency jurisdiction understanding includes knowing which federal and state agencies oversee different aspects of credit reporting and how to access appropriate regulatory assistance. Jurisdictional knowledge helps ensure that regulatory strategies target appropriate oversight bodies.

Examination cycle awareness involves understanding when credit bureaus face regulatory examinations and how these periods affect their responsiveness to consumer complaints and disputes. Strategic timing around examination cycles can enhance dispute effectiveness.

Enforcement priority recognition includes understanding current regulatory focus areas and how to align consumer complaints with agency priorities for maximum attention. Priority alignment helps ensure that regulatory strategies receive appropriate agency consideration.

Regulatory relationship dynamics involve understanding how agencies interact with credit bureaus and how consumer complaints fit into broader regulatory oversight activities. Dynamic understanding helps optimize regulatory strategy effectiveness.

Complaint timing optimization includes understanding when regulatory complaints are most likely to receive attention and produce favorable outcomes. Strategic timing helps maximize regulatory assistance effectiveness.

Evidence presentation for regulatory purposes involves organizing documentation and arguments to align with agency procedures and priorities. Effective presentation helps ensure that regulatory complaints receive serious consideration and appropriate action.

Follow-up procedures with regulatory agencies include understanding how to maintain agency attention and provide additional information when requested. Systematic follow-up helps optimize regulatory assistance outcomes.

Inter-agency coordination involves understanding how different agencies work together and how to leverage multiple regulatory relationships for enhanced outcomes. Coordinated regulatory strategies often produce better results than single-agency approaches.

Political environment awareness includes understanding how regulatory priorities change with political leadership and how to adapt strategies accordingly. Environmental awareness helps maintain regulatory strategy effectiveness through changing circumstances.

Industry pressure dynamics involve understanding how regulatory oversight affects credit bureau operations and how consumer complaints contribute to broader regulatory pressure. Understanding dynamics helps leverage regulatory influence effectively.

Regulatory trend monitoring includes staying current with agency guidance, enforcement actions, and policy developments that affect credit reporting oversight. Trend awareness helps adapt regulatory strategies to changing oversight environments.

Professional regulatory advocacy involves working with consumer attorneys and advocacy organizations that have specialized regulatory expertise and relationships. Professional advocacy help can significantly enhance regulatory strategy effectiveness.

Emerging technology impacts on advanced dispute strategies include understanding how artificial intelligence, blockchain, automated systems, and other technological developments affect credit reporting and create new opportunities for strategic consumer advocacy. Technology awareness helps adapt strategies to evolving industry practices.

Artificial intelligence applications in credit bureau operations affect dispute processing, investigation procedures, and decision-making systems. Understanding AI impacts helps identify new strategic opportunities and potential system vulnerabilities for advanced dispute approaches.

Blockchain technology potential for credit reporting includes immutable record-keeping, enhanced verification procedures, and decentralized reporting systems. Blockchain awareness helps anticipate future industry changes and strategic adaptation requirements.

Automated dispute processing systems used by credit bureaus create both opportunities and challenges for advanced strategies. Understanding automation helps identify system limitations and optimization opportunities for strategic exploitation.

Data analytics applications by credit bureaus affect investigation procedures, pattern recognition, and quality control systems. Analytics awareness helps understand bureau decision-making processes and identify strategic approach opportunities.

Digital verification methods change how furnishers and credit bureaus confirm information accuracy during dispute investigations. Understanding digital verification helps adapt dispute strategies to new technological environments.

Electronic evidence standards continue evolving as courts and agencies adapt to digital documentation and communication methods. Standard awareness helps optimize evidence development and presentation for technological environments.

Cybersecurity considerations affect how consumer information is protected and how disputes are processed securely. Security awareness helps ensure that advanced strategies maintain privacy protection while optimizing effectiveness.

Mobile technology integration in credit reporting affects consumer access, dispute submission methods, and monitoring capabilities. Mobile awareness helps leverage technological convenience while maintaining strategic effectiveness.

Privacy regulation evolution includes understanding how data protection laws affect credit reporting and consumer rights. Regulatory awareness helps identify new protection opportunities and strategic approaches.

International technology standards affect credit reporting through global data sharing, cross-border verification, and international privacy requirements. International awareness helps address complex credit situations involving foreign elements.

Future technology anticipation involves staying current with emerging developments that might affect credit reporting and strategic opportunities. Forward-thinking technology awareness helps maintain strategic advantages as industry practices evolve.

Strategic technology integration involves incorporating appropriate technological tools into advanced dispute strategies while maintaining focus on fundamental legal principles and strategic objectives. Balanced integration helps optimize technology benefits without losing strategic focus.

Quality control and continuous improvement for advanced dispute strategies involve systematic evaluation, refinement, and optimization of strategic approaches to maintain effectiveness and adapt to changing circumstances. Quality management helps ensure that advanced strategies continue producing optimal outcomes over time.

Performance monitoring systems should track multiple effectiveness indicators across different strategy components and time periods. Comprehensive monitoring helps identify successful approaches and areas requiring improvement or adjustment.

Strategy refinement procedures involve analyzing outcomes, identifying improvement opportunities, and implementing strategic adjustments based on experience and changing circumstances. Systematic refinement helps maintain strategy effectiveness through ongoing optimization.

Best practice identification includes recognizing most effective approaches for different circumstances and codifying successful strategies for consistent application. Best practice development helps ensure that effective strategies are preserved and replicated.

Error analysis procedures involve understanding why certain strategies fail to produce expected outcomes and developing improvements to prevent similar failures. Strategic error analysis helps optimize future effectiveness through experience-based learning.

Adaptation protocols help modify strategies based on changing credit bureau procedures, regulatory requirements, and industry practices. Systematic adaptation helps maintain strategy relevance and effectiveness as conditions evolve.

Benchmarking procedures involve comparing strategy outcomes against industry standards, professional service results, and optimal theoretical outcomes. Strategic benchmarking helps evaluate performance and identify improvement opportunities.

Documentation improvement includes enhancing evidence development, presentation methods, and record-keeping procedures based on experience and effectiveness analysis. Documentation optimization helps improve strategy outcomes through better evidence quality.

Training and skill development involve ongoing education about credit laws, industry practices, and strategic techniques to maintain and enhance strategic capabilities. Continuous learning helps ensure that advanced strategies remain current and effective.

Professional consultation evaluation includes assessing when and how to incorporate expert assistance into strategic approaches. Professional evaluation helps optimize assistance benefits while maintaining cost-effectiveness.

Technology integration assessment involves evaluating how emerging tools and capabilities can enhance strategy effectiveness without compromising fundamental strategic principles. Technology assessment helps maintain competitive advantages through appropriate innovation adoption.

Success criteria evolution involves updating performance standards and objectives based on achieved outcomes and changing circumstances. Criteria evolution helps ensure that strategies remain aligned with current objectives and realistic expectations.

Long-term effectiveness maintenance includes planning for sustained strategy implementation and ongoing optimization over extended periods. Maintenance planning helps ensure that advanced strategies continue producing benefits throughout extended credit improvement processes.

Advanced dispute strategy troubleshooting involves identifying and resolving common problems that can undermine strategy effectiveness and developing systematic approaches for overcoming obstacles. Effective troubleshooting helps maintain strategy momentum when challenges arise.

Resistance pattern identification includes recognizing common defensive responses from credit bureaus and furnishers to develop targeted counter-strategies. Pattern recognition helps anticipate obstacles and prepare effective responses.

Stalled investigation resolution involves strategies for addressing situations where credit bureaus fail to complete investigations, provide inadequate responses, or ignore procedural requirements. Resolution strategies help restart stalled processes and ensure compliance.

Communication breakdown recovery includes procedures for reestablishing productive dialogue when relationships with credit bureaus or furnishers become adversarial or unresponsive. Recovery strategies help restore strategic effectiveness after communication problems.

Documentation gap remediation involves strategies for addressing situations where insufficient evidence initially weakens strategic positions. Gap remediation helps strengthen positions through additional evidence development and alternative strategic approaches.

Timeline violation responses include specific procedures for addressing credit bureau failures to meet investigation deadlines or other procedural requirements. Violation responses help enforce compliance while maintaining strategic momentum.

Escalation failure management involves strategies for situations where internal escalation, regulatory complaints, or other escalation attempts fail to produce desired outcomes. Failure management helps identify alternative approaches and maintain progress.

Resource depletion adaptation includes strategies for maintaining effectiveness when time, financial, or energy resources become constrained. Adaptation strategies help optimize limited resources for maximum strategic impact.

Motivation maintenance during extended strategic implementation involves procedures for sustaining effort and focus through challenging periods when progress seems slow. Motivation strategies help ensure continued strategic effectiveness.

Legal complication navigation includes understanding how to address situations where advanced strategies encounter legal obstacles or conflicts. Navigation strategies help resolve complications while preserving strategic objectives.

Professional relationship repair involves strategies for restoring productive relationships with credit industry personnel after conflicts or misunderstandings. Repair strategies help maintain long-term strategic effectiveness.

Alternative strategy development includes procedures for identifying and implementing different approaches when primary strategies encounter insurmountable obstacles. Alternative development helps ensure continued progress toward objectives.

Exit strategy implementation involves procedures for concluding advanced strategic activities gracefully while preserving gains and maintaining future options. Implementation strategies help optimize transitions while protecting achieved outcomes.

Advanced dispute strategy integration with broader financial planning ensures that credit improvement efforts support overall wealth-building objectives and coordinate effectively with other financial management activities. Strategic integration helps maximize the long-term value of advanced dispute investments.

Credit improvement goal alignment involves ensuring that advanced dispute strategies support broader financial objectives such as homeownership, business development, or retirement planning. Goal alignment helps optimize strategy selection and resource allocation for maximum long-term benefit.

Timeline coordination with major financial decisions includes planning advanced dispute activities to support mortgage applications, business loans, insurance rate reviews, and other credit-dependent financial milestones. Strategic coordination helps ensure that credit improvements occur when needed most.

Investment prioritization involves balancing time and resources between advanced dispute activities and other wealth-building opportunities. Strategic prioritization helps optimize overall financial outcomes through balanced resource allocation.

Risk management integration includes understanding how advanced dispute activities affect overall financial risk profiles and ensuring that strategies support rather than undermine financial security. Integrated risk management helps optimize outcomes while maintaining financial stability.

Professional team coordination involves working effectively with financial advisors, attorneys, accountants, and other professionals to ensure that credit improvement strategies support comprehensive financial planning. Team coordination helps leverage professional expertise for optimal outcomes.

Tax consideration integration includes understanding how advanced dispute outcomes, professional service costs, and related activities affect tax planning and compliance. Tax integration helps optimize after-tax benefits from credit improvement investments.

Insurance impact assessment involves understanding how credit improvements affect insurance rates, coverage availability, and overall insurance planning. Impact assessment helps quantify broader benefits from credit improvement activities.

Business planning integration includes understanding how personal credit improvement affects business financing opportunities, professional reputation, and entrepreneurial activities. Business integration helps optimize credit improvement benefits for professional development.

Estate planning considerations involve understanding how credit improvement activities affect wealth transfer planning and legacy financial management. Estate integration helps ensure that credit improvement supports long-term family financial objectives.

Retirement planning coordination includes understanding how credit improvement affects retirement financing opportunities and fixed-income financial management. Retirement coordination helps optimize credit improvement benefits for long-term financial security.

Educational investment planning involves understanding how credit improvement affects education financing opportunities for personal and family educational goals. Education integration helps optimize credit improvement benefits for human capital development.

Wealth preservation strategies include understanding how credit improvement contributes to overall asset protection and financial security planning. Preservation integration helps ensure that credit improvement supports long-term wealth maintenance and growth.

Advanced dispute strategy mastery represents the culmination of sophisticated understanding, systematic implementation, and strategic integration of complex credit repair approaches. Mastery enables consumers to navigate the most challenging credit reporting problems while optimizing outcomes through comprehensive strategic thinking.

Mastery characteristics include deep understanding of credit reporting legal frameworks, systematic approach to strategy development and implementation, sophisticated evidence development and presentation capabilities, and strategic integration of multiple approaches for optimal outcomes.

Professional-level competency involves understanding credit reporting at levels comparable to industry professionals while maintaining consumer advocacy perspectives. Professional competency enables advanced strategy implementation that rivals paid professional services.

Strategic thinking development includes understanding how to analyze complex credit situations, identify optimal strategic approaches, and coordinate multiple strategies for cumulative effectiveness. Strategic thinking helps optimize advanced strategy selection and implementation.

Leadership in credit improvement involves understanding how to guide family members, friends, or business associates through credit improvement processes while maintaining ethical standards and professional competency. Leadership capabilities help extend advanced strategy benefits beyond individual applications.

Innovation capacity includes understanding how to adapt strategies to unique circumstances, develop novel approaches for unusual problems, and integrate emerging opportunities into strategic frameworks. Innovation capability helps maintain strategic advantages in evolving environments.

Teaching and mentoring abilities involve understanding how to share advanced strategy knowledge with others while maintaining appropriate boundaries and ethical standards. Teaching capabilities help extend advanced strategy benefits through knowledge sharing.

Ethical leadership includes understanding how to implement advanced strategies while maintaining honesty, integrity, and respect for legitimate business interests. Ethical leadership helps ensure that advanced strategies serve legitimate consumer protection objectives.

Continuous learning commitment involves understanding that advanced strategy mastery requires ongoing education, adaptation, and improvement throughout changing credit industry environments. Learning commitment helps maintain strategic effectiveness over time.

Professional recognition may result from advanced strategy mastery through consultation opportunities, speaking engagements, or advocacy activities. Recognition opportunities help extend advanced strategy benefits while building professional relationships.

Legacy development involves understanding how advanced strategy mastery can contribute to broader consumer protection advocacy and industry improvement efforts. Legacy development helps ensure that individual mastery contributes to systemic improvements.

Impact measurement includes understanding how to evaluate the broader effects of advanced strategy mastery on personal financial outcomes, family financial security, and community financial empowerment. Impact measurement helps optimize the long-term value of advanced strategy mastery.

Mastery maintenance involves understanding how to preserve and enhance advanced strategy capabilities through continued practice, education, and adaptation to changing circumstances. Maintenance strategies help ensure that mastery remains current and effective throughout changing industry conditions.

CHAPTER 11

DEALING WITH FURNISHERS DIRECTLY

Direct furnisher negotiations represent a powerful but often overlooked component of comprehensive credit repair strategies. While most consumers focus exclusively on credit bureau disputes, approaching furnishers directly can yield superior results because these entities have complete access to account records, authority to make immediate corrections, and strong incentives to resolve disputes efficiently to avoid regulatory scrutiny and customer relations problems.

Understanding the distinction between different types of furnishers is crucial for developing effective direct negotiation strategies. Original creditors, collection agencies, debt buyers, and credit reporting agencies each operate under different business models, regulatory requirements, and operational constraints that affect their willingness and ability to negotiate favorable resolutions.

The legal framework governing furnisher obligations has expanded significantly since the original FCRA, particularly through the FACT Act amendments that established direct dispute rights and accuracy standards for information providers. These enhanced obligations create multiple leverage points for consumers who understand how to approach furnishers strategically.

Direct furnisher negotiations often prove more effective than credit bureau disputes because furnishers have better access to account documentation, more flexibility in resolution options, and stronger business incentives to resolve disputes quickly. Credit bureaus typically act as intermediaries with limited authority, while furnishers can make definitive decisions about account status and reporting.

The business relationships between furnishers and credit bureaus create additional opportunities for strategic influence. Furnishers who maintain good relationships with credit bureaus often receive preferential treatment in dispute processing, while regulatory pressure on furnishers can cascade into improved credit bureau responsiveness.

Timing considerations for direct furnisher negotiations include understanding business cycles, regulatory examination periods, and organizational changes that might affect furnisher responsiveness to consumer negotiations. Strategic timing can significantly improve negotiation outcomes.

Documentation requirements for effective furnisher negotiations differ from credit bureau disputes and often require more comprehensive evidence presentation and clearer articulation of desired outcomes. Understanding these requirements helps optimize negotiation effectiveness.

Professional communication standards become particularly important in furnisher negotiations since these interactions often involve direct contact with decision-makers who have authority to resolve disputes definitively. Professional presentation can significantly influence negotiation outcomes.

The intersection of furnisher negotiations with other credit repair strategies creates opportunities for coordinated approaches that leverage multiple pressure points simultaneously. Understanding these intersections helps optimize overall credit repair effectiveness.

Risk management in furnisher negotiations involves understanding potential adverse consequences and implementing safeguards to protect consumer interests while pursuing favorable outcomes. Strategic risk management helps optimize negotiation benefits while minimizing potential negative impacts.

Original creditor negotiations offer unique opportunities and challenges compared to other furnisher types because these entities have complete account histories, ongoing customer relationships, and comprehensive authority to modify account terms and reporting. Understanding original creditor dynamics helps optimize negotiation strategies for maximum effectiveness.

Customer relationship leverage represents a significant advantage in original creditor negotiations since these entities have ongoing business interests in maintaining positive customer relationships and avoiding negative publicity. Long-standing customers often receive more favorable consideration than unknown consumers.

Account history access gives original creditors comprehensive information about payment patterns, account management, and customer communications that can support favorable negotiations when consumers can demonstrate reasonable explanations for credit problems. Historical context often influences negotiation outcomes significantly.

Business reputation concerns motivate original creditors to resolve disputes efficiently and favorably to avoid regulatory attention, customer complaints, and negative publicity that could affect their broader business operations. Reputation concerns create leverage for professional, well-documented negotiations.

Regulatory compliance obligations require original creditors to maintain accurate reporting and investigate consumer disputes thoroughly. Understanding these obligations helps structure negotiations that leverage compliance requirements for favorable outcomes.

Settlement authority within original creditor organizations varies significantly, with customer service representatives typically having limited authority while supervisory personnel and specialized departments often having broader negotiation flexibility. Understanding authority structures helps direct negotiations to appropriate personnel.

Documentation advantages in original creditor negotiations include access to complete account records that can clarify disputes and support favorable resolutions when consumers can demonstrate legitimate explanations for account problems. Comprehensive documentation often facilitates faster resolution.

Goodwill considerations may influence original creditor negotiations when consumers can demonstrate extenuating circumstances, improved financial stability, or long-term customer relationships that justify favorable treatment. Goodwill negotiations often succeed when supported by appropriate evidence.

Regulatory pressure on original creditors through examination oversight, consumer complaints, and enforcement actions creates additional leverage for negotiations that highlight compliance concerns or systematic problems. Regulatory awareness helps structure effective negotiation strategies.

Industry-specific considerations affect original creditor negotiations differently depending on business type, regulatory environment, and competitive pressures. Understanding industry dynamics helps adapt negotiation strategies for specific creditor types and business environments.

Legal exposure concerns may influence original creditor willingness to negotiate favorably when disputes involve potential violations of lending laws, consumer protection requirements, or account management obligations. Legal awareness helps identify appropriate negotiation leverage.

Long-term relationship potential with original creditors creates opportunities for negotiated resolutions that support ongoing business relationships while addressing credit reporting concerns. Relationship-based negotiations often produce more comprehensive and durable outcomes.

Collection agency negotiations require understanding the unique business model, operational constraints, and legal obligations that govern third-party debt collection activities. Collection agencies operate under different incentives and regulatory requirements than original creditors, creating distinct opportunities and challenges for direct negotiations.

Profit motive understanding is crucial for collection agency negotiations since these entities typically work on commission or contingency basis, creating strong incentives to collect rather than negotiate favorable credit reporting terms. Understanding profit motives helps structure negotiations that align with agency interests.

Documentation limitations often affect collection agencies since they may receive incomplete account information from original creditors or prior collection agencies. These limitations create opportunities for verification challenges and negotiated resolutions when agencies cannot adequately document account details.

FDCPA compliance obligations create additional leverage points for collection agency negotiations since violations can result in legal liability and regulatory sanctions. Understanding FDCPA requirements helps structure negotiations that leverage compliance concerns effectively.

Authority restrictions may limit collection agency ability to negotiate certain types of resolutions, particularly when agencies work under specific contracts with original creditors or debt buyers. Understanding authority limitations helps set realistic negotiation expectations.

Business relationship pressures affect collection agencies through their relationships with clients who expect results but also want to avoid regulatory problems and negative publicity. These pressures can create opportunities for negotiations that serve multiple stakeholder interests.

Regulatory oversight of collection agencies has intensified significantly through CFPB supervision and state licensing requirements, creating additional pressure for compliance and professional operation. Regulatory pressure can enhance negotiation leverage when properly understood and applied.

Competition factors among collection agencies create pressure to resolve accounts efficiently and move on to new collection opportunities. Understanding competitive pressures helps structure negotiations that align with agency business interests.

Technology limitations in collection agency operations may affect their ability to access complete account information or implement sophisticated payment arrangements. Understanding technological constraints helps structure realistic negotiation proposals.

Training variations among collection agency personnel affect negotiation quality and outcomes, with some agencies providing comprehensive training while others operate with minimal personnel development. Understanding training levels helps adapt negotiation approaches appropriately.

Quality control systems in collection agencies vary significantly, with some maintaining comprehensive oversight while others operate with minimal supervision. Understanding quality systems helps identify optimal contact points and negotiation strategies.

Legal liability concerns affect collection agency willingness to negotiate when disputes involve potential FDCPA violations, state law compliance issues, or documentation inadequacies. Legal awareness helps identify appropriate negotiation leverage and resolution opportunities.

Debt buyer negotiations present unique challenges and opportunities because these entities purchase debts at significant discounts and often lack comprehensive account documentation, creating both leverage opportunities and verification challenges for consumers seeking favorable credit reporting resolutions.

Purchase price leverage recognizes that debt buyers typically acquire debts for pennies on the dollar, creating opportunities for settlement negotiations that provide buyers with profitable outcomes while offering consumers favorable resolution terms including credit report removal agreements.

Documentation gaps represent common weaknesses in debt buyer operations since account information often degrades through multiple transfers between original creditors, collection agencies, and successive debt buyers. These gaps create opportunities for verification challenges and negotiated resolutions.

Chain of title issues affect debt buyer authority to collect and report debts when ownership transfers lack proper documentation or when assignments contain errors or omissions. Understanding title issues helps identify negotiation leverage and potential dispute grounds.

Verification challenges arise when debt buyers cannot adequately document account details, original terms, payment history, or legal authority to collect. These challenges create opportunities for negotiations that address verification inadequacies.

Portfolio management pressures affect debt buyer operations since these entities typically acquire large numbers of accounts and may prioritize efficient resolution over extended collection efforts. Understanding portfolio pressures helps structure negotiations that align with buyer interests.

Regulatory compliance concerns affect debt buyers through FDCPA obligations, FCRA accuracy requirements, and state licensing restrictions. Compliance concerns create leverage for negotiations that highlight potential violations or systematic problems.

Statute of limitations considerations may affect debt buyer negotiations when debts approach or exceed legal collection periods, creating pressure for resolution before time-based defenses eliminate collection viability. Timing awareness helps optimize negotiation strategies.

Business model understanding helps structure negotiations that recognize debt buyer profit requirements while creating opportunities for favorable consumer outcomes through efficient resolution and risk management considerations.

Technology dependencies in debt buyer operations may affect account access, payment processing capabilities, and reporting accuracy. Understanding technological limitations helps structure realistic negotiation proposals and identify potential system-based leverage.

Legal exposure concerns affect debt buyer willingness to negotiate when disputes involve documentation inadequacies, compliance violations, or potential challenges to collection authority. Legal awareness helps identify negotiation opportunities and appropriate leverage.

Industry consolidation trends affect debt buyer operations through changing ownership, operational procedures, and compliance standards. Understanding industry trends helps anticipate negotiation opportunities and challenges.

Specialized negotiation strategies for debt buyers should recognize their unique position in the debt collection ecosystem and structure approaches that address their specific business needs while achieving favorable consumer outcomes.

Pay-for-delete negotiations represent one of the most valuable direct furnisher strategies, involving agreements where furnishers accept payment in exchange for removing negative items from credit reports entirely. While controversial within the credit industry, pay-for-delete agreements can provide immediate and significant credit score improvements when executed properly.

Legal framework for pay-for-delete agreements exists within a gray area where no specific laws prohibit the practice, but credit bureau policies officially discourage it. Understanding this framework helps structure agreements that maximize enforceability while minimizing potential complications.

Industry resistance to pay-for-delete stems from credit bureau concerns about data integrity and furnisher worries about setting precedents for similar requests. Despite this resistance, many furnishers continue to offer pay-for-delete arrangements when they serve business interests.

Negotiation positioning for pay-for-delete should emphasize mutual benefits including immediate payment for furnishers, account resolution, and reduced administrative costs compared to ongoing collection efforts. Effective positioning helps overcome furnisher resistance to deletion agreements.

Documentation requirements for pay-for-delete agreements should include written confirmation of deletion terms, payment amounts, timing specifications, and furnisher commitments to report deletions to all credit bureaus. Comprehensive documentation helps ensure agreement enforcement.

Payment structure considerations include whether to pay before or after deletion, use of escrow arrangements, partial payments for partial deletion, and protection against re-reporting of deleted items. Strategic payment structuring helps optimize consumer protection while satisfying furnisher requirements.

Verification procedures ensure that agreed-upon deletions are actually implemented across all credit bureaus and that deleted items don't reappear on future credit reports. Systematic verification helps maintain pay-for-delete benefits over time.

Alternative arrangements when furnishers refuse complete deletion might include agreements for "paid as agreed" reporting, account closure with positive status, or partial deletion of specific negative elements. Understanding alternatives helps optimize negotiation outcomes.

Enforceability considerations for pay-for-delete agreements include contract law principles, consumer protection requirements, and practical enforcement mechanisms when furnishers fail to honor agreements. Legal awareness helps structure enforceable agreements.

Credit score impact from successful pay-for-delete negotiations can be immediate and substantial, particularly when agreements remove recent negative items or accounts with high negative impact. Understanding impact helps prioritize negotiation targets for maximum benefit.

Industry variations in pay-for-delete willingness differ significantly between original creditors, collection agencies, and debt buyers, with each type having different business incentives and policy constraints. Understanding variations helps target negotiations appropriately.

Regulatory implications of pay-for-delete agreements continue evolving as agencies scrutinize the practice and consider policy guidance. Staying current with regulatory developments helps maintain compliant negotiation strategies.

Goodwill letters and appeals represent a diplomatic approach to furnisher negotiations that acknowledges account accuracy while requesting favorable consideration based on extenuating circumstances, improved financial stability, or customer relationship factors. These approaches often succeed when supported by compelling narratives and appropriate evidence.

Emotional appeal effectiveness depends on crafting genuine, compelling stories that explain credit problems while demonstrating responsibility and commitment to financial improvement. Authentic narratives often resonate more effectively than generic template approaches.

Timing considerations for goodwill appeals include optimal periods such as account anniversaries, after making consistent payments, during creditor examination periods, or following major life improvements. Strategic timing can significantly influence appeal outcomes.

Supporting documentation for goodwill appeals might include medical records for health-related financial problems, divorce decrees for marital dissolution impacts, unemployment records for job loss situations, or evidence of financial counseling and improvement efforts. Relevant documentation strengthens appeal credibility.

Relationship history leverage involves demonstrating long-term customer relationships, consistent payment patterns prior to credit problems, or ongoing business relationships that justify favorable consideration. Historical context often influences goodwill appeal outcomes.

Improvement demonstration through recent payment history, increased account usage, or enhanced financial stability shows creditors that problems were temporary and that favorable treatment supports continued positive relationships. Improvement evidence strengthens goodwill appeals significantly.

Industry-specific approaches recognize that different types of creditors respond to different appeal strategies, with banks often emphasizing relationship factors while retailers might focus on continued business potential. Understanding industry preferences helps optimize appeal strategies.

Professional presentation through well-written letters, organized documentation, and respectful communication demonstrates seriousness and competence that often influences appeal consideration favorably. Professional presentation can distinguish appeals from routine requests.

Follow-up procedures for goodwill appeals include appropriate timing for response expectations, escalation to supervisory personnel when initial appeals are unsuccessful, and integration with other negotiation strategies. Systematic follow-up helps optimize appeal effectiveness.

Success factors for goodwill appeals include genuine circumstances that explain credit problems, demonstrated improvement since problem periods, ongoing customer relationships, and professional presentation that resonates with decision-makers. Understanding success factors helps craft effective appeals.

Alternative outcomes when complete removal isn't granted might include partial improvement such as late payment reduction, account status upgrades, or removal of specific negative elements. Understanding alternatives helps optimize appeal benefits even when complete success isn't achieved.

Integration with other strategies allows goodwill appeals to complement verification challenges, pay-for-delete negotiations, or dispute activities for comprehensive approaches that maximize favorable outcome potential. Strategic integration helps optimize overall negotiation effectiveness.

Settlement negotiations with furnishers extend beyond simple payment arrangements to encompass comprehensive resolutions that address both debt obligations and credit reporting concerns. Effective settlement strategies recognize that furnishers often prefer definitive resolution over ongoing collection efforts and regulatory exposure.

Settlement authority identification involves understanding which furnisher personnel have authority to negotiate comprehensive agreements and how to access decision-makers who can approve both payment terms and credit reporting modifications. Authority identification helps ensure productive negotiations.

Leverage development for settlement negotiations includes understanding furnisher vulnerabilities such as documentation problems, compliance concerns, statute of limitations issues, or potential disputes that create pressure for favorable resolution. Effective leverage helps achieve better settlement terms.

Payment capacity assessment involves realistic evaluation of available resources while understanding that furnishers may accept significantly reduced payments when combined with immediate resolution and reduced administrative costs. Honest capacity assessment helps structure viable proposals.

Credit reporting components of settlements should address not only account removal but also timing of reporting changes, confirmation procedures, and protection against future negative reporting of settled accounts. Comprehensive credit terms help maximize settlement benefits.

Documentation requirements for settlement agreements should include written confirmation of all terms, payment schedules, credit reporting commitments, and mutual releases that protect both parties from future claims. Proper documentation helps ensure settlement enforceability.

Tax implications of debt settlement may include taxable income from forgiven debt amounts, though certain exceptions apply for insolvency or qualified student loans. Understanding tax consequences helps evaluate true settlement costs and benefits.

Timing strategies for settlement offers include periods when furnishers face examination pressure, portfolio sales, or operational changes that create motivation for efficient resolution. Strategic timing can significantly improve settlement outcomes.

Negotiation tactics for settlement discussions include initial low offers, incremental increases, deadline pressure, and alternative proposal presentation that provides furnishers with face-saving resolution options. Effective tactics help optimize settlement terms.

Alternative structures for settlements might include payment plans, partial payments for partial credit improvements, or contingent agreements based on future financial performance. Understanding alternatives helps create mutually acceptable arrangements.

Legal protection in settlement agreements includes ensuring that settlements don't waive legitimate consumer protection rights or create admissions that could harm future disputes with other creditors. Legal awareness helps structure protective settlements.

Integration with comprehensive credit repair strategies ensures that settlement activities support overall credit improvement goals and coordinate effectively with other furnisher negotiations and credit bureau disputes. Strategic integration helps optimize overall outcomes.

Specialized furnisher negotiation strategies address unique circumstances and furnisher types that require adapted approaches beyond standard negotiation techniques. Understanding these specializations helps optimize outcomes for complex situations and unusual furnisher relationships.

Medical debt negotiations often benefit from unique considerations including insurance billing complexities, provider billing errors, and special regulatory protections for medical debt reporting. Understanding medical debt dynamics helps structure effective specialized negotiations.

Student loan furnisher negotiations involve complex federal regulations, rehabilitation programs, and servicer transfer issues that create specialized opportunities and constraints. Student loan expertise helps navigate these unique negotiation environments effectively.

Utility and service provider negotiations may involve different business models and regulatory requirements than traditional creditors, creating opportunities for specialized approaches that recognize these entities' unique operational constraints and business interests.

Mortgage servicer negotiations require understanding complex servicing regulations, investor requirements, and foreclosure prevention programs that affect servicer authority and willingness to negotiate favorable credit reporting terms. Specialized mortgage knowledge helps optimize servicer negotiations.

Government entity negotiations involve unique procedural requirements, political considerations, and regulatory constraints that differ significantly from private sector negotiations. Understanding government dynamics helps structure effective public sector negotiation strategies.

Small business creditor negotiations may offer more personal relationships and flexibility than large corporate creditors, creating opportunities for individualized approaches that recognize small business operational realities and relationship factors.

Bankruptcy-related furnisher negotiations involve complex discharge protections, automatic stay provisions, and post-bankruptcy reporting requirements that create specialized legal frameworks and negotiation opportunities. Bankruptcy expertise helps navigate these complex situations.

Identity theft victim negotiations require understanding specialized procedures for fraud claims, documentation requirements, and furnisher obligations to investigate and resolve identity theft situations appropriately. Identity theft expertise helps ensure proper resolution.

Estate-related negotiations involve unique legal considerations when deceased persons' accounts affect surviving family members' credit reports or when estate representatives need to resolve account issues. Estate expertise helps navigate these sensitive situations.

International furnisher negotiations may involve foreign entities, cross-border transactions, and complex jurisdictional issues that require specialized approaches and understanding of international business practices. International expertise helps address complex global credit issues.

Technology company negotiations may involve specialized business models, regulatory environments, and operational considerations that differ from traditional financial service providers. Technology sector expertise helps optimize negotiations with these emerging credit participants.

Professional service provider negotiations involve licensed professionals such as attorneys, doctors, or accountants who may have unique ethical obligations and business considerations that affect negotiation strategies and outcomes.

Furnisher compliance leverage involves understanding and utilizing the comprehensive regulatory framework that governs furnisher accuracy obligations, investigation requirements, and reporting standards to create pressure for favorable negotiations and resolution outcomes.

FCRA furnisher provisions establish specific obligations for accuracy, investigation procedures, and correction requirements that create enforceable standards for furnisher compliance. Understanding these provisions helps identify leverage opportunities and structure effective negotiations.

CFPB supervision of larger furnishers provides ongoing regulatory oversight that creates compliance pressure and potential enforcement action exposure. Leveraging supervisory attention can enhance negotiation effectiveness through regulatory pressure.

State law compliance requirements vary significantly between jurisdictions but often provide additional furnisher obligations beyond federal requirements. Understanding state law variations helps identify additional leverage opportunities and compliance pressure points.

Documentation standards required by various regulations create obligations for furnishers to maintain adequate records supporting their credit reporting activities. Understanding documentation requirements helps identify potential compliance weaknesses and negotiation leverage.

Investigation obligations under FCRA amendments require furnishers to investigate consumer disputes and correct inaccurate reporting when errors are identified. Leveraging investigation requirements helps ensure proper dispute handling and favorable resolutions.

Accuracy standards established by regulations require furnishers to implement reasonable procedures to ensure reporting accuracy and to correct errors when identified. Understanding accuracy standards helps identify compliance violations and negotiation leverage.

Timing requirements for furnisher responses to disputes and credit bureau verification requests create enforceable deadlines that can provide leverage when furnishers fail to meet compliance timelines. Understanding timing requirements helps enforce proper procedures.

Quality control obligations require furnishers to maintain systems ensuring ongoing compliance with accuracy and investigation requirements. Understanding quality obligations helps identify systematic compliance problems and negotiation opportunities.

Training requirements for furnisher personnel handling credit reporting and disputes create standards that can provide leverage when inadequate training contributes to compliance violations. Understanding training obligations helps identify compliance weaknesses.

Regulatory guidance from CFPB and other agencies provides evolving standards for furnisher compliance that create additional pressure points for negotiations. Staying current with guidance helps identify emerging leverage opportunities.

Enforcement actions against furnishers provide precedents for compliance requirements and demonstrate regulatory priorities that can enhance negotiation leverage. Understanding enforcement patterns helps identify effective compliance pressure strategies.

Industry best practices that exceed minimum regulatory requirements create additional standards that furnishers may feel obligated to meet, providing negotiation leverage beyond basic compliance requirements. Understanding best practices helps identify additional pressure points.

Communication strategies for furnisher negotiations require sophisticated understanding of business psychology, organizational dynamics, and professional presentation techniques that optimize persuasive impact while maintaining productive relationships for potential future interactions.

Professional presentation standards involve demonstrating competence, seriousness, and legitimate basis for negotiations through high-quality documentation, clear communication, and systematic approach implementation. Professional presentation significantly influences negotiation reception and outcomes.

Authority identification techniques help ensure that negotiations reach decision-makers who have authority to approve comprehensive resolutions rather than customer service personnel with limited negotiation flexibility. Effective authority identification helps optimize negotiation efficiency and outcomes.

Relationship building strategies recognize that long-term success often depends on establishing professional relationships with furnisher personnel who can provide ongoing assistance and favorable consideration. Strategic relationship development helps optimize long-term negotiation effectiveness.

Pressure application methods involve understanding how to create appropriate motivation for favorable resolutions without triggering defensive responses or relationship damage. Effective pressure application helps achieve outcomes while maintaining productive relationships.

Problem-solving approaches that frame negotiations as mutual problem-solving rather than adversarial conflicts often produce better outcomes and preserve relationships for future interactions. Collaborative framing helps optimize negotiation effectiveness and relationship preservation.

Documentation presentation techniques involve organizing evidence and arguments for maximum persuasive impact while maintaining clarity and professionalism. Effective presentation helps ensure that strong cases receive appropriate consideration and favorable outcomes.

Follow-up procedures for ongoing negotiations include appropriate timing, escalation strategies, and persistence techniques that maintain momentum without appearing harassing or unreasonable. Strategic follow-up helps optimize negotiation outcomes through sustained professional effort.

Escalation strategies for unsuccessful initial negotiations include accessing supervisory personnel, regulatory complaint threats, and alternative pressure mechanisms that can restart stalled negotiations. Effective escalation helps achieve outcomes when initial approaches prove insufficient.

Cultural adaptation techniques recognize that different furnisher organizations have varying corporate cultures, communication preferences, and decision-making processes that affect optimal negotiation strategies. Cultural awareness helps optimize approach selection for specific organizational environments.

Technology integration in furnisher communications includes understanding preferred communication channels, electronic documentation methods, and digital signature processes that can expedite negotiation implementation. Technology awareness helps optimize negotiation efficiency and implementation.

Legal compliance in furnisher communications ensures that negotiation strategies don't violate debt collection laws, harassment prohibitions, or other regulatory requirements that could create legal liability or harm negotiation positions. Compliance awareness helps maintain effective and legal negotiation strategies.

Success measurement for furnisher negotiations involves evaluating outcomes against objectives while understanding that partial success often provides significant benefits even when complete objectives aren't achieved. Realistic measurement helps optimize satisfaction and strategic planning.

Enforcement and follow-up procedures ensure that successful furnisher negotiations result in actual implementation of agreed-upon terms and that negotiated benefits are preserved over time. Systematic enforcement helps maximize the long-term value of negotiation investments.

Agreement documentation standards should include written confirmation of all negotiated terms, implementation timelines, responsible parties, and enforcement mechanisms that ensure accountability for agreement performance. Comprehensive documentation helps ensure successful implementation.

Implementation monitoring involves systematic tracking of furnisher compliance with negotiated agreements, including credit report changes, account status updates, and cessation of collection activities. Active monitoring helps ensure that agreements produce promised benefits.

Verification procedures for credit report changes include obtaining updated reports from all three bureaus to confirm that negotiated modifications are implemented consistently and accurately. Comprehensive verification helps ensure complete agreement implementation.

Timeline enforcement involves monitoring furnisher compliance with agreed-upon implementation deadlines and taking appropriate action when furnishers fail to meet commitment timelines. Timeline enforcement helps ensure prompt agreement implementation.

Quality assurance for implemented changes includes verifying that credit report modifications are accurate, complete, and consistent with negotiated terms. Quality assurance helps prevent implementation errors that could reduce agreement benefits.

Backup enforcement mechanisms include regulatory complaints, legal action threats, and alternative pressure strategies that can motivate compliance when furnishers fail to honor negotiated agreements. Effective backup mechanisms help ensure agreement enforceability.

Long-term monitoring procedures ensure that negotiated benefits are preserved over time and that removed items don't reappear on future credit reports. Ongoing monitoring helps maintain negotiation benefits throughout extended periods.

Documentation preservation involves maintaining comprehensive records of negotiations, agreements, and implementation for potential future reference or enforcement action. Proper preservation helps protect negotiation investments and provide evidence for enforcement activities.

Communication protocols for implementation issues include procedures for contacting appropriate furnisher personnel when problems arise and escalation strategies for resolving implementation difficulties. Effective protocols help ensure prompt problem resolution.

Legal recourse options when furnishers fail to honor agreements include contract enforcement actions, consumer protection law violations, and regulatory complaint procedures. Understanding legal options helps ensure that agreements remain enforceable and valuable.

Relationship maintenance during enforcement activities involves balancing enforcement necessity with relationship preservation to maintain future negotiation opportunities. Strategic relationship management helps optimize long-term furnisher interaction effectiveness.

Success preservation strategies ensure that negotiated benefits continue supporting credit improvement goals and that enforcement activities contribute to rather than detract from ongoing credit repair efforts. Strategic preservation helps maximize long-term negotiation value.

Advanced furnisher negotiation techniques involve sophisticated strategies that leverage deep understanding of furnisher operations, regulatory requirements, and business pressures to achieve optimal outcomes in complex situations requiring specialized approaches.

Portfolio analysis techniques help understand furnisher business models, operational pressures, and strategic priorities that affect their willingness to negotiate favorable resolutions. Portfolio understanding helps structure negotiations that align with furnisher business interests.

Competitive pressure leverage involves understanding furnisher relationships with competitors, market position concerns, and reputation management priorities that can create additional motivation for favorable resolution. Competitive awareness helps identify additional pressure points.

Regulatory cycle timing involves coordinating negotiation activities with examination periods, enforcement actions, and policy developments that affect furnisher compliance priorities and negotiation responsiveness. Regulatory timing helps optimize negotiation effectiveness.

Industry expertise demonstration involves showing furnishers that you understand their business environment, operational constraints, and regulatory requirements to establish credibility and facilitate productive negotiations. Expertise demonstration helps ensure serious consideration and respect.

Systematic approach implementation involves developing comprehensive negotiation strategies that address multiple furnisher relationships and coordinate various negotiation activities for cumulative effectiveness.

Systematic approaches often produce better outcomes than isolated negotiations.

Professional network leverage involves utilizing relationships with attorneys, financial advisors, and industry professionals to enhance negotiation credibility and access specialized expertise. Network leverage helps optimize negotiation effectiveness and access.

Technology integration involves understanding furnisher technology systems, operational processes, and communication preferences to optimize negotiation efficiency and implementation. Technology awareness helps structure effective and efficient negotiations.

Risk assessment procedures help evaluate potential adverse consequences from aggressive negotiation strategies and implement safeguards that protect consumer interests while pursuing optimal outcomes. Risk management helps optimize negotiation benefits while minimizing potential negative impacts.

Quality control systems for advanced negotiations involve systematic evaluation of strategy effectiveness, outcome optimization, and continuous improvement based on experience and results. Quality control helps ensure that advanced techniques continue producing optimal outcomes.

Integration with legal strategies involves coordinating furnisher negotiations with potential legal action to preserve rights while maximizing opportunities for favorable resolution without litigation. Legal integration helps optimize overall strategy effectiveness.

Performance measurement for advanced techniques involves sophisticated evaluation methods that assess cumulative outcomes, strategic effectiveness, and long-term benefits rather than simple negotiation success rates. Advanced measurement helps optimize strategy selection and resource allocation.

Mastery development in furnisher negotiations involves continuous learning, skill refinement, and strategic adaptation that enables consistently superior outcomes across diverse situations and furnisher types. Mastery development helps ensure sustained negotiation effectiveness.

Specialized industry considerations recognize that different types of furnishers operate under varying business models, regulatory requirements, and operational constraints that require adapted negotiation strategies for optimal effectiveness.

Financial institution negotiations involve understanding banking regulations, examination oversight, and institutional policies that affect negotiation flexibility and outcomes. Banking expertise helps optimize negotiations with traditional financial service providers.

Healthcare provider negotiations require understanding medical billing complexities, insurance interactions, and industry-specific regulations that create unique opportunities and constraints. Healthcare expertise helps navigate these specialized negotiation environments.

Telecommunications provider negotiations involve understanding service industry dynamics, regulatory oversight, and customer relationship management practices that differ from traditional credit relationships. Telecommunications expertise helps optimize these specialized negotiations.

Retail creditor negotiations may involve different business priorities, customer relationship factors, and operational considerations than financial institutions. Retail expertise helps structure effective approaches for these specialized creditor relationships.

Utility company negotiations require understanding regulatory oversight, service provision obligations, and public utility dynamics that create unique negotiation environments. Utility expertise helps navigate these specialized regulatory environments effectively.

Government creditor negotiations involve unique procedural requirements, political considerations, and legal constraints that differ significantly from private sector negotiations. Government expertise helps structure effective public sector negotiation strategies.

Insurance company negotiations require understanding claims processing, regulatory oversight, and risk management practices that affect negotiation strategies and outcomes. Insurance expertise helps optimize these specialized negotiation approaches.

Professional service provider negotiations involve understanding licensing requirements, ethical obligations, and professional relationship dynamics that affect negotiation strategies. Professional service expertise helps navigate these unique business relationships.

Technology company negotiations may involve specialized business models, intellectual property considerations, and regulatory environments that require adapted approaches. Technology expertise helps optimize negotiations with emerging credit participants.

Real estate industry negotiations involve understanding property-related credit obligations, regulatory oversight, and market dynamics that affect negotiation strategies and outcomes. Real estate expertise helps navigate these specialized industry relationships.

Transportation industry negotiations may involve specialized financing arrangements, regulatory oversight, and operational considerations that require adapted negotiation approaches. Transportation expertise helps optimize these specialized negotiations.

Educational institution negotiations involve understanding federal regulations, financial aid interactions, and institutional policies that create unique negotiation environments. Educational expertise helps navigate these specialized academic relationships effectively.

International furnisher considerations address the increasing complexity of cross-border credit relationships, foreign creditor negotiations, and international regulatory compliance that affect modern credit management and repair strategies.

Jurisdictional complexity in international furnisher relationships involves understanding which laws apply, enforcement mechanisms across borders, and practical limitations on negotiation effectiveness. Jurisdictional awareness helps structure realistic international negotiation strategies.

Cultural adaptation for international negotiations requires understanding business cultures, communication preferences, and relationship dynamics that vary significantly across different countries and regions. Cultural sensitivity helps optimize international negotiation effectiveness.

Language considerations in international negotiations may require translation services, cultural interpretation, and adaptation of persuasive techniques for different linguistic contexts. Language awareness helps ensure effective communication across cultural boundaries.

Currency and payment considerations involve understanding exchange rate impacts, international payment methods, and currency conversion effects on negotiation terms. Currency awareness helps structure practical international agreements.

Legal framework differences between countries create varying consumer protection standards, enforcement mechanisms, and negotiation opportunities that require specialized understanding. Legal awareness helps identify appropriate strategies for different international contexts.

Documentation requirements for international negotiations may involve authentication procedures, translation services, and compliance with foreign legal standards. Documentation expertise helps ensure effective international agreement implementation.

Time zone coordination for international negotiations requires understanding business hours, communication preferences, and scheduling considerations across different regions. Timing awareness helps optimize international negotiation efficiency.

Regulatory compliance across borders involves understanding multiple regulatory requirements, enforcement limitations, and coordination between different regulatory systems. Compliance awareness helps structure effective and legal international strategies.

Technology considerations for international furnisher interactions include understanding communication systems, payment technologies, and digital infrastructure differences that affect negotiation implementation. Technology awareness helps optimize international negotiation efficiency.

Enforcement challenges in international agreements include jurisdiction limitations, service of process difficulties, and judgment enforcement problems across borders. Enforcement understanding helps structure realistic and enforceable international agreements.

Professional assistance for international negotiations may require specialized expertise in international law, foreign business practices, and cross-border enforcement mechanisms. Professional awareness helps identify when specialized assistance becomes necessary.

Future trends in international credit reporting include increasing globalization, standardization efforts, and technology integration that will affect international furnisher negotiation strategies. Trend awareness helps anticipate future international negotiation opportunities and challenges.

Technology integration in furnisher negotiations involves leveraging digital tools, communication platforms, and electronic processes to enhance negotiation efficiency, documentation quality, and implementation effectiveness while maintaining professional standards and legal compliance.

Digital communication strategies include understanding furnisher preferences for email, portal systems, and electronic messaging that can expedite negotiation processes while maintaining proper documentation and professional presentation. Digital efficiency helps optimize negotiation timelines and accessibility.

Electronic documentation systems involve using digital signature platforms, cloud storage solutions, and electronic filing systems that facilitate agreement implementation and record-keeping. Electronic systems help improve efficiency while maintaining comprehensive documentation standards.

Payment technology integration includes understanding electronic fund transfer options, online payment systems, and digital escrow services that can facilitate settlement implementation and provide security for both parties. Payment technology helps optimize agreement implementation and protection.

Automated monitoring systems can track credit report changes, account status updates, and agreement implementation to ensure that negotiated terms are properly executed. Monitoring automation helps ensure comprehensive oversight while reducing manual monitoring requirements.

Database management systems help organize furnisher contact information, negotiation history, and outcome tracking for multiple relationships over time. Database organization helps optimize relationship management and strategic planning for ongoing negotiations.

Communication platforms that support secure messaging, document sharing, and collaborative problem-solving can enhance negotiation effectiveness while maintaining privacy protection and professional standards. Platform integration helps optimize collaborative negotiation processes.

Analytics tools can help evaluate negotiation effectiveness, identify successful strategies, and optimize future approach selection based on historical data and outcome analysis. Analytics integration helps improve strategic decision-making and resource allocation.

Mobile technology integration enables remote negotiation management, real-time communication, and convenient access to documentation and monitoring systems. Mobile capability helps maintain negotiation effectiveness regardless of location or schedule constraints.

Security considerations for technology integration include protecting sensitive financial information, maintaining communication privacy, and ensuring compliance with data protection requirements. Security awareness helps balance technology benefits with privacy protection and legal compliance.

Integration challenges may include furnisher technology limitations, system compatibility issues, and training requirements for effective technology utilization. Challenge awareness helps structure realistic technology integration strategies that account for practical limitations.

Future technology trends include artificial intelligence applications, blockchain verification systems, and enhanced automation that may affect furnisher negotiation processes and opportunities. Trend awareness helps anticipate future technology integration opportunities.

Professional standards for technology integration ensure that digital tools enhance rather than compromise negotiation professionalism, legal compliance, and relationship quality. Standards awareness helps maintain effectiveness while leveraging technology benefits appropriately.

Quality control and performance optimization for furnisher negotiations involve systematic evaluation, continuous improvement, and strategic refinement of negotiation approaches to ensure consistently superior outcomes and maximum value from negotiation investments.

Performance metrics for furnisher negotiations should include success rates, outcome quality, relationship preservation, implementation effectiveness, and long-term benefit durability. Comprehensive metrics help evaluate true negotiation value and identify improvement opportunities.

Success criteria definition involves establishing clear objectives, realistic expectations, and meaningful measurement standards that recognize partial success and optimize resource allocation. Clear criteria help evaluate performance accurately and make informed strategic adjustments.

Strategy effectiveness analysis involves evaluating which approaches produce optimal outcomes for different furnisher types, situation characteristics, and negotiation objectives. Effectiveness analysis helps optimize approach selection and resource allocation for maximum results.

Continuous improvement procedures include regular strategy review, outcome analysis, and approach refinement based on experience and changing circumstances. Improvement procedures help ensure that negotiation capabilities continue developing and adapting to optimize effectiveness.

Documentation quality assessment involves evaluating evidence development, presentation effectiveness, and record-keeping adequacy to ensure that documentation supports rather than undermines negotiation objectives. Quality assessment helps optimize documentation standards and effectiveness.

Relationship management evaluation includes assessing long-term relationship quality, ongoing cooperation potential, and relationship preservation effectiveness alongside immediate negotiation outcomes. Relationship evaluation helps balance short-term gains with long-term strategic value.

Professional development planning involves identifying skill enhancement opportunities, knowledge development needs, and strategic capability expansion that can improve future negotiation effectiveness. Development planning helps ensure sustained improvement and mastery development.

Technology optimization involves evaluating digital tool effectiveness, identifying enhancement opportunities, and implementing technology improvements that support negotiation objectives. Technology optimization helps maintain competitive advantages through appropriate innovation adoption.

Resource allocation optimization involves evaluating time investment, financial costs, and effort distribution across different negotiation activities to ensure maximum return on negotiation investments. Resource optimization helps maintain sustainable and effective negotiation activities.

Risk management assessment involves evaluating potential adverse consequences, implementing appropriate safeguards, and balancing aggressive strategies with prudent risk management. Risk assessment helps optimize outcomes while protecting consumer interests and maintaining strategic flexibility.

Integration assessment involves evaluating how furnisher negotiations coordinate with other credit repair activities and overall financial planning to ensure comprehensive strategy effectiveness. Integration assessment helps optimize coordination and avoid conflicts between different improvement activities.

Outcome durability evaluation involves assessing how well negotiated benefits are preserved over time and what factors contribute to lasting positive results versus temporary improvements. Durability evaluation helps optimize long-term value from negotiation investments.

Regulatory environment navigation for furnisher negotiations involves understanding the complex oversight landscape, compliance requirements, and enforcement mechanisms that affect furnisher behavior and create leverage opportunities for strategic negotiations.

CFPB oversight impact on furnisher negotiations includes understanding examination schedules, enforcement priorities, and regulatory pressure that affects furnisher responsiveness to consumer negotiations. CFPB awareness helps leverage regulatory pressure for enhanced negotiation effectiveness.

State regulatory considerations vary significantly between jurisdictions but often provide additional leverage through licensing requirements, examination oversight, and enforcement mechanisms beyond federal regulation. State awareness helps identify additional pressure points and compliance leverage.

Industry-specific regulation affects different furnisher types through specialized oversight, compliance requirements, and enforcement mechanisms that create unique negotiation opportunities and constraints. Industry awareness helps adapt strategies for specific regulatory environments.

Examination cycle awareness involves understanding when furnishers face regulatory scrutiny and how examination periods affect their willingness to resolve consumer complaints efficiently. Examination timing helps optimize negotiation scheduling for maximum regulatory leverage.

Enforcement action monitoring includes tracking regulatory actions against furnishers to understand compliance priorities, identify systematic problems, and leverage enforcement pressure for improved negotiation outcomes. Enforcement awareness helps identify strategic opportunities.

Compliance guidance interpretation involves understanding how regulatory guidance affects furnisher obligations and creates new leverage opportunities for consumer negotiations. Guidance awareness helps identify emerging compliance pressure points.

Regulatory complaint coordination involves strategically timing regulatory complaints with negotiation activities to provide additional pressure for favorable resolution while avoiding conflicts between different enforcement mechanisms. Complaint coordination helps optimize combined pressure strategies.

Agency coordination procedures help ensure that interactions with different regulatory agencies support rather than conflict with negotiation objectives and that regulatory assistance enhances rather than undermines direct negotiation effectiveness. Coordination helps optimize combined approaches.

Political environment awareness includes understanding how regulatory priorities change with political leadership and how to adapt negotiation strategies to leverage current regulatory focus areas. Political awareness helps maintain regulatory leverage effectiveness through changing circumstances.

Industry lobbying impact involves understanding how furnisher advocacy affects regulatory policy and enforcement priorities to anticipate changes in negotiation leverage and regulatory support. Lobbying awareness helps adapt strategies to changing regulatory environments.

Future regulatory trends include emerging oversight mechanisms, new compliance requirements, and evolving enforcement priorities that will affect furnisher negotiation strategies and opportunities. Trend awareness helps anticipate future regulatory leverage opportunities.

Professional regulatory advocacy involves working with consumer attorneys and advocacy organizations that have specialized regulatory expertise and relationships to enhance regulatory pressure and support for negotiation objectives. Professional advocacy helps optimize regulatory strategy effectiveness.

Risk management and mitigation strategies for furnisher negotiations involve understanding potential adverse consequences and implementing safeguards that protect consumer interests while pursuing optimal outcomes through sophisticated negotiation approaches.

Relationship damage prevention involves structuring negotiations to achieve favorable outcomes while preserving productive relationships with furnishers who may provide ongoing services or future cooperation. Relationship preservation helps maintain long-term strategic value.

Legal exposure minimization includes understanding how negotiation strategies might create legal vulnerabilities and implementing approaches that achieve objectives while avoiding potential liability or adverse legal consequences. Legal protection helps ensure that negotiations support rather than compromise legal positions.

Privacy protection during negotiations involves securing sensitive financial information while maintaining effective communication and documentation. Privacy safeguards help prevent identity theft and information misuse while preserving negotiation effectiveness.

Documentation vulnerability assessment involves ensuring that comprehensive evidence development doesn't inadvertently create damaging admissions or undermine consumer positions in future disputes or legal proceedings. Documentation protection helps maintain strategic advantages.

Escalation risks include understanding how aggressive negotiation strategies might trigger defensive responses or relationship damage that makes future negotiations more difficult. Escalation management helps balance assertiveness with strategic relationship preservation.

Credit impact considerations involve understanding how negotiation activities might temporarily affect credit scores or credit availability during negotiation periods. Impact awareness helps manage timing for important financial decisions and optimize negotiation scheduling.

Financial cost management includes understanding resource requirements for comprehensive negotiation strategies and ensuring sustainable approaches that don't exceed available resources or compromise other financial priorities. Cost management helps maintain effective and sustainable negotiation activities.

Professional relationship effects involve ensuring that negotiation strategies don't damage relationships with attorneys, financial advisors, or other professional assistance providers. Professional preservation helps maintain access to expertise and support throughout credit improvement processes.

Regulatory attention risks include understanding when negotiation activities might attract unwanted regulatory scrutiny or create complications with ongoing regulatory compliance. Regulatory management helps optimize regulatory leverage while avoiding adverse attention.

Competition risks involve understanding how successful negotiations with one furnisher might affect relationships or negotiation opportunities with other creditors. Competition awareness helps optimize overall negotiation strategy while maintaining multiple relationship options.

Time investment optimization involves balancing negotiation effort against potential benefits to ensure efficient resource allocation and sustainable activity levels. Time management helps maintain effective negotiation activities without overwhelming other priorities.

Alternative strategy preservation involves maintaining options for different approaches when negotiation strategies encounter obstacles or prove less effective than anticipated. Strategy flexibility helps ensure continued progress regardless of individual negotiation outcomes.

Advanced furnisher relationship management involves developing sophisticated approaches to long-term creditor relationships that support ongoing financial objectives while optimizing credit repair and management outcomes through strategic interaction and professional development.

Long-term relationship strategy development includes understanding how current negotiations affect future business opportunities, credit availability, and ongoing account management relationships. Strategic relationship planning helps optimize immediate negotiation outcomes while preserving long-term value.

Customer lifecycle management involves understanding different phases of customer relationships and how to optimize interactions during account opening, active management, problem resolution, and account closure periods. Lifecycle awareness helps maintain optimal relationships throughout changing circumstances.

Professional reputation development includes building credibility with furnisher personnel through consistent professionalism, reliable communication, and ethical interaction that enhances future negotiation effectiveness. Reputation development helps ensure continued access and favorable consideration.

Account management optimization involves understanding how to maintain positive ongoing relationships with creditors while addressing credit repair objectives and managing account performance. Account optimization helps balance multiple objectives through strategic account management.

Communication system development includes establishing preferred contact methods, maintaining current contact information, and developing efficient communication protocols that support ongoing relationship management. Communication systems help optimize relationship efficiency and effectiveness.

Problem prevention strategies involve understanding common relationship problems and implementing preventive measures that maintain positive relationships while addressing credit repair objectives. Prevention strategies help avoid relationship damage while achieving improvement goals.

Conflict resolution procedures include systematic approaches for addressing relationship problems when they arise and restoring productive interactions that support ongoing objectives. Resolution procedures help maintain relationship value even when conflicts occur.

Value demonstration involves showing furnishers the benefits of maintaining positive relationships through reliable communication, prompt problem resolution, and ongoing business potential. Value demonstration helps motivate furnisher cooperation and favorable treatment.

Mutual benefit identification includes understanding how positive relationships serve both consumer and furnisher interests through reduced administrative costs, improved account performance, and enhanced business outcomes. Benefit alignment helps create sustainable positive relationships.

Professional network integration involves connecting furnisher relationships with broader professional networks including attorneys, financial advisors, and business associates to enhance relationship value and strategic positioning. Network integration helps optimize relationship benefits.

Industry position awareness includes understanding how to maintain relationships that support broader industry reputation and professional development while achieving specific credit repair objectives. Position awareness helps optimize long-term professional development through strategic relationship management.

Legacy relationship planning involves understanding how current relationship investments affect long-term financial opportunities and ensuring that relationship strategies support lasting financial success and professional development. Legacy planning helps optimize strategic relationship investments for maximum long-term value.

Furnisher negotiation mastery represents the culmination of sophisticated understanding, systematic implementation, and strategic integration of comprehensive approaches to direct creditor interaction that optimize outcomes while building lasting professional capabilities and relationship assets.

Mastery characteristics include deep understanding of furnisher business models and operational constraints, systematic approach to negotiation strategy development and implementation, sophisticated relationship management capabilities that preserve long-term value, and strategic integration of multiple approaches for optimal cumulative outcomes.

Professional competency development involves building expertise comparable to industry professionals while maintaining consumer advocacy perspectives and ethical standards. Professional development enables advanced negotiation implementation that rivals paid professional services while preserving consumer interests.

Strategic thinking mastery includes understanding how to analyze complex credit situations, identify optimal negotiation approaches, and coordinate multiple furnisher relationships for comprehensive effectiveness. Strategic mastery helps optimize approach selection and resource allocation for maximum benefit.

Industry expertise demonstration involves showing furnishers that you understand their business environment, regulatory requirements, and operational realities to establish credibility and facilitate productive negotiations. Expertise demonstration helps ensure serious consideration and professional respect.

Communication excellence includes developing superior presentation skills, persuasive capabilities, and relationship management abilities that optimize negotiation effectiveness and preserve long-term relationship value. Communication excellence helps achieve optimal outcomes while maintaining professional relationships.

Ethical leadership involves implementing advanced strategies while maintaining honesty, integrity, and respect for legitimate business interests and regulatory requirements. Ethical leadership helps ensure that negotiation mastery serves legitimate consumer protection objectives.

Innovation capacity includes understanding how to adapt strategies to unique circumstances, develop novel approaches for unusual problems, and integrate emerging opportunities into negotiation frameworks. Innovation capability helps maintain strategic advantages in evolving business environments.

Teaching and mentoring abilities involve understanding how to share negotiation expertise with others while maintaining appropriate boundaries and professional standards. Teaching capabilities help extend negotiation mastery benefits through knowledge sharing and professional development.

Quality control systems for mastery involve systematic evaluation of negotiation effectiveness, continuous improvement procedures, and strategic refinement based on experience and changing circumstances. Quality systems help ensure that mastery continues developing and adapting for optimal effectiveness.

Professional recognition opportunities may result from negotiation mastery through consultation opportunities, speaking engagements, or advocacy activities that extend expertise benefits while building professional networks. Recognition opportunities help leverage mastery for broader professional development.

Legacy development involves understanding how negotiation mastery contributes to broader consumer protection advocacy and industry improvement efforts while supporting personal financial objectives. Legacy development helps ensure that individual mastery contributes to systemic improvements.

Impact optimization includes understanding how to leverage negotiation mastery for maximum personal financial benefit while contributing to broader consumer protection and industry improvement efforts. Impact optimization helps ensure that mastery investments produce comprehensive and lasting benefits.

CHAPTER 12

REMOVING SPECIFIC NEGATIVE ITEMS

Different types of negative items on credit reports require specialized removal strategies that address the unique characteristics, legal frameworks, and reporting requirements associated with each category. Understanding these distinctions is crucial for developing effective removal approaches that leverage the specific vulnerabilities and regulatory requirements affecting different negative item types.

The landscape of negative credit reporting has evolved significantly as regulatory oversight has intensified and consumer protection laws have expanded. Modern removal strategies must account for enhanced furnisher obligations, stricter accuracy requirements, and increased regulatory scrutiny that affects how different negative items can be challenged and removed.

Strategic prioritization of negative item removal involves understanding which items have the greatest impact on credit scores and future credit opportunities. Recent negative items typically carry more weight than older ones, but high-balance items, charge-offs, and public records can have disproportionate effects that justify prioritized attention regardless of age.

Legal frameworks governing different negative item types vary significantly, with collections subject to FDCPA protections, medical debt receiving special treatment under recent regulatory changes, and public records governed by court procedures and state law variations. Understanding these frameworks helps identify optimal removal strategies.

The timing of removal efforts can significantly affect success rates, with certain periods offering enhanced opportunities due to regulatory examination cycles, furnisher business changes, or legal developments that create pressure for favorable resolution. Strategic timing maximizes removal effectiveness.

Documentation requirements differ substantially between negative item types, with collections often having documentation gaps, public records requiring court research, and original creditor items needing account history analysis.

Comprehensive documentation research forms the foundation of effective removal strategies.

Verification standards vary between different negative item types, with some requiring minimal documentation while others demand extensive proof of accuracy. Understanding these standards helps target removal efforts toward items with the highest probability of successful challenge.

Industry-specific considerations affect removal strategies differently depending on whether negative items originated from banks, collection agencies, medical providers, government entities, or other specialized sectors. Each industry operates under different constraints and pressures that affect removal opportunities.

The interconnected nature of modern credit reporting means that removing one negative item can sometimes trigger changes in related items or create opportunities for additional removals. Understanding these connections helps develop comprehensive removal strategies.

Technology impacts on negative item removal include automated verification systems, electronic documentation requirements, and digital communication platforms that change how removal strategies are implemented and how furnishers respond to challenges.

Collection account removal represents one of the most common and potentially rewarding negative item removal challenges, as collection accounts often involve documentation problems, procedural violations, and business pressures that create multiple removal opportunities for informed consumers.

The collection industry's business model creates inherent vulnerabilities for removal strategies since collection agencies typically purchase or accept debts with incomplete documentation, operate under tight profit margins, and face extensive regulatory compliance requirements. Understanding these vulnerabilities helps identify optimal removal approaches.

Documentation gaps in collection accounts arise from multiple transfers between original creditors and collection agencies, incomplete record preservation during account transfers, and collection agencies' limited access to original account documentation. These gaps create opportunities for verification challenges and removal strategies.

FDCPA compliance issues affect virtually all collection accounts since collection agencies must comply with extensive procedural requirements, validation obligations, and communication restrictions. Violations of these requirements can provide leverage for removal negotiations or legal challenges.

Verification challenges for collection accounts often succeed because collection agencies may lack adequate documentation to verify account details, payment history, or original debt terms. Strategic verification challenges can expose these documentation inadequacies and force account removal.

Statute of limitations considerations affect collection account removal strategies since old debts may be beyond legal collection periods, creating pressure for removal rather than continued collection efforts. Understanding limitation periods helps identify removal opportunities based on debt age.

Portfolio sales and transfers create opportunities for removal challenges when collection agencies cannot adequately document ownership chains or when account information degrades during multiple transfers. Chain of title challenges can be particularly effective for heavily traded accounts.

Regulatory pressure on collection agencies through CFPB oversight, state licensing requirements, and industry examination creates additional motivation for favorable resolution of consumer challenges. Leveraging regulatory pressure can enhance removal negotiation effectiveness.

Pay-for-delete opportunities with collection agencies often prove more successful than with original creditors since collection agencies purchased debts at significant discounts and may accept reduced payments in exchange for complete removal. Strategic pay-for-delete negotiations can provide immediate removal benefits.

Settlement leverage increases when collection accounts involve documentation problems, FDCPA violations, or verification inadequacies that create legal exposure for collection agencies. These issues often motivate favorable settlements that include account removal.

Industry variations among collection agencies affect removal strategies differently depending on agency size, specialization, compliance sophistication, and business model. Understanding these variations helps target removal efforts appropriately.

Medical debt collection removal often benefits from special regulatory protections, insurance billing complexities, and industry-specific dynamics that create enhanced removal opportunities compared to traditional collection accounts.

Charge-off removal strategies address one of the most damaging types of negative credit reporting, requiring sophisticated approaches that understand the business and regulatory factors affecting original creditors' willingness to modify or remove charge-off reporting.

The charge-off designation represents a significant business decision by original creditors to write off debts for accounting and tax purposes, creating complex considerations that affect removal strategies. Understanding charge-off business implications helps structure effective removal approaches.

Original creditor relationships provide advantages for charge-off removal since these entities have complete account documentation, ongoing customer relationship interests, and comprehensive authority to modify account reporting. Leveraging these relationships helps optimize removal opportunities.

Accounting implications of charge-offs create business considerations that may affect creditor willingness to modify reporting, as charge-off reversals can have tax and regulatory reporting consequences. Understanding accounting factors helps structure realistic removal proposals.

Payment history accuracy becomes crucial for charge-off removal challenges since errors in reported payment patterns, charge-off timing, or account status can provide grounds for correction or removal. Detailed payment history analysis helps identify challenge opportunities.

Goodwill negotiations with original creditors often prove effective for charge-off removal when supported by compelling circumstances, improved financial stability, or ongoing customer relationships. Strategic goodwill appeals can achieve removal when verification challenges fail.

Settlement negotiations for charge-off removal may involve payment arrangements combined with reporting modifications, creating opportunities for favorable outcomes that serve both creditor collection interests and consumer credit repair objectives.

Verification challenges for charge-offs typically require more sophisticated approaches than collection account challenges since original creditors usually have comprehensive documentation. However, procedural violations or reporting errors can still provide removal opportunities.

Industry-specific considerations affect charge-off removal strategies differently depending on creditor type, with banks often having different policies and constraints than credit card companies, retailers, or specialty finance companies. Industry awareness helps optimize approach selection.

Regulatory compliance issues may affect charge-off removal when original creditors violate reporting requirements, investigation obligations, or account management regulations. Leveraging compliance issues can provide additional removal pressure.

Timing strategies for charge-off removal include optimal periods such as account anniversaries, customer relationship milestones, or regulatory examination periods when creditors may be more receptive to favorable resolution.

Documentation preservation becomes particularly important for charge-off removal since original creditors typically maintain comprehensive records that must be addressed through strategic rather than verification-based challenges.

Legal considerations for charge-off removal include understanding how removal affects debt collection rights, tax implications, and regulatory reporting requirements that may influence creditor decision-making.

Public record removal involves complex procedures that vary significantly between different types of public records and jurisdictions, requiring specialized knowledge of court systems, government procedures, and legal requirements that differ from traditional credit reporting challenges.

Bankruptcy reporting removal after the appropriate time periods requires understanding federal bankruptcy law, credit bureau procedures, and specific requirements for updating bankruptcy information. Strategic approaches can expedite removal when credit bureaus fail to implement automatic deletion procedures.

Tax lien removal has become less common since major credit bureaus voluntarily removed most tax liens from credit reports, but liens may still appear on specialty reports and affect credit decisions. Understanding current lien reporting helps address remaining lien issues.

Judgment removal strategies vary significantly between jurisdictions due to different state court procedures, reporting requirements, and credit bureau access to court records. State-specific knowledge helps optimize judgment removal approaches.

Court procedure understanding becomes crucial for public record removal since these items originate from official court proceedings that require different challenge approaches than traditional credit reporting disputes. Legal procedure knowledge helps identify removal opportunities.

Satisfaction documentation for paid public records requires understanding court procedures for recording satisfaction, credit bureau notification processes, and timing requirements for reporting updates. Proper satisfaction procedures help ensure timely credit report updates.

Jurisdiction variations create significant differences in public record reporting, challenge procedures, and removal opportunities between different states and court systems. Jurisdictional awareness helps adapt removal strategies appropriately.

Appeal procedures for erroneous public records may involve court challenges, administrative appeals, or credit bureau disputes depending on the nature of errors and reporting procedures. Understanding appeal options helps identify optimal correction approaches.

Identity theft considerations for public records require specialized procedures for challenging fraudulent court records and ensuring that identity theft victims aren't held responsible for fraudulent legal proceedings. Identity theft procedures help protect victims from fraudulent public record reporting.

Statute of limitations for public records varies between record types and jurisdictions, with some records having automatic removal periods while others may remain reportable indefinitely. Understanding limitation periods helps identify removal timing opportunities.

Settlement effects on public records may involve court approval procedures, creditor cooperation requirements, and specific notification processes to ensure that settled public records are properly updated on credit reports.

Professional assistance for public record removal often proves valuable due to complex legal procedures, jurisdictional variations, and specialized knowledge requirements that exceed typical consumer expertise. Professional evaluation helps identify when specialized assistance becomes necessary.

Preventive strategies for public record problems include understanding court procedures, maintaining current address information, and monitoring court records to identify problems early when correction opportunities are optimal.

Inquiry removal strategies address both unauthorized credit inquiries and legitimate inquiries that remain on credit reports longer than permitted or affect credit scores disproportionately. While inquiry impact decreases over time, strategic removal can provide immediate credit score benefits.

Unauthorized inquiry identification involves understanding permissible purposes for credit report access and identifying inquiries that lack proper authorization or legitimate business purposes. Unauthorized inquiry challenges often succeed when proper documentation is provided.

Identity theft inquiry removal requires specialized procedures for challenging inquiries that result from fraudulent credit applications or unauthorized account opening attempts. Identity theft procedures provide enhanced protection and removal rights.

Promotional inquiry challenges address situations where consumers receive inquiries from prescreened credit offers without proper opt-out compliance or authorization. Understanding promotional inquiry rules helps challenge inappropriate promotional access.

Employment inquiry issues may arise when employers access credit reports without proper authorization or fail to comply with FCRA employment procedures. Employment inquiry challenges help protect against unauthorized workplace credit reporting.

Duplicate inquiry removal addresses situations where the same credit application generates multiple inquiries or where inquiries appear incorrectly due to credit bureau processing errors. Duplicate inquiry challenges help ensure accurate inquiry reporting.

Timing challenges for inquiry removal involve understanding the two-year reporting period for inquiries and ensuring that old inquiries are removed promptly when reporting periods expire. Timing challenges help enforce automatic removal requirements.

Hard versus soft inquiry clarification addresses situations where soft inquiries appear as hard inquiries or where inquiry types are misreported. Proper inquiry categorization helps ensure accurate credit score calculations.

Creditor cooperation for inquiry removal may involve contacting creditors who made inquiries to request removal or correction when inquiries were unauthorized or resulted from processing errors. Creditor cooperation can expedite inquiry resolution.

Verification procedures for inquiry challenges require documentation of authorization status, inquiry purposes, and consumer consent for credit report access. Proper verification helps ensure that inquiry challenges address legitimate unauthorized access.

Impact assessment for inquiry removal involves understanding how inquiry removal affects credit scores and prioritizing removal efforts based on score impact potential. Strategic prioritization helps optimize inquiry removal benefits.

Prevention strategies for unauthorized inquiries include credit monitoring, fraud alerts, and security freeze utilization that prevent unauthorized access while maintaining legitimate credit opportunities.

Regulatory oversight of inquiry practices through CFPB supervision and enforcement actions creates additional protection against unauthorized credit report access and provides complaint mechanisms for inquiry violations.

Personal information correction involves addressing errors in identifying information that can affect credit reporting accuracy, account matching, and identity verification procedures. While personal information errors may seem minor, they can indicate serious problems and affect credit access.

Name variation corrections address situations where credit reports contain incorrect names, name spellings, or name variations that don't belong to consumers. Name corrections help prevent file mixing and ensure accurate identity verification.

Address error correction involves updating incorrect current or previous addresses that may affect credit report accuracy or account verification procedures. Address corrections help ensure accurate reporting and prevent identity confusion.

Social Security number errors require immediate attention since SSN errors can indicate identity theft, file mixing, or serious data quality problems. SSN corrections help protect against fraud and ensure accurate identity verification.

Date of birth corrections address errors that may affect credit report matching, account verification, or age-related credit protections. Birth date accuracy helps ensure proper credit report maintenance and regulatory compliance.

Employment information accuracy affects credit applications and verification procedures, making employment correction important for consumers seeking credit or facing employment-related credit reviews. Employment accuracy helps optimize credit application outcomes.

Phone number corrections help ensure that creditors and credit bureaus can contact consumers appropriately and that contact information supports rather than hinders credit repair and management activities.

Previous address completeness affects credit report accuracy and account history matching, making address history correction important for comprehensive credit report accuracy. Complete address history helps ensure accurate account reporting.

Alias and AKA removal addresses situations where credit reports contain names or aliases that don't belong to consumers or result from identity theft or file mixing. Alias removal helps prevent identity confusion and fraud.

File mixing correction requires comprehensive approaches when credit reports contain information from other consumers due to similar identifying information or credit bureau processing errors. File mixing correction helps ensure report accuracy and prevent ongoing problems.

Identity verification enhancement through personal information correction helps ensure that credit applications, account access, and verification procedures work smoothly without identity confusion or processing delays.

Fraud prevention through personal information accuracy helps protect against identity theft and unauthorized account opening by ensuring that credit reports contain accurate identifying information that supports rather than hinders fraud detection.

Regulatory compliance for personal information accuracy involves understanding credit bureau obligations to maintain accurate identifying information and correct errors promptly when identified. Compliance awareness helps enforce correction requirements.

Medical debt removal strategies leverage special regulatory protections, industry-specific dynamics, and unique billing characteristics that create enhanced removal opportunities compared to traditional debt collection situations.

Regulatory protections for medical debt include enhanced dispute rights, longer waiting periods before initial reporting, and automatic removal requirements when insurance payments satisfy debts. Understanding these protections helps optimize medical debt removal strategies.

Insurance billing complexities create documentation problems and verification challenges that often benefit consumers seeking medical debt removal. Insurance coordination errors frequently provide grounds for successful dispute challenges.

Provider billing errors are common in medical billing due to complex coding requirements, insurance interactions, and administrative processing issues. Billing error identification helps support medical debt removal challenges.

HIPAA privacy considerations affect medical debt collection and reporting by limiting information sharing and creating additional procedural requirements. Privacy protections may provide additional leverage for medical debt removal.

Charity care and financial assistance programs offered by many medical providers can provide removal opportunities when patients qualify for assistance programs that weren't initially applied to accounts. Assistance program exploration helps identify removal opportunities.

Payment plan options with medical providers often provide alternatives to collection reporting and may include agreements to remove negative reporting upon successful payment plan completion. Payment plan negotiations help achieve removal while addressing payment obligations.

Verification challenges for medical debt often succeed due to complex billing systems, multiple provider involvement, and documentation gaps that arise from insurance processing and payment coordination issues.

Statute of limitations considerations for medical debt vary by state and may provide removal leverage when debts exceed legal collection periods. Understanding limitation periods helps identify timing-based removal opportunities.

Settlement negotiations with medical providers may include favorable terms due to providers' primary focus on patient care rather than debt collection. Medical provider negotiations often achieve better outcomes than traditional collection negotiations.

Collection agency challenges for medical debt benefit from FDCPA protections plus medical debt-specific regulations that create enhanced consumer rights and collection restrictions. Combined protections provide multiple challenge opportunities.

Dispute timing for medical debt should consider insurance processing periods, appeal deadlines, and provider billing cycles that may affect dispute outcomes. Strategic timing helps optimize medical debt removal effectiveness.

Professional assistance for complex medical debt situations may include patient advocacy services, healthcare billing specialists, and consumer attorneys with medical debt expertise. Professional evaluation helps identify when specialized assistance becomes beneficial.

Student loan credit issues require specialized understanding of federal regulations, servicer obligations, and unique rehabilitation programs that create removal opportunities not available for other debt types. Student loan credit repair involves complex federal program coordination and specialized dispute strategies.

Default removal through rehabilitation programs provides unique opportunities for student loan borrowers to remove default reporting after completing approved rehabilitation requirements. Rehabilitation programs offer complete default removal that's unavailable for other debt types.

Servicer error correction addresses common problems in student loan servicing including payment misapplication, incorrect status reporting, and administrative errors that affect credit reporting. Servicer error identification helps support correction and removal efforts.

Consolidation impact on credit reporting involves understanding how loan consolidation affects existing credit reporting and creates opportunities for improved reporting status. Strategic consolidation can provide credit reporting benefits beyond payment simplification.

Deferment and forbearance reporting accuracy requires understanding proper status reporting during approved non-payment periods and challenging incorrect delinquency reporting during authorized postponement periods.

Income-driven repayment plan effects on credit reporting include understanding how payment plan participation affects credit status and ensuring that plan participation is reported accurately rather than as delinquency or default.

Discharge program eligibility for certain student loan forgiveness programs can provide complete removal opportunities when borrowers qualify for programs such as public service forgiveness, disability discharge, or closed school discharge.

Documentation requirements for student loan disputes often involve federal program documentation, servicer correspondence, and payment history analysis that differs from traditional credit disputes. Comprehensive documentation helps support student loan challenges.

Federal oversight of student loan servicers provides additional leverage through regulatory complaints and oversight mechanisms that may enhance dispute resolution effectiveness. Regulatory leverage helps optimize servicer responsiveness.

Transfer complications between servicers create opportunities for disputes when account information degrades during transfers or when new servicers report information incorrectly. Transfer-related problems often provide dispute opportunities.

Borrower defense applications and related federal programs may affect credit reporting when borrowers successfully challenge loan validity or obtain discharge relief. Program participation helps address both debt obligations and credit reporting.

Professional assistance for complex student loan issues may include student loan attorneys, financial aid specialists, and consumer advocates with federal program expertise. Professional evaluation helps navigate complex federal requirements and optimize outcomes.

Inquiry management and optimization strategies focus on minimizing negative inquiry impact while maintaining credit access and optimizing credit application timing for maximum score benefit and minimal score impact.

Strategic inquiry timing involves coordinating credit applications to minimize score impact through rate shopping windows, application clustering, and optimal timing around major financial decisions. Strategic timing helps optimize inquiry impact management.

Rate shopping window utilization allows multiple inquiries for the same credit type within specific time periods to count as single inquiries for scoring purposes. Understanding rate shopping helps minimize inquiry impact during credit shopping.

Application clustering strategies involve grouping credit applications within optimal time periods to minimize cumulative inquiry impact while maintaining access to multiple credit opportunities. Clustering helps optimize inquiry management for credit building.

Prequalification utilization involves using soft inquiry prequalification tools to evaluate credit opportunities without hard inquiry impact. Strategic prequalification helps optimize application success rates while minimizing inquiry impact.

Credit monitoring for inquiry tracking helps identify unauthorized inquiries quickly and provides documentation for inquiry disputes when unauthorized access occurs. Monitoring helps maintain inquiry accuracy and prevent fraud.

Inquiry impact assessment involves understanding how different inquiry types affect credit scores and prioritizing inquiry management efforts based on score impact potential. Impact assessment helps optimize inquiry management strategies.

Authorization documentation for legitimate inquiries helps protect against unauthorized access claims while ensuring that authorized inquiries are properly documented and defensible. Documentation helps maintain inquiry accuracy.

Dispute preparation for inquiry challenges requires understanding permissible purposes, authorization requirements, and proper dispute procedures for different inquiry types. Preparation helps optimize inquiry dispute effectiveness.

Prevention strategies for unauthorized inquiries include fraud alerts, security freezes, and credit monitoring that prevent unauthorized access while maintaining legitimate credit opportunities. Prevention helps avoid inquiry problems proactively.

Industry-specific inquiry considerations recognize that different types of creditors have varying inquiry practices, authorization procedures, and removal willingness. Industry awareness helps optimize inquiry management for different creditor types.

Professional guidance for inquiry optimization may include credit counselors, mortgage professionals, and financial advisors who understand inquiry impact and application timing strategies. Professional evaluation helps optimize inquiry management decisions.

Long-term inquiry strategy involves understanding how inquiry patterns affect credit profiles over time and planning inquiry timing to support long-term credit goals and major financial decisions. Strategic planning helps optimize long-term inquiry impact.

Specialized removal techniques address unique situations and complex negative items that require sophisticated approaches beyond standard dispute and negotiation strategies. These techniques leverage advanced legal principles, industry knowledge, and strategic pressure application.

Statute of limitations challenges involve identifying time-barred debts and leveraging legal collection limitations to pressure for removal rather than continued reporting. While time-barred debts may remain reportable under FCRA, collection limitations create negotiation leverage.

Successor liability issues arise when creditors merge, sell portfolios, or transfer obligations to entities that may lack proper documentation or legal authority. Successor liability challenges can provide removal opportunities when ownership chains are inadequate.

Bankruptcy discharge violations occur when creditors continue reporting discharged debts or fail to update reporting to reflect discharge status. Discharge violation challenges provide strong removal leverage and potential legal remedies.

Identity theft recovery involves comprehensive procedures for removing fraudulent accounts and repairing credit damage from identity theft. Recovery procedures provide enhanced rights and removal opportunities beyond standard dispute processes.

Mixed file corrections address situations where credit reports contain information from multiple consumers due to similar identifying information or processing errors. Mixed file correction requires systematic approaches to separate and remove inappropriate information.

Account duplication removal involves identifying and challenging duplicate reporting of the same debt by multiple furnishers or collection agencies. Duplication challenges help ensure accurate debt representation and prevent artificial inflation of negative information.

Procedural violation leverage involves identifying and challenging credit bureau or furnisher failures to comply with specific FCRA requirements during dispute processing or reporting procedures. Procedural violations can provide removal leverage regardless of information accuracy.

Industry expert consultation for complex removal situations may involve attorneys, forensic accountants, or industry specialists who can provide expertise for unusual circumstances requiring specialized knowledge. Expert assistance helps address complex situations effectively.

Documentation forensics involves detailed analysis of account documentation to identify errors, inconsistencies, or procedural violations that support removal challenges. Forensic analysis helps identify removal opportunities that standard reviews might miss.

Regulatory intervention for systematic problems may involve CFPB complaints, state attorney general involvement, or other regulatory assistance when removal efforts reveal broader compliance problems. Regulatory intervention can provide resolution assistance beyond individual removal efforts.

Class action considerations may arise when removal efforts identify systematic problems affecting multiple consumers. Class action awareness helps determine when individual efforts might benefit from or contribute to broader legal challenges.

Professional network utilization involves leveraging relationships with attorneys, financial professionals, and industry experts to access specialized knowledge and assistance for complex removal situations. Network utilization helps optimize removal effectiveness through professional collaboration.

Account closure strategies recognize that how accounts are closed can significantly affect ongoing credit reporting and create opportunities for improved reporting status or complete removal of negative information.

Voluntary closure procedures involve understanding how to close accounts strategically to minimize negative impact while preserving positive credit history and account age benefits. Strategic closure helps optimize credit profile effects.

Closure timing considerations include optimal periods for account closure that support credit score improvement, major financial goals, and overall credit management strategies. Strategic timing helps optimize closure benefits.

Negative account closure may involve negotiating with creditors to close accounts with favorable reporting status rather than allowing continued negative reporting through charge-off or collection placement. Closure negotiations help minimize negative impact.

Settlement closure agreements can include provisions for account closure with agreed-upon reporting status, providing opportunities for improved final reporting compared to continued negative status. Settlement closure helps optimize final account status.

Documentation requirements for account closure include written confirmation of closure terms, final payment status, and reporting commitments to ensure that closure produces intended credit reporting benefits. Proper documentation helps ensure closure effectiveness.

Credit utilization impact from account closures requires understanding how closures affect available credit and utilization calculations for credit scoring purposes. Utilization planning helps minimize negative closure effects.

Age of accounts considerations involve understanding how account closures affect credit history length and account age calculations for credit scoring. Age preservation helps maintain credit score benefits from long-term accounts.

Reopen opportunities with closed accounts may exist when circumstances change or when account closure was based on temporary financial difficulties. Understanding reopen procedures helps maintain future credit access options.

Industry variations in closure procedures differ between banks, credit card companies, retailers, and other creditor types. Industry awareness helps optimize closure strategies for different account types.

Professional guidance for account closure decisions may include financial advisors, credit counselors, and credit repair professionals who understand closure impact on credit scores and financial goals. Professional evaluation helps optimize closure decisions.

Monitoring closed accounts ensures that closure is properly implemented and that closed accounts continue reporting accurately without inappropriate negative information. Closure monitoring helps maintain closure benefits over time.

Strategic closure sequencing involves planning closure timing across multiple accounts to optimize overall credit impact and support broader credit management objectives. Sequential planning helps maximize closure strategy effectiveness.

Comprehensive removal planning involves developing systematic approaches that address multiple negative items strategically while optimizing overall credit improvement and supporting broader financial objectives.

Priority assessment for negative item removal helps identify which items to address first based on credit score impact, removal probability, and resource requirements. Strategic prioritization helps optimize removal effectiveness and resource allocation.

Timeline development for comprehensive removal involves understanding typical removal periods and coordinating removal efforts with major financial goals and credit needs. Timeline planning helps ensure that removal efforts support important financial decisions.

Resource allocation across multiple removal efforts requires balancing time, effort, and costs among different negative items while maintaining sustainable activity levels. Resource planning helps optimize removal effectiveness within available constraints.

Coordination strategies ensure that different removal efforts support rather than conflict with each other and that removal activities integrate effectively with other credit repair strategies. Coordination helps maximize cumulative removal effectiveness.

Success measurement for comprehensive removal involves tracking multiple outcomes including credit score improvements, negative item reductions, and progress toward broader financial goals. Comprehensive measurement helps evaluate removal strategy effectiveness.

Adaptation procedures help modify removal strategies based on initial results, changing circumstances, and emerging opportunities. Strategic adaptation helps maintain removal effectiveness through changing conditions.

Documentation organization for multiple removal efforts requires systematic record-keeping that supports ongoing activities while providing evidence for potential legal action or regulatory complaints. Organization helps optimize removal management efficiency.

Professional assistance coordination involves working effectively with attorneys, credit repair companies, and financial advisors across multiple removal efforts. Professional coordination helps optimize assistance benefits while maintaining strategic coherence.

Integration with credit building ensures that removal efforts coordinate effectively with positive credit building activities to maximize overall credit improvement effectiveness. Integration helps optimize comprehensive credit repair outcomes.

Long-term monitoring ensures that removal benefits are preserved over time and that removed items don't reappear on future credit reports. Monitoring helps maintain removal investments and prevent problem recurrence.

Quality control procedures help ensure that removal efforts maintain high standards and produce lasting benefits rather than temporary improvements. Quality control helps optimize removal strategy effectiveness and durability.

Strategic exit planning involves understanding when removal efforts have achieved their objectives and when to transition to maintenance monitoring rather than active removal activities. Exit planning helps optimize transition to credit maintenance phases.

Technology integration in negative item removal involves leveraging digital tools, monitoring services, and automated systems to enhance removal effectiveness while maintaining comprehensive oversight of credit reporting accuracy.

Credit monitoring integration provides real-time updates on credit report changes and helps identify new negative items or verify removal outcomes quickly. Monitoring integration helps optimize removal timing and effectiveness verification.

Document management systems help organize evidence, correspondence, and tracking information for multiple removal efforts efficiently. Digital organization significantly improves removal management and evidence accessibility.

Automated dispute tracking helps manage multiple dispute timelines, follow-up requirements, and outcome verification across different negative items and credit bureaus. Tracking automation helps ensure comprehensive dispute management.

Communication platforms that support secure messaging and document sharing can enhance removal negotiations while maintaining privacy protection and professional presentation. Platform integration helps optimize removal communication effectiveness.

Research tools help identify furnisher information, regulatory actions, and industry changes that may affect removal strategies and opportunities. Research integration helps maintain current removal strategy effectiveness.

Analytics capabilities help evaluate removal effectiveness patterns, identify successful strategies, and optimize future approach selection based on historical data. Analytics integration helps improve removal decision-making through data-driven insights.

Mobile access enables remote removal management, real-time monitoring, and convenient access to removal documentation and tracking systems. Mobile capability helps maintain removal effectiveness regardless of location constraints.

Security measures protect sensitive financial information and removal documentation while ensuring privacy protection throughout removal activities. Security integration helps balance technology benefits with privacy protection requirements.

Integration challenges may include system compatibility issues, technology learning requirements, and cost considerations for comprehensive technology solutions. Challenge awareness helps structure realistic technology integration strategies.

Future technology trends include artificial intelligence applications, automated verification systems, and enhanced monitoring capabilities that may affect removal strategies and opportunities. Trend awareness helps anticipate future technology benefits.

Professional technology consultation may help identify optimal technology solutions and integration strategies for complex removal situations requiring sophisticated management systems. Professional evaluation helps optimize technology investment decisions.

Backup and redundancy systems ensure that technology failures don't compromise removal efforts or result in loss of important documentation and tracking information. Backup planning helps protect removal investments against technology failures.

Legal action considerations for negative item removal involve understanding when legal remedies become appropriate and how to coordinate legal action with other removal strategies for optimal outcomes.

FCRA violation assessment involves identifying credit bureau or furnisher failures that create grounds for legal action while pursuing other removal strategies. Violation identification helps evaluate legal action potential and coordination opportunities.

FDCPA violation evaluation for collection accounts helps identify illegal collection practices that provide legal remedies and removal leverage. Violation evaluation helps determine when legal action enhances removal effectiveness.

Damage calculation for legal action involves understanding potential financial recovery for credit reporting violations while evaluating litigation costs and benefits. Damage assessment helps make informed legal action decisions.

Attorney consultation timing involves understanding when legal expertise becomes necessary for complex removal situations requiring specialized knowledge or legal action coordination. Consultation timing helps optimize legal assistance benefits.

Settlement leverage from potential legal action often motivates favorable removal negotiations when furnishers face liability exposure for violations. Legal leverage helps enhance removal negotiation effectiveness.

Evidence development for legal action involves systematic documentation that supports both removal efforts and potential litigation. Evidence development helps maintain legal options while pursuing other removal strategies.

Statute of limitations for legal action requires understanding deadlines for different types of violations to preserve legal rights while pursuing removal through other methods. Limitation awareness helps maintain legal option viability.

Class action opportunities may arise when removal efforts identify systematic violations affecting multiple consumers. Class action evaluation helps determine when individual efforts might benefit from broader legal challenges.

Regulatory complaint coordination with potential legal action helps maximize pressure for favorable resolution while preserving legal rights and remedies. Coordination helps optimize combined pressure strategies.

Cost-benefit analysis for legal action involves evaluating potential recovery against litigation costs while considering removal benefits beyond monetary damages. Analysis helps make informed legal action decisions.

Professional representation evaluation includes finding attorneys with appropriate expertise in consumer protection law and credit reporting violations. Representation evaluation helps optimize legal assistance quality and effectiveness.

Alternative dispute resolution options may provide more efficient remedies than traditional litigation for some credit reporting violations. Alternative resolution evaluation helps identify optimal legal remedy approaches.

Quality assurance and verification procedures ensure that negative item removal efforts produce lasting benefits and that removed items don't reappear on future credit reports due to inadequate implementation or verification.

Removal verification procedures involve obtaining updated credit reports from all three bureaus to confirm that removal efforts produced intended results across all reporting systems. Comprehensive verification helps ensure complete removal implementation.

Implementation monitoring tracks whether removal agreements are properly executed and that furnishers comply with negotiated terms and timelines. Active monitoring helps ensure that removal efforts produce promised benefits.

Credit score impact assessment helps determine whether removal efforts translate into expected credit score improvements and identifies additional optimization opportunities. Impact assessment helps evaluate removal effectiveness.

Long-term monitoring ensures that removed items don't reappear on future credit reports due to processing errors, system glitches, or furnisher non-compliance with removal agreements. Ongoing monitoring helps preserve removal benefits.

Documentation preservation maintains comprehensive records of removal efforts, agreements, and outcomes for potential future reference or enforcement needs. Preservation helps protect removal investments and provide evidence for enforcement.

Quality control standards ensure that removal efforts maintain high effectiveness levels and produce durable benefits rather than temporary improvements. Standards help optimize removal strategy effectiveness and sustainability.

Error correction procedures address situations where removal implementation contains errors or incomplete execution. Correction procedures help ensure that removal efforts achieve complete intended benefits.

Relationship maintenance during verification activities involves balancing verification necessity with relationship preservation to maintain future cooperation and effectiveness. Maintenance helps optimize long-term removal relationship benefits.

Follow-up procedures for incomplete removal help address situations where removal efforts achieve partial success requiring additional work or alternative approaches. Follow-up procedures help optimize removal outcome completion.

Professional assistance for verification may include credit monitoring services, legal consultation, or specialized verification assistance for complex removal situations. Professional evaluation helps identify when verification assistance becomes beneficial.

Technology integration for verification includes automated monitoring, alert systems, and tracking tools that help maintain comprehensive oversight of removal outcomes. Technology integration helps optimize verification efficiency and effectiveness.

Success preservation strategies ensure that removal benefits continue supporting credit improvement goals and that verification activities contribute to rather than detract from ongoing credit repair efforts. Preservation strategies help maximize long-term removal value.

Advanced removal strategies for complex situations involve sophisticated approaches that address unusual circumstances, systematic problems, and challenging negative items requiring specialized expertise and strategic coordination.

Forensic analysis techniques involve detailed examination of account documentation, reporting procedures, and industry practices to identify removal opportunities that standard approaches might miss. Forensic analysis helps uncover hidden removal leverage.

Pattern recognition across multiple accounts helps identify systematic problems, furnisher violations, or industry practices that create broader removal opportunities. Pattern recognition helps optimize removal strategy scope and effectiveness.

Expert witness utilization for complex removal situations may involve industry professionals, legal experts, or technical specialists who can provide testimony or analysis supporting removal efforts. Expert assistance helps address sophisticated removal challenges.

Regulatory intervention coordination involves leveraging federal and state oversight to address systematic problems while pursuing individual removal objectives. Intervention coordination helps optimize regulatory assistance for removal efforts.

Industry expertise development includes understanding specific sector practices, compliance requirements, and business pressures that affect removal opportunities within different industries. Expertise development helps optimize industry-specific removal strategies.

Innovative approach development involves creating novel removal strategies for unique circumstances or emerging industry practices not addressed by standard approaches. Innovation helps maintain removal effectiveness in evolving credit reporting environments.

Professional network utilization involves leveraging relationships with attorneys, industry experts, and consumer advocates to access specialized knowledge and assistance for complex removal situations. Network utilization helps optimize professional collaboration benefits.

Strategic patience for complex removal involves understanding that sophisticated approaches often require extended timeframes and sustained effort to achieve optimal outcomes. Patience helps maintain effectiveness through challenging removal processes.

Risk management for advanced strategies includes understanding potential adverse consequences and implementing safeguards that protect consumer interests while pursuing sophisticated removal approaches. Risk management helps optimize advanced strategy benefits while minimizing potential negative impacts.

Integration coordination ensures that advanced removal strategies support overall credit repair objectives and coordinate effectively with other improvement activities. Coordination helps maximize advanced strategy contribution to comprehensive credit improvement.

Performance measurement for advanced techniques involves sophisticated evaluation methods that assess complex strategy effectiveness and optimize resource allocation for maximum removal benefits. Advanced measurement helps ensure optimal advanced strategy implementation.

Mastery development in advanced removal involves continuous learning, skill refinement, and strategic adaptation that enables consistently superior outcomes across diverse situations and negative item types. Mastery development helps ensure sustained advanced removal effectiveness.

Preventive strategies for avoiding future negative items focus on proactive credit management, early intervention, and systematic monitoring that prevent credit problems before they require removal efforts.

Early warning systems help identify potential credit problems before they result in negative reporting, providing opportunities for preventive intervention and problem resolution. Warning systems help avoid removal necessity through proactive management.

Account monitoring procedures involve systematic oversight of all credit accounts to identify problems quickly and address issues before they escalate to negative reporting. Monitoring helps prevent negative items through early intervention.

Communication protocols with creditors establish procedures for addressing account problems proactively and maintaining positive relationships that support problem prevention. Protocol development helps prevent problems through improved creditor communication.

Financial management systems help maintain stable payment patterns and avoid circumstances that lead to negative credit reporting. Management systems help prevent negative items through improved financial stability.

Emergency response plans provide procedures for addressing unexpected financial difficulties before they result in negative credit reporting. Response planning helps prevent negative items during financial emergencies.

Professional assistance utilization includes working with financial counselors, credit advisors, and other professionals who can provide guidance for preventing credit problems. Professional assistance helps optimize prevention effectiveness through expert guidance.

Insurance and protection strategies help minimize financial disruption from unexpected events that might otherwise result in negative credit reporting. Protection strategies help prevent negative items through risk management.

Education and skill development in credit management helps maintain knowledge and capabilities necessary for effective credit problem prevention. Education helps optimize prevention effectiveness through improved credit management skills.

Technology integration for prevention includes automated monitoring, alert systems, and management tools that support proactive credit problem prevention. Technology integration helps optimize prevention efficiency and effectiveness.

Industry awareness helps understand changing credit industry practices, regulatory requirements, and economic conditions that might affect credit management and problem prevention. Awareness helps adapt prevention strategies to changing conditions.

Long-term planning for credit management ensures that prevention strategies support broader financial goals and maintain effectiveness through changing life circumstances. Planning helps optimize prevention strategy sustainability and effectiveness.

Quality assurance for prevention involves regular evaluation of prevention effectiveness and strategic refinement based on experience and changing circumstances. Quality assurance helps ensure that prevention strategies continue optimizing credit protection over time.

Case study:

Case study applications demonstrate how theoretical removal strategies translate into practical results across different negative item types and consumer circumstances. Understanding real-world applications helps optimize strategy selection and implementation for specific situations.

Collection account removal case study involves a consumer facing multiple collection accounts from medical debt consolidation. The strategic approach began with verification challenges targeting the collection agency's documentation gaps, followed by FDCPA compliance analysis that revealed validation notice violations. The combination of verification inadequacies and legal violations created leverage for negotiated removal agreements that eliminated all collection accounts within four months.

Charge-off removal case study demonstrates successful removal of a credit card charge-off through goodwill negotiation combined with settlement terms. The consumer leveraged a long-standing customer relationship, documented medical emergency circumstances, and improved financial stability to negotiate charge-off removal in exchange for a settlement payment. The approach required three months of strategic communication and relationship building with the original creditor.

Public record removal case study illustrates successful bankruptcy notation removal after the ten-year reporting period expired but credit bureaus failed to implement automatic deletion. The consumer's systematic dispute campaign included documentation of discharge dates, timeline calculations, and regulatory compliance requirements that forced bureau compliance within sixty days of initial disputes.

Medical debt removal case study showcases the effectiveness of specialized medical debt strategies including insurance billing error identification, provider billing dispute procedures, and charity care program application. The comprehensive approach eliminated over $15,000 in medical debt reporting within six months through coordinated provider negotiations and insurance company intervention.

Student loan default removal case study demonstrates successful rehabilitation program completion that removed default status reporting. The consumer's strategic approach included servicer error correction, payment plan negotiation, and federal program compliance that restored positive reporting status and eliminated default notation after twelve months of consistent rehabilitation payments.

Inquiry removal case study shows systematic unauthorized inquiry challenges that removed multiple inquiries resulting from identity theft. The consumer's documentation included police reports, identity theft affidavits, and creditor correspondence that supported comprehensive inquiry removal across all three credit bureaus within ninety days.

Mixed file correction case study illustrates successful separation of credit files that had been mixed due to similar names and social security numbers. The comprehensive correction process required systematic documentation, identity verification, and coordination with multiple credit bureaus to ensure complete file separation and accuracy.

Comprehensive removal case study demonstrates coordinated removal of multiple negative item types through integrated strategy implementation. The consumer's eighteen-month campaign addressed collections, charge-offs, inquiries, and personal information errors through systematic priority-based removal that improved credit scores by over 150 points.

Industry-specific removal case study showcases successful removal strategies adapted for telecommunications debt involving regulatory compliance issues and industry-specific business practices. The specialized approach leveraged telecommunications regulations and industry oversight to achieve favorable removal outcomes.

Success measurement and outcome optimization involve systematic evaluation of removal strategy effectiveness and continuous improvement procedures that maximize long-term benefits from negative item removal investments.

Performance metrics for removal effectiveness should include success rates by negative item type, timeline efficiency, credit score improvement correlation, and long-term outcome durability. Comprehensive metrics help evaluate true removal strategy value and identify optimization opportunities.

Credit score impact correlation helps understand which removal efforts produce the greatest score improvements and how to prioritize removal activities for maximum scoring benefit. Impact correlation helps optimize removal strategy selection for score improvement goals.

Timeline analysis evaluates removal strategy efficiency and identifies factors that accelerate or delay successful outcomes. Timeline analysis helps optimize removal planning and resource allocation for maximum efficiency.

Cost-effectiveness evaluation includes measuring resource investments against achieved outcomes to identify the most efficient removal strategies for different circumstances. Effectiveness evaluation helps optimize approach selection and resource management.

Durability assessment measures how well removal benefits are preserved over time and what factors contribute to lasting positive results versus temporary improvements. Durability assessment helps optimize long-term removal strategy value.

Success factor identification involves analyzing successful removal outcomes to understand which approaches, timing factors, and circumstances contribute most significantly to positive results. Factor identification helps replicate successful strategies and avoid ineffective approaches.

Failure analysis examines unsuccessful removal attempts to understand obstacles, identify improvement opportunities, and refine strategies for better future outcomes. Failure analysis helps optimize strategy effectiveness through experience-based learning.

Benchmark establishment provides standards for evaluating removal performance and identifying areas requiring improvement or strategic adjustment. Benchmarking helps maintain consistent performance evaluation and optimization.

Continuous improvement procedures involve regular strategy review, outcome analysis, and approach refinement based on accumulated experience and changing circumstances. Improvement procedures help ensure that removal capabilities continue developing and adapting.

Professional development planning includes identifying skill enhancement opportunities and knowledge development needs that can improve future removal effectiveness. Development planning helps ensure sustained improvement in removal capabilities.

Technology optimization involves evaluating digital tool effectiveness and implementing technology improvements that support removal objectives. Technology optimization helps maintain competitive advantages through appropriate innovation adoption.

Integration assessment evaluates how removal efforts coordinate with other credit repair activities and overall financial planning to ensure comprehensive strategy effectiveness. Integration assessment helps optimize removal contribution to broader financial objectives.

Future trends and emerging opportunities in negative item removal include regulatory developments, technology innovations, and industry changes that will affect removal strategies and create new opportunities for consumer credit repair.

Regulatory evolution in credit reporting oversight continues expanding consumer protections through enhanced accuracy requirements, stricter furnisher obligations, and increased enforcement activity. Regulatory trends help anticipate new removal opportunities and leverage points.

Technology advancement in credit reporting systems includes artificial intelligence applications, blockchain verification systems, and automated dispute processing that will change how removal strategies are implemented and how furnishers respond to challenges.

Industry consolidation trends affect removal strategies through changing ownership, operational procedures, and compliance standards across credit reporting participants. Consolidation awareness helps anticipate removal strategy adaptations for changing industry structure.

Consumer protection enhancement through legislative proposals and regulatory guidance continues expanding removal opportunities and strengthening consumer rights. Protection enhancement helps identify emerging removal leverage and strategy opportunities.

Data accuracy improvement initiatives by credit bureaus and regulatory agencies create additional removal opportunities through enhanced verification requirements and quality control standards. Accuracy initiatives help identify new removal pressure points.

International coordination in credit reporting standards may affect American consumers through global data sharing, cross-border verification, and international privacy requirements. International trends help anticipate complex removal challenges and opportunities.

Alternative data integration in credit reporting creates new positive reporting opportunities while potentially introducing new negative item categories requiring specialized removal strategies. Alternative data awareness helps anticipate future removal challenges.

Artificial intelligence applications in dispute processing may change how credit bureaus handle removal challenges and how consumers can effectively present removal arguments. AI trends help anticipate strategy adaptation requirements.

Regulatory technology (RegTech) adoption by furnishers may improve compliance and accuracy while creating new removal opportunities through enhanced verification and documentation requirements. RegTech trends help identify emerging removal leverage points.

Consumer education initiatives by regulatory agencies and industry organizations continue improving consumer understanding of removal rights and strategies. Education trends help anticipate improved consumer advocacy capabilities.

Professional service evolution in credit repair includes enhanced service offerings, improved technology integration, and specialized expertise development that may affect removal strategy accessibility and effectiveness. Service evolution helps anticipate professional assistance developments.

Innovation opportunities in removal strategies include novel approaches for emerging credit reporting practices, technology-enhanced removal techniques, and coordinated advocacy efforts that may improve removal effectiveness and accessibility for consumers seeking credit repair assistance.

CHAPTER 13

SECURED CREDIT CARDS AND CREDIT BUILDING

Secured credit cards represent one of the most effective and accessible tools for building or rebuilding credit, providing a pathway to positive credit history for consumers who cannot qualify for traditional unsecured credit cards. Understanding how to select, manage, and optimize secured credit cards can significantly accelerate credit improvement while establishing the foundation for long-term credit success.

The fundamental mechanism of secured credit cards involves depositing money with the card issuer as collateral, which typically becomes your credit limit. This security deposit eliminates the issuer's risk while allowing consumers with poor or no credit history to access credit reporting opportunities that build positive payment history and demonstrate creditworthiness to future lenders.

Modern secured credit cards have evolved far beyond basic deposit-secured accounts to include sophisticated features, graduation pathways, and integration with broader credit building programs. Understanding these advanced features helps optimize secured card selection and utilization for maximum credit building effectiveness.

The credit building power of secured cards stems from their reporting to major credit bureaus as regular credit accounts, without distinguishing them as secured products on credit reports. This means that properly managed secured cards contribute to credit scores exactly like unsecured cards, providing genuine credit building value rather than merely educational benefits.

Strategic secured card utilization goes beyond simple payment compliance to encompass sophisticated credit management techniques including optimal utilization ratios, payment timing strategies, and account management practices that maximize credit score improvement while preparing for graduation to unsecured products.

The secured card market includes diverse options ranging from basic deposit-secured cards to sophisticated products offering rewards, graduation pathways, and integrated financial services. Understanding this diversity helps identify optimal products for specific credit building objectives and financial circumstances.

Timing considerations for secured card applications include understanding how new accounts affect credit scores, coordinating applications with other credit building activities, and optimizing application timing for major financial goals such as mortgage applications or car loans.

Cost-benefit analysis for secured cards involves evaluating fees, deposit requirements, and feature benefits against alternative credit building strategies to ensure that secured cards provide optimal value for specific credit improvement objectives.

The relationship between secured cards and future credit opportunities extends beyond immediate credit building to include establishing banking relationships, demonstrating creditworthiness patterns, and creating foundations for comprehensive financial service access.

Regulatory protections for secured card users include CARD Act provisions, CFPB oversight, and state consumer protection laws that ensure fair treatment and transparent terms for secured card products.

Secured card selection criteria involve comprehensive evaluation of product features, costs, policies, and issuer characteristics that affect both immediate credit building effectiveness and long-term financial benefits. Strategic selection significantly impacts credit building outcomes and overall value.

Deposit requirements vary significantly between secured card products, with some requiring minimum deposits as low as $200 while others accept deposits up to $5,000 or more. Understanding deposit flexibility helps optimize credit limit establishment and account accessibility.

Fee structures for secured cards include annual fees, monthly maintenance fees, application fees, and various transaction charges that significantly affect product value. Comprehensive fee analysis helps identify cards that provide optimal value while minimizing unnecessary costs.

Credit limit policies determine how deposits translate into available credit, with some cards matching deposits dollar-for-dollar while others provide higher credit limits than deposit amounts. Understanding limit policies helps optimize deposit allocation and credit availability.

Reporting practices to credit bureaus vary between secured card issuers, with some reporting to all three major bureaus while others report selectively. Comprehensive reporting ensures maximum credit building benefit and score improvement potential.

Graduation pathways represent crucial secured card features that determine how accounts transition to unsecured status and deposit refund procedures. Strong graduation policies provide clear pathways to unsecured credit without account closure or credit history interruption.

Interest rates and APR terms affect costs for consumers who carry balances, though optimal secured card management typically involves paying balances in full to avoid interest charges while building credit history.

Additional features such as online account management, mobile apps, customer service quality, and financial education resources enhance secured card value and usability for ongoing credit management.

Issuer reputation and stability affect long-term account relationships and service quality, making issuer research important for secured card selection. Established issuers typically provide better service and more reliable graduation pathways.

Product evolution potential includes understanding how secured cards may upgrade to better products or additional services over time, providing pathways for expanded financial relationships and improved benefits.

Geographic and eligibility restrictions may limit secured card availability for some consumers, making alternative option research important for comprehensive selection evaluation.

Integration capabilities with other financial products help establish comprehensive banking relationships that support broader financial goals beyond immediate credit building.

Customer support quality becomes particularly important for secured card users who may need assistance with credit building strategies, account management, and graduation procedures.

Application strategies for secured credit cards involve timing, preparation, and optimization techniques that maximize approval chances while setting up accounts for successful credit building and future graduation opportunities.

Application timing considerations include understanding how new credit applications affect credit scores, coordinating secured card applications with other credit activities, and optimizing timing for major financial decisions requiring strong credit profiles.

Documentation preparation for secured card applications involves gathering required identification, income verification, and banking information that streamlines application processing and prevents delays or rejections due to incomplete submissions.

Income considerations for secured card applications include understanding how issuers evaluate income relative to credit limits and how to present income information that supports application approval and optimal credit limit establishment.

Bank relationship advantages may provide benefits for consumers applying for secured cards from existing banking providers, including expedited processing, fee reductions, or enhanced product features for established customers.

Multiple application strategies involve understanding when applying for multiple secured cards simultaneously makes sense versus sequential applications that build credit history progressively.

Denial response procedures help address situations where secured card applications are rejected despite adequate deposits, including appeal processes, alternative issuer options, and application improvement strategies.

Credit limit optimization involves maximizing initial credit limits through appropriate deposit amounts while balancing account costs and credit utilization management requirements.

Account setup procedures include establishing automatic payments, online account access, and monitoring systems that support effective ongoing account management and credit building.

Initial utilization planning involves determining optimal initial spending and payment patterns that establish positive credit history while demonstrating responsible credit management to the issuer.

Communication establishment with card issuers creates relationships that support account management, graduation timeline discussions, and problem resolution when issues arise.

Integration planning with existing financial accounts helps establish comprehensive money management systems that support secured card success and broader financial goal achievement.

Security considerations for secured card accounts include protecting account information, monitoring for unauthorized activity, and establishing fraud protection procedures that safeguard deposits and credit history.

Optimal utilization strategies for secured credit cards focus on credit building techniques that maximize positive credit reporting while demonstrating creditworthiness patterns that support graduation to unsecured products and future credit opportunities.

Utilization ratio management represents the most critical secured card strategy, involving maintaining low balance-to-limit ratios that optimize credit scores while providing sufficient account activity to demonstrate active credit management.

The 30% utilization threshold serves as a maximum guideline, but optimal secured card utilization typically involves keeping balances below 10% of credit limits for maximum score benefit. Understanding utilization impact helps optimize credit building effectiveness.

Statement balance versus current balance timing affects credit reporting and score calculations, making payment timing strategies important for managing reported utilization ratios independent of actual spending patterns.

Multiple payment strategies can help maintain low reported utilization while using secured cards for regular spending, including mid-cycle payments, early payments, and balance spreading techniques across different reporting periods.

Purchase diversification demonstrates responsible credit management across different spending categories while avoiding patterns that might suggest cash advance usage or other risky behaviors that could affect graduation prospects.

Payment history perfection requires establishing automatic payment systems and backup procedures that ensure 100% on-time payment performance, as payment history represents the most important credit scoring factor.

Account activity consistency involves maintaining regular but reasonable account usage that demonstrates ongoing creditworthiness without appearing dependent on credit or engaging in risky spending patterns.

Limit increase strategies help expand available credit over time through responsible usage demonstration, request procedures, and additional deposit options that enhance credit building potential.

Cross-bureau optimization ensures that secured card benefits extend across all three major credit bureaus through issuer reporting verification and dispute procedures when reporting inconsistencies occur.

Credit building timeline understanding helps establish realistic expectations for secured card credit improvement and graduation timing based on usage patterns and issuer policies.

Integration with other credit building activities ensures that secured card management supports broader credit improvement strategies without conflicts or counterproductive account management decisions.

Graduation preparation involves establishing usage patterns and account management practices that position accounts for successful transition to unsecured status when eligibility requirements are met.

Payment timing and balance management techniques for secured credit cards involve sophisticated strategies that optimize credit reporting while minimizing costs and maximizing credit building effectiveness through strategic account management.

Reporting date identification involves understanding when secured card issuers report account information to credit bureaus, typically occurring monthly on specific dates that determine what balance and payment information appears on credit reports.

Payment timing optimization involves scheduling payments relative to reporting dates to ensure that credit reports reflect optimal utilization ratios regardless of actual spending patterns or payment convenience preferences.

Zero balance reporting strategies can provide maximum credit score benefits by ensuring that one or more secured cards report zero balances while maintaining activity on other accounts to demonstrate ongoing credit management.

Multiple payment techniques include making several payments per month to manage utilization, spreading payments across different weeks to optimize cash flow, and using early payments to reduce reported balances before statement closing dates.

Statement date manipulation through payment timing allows consumers to control reported balances independently of actual spending by ensuring that payments post before statement generation and credit bureau reporting.

Autopay optimization involves setting up automatic payments that ensure perfect payment history while maintaining flexibility for additional payments that optimize utilization reporting and credit building effectiveness.

Balance distribution across multiple secured cards helps optimize utilization reporting by spreading balances to keep individual card utilization low while maintaining aggregate credit utilization within optimal ranges.

Cash flow coordination with secured card payments ensures that payment strategies support overall financial management while optimizing credit building without creating budgetary strain or financial instability.

Emergency payment procedures provide backup systems for ensuring payment timeliness when automatic systems fail or when unexpected circumstances affect normal payment processing.

Interest minimization strategies help avoid finance charges through balance management and payment timing while maintaining credit building effectiveness for consumers who occasionally carry balances.

Credit limit cycling involves understanding how payment timing affects available credit for ongoing spending while maintaining optimal utilization ratios throughout monthly cycles.

Monitoring and adjustment procedures help track payment effectiveness and optimize strategies based on credit report updates and score changes resulting from different payment timing approaches.

Graduation pathways and unsecured conversion represent the ultimate goal of secured credit card strategies, involving understanding issuer policies, qualification requirements, and optimization techniques that facilitate transition to unsecured credit without account closure or credit history interruption.

Graduation timeline expectations vary significantly between secured card issuers, with some providing conversion opportunities after six months of responsible use while others require twelve to eighteen months or more before considering unsecured conversion.

Qualification criteria for graduation typically include consistent payment history, appropriate utilization management, stable income demonstration, and overall creditworthiness improvement that satisfies issuer requirements for unsecured credit extension.

Automatic versus manual graduation processes differ between issuers, with some cards providing automatic conversion when criteria are met while others require consumer requests or applications for unsecured conversion consideration.

Credit score requirements for graduation may involve specific score thresholds that consumers must achieve before becoming eligible for unsecured conversion, making score monitoring and improvement crucial for graduation timing.

Income verification for graduation may require updated income documentation or employment verification that demonstrates ability to handle unsecured credit responsibilities without collateral protection.

Account history evaluation for graduation includes issuer review of payment patterns, utilization management, and overall account relationship quality that influences graduation approval and conversion terms.

Deposit refund procedures vary between graduation programs, with some providing immediate deposit return upon conversion while others may require waiting periods or specific account performance after conversion.

Credit limit determination for graduated accounts may differ from original secured limits, with some issuers maintaining existing limits while others reassess appropriate credit limits based on current creditworthiness.

Alternative product options during graduation may include opportunities to convert to different unsecured cards with better features, rewards programs, or terms than direct conversion of existing secured accounts.

Graduation acceleration techniques include strategies for optimizing account management to meet graduation criteria more quickly while maintaining account health and demonstrating consistent creditworthiness.

Relationship building with issuers throughout the secured card period helps establish positive customer relationships that may influence graduation decisions and conversion opportunities.

Post-graduation account management involves transitioning from secured card strategies to unsecured credit management while maintaining the positive credit building momentum established during the secured card period.

Secured card fees and cost optimization involve understanding the comprehensive cost structure of secured credit products and implementing strategies that minimize unnecessary expenses while maximizing value from secured card credit building investments.

Annual fee evaluation requires comparing fee amounts against card benefits, graduation pathways, and alternative product options to ensure that annual fees provide appropriate value for credit building objectives and account features.

Monthly maintenance fees represent ongoing costs that can significantly impact secured card value over time, making fee-free alternatives important considerations for long-term credit building strategies.

Application fee assessment involves understanding one-time charges for account establishment and comparing these costs against alternative secured card options that may offer similar benefits without application fees.

Security deposit opportunity costs include understanding how deposit amounts could earn returns in savings accounts, investments, or other financial products versus remaining on deposit with card issuers.

Transaction fee analysis covers charges for cash advances, foreign transactions, overlimit fees, and other usage-based costs that can be minimized through strategic account management and usage pattern optimization.

Late payment fee avoidance through automatic payment systems and backup procedures helps eliminate unnecessary costs while maintaining perfect payment history for credit building effectiveness.

Cost comparison methodologies help evaluate total secured card costs against alternative credit building strategies to ensure optimal value and resource allocation for credit improvement objectives.

Fee negotiation opportunities may exist with some secured card issuers, particularly for existing banking customers or consumers with improving credit profiles that justify fee reductions or elimination.

Upgrade cost considerations involve understanding how graduation to unsecured products affects ongoing account costs and whether conversion provides appropriate value improvement to justify continued account maintenance.

Alternative product evaluation includes comparing secured card costs against other credit building options such as credit builder loans, authorized user positions, or alternative credit cards with different cost structures.

Long-term cost projection involves calculating total secured card expenses over expected usage periods to ensure that credit building benefits justify ongoing financial commitments.

Value optimization strategies help maximize secured card benefits while minimizing costs through strategic usage, fee avoidance, and upgrade planning that optimizes return on credit building investments.

Advanced secured card strategies involve sophisticated techniques that maximize credit building effectiveness while preparing for comprehensive credit portfolio development and optimal integration with broader financial planning objectives.

Multiple secured card coordination involves strategically managing several secured cards simultaneously to optimize credit building through increased available credit, diversified account types, and enhanced payment history development across multiple tradelines.

Issuer diversification through multiple secured cards from different financial institutions provides broader banking relationships, varied graduation pathways, and reduced dependence on single issuer policies or problems.

Credit mix optimization includes using secured cards alongside other credit building tools such as credit builder loans, authorized user accounts, and store credit cards to create comprehensive credit profiles that demonstrate diverse credit management capabilities.

Balance distribution strategies across multiple secured cards help optimize utilization reporting by maintaining low individual card utilization while maximizing aggregate credit availability and account activity demonstration.

Graduation timing coordination involves planning secured card conversions strategically to maintain continuous credit building momentum while optimizing overall credit profile development and future credit opportunities.

Advanced payment strategies include sophisticated timing techniques that optimize credit reporting across multiple cards while minimizing administrative complexity and maintaining perfect payment performance across all accounts.

Relationship building with multiple issuers creates diverse banking connections that support future credit opportunities while providing backup options when problems arise with individual secured card accounts.

Credit limit expansion techniques involve strategic deposit increases, usage demonstration, and relationship development that maximize available credit while maintaining optimal utilization ratios across expanded credit lines.

Integration with investment strategies may include coordinating secured card deposits with broader investment planning to optimize returns while maintaining credit building effectiveness and graduation pathway progress.

Professional credit profile development through advanced secured card management demonstrates sophisticated financial management that supports future credit applications and business credit development opportunities.

Portfolio transition planning involves preparing for graduation from secured cards to comprehensive unsecured credit portfolios while maintaining credit building momentum and optimizing long-term credit management strategies.

Mastery demonstration through advanced secured card management provides foundation skills and knowledge that support broader credit management excellence and financial planning sophistication throughout changing life circumstances.

Secured card troubleshooting addresses common problems and challenges that arise during secured card management while providing systematic solutions that protect credit building progress and account relationships.

Application denial resolution involves understanding reasons for secured card rejections and implementing corrective strategies that address underlying issues while pursuing alternative credit building options.

Deposit processing delays can affect account establishment and credit building timeline, requiring follow-up procedures and alternative planning that maintains credit improvement momentum during processing delays.

Reporting inconsistencies between credit bureaus require monitoring and dispute procedures that ensure secured cards provide comprehensive credit building benefits across all major credit reporting agencies.

Graduation denial responses include understanding issuer reasons for refusing unsecured conversion and implementing improvement strategies that address deficiencies while maintaining account health and credit building progress.

Account closure threats may arise from issuer policy changes or account management issues, requiring negotiation strategies and alternative planning that protect established credit history and relationships.

Limit decrease problems can affect utilization ratios and available credit, requiring response strategies that address issuer concerns while maintaining optimal credit management and building effectiveness.

Customer service problems with secured card issuers require escalation procedures and relationship management that resolve issues while protecting account status and credit building benefits.

Fee increase notifications require evaluation and response strategies that protect account value while considering alternative options and negotiation opportunities for fee reduction or elimination.

Credit report error correction for secured card information involves dispute procedures and issuer coordination that ensure accurate reporting supports rather than undermines credit building objectives.

Identity theft protection for secured card accounts includes monitoring procedures and response systems that protect deposits and credit history from fraudulent activity while maintaining account security.

Account management system failures require backup procedures and alternative access methods that maintain payment timeliness and account monitoring during technical problems or system outages.

Problem escalation procedures help resolve complex secured card issues through appropriate channels while maintaining relationships and protecting

credit building investments when standard customer service proves inadequate.

Integration with comprehensive credit building involves coordinating secured card strategies with other credit improvement activities to create systematic approaches that optimize overall credit development while supporting broader financial planning objectives.

Credit builder loan coordination with secured cards creates complementary credit building that demonstrates diverse credit management while maximizing tradeline development and payment history establishment across different account types.

Authorized user strategy integration involves timing secured card applications and management with authorized user opportunities to optimize credit building while avoiding negative interactions between different credit building approaches.

Alternative credit reporting integration includes leveraging services that report rent, utilities, and other payments to credit bureaus while maintaining secured card management for comprehensive credit profile development.

Debt consolidation coordination ensures that secured card strategies support broader debt management objectives while optimizing credit utilization and payment history across all credit obligations.

Credit monitoring integration provides systematic oversight of secured card progress while tracking overall credit improvement across multiple credit building activities and credit repair efforts.

Budget planning integration ensures that secured card management supports overall financial planning while optimizing credit building within available resources and broader financial objectives.

Goal timeline coordination aligns secured card strategies with major financial milestones such as mortgage applications, business loans, or other credit-dependent objectives that require strategic timing and preparation.

Professional assistance coordination involves working effectively with credit counselors, financial advisors, and other professionals while maintaining secured card management excellence and integrated credit building strategies.

Emergency planning integration includes incorporating secured card management into broader financial emergency procedures while maintaining credit building effectiveness during unexpected financial difficulties.

Long-term financial planning integration ensures that secured card strategies support wealth building, retirement planning, and other long-term objectives while optimizing immediate credit improvement benefits.

Education and skill development integration includes ongoing learning about credit management excellence while implementing secured card strategies that demonstrate and develop advanced financial management capabilities.

Success measurement integration involves tracking secured card effectiveness within broader credit improvement evaluation while optimizing resource allocation and strategy refinement across comprehensive credit building activities.

Secured card industry trends and innovations include emerging product features, regulatory developments, and market changes that affect secured card selection, management, and credit building effectiveness for consumers seeking optimal credit improvement strategies.

Product innovation in secured cards includes new features such as rewards programs, cashback opportunities, and enhanced digital banking integration that provide additional value while maintaining credit building effectiveness.

Graduation pathway improvements by secured card issuers include faster conversion timelines, automatic upgrade procedures, and enhanced unsecured product options that optimize consumer benefits from secured card relationships.

Technology integration enhancements include mobile app improvements, digital payment integration, and automated account management tools that optimize secured card usability while supporting effective credit building strategies.

Regulatory development impacts include CFPB oversight enhancements, CARD Act implementation improvements, and state consumer protection developments that strengthen secured card consumer protections and transparency.

Market competition increases among secured card issuers continue improving consumer options through reduced fees, enhanced features, and better graduation pathways that optimize secured card value and accessibility.

Alternative credit integration includes secured card issuer adoption of alternative credit data, rent reporting, and other non-traditional credit information that enhances credit building effectiveness and graduation qualification.

Financial education integration by secured card issuers includes enhanced consumer education programs, credit building guidance, and financial literacy resources that support optimal secured card management and broader financial success.

Fintech innovation in secured card products includes new technology applications, alternative verification methods, and innovative credit building features that expand secured card accessibility and effectiveness.

Banking integration trends include secured card incorporation into comprehensive banking relationships with enhanced cross-selling, relationship benefits, and integrated financial service offerings.

International expansion of secured card options includes products for immigrants, international students, and consumers with foreign credit history that address specialized credit building needs and circumstances.

Environmental and social responsibility features in secured card products include sustainable materials, social impact programs, and responsible lending practices that align with consumer values while maintaining credit building effectiveness.

Future development anticipation includes emerging trends in credit reporting, scoring, and lending that will affect secured card value and strategy while creating new opportunities for credit building and financial development.

Professional secured card management involves developing expertise and systematic approaches that optimize secured card benefits while building foundation skills for comprehensive credit management throughout changing financial circumstances and evolving credit needs.

Expertise development in secured card management includes understanding product complexities, optimization strategies, and advanced techniques that maximize credit building effectiveness while preparing for broader credit management challenges.

Systematic approach implementation involves creating organized procedures for secured card selection, management, and optimization that ensure consistent results while supporting broader financial planning and credit development objectives.

Performance measurement systems help track secured card effectiveness through comprehensive metrics that evaluate credit building progress, cost optimization, and goal achievement while identifying improvement opportunities and strategy refinement needs.

Quality control procedures ensure that secured card management maintains high standards while adapting to changing circumstances and continuing to support credit building objectives throughout different life stages and financial situations.

Strategic thinking development through secured card management provides foundation skills for broader financial planning while demonstrating analytical capabilities and systematic approach implementation that supports comprehensive financial success.

Relationship management skills developed through secured card issuer interactions provide valuable experience for broader financial relationship development while building communication and negotiation capabilities that support ongoing financial management.

Problem-solving capability development through secured card challenge resolution provides experience and skills that transfer to broader financial problem-solving while building confidence and competence in financial management situations.

Professional network development through secured card relationships may include banking connections, financial advisor relationships, and industry knowledge that supports broader financial planning and credit management excellence.

Teaching and mentoring opportunities may arise from secured card expertise that enables helping others while building leadership capabilities and contributing to broader financial literacy and consumer protection efforts.

Innovation capacity through secured card strategy development provides experience in financial innovation and optimization that supports broader financial planning creativity while building adaptability for changing financial environments.

Legacy planning considerations include understanding how secured card expertise and relationships contribute to long-term financial success while building capabilities that support sustained financial excellence throughout changing circumstances.

Mastery achievement in secured card management represents comprehensive understanding and capability that provides foundation for broader credit management excellence while demonstrating financial management sophistication that supports comprehensive financial success and professional development opportunities.

Secured card mastery integration with broader financial planning ensures that credit building expertise supports comprehensive wealth development while optimizing secured card benefits within broader financial management strategies and long-term goal achievement.

Wealth building integration includes understanding how secured card credit building supports broader financial goal achievement through improved credit access, reduced borrowing costs, and enhanced financial opportunity availability that multiplies wealth building effectiveness.

Investment planning coordination ensures that secured card strategies complement investment activities while optimizing deposit allocation and graduation timing to support broader financial portfolio development and return optimization.

Business credit development integration includes using secured card expertise as foundation for business credit building while establishing personal credit excellence that supports entrepreneurial activities and business financing opportunities.

Real estate financing preparation through secured card credit building provides foundation for mortgage qualification while optimizing credit profiles for real estate investment and homeownership opportunity achievement.

Insurance optimization through credit improvement via secured cards helps reduce insurance costs while improving coverage availability and supporting comprehensive risk management planning for financial protection and wealth preservation.

Retirement planning integration includes understanding how secured card credit building supports retirement financing opportunities while optimizing long-term financial security through improved credit access and reduced borrowing costs throughout retirement.

Education financing optimization through secured card credit building supports educational investment opportunities while providing foundation for family education planning and human capital development through improved credit access.

Emergency planning integration includes incorporating secured card management into comprehensive financial emergency procedures while maintaining credit building effectiveness during unexpected circumstances and financial challenges.

Professional development support through secured card expertise may include consulting opportunities, educational activities, and industry involvement that leverage credit management knowledge for professional advancement and income enhancement.

Tax planning coordination ensures that secured card strategies support tax optimization while understanding tax implications of credit improvement and financial planning integration for comprehensive tax efficiency achievement.

Estate planning integration includes understanding how secured card credit building supports estate development while optimizing long-term wealth transfer planning and family financial security through improved credit management and financial capability development.

Impact measurement for secured card mastery involves evaluating comprehensive benefits including credit improvement, financial capability development, wealth building enhancement, and professional development achievement that optimize long-term value from secured card expertise and financial management mastery.

Secured card evolution and future opportunities include understanding emerging trends, regulatory developments, and market innovations that will affect secured card value while creating new credit building opportunities and optimization strategies for evolving financial environments.

Technology advancement in secured card products includes artificial intelligence applications, blockchain verification systems, and digital integration enhancements that will improve credit building effectiveness while creating new management opportunities and optimization strategies.

Regulatory evolution in secured card oversight includes enhanced consumer protections, improved transparency requirements, and strengthened graduation pathway standards that will benefit consumers while creating new optimization opportunities and protection mechanisms.

Market expansion in secured card accessibility includes products for underserved populations, international consumers, and specialized circumstances that will broaden credit building opportunities while addressing diverse consumer needs and financial situations.

Integration innovation with other financial products includes secured card coordination with investment accounts, savings programs, and comprehensive banking relationships that will enhance value while supporting broader financial planning integration.

Alternative credit integration includes secured card coordination with rent reporting, utility payment credit building, and other emerging credit building opportunities that will enhance effectiveness while providing comprehensive credit profile development.

Financial education enhancement through secured card programs includes expanded consumer education, financial literacy integration, and decision-making support that will improve consumer outcomes while building financial capability and management excellence.

Sustainability and responsibility trends in secured card products include environmental considerations, social impact programs, and ethical lending practices that will align with consumer values while maintaining credit building effectiveness.

Global expansion of secured card opportunities includes international products, cross-border credit building, and global financial integration that will address increasingly global consumer needs while providing expanded opportunities for credit development.

Innovation anticipation in credit building includes emerging technologies, new credit scoring methods, and alternative credit assessment approaches that will affect secured card value while creating new optimization opportunities and strategic considerations.

Professional development opportunities through secured card expertise include consulting, education, and advocacy activities that will leverage credit building knowledge while contributing to broader consumer protection and financial literacy advancement.

Community impact potential through secured card expertise includes helping others achieve credit building success while contributing to broader financial inclusion and consumer protection efforts that benefit communities and society.

Future mastery development in secured card strategies includes continuous learning, adaptation capability, and innovation capacity that will maintain effectiveness while building comprehensive financial management excellence that supports long-term success and professional development throughout changing financial environments and evolving consumer needs.

Secured card program evaluation and selection criteria involve comprehensive assessment methodologies that optimize secured card choice while ensuring alignment with individual credit building objectives, financial circumstances, and long-term planning goals.

Comparative analysis frameworks help evaluate multiple secured card options through systematic comparison of features, costs, benefits, and graduation pathways that ensure optimal product selection for specific credit building objectives and financial situations.

Due diligence procedures for secured card selection include issuer research, product feature verification, customer review analysis, and regulatory standing evaluation that ensure reliable product selection and avoid problematic issuers or products.

Cost-benefit modeling for secured card evaluation includes comprehensive analysis of fees, deposit requirements, opportunity costs, and credit building benefits that ensure optimal value and resource allocation for credit improvement investments.

Feature prioritization methodologies help identify which secured card characteristics are most important for individual circumstances while balancing immediate needs against long-term optimization objectives and graduation pathway requirements.

Risk assessment procedures for secured card selection include evaluation of issuer stability, product policy risks, and potential problems that could affect credit building effectiveness or account relationship quality over time.

Timeline coordination for secured card implementation includes understanding how product selection timing affects credit building objectives while optimizing coordination with other credit building activities and major financial goals.

Integration planning for secured card selection ensures that product choice supports broader financial planning while optimizing coordination with existing financial relationships and comprehensive wealth building strategies.

Performance projection methodologies help estimate secured card effectiveness for specific circumstances while setting realistic expectations and optimization targets for credit building progress and goal achievement.

Alternative evaluation includes comparing secured cards against other credit building options to ensure that secured card selection provides optimal value compared to credit builder loans, authorized user opportunities, or other credit building alternatives.

Professional consultation evaluation includes understanding when expert assistance becomes valuable for secured card selection while balancing consultation costs against selection optimization benefits and expertise access value.

Decision-making frameworks help organize secured card evaluation and selection processes while ensuring systematic consideration of all relevant factors and optimization of product choice for maximum credit building effectiveness and value achievement.

Secured card account management excellence involves implementing systematic procedures and optimization techniques that maximize credit building effectiveness while maintaining account health and preparing for successful graduation to unsecured credit opportunities.

Daily management routines for secured cards include spending monitoring, balance tracking, and payment scheduling that optimize credit building while maintaining account control and preventing problems that could affect credit improvement progress.

Weekly monitoring procedures include account balance verification, payment confirmation, and credit report tracking that ensure secured card effectiveness while identifying problems early when correction opportunities are optimal for maintaining credit building momentum.

Monthly optimization activities include utilization analysis, payment timing evaluation, and account performance assessment that optimize credit building effectiveness while identifying improvement opportunities and strategy refinement needs.

Quarterly performance evaluation includes comprehensive assessment of credit building progress, cost analysis, and graduation pathway advancement that ensure secured card strategies remain aligned with objectives while adapting to changing circumstances.

Annual strategic review includes secured card relationship evaluation, market comparison, and goal alignment assessment that optimize long-term secured card value while planning for graduation and transition to advanced credit management strategies.

Problem prevention procedures include fraud monitoring, account security maintenance, and relationship management that protect secured card investments while ensuring consistent credit building effectiveness and account stability.

Emergency response protocols include procedures for handling account problems, payment processing issues, and issuer relationship challenges that protect credit building progress while maintaining account status during difficult circumstances.

Documentation organization for secured card management includes record keeping for deposits, payments, correspondence, and account changes that support effective management while providing evidence for problem resolution when necessary.

Communication management with secured card issuers includes relationship building, customer service optimization, and escalation procedures that ensure effective account management while building positive relationships that support graduation and optimization opportunities.

Integration maintenance with broader financial planning ensures that secured card management continues supporting comprehensive financial objectives while adapting to changing circumstances and evolving financial goals throughout different life stages.

Continuous improvement implementation includes ongoing optimization of secured card strategies based on experience, results, and changing circumstances while maintaining effectiveness and adapting to new opportunities for enhanced credit building and account management.

Excellence measurement for secured card management includes comprehensive evaluation of account performance, credit building effectiveness, and goal achievement that ensure optimal value while identifying mastery development opportunities and strategic enhancement potential.

Secured card graduation optimization involves strategic preparation and execution techniques that maximize conversion success while ensuring optimal transition to unsecured credit without interruption of credit building momentum or relationship benefits.

Pre-graduation preparation includes establishing qualification criteria understanding, account performance optimization, and relationship building with issuers that enhance graduation prospects while ensuring readiness for unsecured credit management responsibilities.

Qualification timeline tracking involves monitoring progress toward graduation requirements while optimizing account management to meet criteria efficiently and positioning accounts for favorable conversion consideration when eligibility is achieved.

Documentation compilation for graduation includes gathering income verification, account performance records, and supporting information that strengthens graduation applications while demonstrating creditworthiness improvement and management capability.

Communication strategy for graduation includes timing requests appropriately, presenting qualification effectively, and building issuer relationships that support favorable conversion decisions while maintaining professional interaction and account relationship quality.

Alternative evaluation during graduation includes assessing conversion options, upgrade possibilities, and alternative product opportunities that optimize post-graduation account benefits while maintaining credit building momentum and relationship value.

Negotiation techniques for graduation terms include optimizing credit limits, fee structures, and product features while ensuring favorable conversion terms that support continued credit building and enhanced account benefits.

Backup planning for graduation includes preparing alternative strategies when conversion requests are denied while maintaining account health and continuing credit building progress through alternative approaches and timeline extension.

Post-graduation optimization includes account management transition, deposit recovery procedures, and ongoing relationship development that maximize unsecured credit benefits while building foundation for advanced credit management strategies.

Credit building continuation after graduation includes leveraging improved credit status for additional credit opportunities while maintaining account management excellence and continuing credit profile development through enhanced credit access.

Relationship leverage from graduation includes utilizing successful conversion for additional banking services, credit products, and financial relationship enhancement that extends beyond initial secured card benefits to comprehensive financial service access.

Success measurement for graduation includes evaluating conversion outcomes, account benefit improvement, and continued credit building effectiveness that ensure graduation provides intended benefits while supporting broader financial planning objectives.

Mastery demonstration through graduation success provides evidence of credit management capability while building confidence and expertise that supports advanced credit management and comprehensive financial planning excellence throughout changing financial circumstances.

Advanced secured card techniques involve sophisticated strategies that leverage deep understanding of credit building mechanics, issuer operations, and credit scoring optimization to achieve maximum credit improvement effectiveness and accelerated graduation success.

Credit scoring optimization through secured card management includes understanding score calculation nuances, timing strategies, and account management techniques that maximize score improvement while building strong credit profiles that support future credit opportunities.

Multi-bureau optimization ensures that secured card benefits extend across all major credit reporting agencies through strategic account management, reporting verification, and dispute procedures that optimize comprehensive credit building effectiveness.

Account aging acceleration involves strategies that maximize credit history benefits from secured cards while building account age that supports credit scoring and demonstrates long-term credit management capability and stability.

Credit mix enhancement through secured card coordination with other credit types creates comprehensive credit profiles that demonstrate diverse credit management while optimizing scoring factors and creditworthiness demonstration.

Issuer relationship leverage involves building positive relationships with secured card providers that support graduation, additional credit opportunities, and enhanced banking services while demonstrating professional financial management and customer value.

Advanced utilization strategies include sophisticated balance management, payment timing, and credit limit optimization that maximize credit building while demonstrating optimal credit management patterns and financial sophistication.

Rapid graduation techniques involve accelerated qualification strategies, performance optimization, and relationship building that expedite conversion to unsecured credit while maintaining account health and building strong creditworthiness demonstration.

Portfolio integration includes coordinating secured cards with other credit building activities, investment strategies, and financial planning that optimize comprehensive financial development while supporting broader wealth building and financial goal achievement.

Risk management for advanced strategies includes understanding potential complications, implementing safeguards, and maintaining account protection while pursuing aggressive optimization techniques that maximize credit building effectiveness.

Innovation development through secured card mastery includes creating novel approaches, optimization techniques, and strategic applications that enhance credit building effectiveness while building financial innovation capability and management excellence.

Professional application of secured card expertise includes consulting opportunities, educational activities, and advisory services that leverage credit building knowledge while contributing to broader consumer protection and financial literacy advancement.

Mastery integration with comprehensive financial planning ensures that secured card expertise supports broader financial success while optimizing credit building benefits within comprehensive wealth development and long-term financial security achievement strategies.

Technology integration for secured card management involves leveraging digital tools, automation, and monitoring systems to optimize credit building effectiveness while enhancing account management efficiency and security throughout the secured card journey.

Digital account management platforms provided by secured card issuers include mobile apps, online banking systems, and automated tools that enhance account control while supporting optimal credit building through convenient access and management capabilities.

Automated payment systems help ensure perfect payment history while optimizing utilization reporting through strategic payment timing and balance management that supports credit building without requiring constant manual account oversight.

Credit monitoring integration includes real-time tracking of secured card impact on credit scores and reports while providing early identification of problems or opportunities that optimize credit building effectiveness and account management.

Budgeting app integration helps coordinate secured card management with broader financial planning while ensuring that credit building activities support rather than compromise overall financial stability and goal achievement.

Alert systems for secured card management include notifications for payment due dates, balance thresholds, and account changes that help maintain optimal account management while preventing problems that could affect credit building progress.

Mobile optimization for secured card access includes smartphone and tablet integration that supports convenient account management while maintaining security and enabling real-time monitoring and optimization of credit building activities.

These tools help track secured card performance through data analysis that identifies optimization opportunities while measuring credit building effectiveness and supporting strategic decision-making for account management enhancement.

Security technologies for secured card protection include fraud monitoring, identity verification, and account security systems that protect deposits and credit building investments while maintaining account integrity and preventing unauthorized access.

Integration platforms that connect secured cards with other financial accounts help optimize overall financial management while ensuring that credit building activities coordinate effectively with broader financial planning and wealth building strategies.

Backup systems for technology failures include manual procedures and alternative access methods that maintain account management effectiveness during system outages while protecting credit building momentum and payment timeliness.

Future technology adoption planning includes staying current with emerging digital tools and capabilities that can enhance secured card management while maintaining competitive advantages in credit building and financial management excellence.

Privacy protection in technology integration ensures that digital tool usage maintains financial information security while optimizing convenience and effectiveness of secured card management through appropriate technology utilization.

Secured card success measurement and optimization involves comprehensive evaluation methodologies that assess credit building effectiveness while identifying improvement opportunities and ensuring that secured card investments produce maximum value and long-term benefit.

Performance metrics for secured card evaluation include credit score improvement tracking, account management quality assessment, and goal achievement measurement that provide comprehensive understanding of secured card effectiveness and optimization opportunities.

Timeline analysis for secured card progress helps evaluate improvement pace while identifying factors that accelerate or delay credit building success, enabling optimization of strategies and realistic expectation setting for graduation and credit improvement.

Cost-effectiveness evaluation includes measuring secured card expenses against credit building benefits while comparing alternative strategies to ensure optimal resource allocation and maximum value achievement from credit building investments.

Credit score correlation analysis helps understand which secured card management techniques produce the greatest score improvements while optimizing strategy selection and account management practices for maximum scoring benefit.

Benchmark establishment for secured card performance provides standards for evaluating success while identifying areas requiring improvement and ensuring that secured card management maintains high effectiveness levels throughout the credit building process.

Continuous improvement procedures include regular strategy review, outcome analysis, and approach refinement based on results and changing circumstances while maintaining secured card effectiveness and adapting to optimization opportunities.

Success factor identification involves analyzing positive outcomes to understand which approaches, timing factors, and management techniques contribute most significantly to secured card success, enabling replication of effective strategies.

Documentation analysis for secured card management includes evaluating record-keeping effectiveness, evidence quality, and information organization that supports optimal account management while providing foundation for problem resolution when necessary.

Goal alignment assessment ensures that secured card activities continue supporting broader financial objectives while adapting to changing circumstances and maintaining relevance for comprehensive financial planning and wealth building strategies.

Integration effectiveness evaluation includes assessing how secured card management coordinates with other financial activities while identifying optimization opportunities for enhanced coordination and comprehensive financial management improvement.

Professional development measurement through secured card expertise includes evaluating skill development, knowledge advancement, and capability building that result from secured card mastery while identifying opportunities for expertise expansion and professional growth.

Long-term value assessment for secured card investments includes comprehensive evaluation of credit building benefits, relationship development, and foundation building for advanced financial management that optimize secured card value throughout changing financial circumstances and evolving credit needs.

CHAPTER 14

AUTHORIZED USER AND PIGGYBACKING STRATEGIES

Authorized user strategies represent one of the most accessible and potentially powerful credit building techniques available to consumers seeking rapid credit improvement. By becoming an authorized user on someone else's credit account, you can benefit from their positive payment history, credit utilization, and account age, often resulting in immediate and significant credit score improvements.

The fundamental mechanism of authorized user benefits stems from credit scoring models that typically include authorized user accounts in credit score calculations exactly like primary accounts. This means that a well-managed authorized user relationship can provide substantial credit building benefits without requiring independent credit qualification or account management responsibility.

Understanding the distinction between authorized users and account co-signers is crucial for optimizing benefits while avoiding unintended responsibilities. Authorized users typically have no legal liability for account debts, while co-signers assume full legal responsibility for account obligations. This distinction makes authorized user status attractive for credit building without debt exposure.

The credit scoring impact of authorized user accounts varies between scoring models, with some versions giving full weight to authorized user accounts while others reduce their impact compared to primary accounts. Understanding these variations helps optimize authorized user strategies for maximum benefit across different scoring scenarios.

Strategic authorized user relationships require careful selection of accounts and account holders that provide optimal credit building benefits while maintaining positive relationships and avoiding potential complications. The quality of the primary account holder's credit management directly affects authorized user benefits.

Modern authorized user strategies have evolved beyond family relationships to include professional services, strategic partnerships, and comprehensive credit building programs that provide authorized user opportunities for consumers without family members who qualify as suitable account holders.

The timing of authorized user account addition and removal requires strategic planning to optimize credit building while avoiding negative impacts during critical credit evaluation periods. Understanding optimal timing helps maximize authorized user benefits for major financial decisions.

Legal and regulatory frameworks governing authorized user relationships include consumer protection requirements, disclosure obligations, and dispute rights that protect authorized users while ensuring fair treatment and transparency in authorized user arrangements.

Risk management for authorized user strategies involves understanding potential negative consequences and implementing safeguards that protect credit profiles while maximizing benefits from authorized user relationships.

The intersection of authorized user strategies with other credit building techniques creates opportunities for comprehensive approaches that leverage multiple credit building methods simultaneously for accelerated credit improvement.

How authorized user accounts work involves understanding the technical mechanisms through which credit bureaus receive, process, and report authorized user information, creating the foundation for effective authorized user strategy development and optimization.

Credit bureau reporting for authorized user accounts typically occurs automatically when primary account holders add authorized users to their accounts. Most major credit card issuers report authorized user information to all three major credit bureaus, though reporting practices can vary between issuers and account types.

Account history inclusion for authorized users often extends back to account opening dates, meaning that newly added authorized users can immediately benefit from years of positive payment history and account aging that would otherwise take years to establish independently.

Payment history transfer represents one of the most valuable authorized user benefits, as authorized users typically receive credit for the primary account holder's payment performance throughout the account's history. This can provide immediate payment history establishment for consumers with limited credit files.

Credit utilization benefits for authorized users include access to the primary account's credit limit and balance information for credit score calculations. Low utilization on the primary account can significantly improve authorized user credit scores, while high utilization can have negative effects.

Account age advantages from authorized user relationships can provide substantial credit score benefits since account age represents a significant scoring factor. Adding authorized users to old, well-managed accounts can immediately improve their average account age calculations.

Credit limit access through authorized user status increases total available credit for credit score calculations, potentially improving utilization ratios across the authorized user's entire credit profile even when the authorized user doesn't actually use the account.

Issuer policy variations affect authorized user reporting, with some credit card companies providing more comprehensive reporting than others. Understanding issuer differences helps optimize authorized user account selection for maximum credit building benefit.

Scoring model differences in authorized user treatment create varying benefits depending on which credit scores are used for specific credit applications. Some scoring models give full weight to authorized user accounts while others apply limitations or restrictions.

International considerations for authorized user accounts include understanding how foreign credit accounts might affect domestic credit reporting and how authorized user strategies work across different credit reporting systems and national boundaries.

Technology impacts on authorized user reporting include real-time reporting systems, automated account management, and digital authorized user addition processes that affect timing and implementation of authorized user strategies.

Future developments in authorized user treatment by credit scoring companies and regulatory agencies may affect the value and implementation of authorized user strategies, making ongoing monitoring important for strategy optimization.

Finding authorized user opportunities requires systematic approaches to identifying suitable accounts and account holders while building relationships that support mutually beneficial authorized user arrangements and long-term credit building success.

Family member opportunities often provide the most accessible authorized user options through parents, spouses, siblings, or other relatives who maintain excellent credit accounts with favorable characteristics for credit building benefits.

Spouse and domestic partner arrangements typically offer comprehensive authorized user opportunities with shared financial interests and coordinated credit building objectives that support household financial planning and individual credit development simultaneously.

Parent-child authorized user relationships can provide substantial credit building benefits for young adults while establishing financial education opportunities and family financial planning coordination that benefits multiple generations.

Extended family networks may include grandparents, aunts, uncles, or cousins who maintain excellent credit accounts and are willing to support family members' credit building efforts through authorized user arrangements.

Friend and personal network opportunities can extend authorized user access beyond family relationships through trusted personal connections who understand credit building benefits and are willing to provide authorized user assistance.

Professional authorized user services have emerged as commercial options for consumers without family or personal authorized user opportunities, providing access to high-quality authorized user accounts through specialized service providers.

Business relationship opportunities may include employers, business partners, or professional associates who can provide authorized user access as part of comprehensive financial planning or employee benefit programs.

Community and group arrangements might include credit building circles, financial cooperatives, or community organizations that facilitate authorized user opportunities among members with shared financial improvement objectives.

Online platform connections through reputable authorized user services provide systematic access to vetted account holders who offer authorized user opportunities as part of structured credit building programs.

Verification procedures for authorized user opportunities include assessing account quality, account holder creditworthiness, and relationship stability that ensure authorized user arrangements provide intended benefits without creating risks or complications.

Negotiation strategies for authorized user requests involve presenting benefits clearly, addressing concerns appropriately, and structuring arrangements that provide value for both authorized users and primary account holders.

Relationship maintenance for ongoing authorized user arrangements requires ongoing communication, appreciation demonstration, and mutual benefit preservation that sustains authorized user relationships throughout changing circumstances.

Evaluating authorized user opportunities involves comprehensive assessment criteria that optimize account selection while ensuring that authorized user arrangements provide maximum credit building benefits with minimal risk exposure.

Account age assessment represents a critical evaluation factor since older accounts typically provide greater credit score benefits through improved average account age calculations. Accounts with 5+ years of history generally provide optimal authorized user benefits.

Payment history evaluation requires understanding the primary account holder's payment performance throughout the account's history, as negative payment history will transfer to authorized users along with positive history. Perfect payment history provides optimal benefits.

Credit utilization analysis involves examining the primary account's balance-to-limit ratios over time, as authorized users inherit the account's utilization patterns for credit score calculations. Consistently low utilization provides the greatest credit building benefits.

Credit limit considerations include evaluating account limits that will be added to authorized user credit profiles, as higher limits can improve overall utilization ratios and provide greater credit building impact through increased available credit.

Account holder creditworthiness assessment involves understanding the primary account holder's overall credit profile, financial stability, and credit management patterns that affect ongoing account performance and authorized user benefits.

Issuer quality evaluation includes assessing credit card company reporting practices, customer service quality, and policy stability that affect authorized user experience and benefit reliability over time.

Account type considerations involve understanding differences between different credit card products, as some account types may provide better authorized user benefits or reporting characteristics than others.

Fee structure analysis includes evaluating any costs associated with authorized user addition, ongoing account maintenance, or authorized user removal that affect the overall value proposition of authorized user arrangements.

Relationship stability assessment involves evaluating the long-term viability of authorized user relationships and the potential for relationship changes that could affect ongoing authorized user benefits or create complications.

Risk factor identification includes understanding potential negative consequences such as account mismanagement, relationship deterioration, or changes in primary account holder circumstances that could affect authorized user benefits.

Documentation requirements for authorized user arrangements include understanding application procedures, identity verification needs, and ongoing reporting requirements that affect authorized user implementation and maintenance.

Exit strategy planning involves understanding authorized user removal procedures, timing considerations, and alternative options that ensure authorized user arrangements can be concluded gracefully when circumstances change.

Optimal timing for authorized user strategies involves understanding when to add or remove authorized user accounts to maximize credit building benefits while supporting major financial goals and credit evaluation periods.

Credit score timing considerations include understanding how quickly authorized user accounts appear on credit reports and affect credit scores, typically occurring within 30-60 days of account addition but varying by credit card issuer and reporting schedules.

Application timing coordination involves adding authorized user accounts well before major credit applications to ensure benefits are reflected in credit reports when lenders evaluate creditworthiness for mortgages, auto loans, or other significant credit decisions.

Reporting cycle awareness helps optimize authorized user timing by understanding when credit card issuers report to credit bureaus, typically monthly around statement closing dates, affecting when authorized user benefits become visible on credit reports.

Seasonal timing strategies consider optimal periods for authorized user addition that align with personal financial planning, family coordination, and major life events that affect credit needs and authorized user relationship management.

Credit building timeline integration ensures that authorized user strategies coordinate effectively with other credit improvement activities while supporting comprehensive credit building plans and avoiding conflicts between different credit improvement approaches.

Removal timing strategies involve understanding when to remove authorized user accounts to avoid potential negative impacts while preserving benefits that support credit profiles without ongoing authorized user relationships.

Emergency timing considerations include understanding how quickly authorized user accounts can be added when urgent credit improvement is needed for time-sensitive financial opportunities or crisis situations requiring rapid credit enhancement.

Market timing factors may include understanding economic conditions, lending environment changes, and regulatory developments that affect the value and implementation of authorized user strategies during different market conditions.

Life event coordination involves timing authorized user strategies around major life changes such as marriage, divorce, career changes, or family developments that affect financial planning and authorized user relationship dynamics.

Age-related timing considerations include understanding optimal ages for young adults to become authorized users and when to transition from authorized user status to independent credit management for comprehensive credit development.

Multiple account timing involves coordinating addition and removal of multiple authorized user accounts to optimize cumulative benefits while avoiding credit profile complications or excessive authorized user dependence.

Long-term timing strategy development includes planning authorized user usage throughout different life stages while building toward independent credit excellence and comprehensive financial management capability.

Authorized user account management involves strategic approaches to maximizing benefits while maintaining positive relationships and ensuring that authorized user arrangements continue supporting credit building objectives effectively.

Usage strategy development for authorized user accounts includes determining whether to actively use authorized user cards or maintain accounts solely for credit building benefits, balancing convenience against relationship complications and account management clarity.

Spending coordination with primary account holders involves establishing clear communication about authorized user spending, payment responsibilities, and account usage that maintains positive relationships while optimizing credit building benefits.

Payment responsibility clarification ensures that authorized user arrangements include clear understanding of who pays account balances and how authorized user spending affects primary account holder obligations and relationship dynamics.

Account monitoring procedures for authorized users include tracking account performance, payment history, and utilization patterns that affect credit building benefits while identifying potential problems early when corrective action is most effective.

Communication protocols with primary account holders establish ongoing dialogue about account performance, authorized user benefits, and relationship maintenance that sustains positive authorized user arrangements over time.

Credit report verification for authorized user accounts includes regular monitoring to ensure that authorized user benefits are properly reflected on credit reports and that account information is accurate and beneficial.

Dispute procedures for authorized user account errors include understanding how to address incorrect reporting of authorized user information while coordinating with primary account holders and credit card issuers for problem resolution.

Relationship maintenance strategies involve ongoing appreciation, communication, and mutual benefit preservation that sustains authorized user relationships through changing circumstances and ensures continued access to credit building benefits.

Problem prevention for authorized user arrangements includes understanding potential complications and implementing safeguards that protect both authorized users and primary account holders from relationship problems or account management difficulties.

Performance optimization for authorized user benefits involves strategic account management that maximizes credit building while supporting primary account holder objectives and maintaining positive relationship dynamics.

Documentation organization for authorized user arrangements includes maintaining records of agreements, account performance, and communication that supports ongoing relationship management and provides evidence for problem resolution when necessary.

Exit planning for authorized user relationships involves preparing for eventual transition from authorized user status while preserving relationship quality and ensuring smooth conclusion of authorized user arrangements when circumstances change.

Professional authorized user services have emerged as commercial alternatives for consumers without family or personal authorized user opportunities, providing access to high-quality authorized user accounts through specialized service providers and structured programs.

Service provider evaluation involves assessing authorized user companies based on account quality, transparency, customer service, pricing, and regulatory compliance that ensure reliable service and optimal authorized user benefits.

Account quality standards for professional services include understanding the characteristics of accounts offered through authorized user services, such as account age, payment history, credit limits, and utilization patterns that affect credit building benefits.

Pricing analysis for authorized user services involves evaluating costs against benefits while comparing different service providers and understanding fee structures that affect the overall value proposition of professional authorized user arrangements.

Service duration options include understanding different authorized user service terms, from short-term arrangements for specific credit building objectives to longer-term relationships that support ongoing credit maintenance and improvement.

Legal compliance for authorized user services includes understanding regulatory requirements, consumer protection standards, and industry best practices that ensure authorized user services operate ethically and provide legitimate credit building benefits.

Risk assessment for professional services involves understanding potential complications, service limitations, and consumer protections that affect authorized user service selection and usage for credit building objectives.

Customer support evaluation includes assessing service provider responsiveness, problem resolution capabilities, and ongoing assistance quality that affect authorized user service experience and benefit optimization.

Performance tracking for professional services includes monitoring credit building results, service delivery quality, and outcome achievement that ensure authorized user services provide intended benefits and justify service costs.

Contract terms analysis for authorized user services involves understanding agreement details, termination procedures, and service obligations that affect authorized user service relationships and consumer rights.

Alternative service comparison includes evaluating different authorized user service providers while understanding market options and selecting services that provide optimal value and benefit for specific credit building circumstances.

Integration planning for professional services ensures that authorized user services coordinate effectively with other credit building activities while supporting comprehensive credit improvement strategies and financial planning objectives.

Regulatory considerations for authorized user services include understanding consumer protection requirements, industry oversight, and compliance standards that affect service provider selection and authorized user service usage.

Authorized user risks and mitigation strategies involve understanding potential negative consequences while implementing safeguards that protect credit profiles and relationships throughout authorized user arrangements.

Credit score risks include potential negative impacts from primary account holder mismanagement, such as late payments, high utilization, or account closure that could harm authorized user credit profiles and score calculations.

Account closure impacts on authorized users can result in immediate credit score decreases when accounts are closed, potentially affecting credit building progress and credit applications that depend on authorized user account benefits.

Relationship deterioration risks include personal or family conflicts that could result in sudden authorized user removal during critical credit evaluation periods, potentially harming credit profiles when stability is most important.

Primary account holder risks involve dependence on others' credit management decisions and financial stability that could affect authorized user benefits through circumstances beyond authorized user control.

Identity exposure concerns include sharing personal information for authorized user addition while protecting against identity theft and unauthorized account access that could result from authorized user arrangements.

Financial liability confusion may arise when authorized users misunderstand their responsibilities or when account management creates unexpected financial obligations or relationship complications.

Legal liability limitations for authorized users typically protect against debt responsibility, but understanding these protections and their limitations helps avoid complications and ensures appropriate authorized user arrangement structuring.

Credit dependency risks include over-reliance on authorized user accounts for credit building while neglecting development of independent credit management skills and primary account establishment.

Fraud protection for authorized user accounts includes understanding security measures and dispute procedures that protect authorized users from unauthorized account activity while maintaining account relationship integrity.

Documentation preservation for risk mitigation includes maintaining records of authorized user arrangements, agreements, and communications that provide protection and evidence for problem resolution when complications arise.

Exit strategy implementation involves having clear procedures for authorized user removal when relationships change or when authorized user arrangements no longer serve credit building objectives effectively.

Professional consultation for risk management may include working with credit counselors, financial advisors, or consumer attorneys who can provide guidance for complex authorized user situations requiring specialized expertise.

Authorized user removal strategies involve understanding when and how to conclude authorized user relationships while preserving credit building benefits and maintaining positive relationships with primary account holders.

Timing considerations for authorized user removal include understanding optimal periods for account removal that minimize negative credit impacts while supporting transition to independent credit management and continued credit building progress.

Gradual transition strategies involve building independent credit before removing authorized user accounts, ensuring that credit profiles maintain strength through primary account development while reducing authorized user dependence.

Credit score impact assessment for removal includes understanding how authorized user account removal affects credit scores and implementing strategies that minimize negative impacts during transition periods.

Alternative account development before removal helps establish independent credit accounts that replace authorized user benefits while maintaining credit building momentum and score stability throughout transition processes.

Communication strategies for removal discussions involve addressing authorized user conclusion professionally while preserving relationships and expressing appreciation for authorized user assistance and support.

Documentation procedures for authorized user removal include understanding issuer requirements, processing timelines, and verification procedures that ensure complete and timely authorized user account removal.

Monitoring procedures after removal include tracking credit report changes and score impacts to ensure that authorized user removal is properly implemented and that credit profiles adjust appropriately to post-removal status.

Relationship preservation during removal involves maintaining positive connections with primary account holders while concluding authorized user arrangements gracefully and preserving opportunities for future assistance or cooperation.

Backup planning for removal complications includes understanding potential problems and alternative strategies when authorized user removal encounters difficulties or when relationships become complicated during conclusion processes.

Readdition possibilities involve understanding circumstances under which authorized user relationships might be renewed and procedures for reestablishing authorized user arrangements when beneficial for both parties.

Professional assistance for complex removal situations may include working with credit repair professionals or consumer advocates who can provide guidance for difficult authorized user conclusions requiring specialized expertise.

Success measurement for removal transitions includes evaluating credit building preservation, relationship maintenance, and transition effectiveness that ensure authorized user removal supports rather than compromises ongoing credit improvement objectives.

Multiple authorized user strategies involve coordinating several authorized user accounts simultaneously to maximize credit building benefits while managing complexity and maintaining positive relationships across multiple arrangements.

Portfolio approach to authorized user management includes strategic selection of multiple accounts with different characteristics that provide comprehensive credit building benefits through diversified authorized user relationships.

Account characteristic diversification involves combining authorized user accounts with different ages, credit limits, utilization patterns, and issuer types that optimize overall credit profile development and scoring benefit maximization.

Timing coordination for multiple accounts includes strategic addition and removal of various authorized user accounts to maintain optimal credit profile characteristics while adapting to changing credit building needs and relationship circumstances.

Relationship management across multiple authorized user arrangements requires systematic communication, appreciation demonstration, and mutual benefit preservation that sustains several authorized user relationships simultaneously.

Risk distribution through multiple accounts helps reduce dependence on single authorized user relationships while providing backup options when individual authorized user arrangements encounter problems or conclude unexpectedly.

Performance monitoring for multiple authorized user accounts includes tracking each account's contribution to credit building while optimizing the collective impact of combined authorized user benefits on credit profiles and scores.

Cost-benefit analysis for multiple arrangements involves evaluating the cumulative value of several authorized user accounts against complexity and relationship management requirements to ensure optimal resource allocation and benefit achievement.

Integration challenges for multiple authorized user accounts include coordinating various arrangements with other credit building activities while maintaining systematic approach implementation and avoiding conflicts or complications.

Documentation organization for multiple relationships requires systematic record-keeping that tracks different authorized user arrangements while providing clear information for relationship management and problem resolution when necessary.

Quality control for multiple accounts includes ensuring that each authorized user relationship maintains high standards while contributing effectively to overall credit building objectives and supporting comprehensive credit improvement strategies.

Graduation planning from multiple authorized user arrangements involves transitioning from authorized user dependence to independent credit management while preserving benefits and maintaining positive relationships throughout evolution processes.

Mastery development through multiple authorized user management provides experience and skills that support advanced credit management while building relationship management capabilities and strategic planning expertise.

Young adult authorized user strategies focus on establishing credit foundations for individuals with limited credit history while building financial education and management skills that support long-term credit success.

Early credit establishment through authorized user accounts provides young adults with immediate credit history development while avoiding the qualification challenges associated with independent credit applications during early career periods.

Educational integration with authorized user benefits includes combining credit building with financial literacy development while establishing responsible credit management patterns that support long-term financial success and independence.

Parent-child authorized user coordination involves strategic family financial planning that supports young adult credit development while maintaining appropriate supervision and education throughout the credit building process.

College student considerations for authorized user accounts include understanding how authorized user benefits can support student financial needs while building credit for post-graduation financial opportunities and independence.

Timeline planning for young adult authorized user usage involves strategic progression from authorized user status to independent credit management while maintaining credit building momentum throughout transition periods.

Credit limit management for young adult authorized users includes understanding how credit limits affect credit building benefits while establishing appropriate usage patterns that demonstrate responsible credit management and financial maturity.

Spending responsibility education through authorized user accounts provides practical experience with credit management while establishing accountability and financial discipline that supports long-term credit success.

Monitoring and supervision strategies for young adult authorized users include appropriate oversight that ensures responsible usage while building independence and decision-making capabilities for future independent credit management.

Transition planning from authorized user status to independent credit includes strategic timeline development for establishing primary accounts while maintaining credit building benefits throughout graduation to financial independence.

Emergency procedures for young adult authorized user problems include understanding how to address account issues, relationship complications, or credit building obstacles while maintaining family relationships and credit building progress.

Professional development through young adult authorized user experience includes building financial management skills and credit knowledge that support career development and comprehensive financial planning throughout changing life circumstances.

Long-term planning integration ensures that young adult authorized user strategies support broader financial education and wealth building objectives while establishing foundation skills for lifelong financial success and credit management excellence.

Authorized user strategies for credit repair involve leveraging authorized user accounts to accelerate credit improvement for consumers with damaged credit histories while addressing underlying credit problems comprehensively.

Rapid improvement potential through authorized user accounts can provide immediate credit score increases for consumers with limited positive credit history while authorized user benefits supplement ongoing credit repair activities.

Strategic account selection for credit repair involves identifying authorized user opportunities that provide maximum credit building impact for damaged credit profiles while addressing specific credit deficiencies and scoring factor improvement needs.

Integration with dispute activities ensures that authorized user strategies complement credit repair efforts while providing positive credit history development during dispute processing periods and credit file improvement activities.

Timeline coordination for credit repair includes optimizing authorized user timing with other credit improvement activities while supporting major financial goals that require improved credit profiles for achievement.

Damage assessment for authorized user planning involves understanding existing credit problems and how authorized user benefits can address specific deficiencies while supporting comprehensive credit repair strategies.

Score improvement targeting through authorized user accounts includes focusing on specific credit scoring factors that provide maximum improvement while addressing credit profile weaknesses through strategic authorized user benefits.

Relationship leveraging for credit repair may include accessing family or personal networks for authorized user opportunities that support credit improvement while building stronger financial relationships and support systems.

Professional service integration for credit repair involves combining authorized user services with other credit repair assistance while optimizing resource allocation and ensuring comprehensive credit improvement strategy implementation.

Monitoring and adjustment for credit repair includes tracking authorized user impact on credit improvement while adapting strategies based on results and ensuring optimal credit repair progress throughout improvement processes.

Exit strategy planning for credit repair involves transitioning from authorized user dependence to independent credit management while maintaining credit improvement momentum and establishing sustainable credit management patterns.

Success measurement for credit repair includes evaluating authorized user contribution to overall credit improvement while ensuring that authorized user strategies support rather than replace comprehensive credit repair and management development.

Business credit development through authorized user strategies involves leveraging personal credit improvement to support business credit building while understanding the connections between personal and business creditworthiness.

Personal credit foundation building through authorized user accounts provides the strong personal credit profiles often required for business credit applications while demonstrating creditworthiness to business credit providers.

Business application preparation through personal credit improvement includes understanding how authorized user benefits enhance business credit qualification while supporting entrepreneurial activities and business financing opportunities.

Timing coordination between personal and business credit development ensures that authorized user strategies support business credit building timelines while optimizing qualification for business financing and credit opportunities.

Professional relationship development through credit building includes establishing banking relationships and financial connections that support both personal and business credit development through comprehensive financial service access.

Documentation organization for business credit development includes maintaining records that support business credit applications while demonstrating personal creditworthiness through authorized user account management and credit profile development.

Risk management for business credit development involves understanding how personal credit affects business opportunities while implementing strategies that protect both personal and business credit throughout development processes.

Integration planning for business and personal credit ensures that authorized user strategies support business development objectives while maintaining personal credit excellence and financial management capabilities.

Professional consultation for business credit development may include working with business advisors, accountants, and credit professionals who understand the connections between personal and business creditworthiness.

Long-term strategy development for business credit includes understanding how authorized user foundations support business growth while building comprehensive financial management capabilities that serve both personal and business objectives.

Success measurement for business development includes evaluating how authorized user strategies contribute to business credit achievement while supporting entrepreneurial goals and comprehensive financial success.

Transition planning from personal to business credit focus includes understanding when and how to shift emphasis while maintaining personal credit excellence and supporting business development through strategic credit management.

Advanced authorized user techniques involve sophisticated strategies that leverage deep understanding of credit scoring, relationship management, and strategic coordination to maximize authorized user benefits while building comprehensive credit management expertise.

Credit scoring optimization through authorized user management includes understanding score calculation nuances and account management techniques that maximize score improvement while building strong credit profiles that support future credit opportunities.

Multiple relationship coordination involves managing several authorized user arrangements strategically while optimizing collective benefits and maintaining positive relationships across different families, friends, or service providers.

Professional service leverage includes combining commercial authorized user services with personal relationships while optimizing cost-effectiveness and ensuring comprehensive authorized user benefit achievement.

Strategic timing mastery involves sophisticated coordination of authorized user addition and removal with credit applications, life events, and financial planning while maximizing benefits and minimizing risks throughout changing circumstances.

Relationship building expertise includes developing skills for creating, maintaining, and concluding authorized user relationships while building networks that support ongoing credit building and financial planning objectives.

Risk management mastery involves understanding and mitigating potential complications while implementing advanced authorized user strategies that provide maximum benefits with minimal risk exposure.

Integration excellence includes coordinating authorized user strategies with comprehensive credit building, debt management, and financial planning while supporting broader wealth building and financial goal achievement.

Documentation and monitoring systems for advanced strategies include sophisticated tracking and management approaches that optimize authorized user benefits while maintaining comprehensive oversight of multiple relationships and arrangements.

Professional development through authorized user expertise includes building knowledge and skills that support consulting, education, and assistance opportunities while contributing to broader financial literacy and consumer protection efforts.

Innovation development in authorized user strategies includes creating novel approaches and optimization techniques while adapting to changing credit industry practices and regulatory requirements.

Teaching and mentoring capabilities through authorized user mastery enable helping others achieve credit building success while building leadership skills and contributing to broader financial education and consumer empowerment.

Mastery integration with comprehensive financial planning ensures that authorized user expertise supports broader financial success while optimizing credit building benefits within comprehensive wealth development and long-term financial security strategies.

Authorized user strategy evaluation and optimization involve comprehensive assessment methodologies that measure effectiveness while identifying improvement opportunities and ensuring that authorized user investments produce maximum long-term value and credit building benefit.

Performance measurement systems for authorized user strategies include tracking credit score improvements, relationship quality, cost-effectiveness, and goal achievement while providing comprehensive evaluation of authorized user strategy success and optimization opportunities.

Success factor analysis involves understanding which authorized user approaches produce optimal results while identifying relationship characteristics, account features, and management techniques that contribute most significantly to credit building success.

Timeline effectiveness evaluation includes assessing how quickly authorized user strategies produce benefits while understanding factors that accelerate or delay credit improvement and optimizing authorized user timing for maximum effectiveness.

Cost-benefit optimization for authorized user strategies involves evaluating expenses against benefits while comparing alternatives and ensuring that authorized user investments provide optimal value within broader credit building and financial planning contexts.

Relationship quality assessment includes evaluating authorized user relationship health, sustainability, and mutual benefit while identifying factors that support long-term relationship success and authorized user arrangement optimization.

Integration effectiveness analysis involves assessing how authorized user strategies coordinate with other credit building activities while identifying optimization opportunities for enhanced coordination and comprehensive credit improvement.

Risk mitigation evaluation includes understanding how well risk management strategies protect against authorized user complications while identifying additional safeguards that enhance authorized user arrangement security and effectiveness.

Documentation quality assessment involves evaluating record-keeping effectiveness and information organization while ensuring that authorized user documentation supports optimal relationship management and problem resolution when necessary.

Professional development measurement through authorized user experience includes evaluating skill development, knowledge advancement, and capability building while identifying opportunities for expertise expansion and financial management mastery.

Innovation assessment for authorized user strategies includes evaluating novel approaches and optimization techniques while identifying creative solutions that enhance authorized user effectiveness and adapt to changing circumstances.

Long-term value evaluation for authorized user investments includes comprehensive assessment of credit building benefits, relationship development, and foundation building for advanced financial management while optimizing authorized user value throughout changing financial circumstances.

Success preservation strategies ensure that authorized user benefits continue supporting credit improvement goals while maintaining relationship quality and building foundation for sustained financial success through changing life circumstances and evolving credit management needs.

CHAPTER 15

ADVANCED CREDIT BUILDING TECHNIQUES

Advanced credit building techniques represent sophisticated strategies that go beyond traditional credit cards and loans to leverage alternative reporting mechanisms, emerging technologies, and comprehensive financial management approaches for accelerated credit improvement and profile optimization. These techniques are particularly valuable for consumers with limited traditional credit history or those seeking to maximize credit building efficiency.

The evolution of credit reporting has expanded beyond traditional credit products to include rent payments, utility bills, bank account management, and other financial behaviors that demonstrate creditworthiness but historically weren't captured in credit reports. Understanding these alternative data sources creates new opportunities for comprehensive credit building strategies.

Alternative credit reporting services have emerged as powerful tools for consumers seeking to build credit through existing financial behaviors rather than acquiring new debt obligations. These services can provide immediate credit profile enhancement by reporting positive payment history that already exists but wasn't previously contributing to credit scores.

The strategic integration of multiple credit building approaches creates synergistic effects that accelerate credit improvement beyond what individual techniques can achieve independently. Understanding how different credit building methods interact helps optimize comprehensive strategies for maximum effectiveness.

Technology-driven credit building solutions include mobile apps, automated systems, and digital platforms that streamline credit building while providing sophisticated monitoring and optimization capabilities. These tools can significantly enhance traditional credit building effectiveness while reducing management complexity.

Emerging financial products specifically designed for credit building include innovative account types, hybrid products, and specialized services that address credit building needs more directly than traditional financial products. Understanding these innovations helps access cutting-edge credit building opportunities.

The regulatory environment supporting alternative credit building continues evolving through CFPB initiatives, industry guidance, and legislative developments that expand credit building opportunities while protecting consumer interests. Staying current with regulatory changes helps leverage new opportunities as they emerge.

Credit scoring model evolution includes increasing recognition of alternative data sources and behavioral indicators that create new credit building opportunities while changing the relative importance of traditional credit factors. Understanding scoring changes helps optimize credit building strategies for current and future scoring models.

Professional credit building services have expanded beyond traditional credit repair to include comprehensive credit building consultation, alternative data integration, and strategic planning that addresses complete credit profile optimization rather than simply correcting errors.

The intersection of credit building with broader financial planning creates opportunities for integrated approaches that support wealth building, risk management, and comprehensive financial goal achievement while building excellent credit profiles that enhance all financial opportunities.

Rent reporting services represent one of the most accessible and immediately beneficial alternative credit building techniques, allowing consumers to receive credit building benefits from housing payments they're already making without changing spending patterns or acquiring additional debt obligations.

The mechanism of rent reporting involves third-party services that verify rent payments with landlords or property management companies and report this payment history to credit bureaus as positive tradeline information. This creates immediate credit building benefits from existing financial behavior.

Major rent reporting services include established platforms such as Rental Kharma, RentTrack, PayYourRent, and others that offer different features, pricing structures, and credit bureau reporting relationships. Understanding service differences helps optimize rent reporting selection for individual circumstances.

Credit bureau integration varies between rent reporting services, with some reporting to all three major bureaus while others focus on specific bureaus or specialized reporting agencies. Comprehensive reporting provides maximum credit building benefit and score improvement potential.

Eligibility requirements for rent reporting services typically include verifiable rental arrangements, landlord cooperation, and payment documentation that enables service providers to confirm rent payment history. Understanding requirements helps identify optimal rent reporting opportunities.

Historical payment reporting capabilities allow many rent reporting services to include past rent payments in credit reports, potentially providing immediate credit building benefits from months or years of positive payment history that wasn't previously contributing to credit scores.

Landlord participation requirements vary between rent reporting services, with some requiring active landlord cooperation while others can verify payments through bank account analysis or other documentation methods. Understanding participation needs helps evaluate rent reporting feasibility.

Cost analysis for rent reporting services includes monthly fees, setup costs, and additional charges that affect the overall value proposition compared to alternative credit building strategies. Comprehensive cost evaluation helps ensure optimal resource allocation for credit building investments.

Credit score impact from rent reporting can be substantial for consumers with limited credit history, often providing immediate score improvements of 20-60 points when positive rent payment history is added to thin credit files.

Integration strategies for rent reporting include coordinating with other credit building activities while ensuring that rent reporting supports comprehensive credit improvement objectives without conflicts or complications.

Documentation requirements for rent reporting typically include lease agreements, payment records, and identity verification that enable service providers to establish legitimate rent reporting relationships and maintain ongoing reporting accuracy.

Monitoring and optimization procedures for rent reporting include tracking credit report updates, verifying reporting accuracy, and maximizing rent reporting benefits through strategic payment timing and account management.

Utility bill credit reporting represents another powerful alternative credit building technique that leverages essential monthly payments for credit building benefits while demonstrating consistent payment behavior and financial responsibility through utility management.

Utility credit reporting mechanisms include specialized services that collect utility payment information from utility companies and report this data to credit bureaus as positive tradeline information, creating credit building opportunities from necessary monthly expenses.

Experian Boost represents the most prominent utility reporting service, allowing consumers to connect bank accounts and automatically report utility, telecom, and streaming service payments to Experian for immediate credit score improvement. The service is free and provides instant score benefits.

UltraFICO integration includes utility and bank account data in credit scoring calculations through opt-in programs that analyze banking behavior and utility payments to provide more comprehensive creditworthiness assessment beyond traditional credit reporting.

Service provider options for utility reporting include multiple platforms and services that work with different utility companies and provide various levels of reporting comprehensiveness and credit bureau integration. Understanding options helps optimize utility reporting strategies.

Eligible utility types for credit reporting typically include electricity, gas, water, sewer, trash, internet, cable, and mobile phone services that demonstrate regular payment responsibility and financial management capability.

Historical payment inclusion capabilities vary between utility reporting services, with some able to include months or years of past positive payment history while others focus only on prospective reporting from service enrollment forward.

Bank account analysis integration in some utility reporting services includes evaluation of account management, balance maintenance, and overdraft avoidance that provides additional positive financial behavior reporting beyond utility payments alone.

Credit score impact from utility reporting varies based on existing credit profile characteristics, with consumers having limited credit history typically experiencing greater score improvements than those with extensive credit profiles.

Setup requirements for utility reporting include identity verification, bank account connection, and utility account authentication that enables service providers to access payment information and establish ongoing reporting relationships.

Monitoring procedures for utility reporting include verifying that reported information appears accurately on credit reports and that utility reporting continues providing intended credit building benefits over time.

Integration optimization ensures that utility reporting coordinates effectively with other credit building strategies while supporting comprehensive credit improvement objectives without creating conflicts or complications.

Safety and security considerations for utility reporting include understanding data privacy protections, account security measures, and service provider reliability that protect financial information while enabling credit building benefits.

Credit builder loans represent specialized financial products designed specifically for credit building rather than traditional lending purposes, providing structured approaches to establish payment history and account diversity while building savings simultaneously.

The fundamental structure of credit builder loans involves depositing loan proceeds into savings accounts or certificates of deposit rather than providing immediate access to funds. Borrowers make monthly payments that build credit history while eventually gaining access to saved funds upon loan completion.

Community development financial institutions (CDFIs) and credit unions represent the primary sources for credit builder loans, often offering these products as part of community development missions and financial inclusion initiatives that support underserved populations.

Self-pay loan variations include products where borrowers make payments into savings accounts that are held as collateral, building both credit history and emergency savings simultaneously. These products provide dual benefits of credit building and forced savings accumulation.

Secured credit builder loans use borrower deposits as collateral while reporting payments to credit bureaus, combining credit building with savings development in structured programs that ensure successful completion and positive credit outcomes.

Payment structure optimization for credit builder loans includes understanding how payment amounts, loan terms, and payment timing affect credit building benefits while balancing affordability with credit improvement effectiveness.

Credit reporting integration for credit builder loans typically includes reporting to all three major credit bureaus, providing comprehensive credit building benefits and ensuring maximum score improvement potential from credit builder loan participation.

Interest rate considerations for credit builder loans often result in net positive returns when interest earned on deposited funds exceeds loan interest charges, creating situations where borrowers earn money while building credit.

Term length optimization involves selecting credit builder loan durations that balance credit building benefits with affordability and timeline coordination with other financial goals requiring improved credit profiles.

Completion benefits for credit builder loans include access to accumulated savings, established credit history, and improved credit scores that create foundations for accessing traditional credit products with better terms and conditions.

Alternative credit builder loan structures include innovative products from fintech companies and online lenders that provide credit building benefits through various mechanisms including savings challenges, micro-lending, and automated savings programs.

Integration strategies for credit builder loans include coordinating with other credit building activities while ensuring that credit builder loans support comprehensive credit improvement objectives and broader financial planning goals.

Performance measurement for credit builder loans includes tracking credit building progress, savings accumulation, and cost-effectiveness to ensure that credit builder loans provide intended benefits and justify program participation costs.

Experian Boost and similar services represent innovative credit building platforms that leverage existing financial behavior for immediate credit score improvement without requiring new debt obligations or credit applications, providing accessible credit building for consumers with limited traditional credit history.

Experian Boost functionality allows consumers to connect bank accounts and automatically receive credit building benefits from utility payments, streaming services, and telecom bills that are already being paid regularly. The service provides instant credit score improvement upon enrollment.

Alternative data integration through Boost-type services includes various types of positive financial behavior that demonstrate creditworthiness but traditionally haven't been included in credit reports, expanding credit building opportunities beyond traditional credit products.

Banking data analysis in these services includes evaluation of account management, positive balance maintenance, and regular payment patterns that provide additional creditworthiness indicators beyond simple payment history reporting.

Instant score improvement capabilities distinguish these services from traditional credit building approaches by providing immediate credit score benefits upon enrollment rather than requiring months of payment history accumulation for credit improvement.

Service provider comparison includes evaluating different alternative data reporting platforms, their credit bureau relationships, eligible payment types, and integration capabilities that affect credit building effectiveness and convenience.

Eligibility assessment for alternative data services includes understanding qualifying payment types, bank account requirements, and minimum payment history needed to generate meaningful credit building benefits from service participation.

Privacy and security considerations for bank account integration include understanding data protection measures, information sharing policies, and account security protocols that protect financial information while enabling credit building benefits.

Optimization strategies for alternative data services include maximizing reported payment types, ensuring consistent payment patterns, and coordinating with other credit building activities for comprehensive credit improvement effectiveness.

Credit score monitoring integration with these services includes tracking score improvements, verifying reported information accuracy, and understanding how alternative data contributes to overall credit profile development and enhancement.

Limitation understanding for alternative data services includes recognizing that benefits typically apply only to specific credit scores and may not affect all scoring models or lender evaluation criteria equally.

Long-term strategy integration ensures that alternative data services support broader credit building objectives while serving as stepping stones to traditional credit product access and comprehensive credit profile development.

Cost-benefit analysis for alternative data services includes evaluating free versus paid service options while understanding how these services compare to alternative credit building strategies in terms of effectiveness and resource allocation.

Store and gas station credit cards represent accessible entry points into traditional credit building that often provide easier approval than general-purpose credit cards while offering opportunities to establish payment history and account diversity.

Approval accessibility for store credit cards often exceeds that of traditional credit cards due to lower credit requirements, specialized underwriting criteria, and retail partnerships that prioritize customer acquisition over strict credit standards.

Credit building effectiveness of retail credit cards equals that of traditional cards when these accounts report to major credit bureaus and demonstrate positive payment history, account management, and appropriate utilization patterns.

Store card variations include closed-loop cards that work only at specific retailers versus open-loop cards that function like traditional credit cards, with open-loop options typically providing greater credit building value and utility.

Gas station credit card opportunities include major petroleum company cards that often provide easier approval while offering rewards for fuel purchases and credit building benefits through major credit bureau reporting.

Promotional financing options with retail credit cards include deferred interest programs and special financing that can provide utility while building credit, though these programs require careful management to avoid interest charges and payment problems.

Credit limit management for retail credit cards includes understanding typically lower initial limits while implementing strategies for limit increases that enhance credit building benefits and overall credit profile development.

Utilization optimization for retail cards requires careful balance management since lower credit limits can result in high utilization ratios that negatively impact credit scores despite positive payment history.

Upgrade pathways from retail credit cards include opportunities to transition to better products with the same issuers while maintaining account age benefits and established payment history that support continued credit building.

Multiple retail card strategies involve strategically acquiring several retail cards to diversify credit mix while managing multiple accounts effectively and avoiding overextension or account management complications.

Rewards optimization for retail credit cards includes leveraging reward programs and special offers while maintaining focus on credit building objectives and avoiding spending increases that compromise financial stability.

Account management excellence for retail cards includes payment timing, balance management, and utilization optimization that maximizes credit building benefits while preparing for graduation to premium credit products.

Integration planning for retail credit cards ensures that these accounts support broader credit building strategies while serving as stepping stones to comprehensive credit portfolios and advanced credit management.

Multiple payment strategies involve sophisticated techniques for optimizing credit reporting through strategic payment timing, frequency, and amount management that maximizes credit building benefits beyond simple on-time payment compliance.

Payment timing optimization includes understanding credit card reporting dates and scheduling payments to ensure optimal utilization reporting while maintaining perfect payment history and demonstrating sophisticated account management capabilities.

Multiple payment techniques involve making several payments per month to manage utilization ratios, reduce finance charges, and demonstrate consistent payment behavior that exceeds minimum requirements and shows exemplary credit management.

Balance management strategies include maintaining optimal utilization ratios through payment timing while using available credit effectively for necessary expenses without compromising credit building objectives or score optimization.

Autopay integration with manual payment strategies combines automated minimum payment protection with strategic additional payments that optimize utilization reporting while ensuring perfect payment history maintenance.

Cross-account payment coordination involves managing payments across multiple credit accounts to optimize overall utilization while maintaining individual account health and demonstrating comprehensive credit management capability.

Early payment benefits include reducing reported balances before statement generation while demonstrating proactive account management and financial discipline that enhances creditworthiness perception by lenders and scoring models.

Payment source diversification includes using different payment methods and sources to fund credit account payments while maintaining payment reliability and demonstrating diverse financial resource access and management.

Emergency payment procedures include backup systems and contingency plans that ensure payment timeliness during unexpected circumstances while maintaining perfect payment history despite temporary financial or logistical challenges.

Technology integration for payment management includes automated systems, mobile apps, and digital tools that optimize payment timing while reducing management complexity and ensuring consistent execution of sophisticated payment strategies.

Cost optimization for multiple payment strategies includes minimizing payment processing fees, transaction costs, and administrative burden while maintaining payment strategy effectiveness and credit building benefit maximization.

Monitoring and adjustment procedures for payment strategies include tracking effectiveness, measuring results, and refining approaches based on credit score changes and credit report updates that demonstrate payment strategy impact.

Integration with comprehensive credit building ensures that payment strategies support broader credit improvement objectives while coordinating effectively with other credit building techniques and financial planning activities.

Alternative credit reporting platforms have expanded beyond traditional services to include comprehensive credit building ecosystems that integrate multiple data sources, financial behaviors, and credit building techniques into unified platforms for accelerated credit improvement.

Comprehensive platform integration includes services that combine rent reporting, utility reporting, bank account analysis, and other alternative data sources into single platforms that provide holistic credit building approaches and simplified management.

Fintech innovation in credit building includes mobile-first platforms, artificial intelligence-driven optimization, and automated credit building programs that leverage technology to enhance traditional credit building effectiveness while reducing complexity.

Subscription service credit building includes platforms that report subscription payments for streaming services, software, fitness memberships, and other recurring payments that demonstrate consistent payment behavior and financial responsibility.

Bank account credit building services analyze checking and savings account management to report positive financial behaviors such as consistent balances, regular deposits, and overdraft avoidance that indicate creditworthiness and financial stability.

Mobile app-based credit building includes smartphone applications that gamify credit building, provide educational content, and automate credit building activities while offering convenient monitoring and optimization capabilities.

Community-based credit building platforms include services that leverage group dynamics, peer support, and social accountability to enhance credit building effectiveness while providing educational resources and motivation for sustained improvement.

Artificial intelligence optimization in credit building platforms includes personalized recommendations, automated strategy adjustment, and predictive analytics that optimize credit building approaches based on individual circumstances and objectives.

Educational integration with credit building platforms includes financial literacy content, credit education resources, and decision-making support that builds knowledge while implementing credit building strategies for comprehensive financial development.

Data aggregation services combine multiple credit building approaches into unified reporting while providing comprehensive credit profile development through diverse alternative data source integration and strategic optimization.

Performance analytics for alternative platforms include sophisticated tracking, measurement, and optimization capabilities that provide detailed insights into credit building effectiveness while identifying improvement opportunities and strategy refinement needs.

Cost efficiency analysis for comprehensive platforms includes evaluating integrated service value against individual service costs while understanding how platform integration affects overall credit building return on investment and resource allocation.

Future development trends in alternative credit building include emerging technologies, new data sources, and innovative approaches that will expand credit building opportunities while creating enhanced effectiveness and accessibility for diverse consumer populations.

Credit building through business credit development represents an advanced technique that leverages business credit establishment to enhance personal credit opportunities while building comprehensive creditworthiness across both personal and business domains.

Business credit fundamentals include understanding how business credit works independently from personal credit while recognizing connections and crossover opportunities that benefit both personal and business creditworthiness development.

EIN establishment and business structure development provide foundations for business credit building while creating separation from personal credit that protects personal assets and enables independent business credit development.

Vendor credit relationships with suppliers and service providers offer initial business credit building opportunities that don't require personal guarantees while establishing payment history and business creditworthiness through trade credit arrangements.

Business credit card strategies include acquiring business credit cards that build business credit while potentially providing personal credit benefits through business account management and payment history demonstration.

Business loan development through credit building provides access to business financing that supports entrepreneurial activities while building business credit history and demonstrating comprehensive creditworthiness across business and personal domains.

Personal credit enhancement through business development includes understanding how business ownership, successful business management, and business credit excellence can enhance personal creditworthiness and lending opportunities.

Cross-guarantee strategies involve understanding when personal guarantees for business credit can provide mutual benefits while managing risks and ensuring that business and personal credit development support each other appropriately.

Business banking relationships through comprehensive business credit development provide access to enhanced financial services while building institutional relationships that support both business and personal financial objectives.

Professional consultation for business credit development includes working with business advisors, accountants, and credit professionals who understand business credit building while ensuring compliance with business credit requirements and optimization.

Risk management for business credit building includes understanding how business credit activities affect personal credit while implementing safeguards that protect personal assets and credit profiles during business development activities.

Integration planning for business and personal credit ensures coordinated development that optimizes both credit profiles while supporting comprehensive financial planning and wealth building through business and personal financial excellence.

Success measurement for business credit development includes tracking both business and personal credit improvement while evaluating how business credit building contributes to overall financial goal achievement and opportunity enhancement.

Technology-enhanced credit building represents the cutting edge of credit improvement strategies, leveraging artificial intelligence, machine learning, and automated systems to optimize credit building effectiveness while reducing management complexity and time investment.

Artificial intelligence credit optimization includes platforms that analyze credit profiles, identify improvement opportunities, and provide personalized recommendations that optimize credit building strategies based on individual circumstances and objectives.

Machine learning applications in credit building include systems that learn from user behavior, adapt strategies based on results, and continuously optimize approaches to maximize credit improvement effectiveness over time.

Automated credit building systems include platforms that execute credit building strategies automatically while monitoring results and adjusting approaches based on performance data and changing circumstances.

Predictive analytics for credit building include systems that forecast credit score changes, identify optimal timing for credit applications, and predict the impact of various credit building strategies before implementation.

Digital credit coaching platforms provide personalized guidance, educational content, and strategic advice through technology-driven interfaces that make expert credit building guidance accessible and affordable.

Blockchain applications in credit building include emerging technologies that may enhance credit reporting accuracy, security, and portability while creating new opportunities for alternative credit building and verification.

Internet of Things (IoT) integration in credit building includes emerging possibilities for reporting payment behavior through connected devices and smart home technologies that demonstrate financial responsibility through various behavioral indicators.

Mobile-first credit building platforms prioritize smartphone accessibility and convenience while providing comprehensive credit building capabilities through mobile interfaces that enable convenient management and monitoring.

API integration for credit building includes platforms that connect with multiple financial services, credit monitoring systems, and credit bureaus to provide comprehensive credit building coordination and optimization through technology integration.

Cybersecurity considerations for technology-enhanced credit building include understanding data protection, privacy safeguards, and security measures that protect financial information while enabling advanced credit building through technology platforms.

Cost-effectiveness analysis for technology solutions includes evaluating sophisticated platform costs against manual credit building approaches while understanding how technology investment affects overall credit building return on investment.

Future technology trends in credit building include emerging innovations, new platforms, and advancing capabilities that will enhance credit building effectiveness while creating new opportunities for accelerated credit improvement and optimization.

Comprehensive credit building program development involves integrating multiple advanced techniques into cohesive strategies that maximize credit improvement effectiveness while supporting broader financial planning objectives and long-term wealth building goals.

Strategic integration methodology includes systematic approaches to combining alternative credit reporting, traditional credit building, and advanced techniques into unified programs that optimize cumulative effectiveness while avoiding conflicts and complications.

Timeline coordination for comprehensive programs includes understanding how different credit building techniques interact over time while optimizing sequencing and timing to maximize results and support major financial milestones and objectives.

Resource allocation optimization across multiple credit building approaches includes balancing time, effort, and financial investments among various techniques while ensuring optimal return on investment and sustainable program implementation.

Performance measurement systems for comprehensive programs include tracking multiple metrics across various credit building approaches while evaluating cumulative effectiveness and identifying optimization opportunities for program refinement.

Risk management for comprehensive credit building includes understanding how multiple strategies interact while implementing safeguards that protect credit profiles and financial interests throughout complex program implementation.

Professional assistance integration includes working effectively with various experts while coordinating professional services across multiple credit building approaches for comprehensive program optimization and expert guidance utilization.

Technology platform coordination includes leveraging multiple technological solutions while ensuring integration effectiveness and avoiding platform conflicts that could compromise program coordination and optimization.

Educational development through comprehensive programs includes building financial literacy, credit management expertise, and strategic planning capabilities while implementing advanced credit building techniques and achieving credit improvement objectives.

Quality control for comprehensive programs includes ensuring that all program components maintain high effectiveness levels while adapting to changing circumstances and continuing to support credit building objectives throughout program evolution.

Success criteria establishment for comprehensive programs includes defining clear objectives, measurement standards, and achievement targets that guide program implementation while providing accountability and motivation for sustained effort.

Adaptation procedures for comprehensive programs include systematic approaches to modifying strategies based on results, changing circumstances, and emerging opportunities while maintaining program effectiveness and objective achievement.

Long-term sustainability planning for comprehensive credit building ensures that programs support ongoing credit excellence while building capabilities for sustained financial success throughout changing life circumstances and evolving financial goals.

Professional credit building consultation involves working with experts who specialize in advanced credit building techniques while understanding when professional assistance becomes valuable and how to optimize professional service utilization for maximum benefit.

Consultation timing includes understanding optimal periods for seeking professional credit building assistance while evaluating circumstances that justify professional investment and coordination with independent credit building efforts.

Professional credential evaluation includes assessing consultant qualifications, experience, and specialization while understanding professional standards and regulatory requirements that ensure quality service and consumer protection.

Service scope definition for credit building consultation includes understanding what services professionals provide while establishing clear expectations, deliverables, and success criteria that optimize professional assistance value and effectiveness.

Cost-benefit analysis for professional services includes evaluating consultation costs against potential benefits while comparing professional assistance against independent credit building approaches for optimal resource allocation decisions.

Collaboration strategies with credit building professionals include maintaining active participation while leveraging professional expertise effectively for optimal outcomes and skill development through professional guidance and mentorship.

Quality assessment for professional services includes evaluating service delivery, result achievement, and professional communication while ensuring that consultation provides intended value and supports credit building objectives effectively.

Documentation coordination with professionals includes providing comprehensive information while understanding how professional assistance affects evidence development and strategic planning for optimal collaboration and outcome achievement.

Integration planning with professional services ensures that consultation supports broader financial planning objectives while coordinating effectively with other financial advisors and professional service providers.

Performance monitoring for professional consultation includes tracking progress, evaluating effectiveness, and ensuring accountability while maintaining clear communication and expectation management throughout professional service relationships.

Termination planning for professional services includes understanding completion criteria and transition procedures while ensuring that professional assistance builds capabilities for independent credit management and ongoing success.

Professional relationship development through consultation includes building networks, ongoing connections, and referral sources while leveraging professional relationships for continued support and advanced financial planning assistance.

Return on investment measurement for professional consultation includes comprehensive evaluation of costs, benefits, and outcomes while understanding how professional assistance contributes to long-term financial success and credit management excellence.

Credit building mastery integration involves developing comprehensive expertise across multiple advanced techniques while building capabilities that support lifelong credit excellence and financial success through changing circumstances and evolving opportunities.

Expertise development across multiple credit building approaches includes building deep knowledge and practical skills while understanding how different techniques interact and complement each other for optimal credit building effectiveness and strategic flexibility.

Strategic thinking advancement through credit building mastery includes developing analytical capabilities, planning skills, and optimization expertise while building comprehensive understanding of credit systems and financial planning integration.

Teaching and mentoring capability development through credit building expertise includes building knowledge transfer skills while contributing to broader financial literacy and consumer protection through education and assistance provision to others.

Innovation capacity building includes developing creativity and adaptation skills while building capability to develop novel approaches and optimize strategies for unique circumstances and emerging opportunities in credit building.

Professional development opportunities through credit building mastery include consulting possibilities, educational activities, and industry involvement while leveraging expertise for career advancement and income enhancement through credit building knowledge.

Leadership development through credit building excellence includes building influence, communication skills, and community impact capability while contributing to broader financial inclusion and consumer protection efforts through expertise application.

Comprehensive financial planning integration ensures that credit building mastery supports broader wealth building while optimizing credit excellence within comprehensive financial management strategies and long-term security planning.

Continuous learning commitment for credit building mastery includes staying current with industry developments while building adaptation capability for changing regulations, technologies, and market conditions that affect credit building effectiveness.

Quality maintenance for credit building expertise includes systematic evaluation, skill refinement, and knowledge updating while ensuring that mastery remains current and effective throughout changing credit industry conditions and requirements.

Impact measurement for credit building mastery includes evaluating personal outcomes, professional development, and community contribution while understanding how expertise creates value and supports broader financial empowerment and consumer protection.

Legacy development through credit building mastery includes building lasting impact through knowledge transfer, professional contribution, and community assistance while creating systems and relationships that extend expertise benefits beyond individual achievement.

Mastery sustainability planning includes understanding how to maintain and enhance credit building expertise throughout changing life circumstances while continuing to provide value and support for ongoing financial excellence and community contribution.

Advanced credit building troubleshooting involves systematic approaches to identifying and resolving complex problems that arise during sophisticated credit building implementation while maintaining progress and protecting credit building investments.

Problem identification methodologies for advanced credit building include systematic diagnosis of complex issues while understanding how multiple credit building approaches interact and affect each other during problem situations.

Solution development for credit building complications includes creating innovative approaches to overcome obstacles while maintaining credit building effectiveness and protecting progress achieved through advanced strategy implementation.

Alternative strategy development includes backup planning and contingency approaches when primary credit building strategies encounter obstacles while ensuring continued progress toward credit improvement objectives despite complications.

Resource reallocation during problem resolution includes optimizing available resources while addressing complications effectively and maintaining overall credit building program effectiveness during challenging periods and unexpected circumstances.

Professional assistance coordination for complex problems includes accessing specialized expertise while coordinating multiple professional service providers for comprehensive problem resolution and continued credit building optimization.

Risk mitigation during problem resolution includes protecting credit profiles and financial interests while addressing complications and ensuring that problem resolution activities support rather than compromise ongoing credit building objectives.

Communication strategies for problem resolution include working effectively with credit bureaus, furnishers, and service providers while maintaining professional relationships and achieving favorable problem resolution outcomes.

Documentation preservation during problem resolution includes maintaining comprehensive records while ensuring that problem resolution activities create appropriate evidence and support continued credit building effectiveness.

Performance monitoring during problem periods includes tracking credit building effectiveness while identifying emerging issues early and maintaining accountability for problem resolution progress and outcome achievement.

Recovery planning after problem resolution includes restoring credit building momentum while implementing improvements that prevent similar problems and enhance overall credit building effectiveness and resilience.

Learning integration from problem resolution includes building expertise and resilience while developing problem-solving capabilities that enhance credit building mastery and professional development through challenging experience.

Prevention planning based on problem resolution experience includes implementing safeguards and improvements while building systems that reduce future problem likelihood and enhance overall credit building program resilience and effectiveness.

Advanced credit building strategy integration with comprehensive financial planning ensures that sophisticated credit building techniques support broader wealth development while optimizing credit excellence within holistic financial management and long-term security planning.

Wealth building integration includes understanding how advanced credit building supports investment opportunities, business development, and asset accumulation while optimizing credit excellence for enhanced financial opportunity access and wealth multiplication.

Risk management coordination includes integrating credit building with comprehensive financial protection while ensuring that credit building activities support rather than compromise overall financial security and wealth preservation strategies.

Tax planning integration includes understanding how credit building activities affect tax optimization while coordinating credit improvement with comprehensive tax planning for optimal after-tax wealth building and financial efficiency.

Estate planning coordination includes understanding how credit excellence affects wealth transfer planning while ensuring that credit building supports legacy development and family financial security through comprehensive estate planning integration.

Business development support through credit building includes leveraging personal credit excellence for business opportunities while building comprehensive creditworthiness that supports entrepreneurial activities and business financing access.

Investment opportunity enhancement through credit building includes understanding how credit excellence affects investment access while leveraging improved creditworthiness for enhanced investment opportunities and wealth building acceleration.

Insurance optimization through credit improvement includes understanding how credit scores affect insurance costs while integrating credit building with comprehensive risk management and insurance planning for optimal financial protection.

Retirement planning integration includes understanding how credit building supports retirement financing while ensuring that credit excellence enhances retirement security and financial independence through improved access to financial opportunities.

Education financing optimization through credit building includes leveraging credit excellence for educational investment opportunities while supporting family education planning and human capital development through improved credit access.

Professional development support through credit excellence includes understanding how credit building enhances career opportunities while leveraging creditworthiness for professional advancement and income enhancement through improved financial access.

Legacy planning through credit building mastery includes understanding how expertise and excellence create lasting value while building capabilities and relationships that support sustained financial success and community contribution.

Impact optimization for comprehensive integration includes measuring how credit building expertise contributes to overall financial success while maximizing value creation through comprehensive financial planning excellence and strategic coordination.

CHAPTER 16

THE SCIENCE OF CREDIT UTILIZATION

Credit utilization represents the most dynamic and immediately controllable factor in credit score calculations, making it the cornerstone of strategic credit management and optimization. Understanding the sophisticated science behind utilization calculations enables consumers to manipulate this critical scoring factor for maximum credit score improvement while maintaining optimal credit management practices.

The mathematical precision of utilization calculations creates opportunities for exact score optimization through strategic balance management and payment timing that can produce immediate and substantial credit score improvements. Unlike other scoring factors that require time to develop, utilization changes can reflect in credit scores within days of credit bureau reporting updates.

Individual card utilization versus aggregate utilization creates complex interactions in credit scoring that require sophisticated understanding for optimal management. While overall utilization across all accounts matters significantly, individual card utilization ratios can have disproportionate impacts that make strategic balance distribution crucial for score optimization.

The psychology of credit utilization extends beyond mathematical calculations to include lender perception factors and risk assessment algorithms that evaluate utilization patterns for creditworthiness determination. Understanding these psychological factors helps optimize utilization management for maximum positive impact on credit decisions.

Modern credit scoring models have evolved to include increasingly sophisticated utilization analysis that considers historical patterns, trend analysis, and utilization stability over time. These advanced calculations create new opportunities for strategic utilization management that goes beyond simple ratio maintenance.

Technology integration in utilization management includes real-time monitoring, automated optimization, and predictive analytics that help consumers maintain optimal utilization ratios while minimizing management complexity and maximizing score improvement effectiveness.

The timing aspects of utilization reporting create opportunities for strategic manipulation through payment scheduling and balance management that can optimize reported utilization independent of actual spending patterns and financial behavior.

Utilization thresholds in credit scoring create specific targets and optimization opportunities that enable precise score improvement through strategic balance management and payment timing that aligns with scoring model mathematics.

Advanced utilization strategies leverage deep understanding of scoring algorithms, reporting mechanics, and credit bureau procedures to achieve maximum score benefits while maintaining practical account management and financial stability.

The business implications of utilization management extend beyond personal credit improvement to include business credit building, lending qualification, and comprehensive financial planning that relies on optimal credit profiles for enhanced opportunities and improved terms.

Utilization calculation methodology involves understanding the precise mathematical formulas and data points that credit scoring models use to evaluate utilization ratios and their impact on credit score calculations and creditworthiness assessment.

Individual account utilization calculation involves dividing current account balances by credit limits to determine per-card utilization ratios that significantly impact credit scores. Most scoring models evaluate each account individually before considering aggregate utilization patterns.

Aggregate utilization computation combines total balances across all revolving credit accounts divided by total available credit limits to create overall utilization ratios that represent another critical scoring factor requiring strategic management.

Balance timing considerations affect utilization calculations based on when credit card companies report account information to credit bureaus, typically occurring monthly around statement closing dates but varying by issuer and potentially creating optimization opportunities.

Credit limit reporting variations between issuers can affect utilization calculations when some accounts report limits while others don't, creating situations where utilization calculations may be skewed or incomplete for scoring purposes.

Zero balance impact on utilization calculations creates complex scoring considerations since having all accounts at zero utilization can sometimes be less optimal than maintaining small balances on one or more accounts for scoring algorithm purposes.

Charge card vs. credit card utilization differences affect calculations since charge cards without preset spending limits are typically excluded from utilization calculations, though they may still influence scoring through other factors.

Business credit card utilization may or may not impact personal credit scores depending on issuer reporting practices and account structure, creating strategic considerations for business and personal credit management coordination.

Credit limit changes affect utilization calculations immediately upon credit bureau reporting, creating opportunities for strategic limit increase requests that can improve utilization ratios without requiring balance reductions.

Account closure impacts on utilization include loss of available credit that can dramatically increase utilization ratios, making strategic account closure timing crucial for maintaining optimal utilization levels.

Promotional balance transfers and special financing arrangements may affect utilization calculations differently than regular purchases, creating opportunities for strategic balance management through promotional programs.

Historical utilization trending in advanced scoring models considers utilization patterns over time rather than just current ratios, making consistent utilization management important for optimal scoring beyond immediate ratio optimization.

Optimal utilization ratios involve understanding specific percentage thresholds that maximize credit score benefits while avoiding utilization levels that trigger negative scoring impacts or suggest financial stress to credit scoring algorithms.

The 30% threshold represents the maximum utilization ratio recommended for maintaining good credit scores, but optimal scoring typically requires much lower utilization levels for maximum score benefits and creditworthiness demonstration.

Single-digit utilization benefits include score improvements that occur when maintaining aggregate utilization below 10%, with some scoring models providing additional benefits for utilization below 5% or even lower thresholds.

Zero utilization considerations create complex scoring situations since having no reported balances can sometimes result in lower scores than maintaining minimal utilization that demonstrates active credit usage and management capability.

The 1% strategy involves maintaining approximately 1% utilization on one account while keeping all other accounts at zero balances, often providing optimal scoring benefits by demonstrating credit usage without suggesting financial stress.

Individual card thresholds include specific ratio targets for each account that optimize scoring while considering that some scoring models penalize individual cards with utilization above certain thresholds regardless of overall utilization levels.

High utilization recovery strategies involve systematic approaches to reducing utilization from dangerous levels (above 50%) to optimal ranges while minimizing negative score impact during the reduction process.

Utilization distribution strategies across multiple accounts help optimize scoring by spreading balances strategically rather than concentrating utilization on single accounts that might trigger individual card penalties.

Industry-specific utilization considerations include understanding how different types of credit accounts may be weighted differently in utilization calculations and how specialized credit products affect utilization optimization strategies.

Credit limit utilization versus available credit considerations include understanding how credit scoring models evaluate utilization relative to original limits versus current available credit after payments and credits.

Seasonal utilization management involves strategies for maintaining optimal ratios during periods of higher spending while ensuring that temporary utilization increases don't create lasting negative scoring impacts.

Emergency utilization protocols include procedures for managing credit utilization during financial emergencies while minimizing negative score impacts and maintaining long-term credit health despite temporary elevated utilization.

Per-card versus overall utilization strategy requires sophisticated understanding of how credit scoring models weight individual account utilization against aggregate utilization to optimize both factors simultaneously for maximum score benefit.

Individual card optimization involves managing each credit account to maintain optimal utilization ratios while understanding that some scoring models apply penalties for individual cards exceeding specific thresholds regardless of overall utilization levels.

Aggregate utilization management focuses on total utilization across all accounts while ensuring that overall ratios remain within optimal ranges for maximum scoring benefits and creditworthiness demonstration.

Scoring model variations in utilization weighting create different optimization requirements depending on which scoring versions are used for specific credit applications, making comprehensive optimization necessary for maximum effectiveness.

Balance distribution strategies involve spreading utilization across multiple accounts rather than concentrating balances on single cards to optimize both individual and aggregate utilization factors simultaneously.

High-limit card utilization advantages include using accounts with higher credit limits for utilization to minimize percentage impacts while maintaining the same dollar amounts of credit usage for practical purposes.

Low-limit card management requires special attention since small balances can create high utilization percentages that trigger scoring penalties disproportionate to actual credit usage amounts.

Account-specific utilization targets include establishing optimal ratio ranges for each individual account based on credit limits, account characteristics, and scoring optimization requirements.

Cross-account balance coordination involves managing payments and spending across multiple accounts to maintain optimal utilization distribution while supporting practical spending needs and payment convenience.

Utilization isolation strategies include designating specific accounts for utilization maintenance while keeping other accounts at zero balances to optimize scoring while maintaining credit availability for emergencies.

Multiple payment strategies for utilization optimization include timing payments across different accounts to achieve optimal utilization reporting while maintaining practical account management and cash flow coordination.

Portfolio approach to utilization management involves viewing all credit accounts as integrated components of utilization optimization rather than managing accounts independently without coordination.

Timing of payments and reporting represents one of the most sophisticated aspects of utilization management, requiring precise understanding of credit card issuer reporting schedules and payment processing to optimize utilization ratios independent of spending patterns.

Statement closing date significance affects utilization reporting since most credit card issuers report account balances to credit bureaus on or shortly after statement closing dates, making payment timing relative to these dates crucial for utilization optimization.

Payment posting timing considerations include understanding how long payments take to process and reflect in account balances, typically requiring 1-3 business days for electronic payments and longer for mailed payments.

Reporting schedule variations between credit card issuers create different optimization opportunities since some issuers report on specific monthly dates while others report throughout the month on varying schedules.

Pre-statement payment strategies involve making payments before statement closing dates to reduce reported balances below optimal utilization thresholds while maintaining spending convenience throughout the month.

Multiple payment techniques include making several payments per month to manage utilization ratios while using credit cards for regular spending without creating suboptimal utilization reporting.

Payment amount calculation for optimal utilization involves determining exact payment amounts needed to achieve target utilization ratios while considering pending transactions and payment processing timing.

Autopay coordination with manual payments combines automated minimum payment protection with strategic additional payments that optimize utilization reporting while ensuring payment security and timing control.

Weekend and holiday payment timing considerations include understanding how payment processing delays during non-business days affect utilization optimization and payment scheduling for optimal reporting.

Credit limit cycling involves understanding how payments restore available credit for continued spending while maintaining optimal utilization ratios throughout monthly spending and payment cycles.

Emergency payment procedures for utilization optimization include rapid payment methods and backup systems that enable quick utilization adjustments when unexpected spending or payment timing issues arise.

Technology integration for payment timing includes automated systems, mobile apps, and alert systems that optimize payment scheduling while reducing management complexity and ensuring consistent utilization optimization.

Balance transfer considerations for utilization optimization involve understanding how balance transfers affect utilization calculations and using transfer strategies to optimize utilization ratios across multiple accounts while managing transfer costs and limitations.

Balance transfer mechanics affect utilization calculations immediately upon transfer completion, creating opportunities for strategic utilization redistribution that optimizes scoring while potentially reducing interest costs through promotional rates.

Promotional rate utilization involves leveraging balance transfer promotions to optimize utilization distribution while taking advantage of reduced interest costs that support balance management and credit building objectives.

Transfer fee evaluation includes analyzing balance transfer costs against utilization optimization benefits while understanding how transfer fees affect overall financial costs and credit building return on investment.

Credit limit utilization for transfers involves understanding how balance transfers affect available credit on both source and destination accounts while optimizing utilization ratios across the entire credit portfolio.

Multiple account transfer strategies include coordinating transfers across several accounts to optimize utilization distribution while taking advantage of multiple promotional offers and credit availability.

Timing considerations for balance transfers include understanding promotional period limitations, transfer processing time, and optimal timing relative to credit applications and other financial planning objectives.

Utilization reset strategies through balance transfers involve using transfers to quickly achieve optimal utilization ratios when payment-based optimization would take too long to support time-sensitive credit needs.

Transfer reversal planning includes understanding how to undo balance transfer strategies when circumstances change while maintaining utilization optimization and minimizing costs and complications.

Credit building integration with balance transfers ensures that transfer strategies support broader credit improvement objectives while optimizing utilization as part of comprehensive credit building programs.

Risk management for balance transfer utilization strategies includes understanding promotional rate expiration, payment requirement implications, and potential negative consequences that could affect credit building and financial stability.

Long-term planning for balance transfer strategies includes understanding how transfers affect ongoing utilization management while building sustainable approaches that don't rely on continuous promotional rate availability.

Credit limit increase strategies represent powerful tools for utilization optimization that can provide immediate score improvements without requiring balance reductions or payment timing manipulation, making limit increases valuable components of comprehensive utilization management.

Automatic limit increase opportunities with many credit card issuers provide regular credit limit growth that improves utilization ratios automatically while demonstrating account management excellence and creditworthiness improvement over time.

Manual limit increase requests involve strategic timing and presentation to maximize approval chances while optimizing request amounts that provide meaningful utilization improvement without triggering issuer concerns about overextension.

Income documentation for limit increases includes preparing current income information and employment verification that supports larger credit limit requests while demonstrating ability to handle increased credit responsibility.

Request timing optimization involves understanding optimal periods for limit increase requests such as after payment history improvement, income increases, or account anniversary dates when issuers may be more receptive to increases.

Multiple account limit increases involve coordinating requests across different credit cards to maximize overall credit availability while managing request timing to avoid appearance of financial distress or overextension.

Soft pull vs. hard pull implications for limit increase requests include understanding which issuers perform hard credit inquiries for limit increases while prioritizing soft-pull increases that don't affect credit scores negatively.

Alternative limit increase strategies include product changes, account upgrades, and issuer-specific programs that provide credit limit growth through methods other than traditional increase requests.

Business credit limit strategies for personal utilization optimization include understanding how business credit cards might provide additional credit availability while maintaining optimal personal credit utilization ratios.

Utilization improvement calculation from limit increases includes determining how much credit limit increase is needed to achieve target utilization ratios while setting realistic expectations for limit increase outcomes.

Relationship building with issuers for limit increases includes maintaining positive account management and customer relationships that support favorable consideration for limit increase requests and ongoing credit line growth.

Integration with credit building strategies ensures that limit increase efforts support broader credit improvement objectives while coordinating with other credit building activities for comprehensive credit optimization.

Utilization and credit score impact involves understanding the precise relationships between utilization ratios and credit score changes to enable accurate prediction and optimization of score improvements through strategic utilization management.

Scoring model weight allocation for utilization typically represents 30% of credit score calculations in FICO models, making utilization the second-most important scoring factor after payment history and creating significant optimization opportunities.

Immediate score impact from utilization changes can occur within days of credit bureau reporting updates, making utilization optimization one of the fastest ways to improve credit scores for time-sensitive credit applications and financial objectives.

Score improvement magnitude from utilization optimization varies based on starting utilization levels, with consumers having high utilization typically experiencing larger score improvements than those already maintaining optimal ratios.

Threshold-based scoring impacts include specific utilization levels that trigger score improvements or penalties, such as crossing below 30%, 10%, or 5% utilization where scoring algorithms provide step-function benefits.

Individual account impact on scores includes understanding how single high-utilization accounts can significantly impact overall scores even when aggregate utilization remains reasonable, making individual account management crucial.

Credit mix interaction with utilization includes understanding how utilization optimization affects other scoring factors and how account diversity influences utilization impact on overall credit score calculations.

Historical utilization trending in advanced scoring models includes evaluation of utilization patterns over time rather than just current snapshots, making consistent utilization management important for optimal long-term scoring.

Utilization volatility impact on scoring includes potential penalties for dramatic utilization changes that might suggest financial instability, making gradual optimization preferable to sudden dramatic changes.

Score prediction modeling for utilization changes enables accurate forecasting of score improvements from specific utilization optimization strategies while setting realistic expectations for utilization management outcomes.

Cross-bureau scoring differences for utilization include understanding how different credit bureaus might report utilization differently and how various scoring models weight utilization factors for comprehensive optimization.

Long-term utilization strategy for sustained score optimization includes building utilization management habits that maintain optimal ratios consistently while supporting ongoing credit building and financial management objectives.

Strategic account management for utilization optimization involves sophisticated approaches to credit account selection, management, and coordination that maximize utilization benefits while supporting broader credit building and financial planning objectives.

Account portfolio design for utilization includes selecting credit accounts with characteristics that support optimal utilization management while providing practical utility and credit building benefits through strategic account acquisition.

High-limit account prioritization involves focusing utilization on accounts with higher credit limits to minimize percentage impacts while maintaining practical spending flexibility and optimal ratio achievement across the credit portfolio.

Low-limit account management requires special strategies for accounts with smaller credit limits that can easily exceed optimal utilization thresholds even with modest spending, potentially requiring dedicated management or strategic closure.

Account aging considerations for utilization include understanding how account age affects credit scores while balancing utilization optimization against account closure decisions that might impact credit history length and scoring.

Product change strategies for utilization optimization include upgrading or changing credit card products to obtain higher limits or better features while maintaining account age and optimizing utilization management capabilities.

Seasonal account management involves adapting utilization strategies for periods of higher or lower spending while maintaining optimal ratios during holiday seasons, vacation periods, and other times when spending patterns change.

Emergency credit planning includes maintaining credit availability for unexpected expenses while preserving optimal utilization ratios through strategic credit reserve management and emergency utilization protocols.

Account closure timing for utilization includes understanding when closing credit accounts might improve or harm utilization ratios while considering broader credit score impacts from account closure decisions.

Multiple issuer relationship management involves maintaining positive relationships with various credit card companies while optimizing utilization across different issuer relationships for maximum benefit and ongoing account management.

Integration with reward optimization includes balancing utilization optimization with credit card reward maximization while ensuring that reward strategies don't compromise optimal utilization ratio maintenance.

Professional credit management through utilization optimization demonstrates sophisticated financial management that can enhance lending relationships and provide advantages in credit applications and financial service access.

Advanced utilization techniques involve sophisticated strategies that leverage deep understanding of credit scoring algorithms, credit bureau reporting mechanics, and credit card issuer procedures to achieve maximum utilization optimization benefits.

Micro-balance management involves maintaining very small balances on specific accounts to optimize individual account utilization while demonstrating credit usage without creating suboptimal aggregate utilization ratios.

Payment frequency optimization includes making multiple payments per week or even daily to maintain optimal utilization while using credit cards for regular spending without compromising utilization ratio targets.

Balance cycling strategies involve systematic rotation of balances across different accounts to optimize utilization distribution while taking advantage of different reporting schedules and payment processing timelines.

Utilization arbitrage opportunities include leveraging differences in credit card terms, promotional rates, and reporting schedules to optimize utilization ratios while potentially reducing overall credit costs through strategic management.

Technology-enhanced utilization management includes using apps, automated systems, and monitoring tools to optimize utilization ratios with minimal manual management while maintaining precision and consistency.

Cross-account coordination involves managing utilization across business and personal credit accounts, store cards, and traditional credit cards to optimize overall credit utilization while maintaining practical account utility.

Promotional balance management includes understanding how promotional financing, deferred interest programs, and special offers affect utilization calculations while leveraging these programs for utilization optimization.

Emergency utilization protocols include rapid response procedures for managing utilization during unexpected financial stress while minimizing negative credit score impacts and maintaining long-term credit health.

International utilization considerations include understanding how foreign credit card usage, currency conversions, and international payment processing affect utilization calculations and optimization strategies.

Professional consultation integration for utilization optimization includes working with credit professionals and financial advisors while maintaining sophisticated utilization management as part of comprehensive financial planning.

Innovation development in utilization strategies includes creating novel approaches for unique circumstances while adapting utilization optimization to changing credit industry practices and scoring model evolution.

Mastery demonstration through utilization excellence provides evidence of sophisticated credit management that supports lending relationships and financial opportunities while building expertise for professional development.

Utilization psychology and lender perception involves understanding how utilization ratios influence lender decision-making beyond credit scores, including risk assessment factors and creditworthiness evaluation that affect lending outcomes and terms.

Risk assessment algorithms used by lenders often include utilization analysis beyond simple ratio calculations, evaluating utilization trends, volatility, and patterns that suggest financial stability or stress independent of credit score impacts.

Underwriter evaluation of utilization includes manual review processes that consider utilization context, explanations, and circumstances that might not be captured in automated scoring but affect lending decisions for significant credit applications.

Utilization trend analysis by lenders includes evaluation of historical utilization patterns to assess financial management capability and predict future credit performance based on utilization management consistency and improvement.

Financial stress indicators through utilization include warning signs that lenders recognize in utilization patterns that might suggest financial difficulties or increased default risk regardless of current credit score levels.

Credit management sophistication demonstration through optimal utilization management can positively influence lender perceptions and support favorable lending decisions that go beyond standard credit scoring criteria.

Industry-specific utilization considerations include understanding how different types of lenders evaluate utilization for various credit products while adapting utilization strategies to specific lending contexts and requirements.

Business lending utilization impact includes understanding how personal credit utilization affects business credit applications while managing personal utilization to support business credit access and entrepreneurial opportunities.

Mortgage lending utilization requirements often include specific utilization thresholds and management expectations that affect mortgage qualification while requiring strategic utilization optimization for home financing.

Auto lending utilization considerations include understanding how utilization affects automotive financing while optimizing utilization for vehicle purchase and lease applications that require strong credit profiles.

Premium credit product qualification through utilization excellence includes understanding how optimal utilization management supports access to high-end credit cards and exclusive financial products with superior terms and benefits.

Long-term relationship building with lenders through consistent utilization excellence helps establish positive institutional relationships that support ongoing financial opportunities and preferential treatment for future credit needs.

Utilization monitoring and automation involves leveraging technology and systematic approaches to maintain optimal utilization ratios with minimal manual management while ensuring consistent optimization and early problem identification.

Real-time monitoring systems provide continuous utilization tracking through mobile apps and online platforms that alert consumers to utilization changes and optimization opportunities while enabling proactive management.

Automated payment systems for utilization optimization include sophisticated autopay arrangements that maintain optimal ratios through strategic payment timing and amount calculation while reducing management complexity.

Alert systems for utilization thresholds include notifications when balances approach suboptimal levels while providing early warning for utilization management and optimization opportunity identification.

Credit monitoring integration includes incorporating utilization tracking with comprehensive credit monitoring services that provide holistic credit management while optimizing utilization as part of broader credit improvement strategies.

Mobile app utilization for credit management includes smartphone applications that provide convenient utilization monitoring and management while enabling real-time optimization and payment scheduling from anywhere.

Spending category analysis through monitoring systems helps identify spending patterns that affect utilization while optimizing spending allocation across different accounts for utilization and reward optimization.

Predictive analytics for utilization management include systems that forecast utilization impacts from planned spending while providing optimization recommendations based on individual spending patterns and financial objectives.

Integration with budgeting systems includes connecting utilization management with broader financial planning while ensuring that utilization optimization supports overall financial management and stability.

Backup monitoring systems include redundant tracking methods that ensure utilization monitoring continues during technology failures while maintaining optimization effectiveness regardless of primary system availability.

Data security for utilization monitoring includes understanding privacy protections and security measures for financial monitoring systems while balancing convenience with information protection requirements.

Performance analytics for utilization monitoring include evaluation of monitoring system effectiveness while identifying optimization opportunities and ensuring that monitoring systems provide intended benefits and support objectives.

Utilization crisis management involves systematic approaches to addressing high utilization situations that threaten credit scores while implementing rapid recovery strategies that minimize negative impacts and restore optimal ratios quickly.

High utilization identification includes recognizing dangerous utilization levels before they severely impact credit scores while understanding threshold levels that require immediate intervention and corrective action.

Emergency payment strategies for utilization reduction include rapid payment methods, emergency fund utilization, and alternative funding sources that enable quick utilization reduction when time-sensitive credit decisions require immediate optimization.

Balance consolidation for utilization improvement includes strategic use of balance transfers, personal loans, and other debt consolidation methods that reduce utilization ratios while potentially improving overall financial management.

Communication with creditors during utilization crises includes negotiating payment arrangements, limit increases, and other accommodations that help manage utilization while maintaining positive creditor relationships.

Credit counseling integration for utilization management includes working with professional counselors during utilization crises while developing sustainable utilization management strategies that prevent future problems.

Prioritization strategies for multiple high-utilization accounts include determining optimal order for utilization reduction across different accounts while maximizing score improvement impact from available resources.

Income acceleration for utilization reduction includes strategies for increasing available funds for utilization reduction while managing cash flow and maintaining financial stability during utilization crisis periods.

Expense reduction for utilization management includes temporary spending cuts and lifestyle adjustments that free up resources for utilization reduction while supporting sustainable financial management.

Timeline planning for utilization recovery includes understanding how long utilization reduction takes to impact credit scores while coordinating recovery efforts with time-sensitive credit applications and financial objectives.

Progress monitoring during utilization crisis includes tracking recovery progress and score improvements while ensuring that crisis management efforts produce intended results and support ongoing financial objectives.

Prevention planning after utilization crisis includes implementing systems and strategies that prevent future utilization problems while building sustainable utilization management habits for long-term credit health.

Industry-specific utilization strategies recognize that different types of credit decisions and lending contexts require adapted utilization approaches while optimizing utilization management for specific financial goals and lending environments.

Mortgage lending utilization requirements often include specific ratio thresholds and timing considerations that affect home loan qualification while requiring strategic utilization optimization for real estate financing applications.

Auto lending utilization optimization includes understanding how vehicle financing evaluates utilization while managing ratios for optimal automotive lending terms and qualification for preferred financing programs.

Business lending utilization impact includes understanding how personal utilization affects business credit applications while managing personal credit to support entrepreneurial activities and business financing access.

Credit card application utilization includes optimizing ratios before applying for new credit cards while understanding how utilization affects approval chances and initial credit limit determination for new accounts.

Student loan utilization considerations include understanding how educational financing evaluates credit utilization while managing utilization to support educational investment and student loan qualification.

Personal loan utilization optimization includes managing ratios for personal loan applications while understanding how personal lending evaluates utilization relative to other creditworthiness factors.

Insurance utilization impact includes understanding how credit utilization affects insurance rates and coverage while optimizing utilization for comprehensive risk management and insurance cost reduction.

Employment utilization considerations include understanding how credit utilization might affect employment opportunities requiring credit checks while managing utilization for career development and professional opportunities.

Rental application utilization includes optimizing ratios for housing applications while understanding how property management companies evaluate credit utilization for rental approval decisions.

Investment account utilization includes understanding how utilization affects margin lending and investment account qualification while optimizing credit management for investment opportunity access.

Professional service utilization includes understanding how credit utilization affects access to professional services requiring credit evaluation while managing utilization for comprehensive professional relationship development.

International utilization considerations include understanding how utilization management translates across different credit systems while optimizing utilization for international financial opportunities and relationships.

Future trends in utilization optimization include emerging developments in credit scoring, technology integration, and industry practices that will affect utilization strategies while creating new opportunities for optimization and credit building.

Artificial intelligence applications in utilization management include automated optimization systems that continuously adjust utilization strategies while learning from individual patterns and optimizing results through machine learning algorithms.

Real-time credit scoring updates may enable immediate utilization optimization benefits while creating opportunities for dynamic utilization management that responds instantly to credit report changes and scoring updates.

Alternative data integration in utilization evaluation includes consideration of bank account management, spending patterns, and financial behavior that supplement traditional utilization analysis while creating new optimization opportunities.

Blockchain applications in credit reporting may affect utilization calculation and reporting while creating new opportunities for accurate, transparent, and immediate utilization optimization and credit management.

Mobile payment integration with utilization management includes seamless coordination between payment systems and utilization optimization while enabling automated utilization management through integrated financial technology platforms.

Predictive utilization modeling includes advanced analytics that forecast optimal utilization strategies while providing personalized recommendations based on individual financial patterns and credit building objectives.

Regulatory evolution in utilization evaluation includes potential changes in credit reporting requirements and scoring model standards that may affect utilization optimization strategies while creating new consumer protections.

Industry consolidation impacts on utilization include understanding how banking industry changes affect credit card issuer policies while adapting utilization strategies to changing issuer relationships and account management practices.

International utilization standardization includes potential development of global credit reporting standards while creating opportunities for international utilization optimization and cross-border credit management.

Consumer education enhancement in utilization management includes improved financial literacy resources while supporting better utilization optimization understanding and implementation across diverse consumer populations.

Professional service evolution in utilization optimization includes enhanced consulting services and technology platforms while providing improved access to sophisticated utilization management expertise and optimization assistance.

Innovation opportunities in utilization management include novel approaches and creative strategies while adapting utilization optimization to changing credit industry practices and emerging financial technology capabilities.

Utilization mastery integration with comprehensive financial planning ensures that sophisticated utilization management supports broader wealth building while optimizing credit excellence within holistic financial management and long-term security planning.

Wealth building integration through utilization optimization includes understanding how optimal credit management supports investment opportunities while leveraging excellent credit for enhanced financial opportunity access and wealth multiplication strategies.

Risk management coordination includes integrating utilization strategies with comprehensive financial protection while ensuring that credit management supports overall financial security and wealth preservation through optimal credit utilization.

Tax planning integration with utilization management includes understanding how credit optimization affects tax strategies while coordinating utilization management with comprehensive tax planning for optimal financial efficiency and wealth building.

Business development support through utilization excellence includes leveraging optimal personal credit utilization for business opportunities while building creditworthiness that supports entrepreneurial activities and business financing access.

Investment opportunity enhancement through utilization optimization includes understanding how credit excellence affects investment access while leveraging improved creditworthiness for enhanced investment opportunities and portfolio development.

Estate planning coordination includes understanding how credit excellence affects wealth transfer while ensuring that utilization mastery supports legacy development and family financial security through comprehensive planning integration.

Professional development through utilization expertise includes building consulting capabilities and educational opportunities while leveraging utilization mastery for career advancement and income enhancement through specialized knowledge.

International financial planning integration includes understanding how utilization optimization supports global financial opportunities while adapting utilization strategies for international investment and business development.

Retirement planning enhancement through credit excellence includes understanding how optimal utilization supports retirement financing while ensuring that credit management excellence enhances retirement security and financial independence.

Insurance optimization through credit improvement includes understanding how utilization affects insurance costs while integrating credit management with comprehensive risk management and financial protection planning.

Legacy creation through utilization mastery includes building lasting financial expertise while contributing to financial literacy and consumer protection through utilization optimization knowledge and community assistance.

Utilization optimization measurement and evaluation involve comprehensive assessment methodologies that track effectiveness while identifying improvement opportunities and ensuring that utilization strategies produce maximum long-term value and credit building benefit.

Performance metrics for utilization optimization include tracking credit score improvements, ratio maintenance consistency, cost-effectiveness, and goal achievement while providing comprehensive evaluation of utilization strategy success and refinement opportunities.

Score correlation analysis helps understand which utilization strategies produce optimal results while identifying specific techniques and ratio targets that contribute most significantly to credit score improvement and creditworthiness enhancement.

Timeline effectiveness evaluation includes assessing how quickly utilization strategies produce benefits while understanding factors that accelerate or delay credit improvement through utilization optimization and strategic management.

Cost-benefit analysis for utilization strategies includes evaluating management effort and potential costs against credit improvement benefits while ensuring optimal resource allocation and strategy selection for maximum return on investment.

Consistency measurement for utilization management includes tracking ratio maintenance over time while identifying factors that support sustained utilization optimization and long-term credit management excellence.

Integration effectiveness assessment includes evaluating how utilization strategies coordinate with other credit building activities while identifying optimization opportunities for enhanced coordination and comprehensive credit improvement.

Technology utilization evaluation includes assessing monitoring systems and automation effectiveness while optimizing technology integration for improved utilization management and reduced complexity.

Relationship impact measurement includes understanding how utilization optimization affects lending relationships while evaluating how credit excellence enhances financial opportunity access and preferential treatment.

Professional development assessment through utilization expertise includes evaluating skill advancement and knowledge development while identifying opportunities for expertise expansion and career enhancement through utilization mastery.

Innovation measurement for utilization strategies includes evaluating novel approaches and creative techniques while identifying successful innovations that enhance utilization optimization effectiveness and adaptability.

Long-term value assessment for utilization optimization includes comprehensive evaluation of credit building benefits, financial opportunity enhancement, and wealth building support while optimizing utilization mastery value throughout changing circumstances.

Success preservation strategies ensure that utilization optimization benefits continue supporting financial objectives while maintaining excellence and building sustainable utilization management habits for lifelong credit success and financial achievement.

Utilization optimization troubleshooting involves systematic approaches to identifying and resolving problems that arise during sophisticated utilization management while maintaining optimization effectiveness and protecting credit building investments.

Problem identification for utilization issues includes recognizing utilization management complications while understanding how system failures, payment processing problems, and account changes affect utilization optimization and credit score impacts.

Solution development for utilization problems includes creating corrective strategies while maintaining utilization optimization effectiveness and minimizing negative impacts during problem resolution periods.

Payment processing problem resolution includes addressing autopay failures, bank account issues, and credit card company problems while maintaining optimal utilization ratios and preventing credit score damage from payment timing issues.

Account change management includes handling credit limit changes, account closures, and issuer policy modifications while adapting utilization strategies to maintain optimization effectiveness despite changing circumstances.

Technology failure backup includes manual utilization management procedures while ensuring optimization continuation during monitoring system outages and automated payment system failures.

Credit bureau reporting error correction includes addressing incorrect utilization reporting while coordinating with credit card issuers and credit bureaus to ensure accurate utilization calculation and score optimization.

Emergency utilization adjustment includes rapid response procedures for unexpected utilization spikes while implementing immediate corrective actions that minimize credit score impacts and restore optimal ratios quickly.

Relationship problem resolution includes addressing credit card issuer issues while maintaining positive relationships and account access that support ongoing utilization optimization and credit management.

Documentation preservation during problem resolution includes maintaining records of utilization management issues while ensuring that problem resolution creates appropriate evidence and supports continued optimization effectiveness.

Professional assistance coordination for complex utilization problems includes accessing specialized expertise while resolving complicated issues that exceed individual problem-solving capabilities and require expert intervention.

Recovery planning after utilization problems includes restoring optimization effectiveness while implementing improvements that prevent similar issues and enhance overall utilization management resilience and sustainability.

Prevention strategies based on problem experience include implementing safeguards while building systems that reduce future problem likelihood and enhance utilization optimization reliability and effectiveness.

Advanced utilization psychology involves understanding the behavioral and emotional aspects of credit utilization management while developing sustainable habits and mindset approaches that support long-term utilization optimization and credit excellence.

Behavioral modification for utilization management includes developing sustainable spending and payment habits while creating psychological frameworks that support consistent utilization optimization without excessive restriction or financial stress.

Emotional regulation during utilization management includes maintaining psychological balance while avoiding anxiety or obsession about utilization ratios that could compromise overall financial well-being and decision-making quality.

Habit formation for utilization optimization includes building automatic behaviors while creating systems that support consistent utilization management without requiring constant conscious attention and decision-making energy.

Stress management during utilization challenges includes maintaining psychological health while addressing utilization problems and implementing corrective strategies without compromising overall mental and emotional well-being.

Motivation maintenance for long-term utilization excellence includes sustaining commitment while building psychological resilience that supports continued utilization optimization through changing circumstances and life challenges.

Goal integration with utilization management includes aligning credit optimization with broader life objectives while ensuring that utilization strategies support rather than conflict with personal values and financial priorities.

Social considerations for utilization management include managing family and relationship dynamics while implementing utilization strategies that coordinate with household financial management and social responsibilities.

Professional psychological development through utilization mastery includes building confidence and expertise while developing leadership capabilities that support broader financial management excellence and community contribution.

Mindfulness applications in utilization management include conscious awareness techniques while developing present-moment focus that enhances utilization decision-making and reduces reactive financial behavior.

Educational psychology for utilization learning includes understanding optimal learning approaches while building utilization expertise through systematic knowledge development and skill building that supports mastery achievement.

Community psychology for utilization advocacy includes understanding group dynamics while contributing to broader financial literacy and consumer protection through utilization optimization knowledge sharing and education.

Therapeutic applications of utilization mastery include understanding how credit excellence supports psychological well-being while building financial confidence and security that enhances overall life satisfaction and mental health.

Utilization optimization legacy and impact involve understanding how mastery of credit utilization creates lasting value while contributing to broader financial empowerment and consumer protection through expertise development and knowledge sharing.

Personal legacy development through utilization expertise includes building lasting financial capabilities while creating foundation skills that support lifelong financial success and provide resilience through changing economic conditions and life circumstances.

Professional legacy creation includes developing consulting capabilities while contributing to broader financial literacy and consumer protection through utilization optimization expertise and educational assistance to others.

Family impact through utilization mastery includes teaching family members while building household financial management excellence that supports multi-generational wealth building and financial security through credit optimization knowledge.

Community contribution through utilization expertise includes sharing knowledge while supporting broader financial inclusion and consumer empowerment through utilization optimization education and assistance programs.

Industry impact through utilization innovation includes contributing to best practices while advancing utilization optimization techniques and supporting industry improvement through expertise development and knowledge sharing.

Educational contribution through utilization mastery includes developing teaching capabilities while supporting financial literacy advancement and consumer education through utilization optimization expertise and instruction.

Policy influence through utilization mastery includes understanding regulatory implications while contributing to consumer protection advancement and credit reporting improvement through expertise application and advocacy activities.

Technology advancement through utilization innovation includes developing new approaches while contributing to fintech development and credit management tool improvement through practical expertise and user experience insights.

Mentoring capability development through utilization excellence includes building guidance skills while supporting others' financial success through utilization optimization knowledge transfer and personal development assistance.

Wealth creation through utilization mastery includes leveraging credit excellence for enhanced financial opportunities while building comprehensive wealth through optimal credit access and preferential lending relationships.

Social impact through utilization expertise includes contributing to financial justice while supporting underserved communities through utilization optimization education and assistance that enhances financial inclusion and empowerment.

Innovation legacy through utilization mastery includes developing creative approaches while contributing to credit optimization advancement and financial management innovation through practical expertise and strategic thinking development.

Knowledge preservation through utilization expertise includes documenting effective strategies while ensuring that utilization optimization knowledge continues benefiting future generations through systematic knowledge transfer and educational resource development.

Sustainable impact through utilization mastery includes building lasting change while creating systems and relationships that continue providing benefit beyond individual achievement through community building and institutional relationship development.

Transformational impact through utilization excellence includes creating significant positive change while contributing to systemic improvement in financial management and consumer protection through comprehensive expertise application and leadership development.

CHAPTER 17

STRATEGIC ACCOUNT MANAGEMENT

Strategic account management represents the sophisticated orchestration of credit accounts to optimize credit profiles, maximize financial benefits, and support long-term wealth building objectives. Unlike basic account management that focuses merely on payment compliance, strategic management leverages deep understanding of credit scoring algorithms, lender preferences, and financial optimization to create comprehensive credit portfolios that enhance all aspects of financial opportunity.

The evolution of credit account management has transformed from simple payment management to complex portfolio optimization that considers account age, credit mix, utilization distribution, and relationship value. Modern strategic account management requires understanding multiple interconnected factors that affect both immediate credit scores and long-term financial opportunities.

Account lifecycle management involves understanding how credit accounts change over time and how to optimize each phase of account ownership for maximum benefit. From initial account acquisition through potential closure, strategic management maximizes value while minimizing risks and costs throughout the entire account relationship.

The portfolio approach to credit account management treats individual accounts as components of an integrated system rather than isolated products. This holistic view enables optimization strategies that leverage account interactions, issuer relationships, and cross-account benefits for superior overall outcomes.

Credit mix optimization through strategic account management involves maintaining diverse account types that demonstrate comprehensive creditworthiness while avoiding unnecessary complexity or accounts that don't contribute meaningfully to credit profiles or financial objectives.

Relationship banking through strategic account management creates comprehensive financial service access through consolidated banking relationships that provide enhanced benefits, preferential treatment, and improved access to financial products and services.

Technology integration in account management includes sophisticated monitoring, automation, and optimization tools that enhance management effectiveness while reducing complexity and ensuring consistent execution of strategic account management principles.

The timing aspects of account management involve understanding optimal periods for account acquisition, modification, and closure while coordinating account management activities with broader financial planning and major life events.

Risk management in strategic account management includes understanding potential complications while implementing safeguards that protect credit profiles and financial interests throughout changing circumstances and market conditions.

Professional account management standards demonstrate financial sophistication that enhances lending relationships and supports preferential treatment from financial institutions while building foundation skills for advanced financial management and wealth building.

When to close accounts versus keeping them open requires sophisticated analysis of multiple factors that affect both immediate credit scores and long-term financial positioning. The decision-making framework must consider credit scoring impacts, financial costs, practical utility, and strategic positioning for future financial opportunities.

Credit score impact analysis for account closure includes understanding how closure affects account age calculations, available credit totals, and credit mix diversity that contribute to credit score calculations and creditworthiness assessment by lenders.

Account age preservation represents one of the most critical factors in closure decisions since account age contributes significantly to credit scores and demonstrates long-term credit management capability. Closing old accounts can substantially reduce average account age and harm credit scores.

Available credit impact from account closure includes understanding how closure reduces total credit limits and potentially increases utilization ratios across remaining accounts, which can significantly impact credit scores even when balances remain unchanged.

Annual fee cost-benefit analysis involves evaluating ongoing account costs against account benefits while considering alternative uses for annual fee payments and whether account benefits justify continued costs throughout changing circumstances.

Credit mix considerations for account closure include understanding how closure affects account type diversity and whether maintaining specific account types provides credit scoring benefits that justify continued account maintenance despite limited practical usage.

Issuer relationship value assessment includes evaluating banking relationships, customer service quality, and potential future product access that might justify maintaining accounts even when immediate benefits are limited or costs are substantial.

Account utility evaluation involves assessing practical usage patterns, reward value, and convenience factors while understanding whether accounts provide sufficient practical benefits to justify continued maintenance and annual fee payments.

Dormancy risk management includes understanding issuer policies regarding inactive accounts while implementing strategies that maintain account activity without unnecessary spending or account management complexity that exceeds account value.

Timing considerations for account closure include understanding optimal periods relative to credit applications, major financial decisions, and life circumstances while minimizing negative impacts during critical credit evaluation periods.

Alternative optimization strategies include account downgrades, product changes, and relationship modifications that might provide account benefits without closure while addressing concerns about fees, terms, or account utility.

Documentation and communication for account closure includes understanding issuer procedures while ensuring proper closure confirmation and credit bureau reporting that prevents ongoing credit report errors or account management complications.

Integration with portfolio strategy ensures that closure decisions support overall credit portfolio optimization while maintaining strategic account positioning and credit building momentum throughout changing financial circumstances and objectives.

Account aging strategies involve understanding how account age affects credit scores while implementing approaches that maximize age-related benefits and position credit profiles for optimal long-term scoring and creditworthiness demonstration.

Average account age calculation includes understanding how credit scoring models weight different accounts while recognizing that newer accounts reduce average age calculations and older accounts provide disproportionate scoring benefits over time.

Account opening timing coordination involves strategic spacing of new account applications while minimizing negative impacts on average account age and ensuring that new accounts support rather than compromise overall credit profile strength.

Authorized user account aging benefits include understanding how authorized user status on old accounts can immediately improve average account age while providing substantial scoring benefits without requiring independent credit qualification or account management.

Account preservation strategies for aging optimization include maintaining old accounts even when practical utility is limited while implementing minimal activity strategies that prevent closure due to dormancy without unnecessary costs or complexity.

Product change considerations for aging include understanding how account modifications affect account age reporting while leveraging product changes to improve account features without sacrificing valuable account age that contributes to credit scoring.

New account impact mitigation includes strategies for minimizing average age reduction when acquiring new accounts while understanding how strategic timing and account selection can optimize aging impacts during credit building phases.

Long-term aging planning involves understanding how current account management decisions affect future credit profiles while building account portfolios that provide sustained aging benefits throughout changing financial circumstances and credit needs.

Industry variations in aging reporting include understanding how different types of accounts contribute to age calculations while optimizing account mix for maximum aging benefits across diverse account types and issuer relationships.

Relationship building through aging includes leveraging long-term account relationships for enhanced customer service, credit line increases, and preferential treatment while building institutional relationships that support ongoing financial opportunities.

Aging optimization integration with other credit factors ensures that age-focused strategies coordinate effectively with utilization management, payment history optimization, and credit mix development for comprehensive credit profile enhancement.

Professional recognition through account aging demonstrates financial stability and long-term credit management capability while building credibility with lenders and supporting enhanced access to financial products and preferential lending terms.

Product change considerations involve understanding when and how to modify existing credit accounts to optimize benefits while preserving valuable account characteristics such as age, credit limits, and issuer relationships.

Upgrade opportunities with existing accounts include transitioning to premium products that offer enhanced benefits while maintaining account age and established credit limits that support continued credit building and financial optimization.

Downgrade strategies for cost reduction include moving to no-fee products when premium benefits no longer justify costs while preserving account age and credit history that contribute to credit score calculations and creditworthiness demonstration.

Feature enhancement through product changes includes accessing improved reward programs, better interest rates, and enhanced account benefits while maintaining established account relationships and credit reporting characteristics.

Credit limit preservation during product changes includes ensuring that account modifications don't reduce available credit while potentially accessing higher credit limits through upgrade opportunities that enhance utilization management capabilities.

Timing optimization for product changes includes understanding optimal periods relative to credit applications and major financial decisions while minimizing any temporary negative impacts during transition periods.

Eligibility assessment for product changes includes understanding issuer requirements and qualification criteria while preparing documentation and account management that supports approval for desired product modifications.

Communication strategies with issuers for product changes include presenting requests professionally while highlighting customer relationship value and account management excellence that supports favorable consideration for product modifications.

Multiple account product change coordination includes managing modifications across different accounts and issuers while ensuring that changes support overall portfolio optimization and strategic account management objectives.

Alternative consideration evaluation includes comparing product change options against new account acquisition while understanding how different approaches affect credit profiles, costs, and long-term financial positioning.

Documentation and confirmation for product changes includes ensuring proper implementation while verifying that changes produce intended benefits and credit reporting reflects product modifications accurately and completely.

Integration with credit building strategies ensures that product changes support broader credit improvement objectives while coordinating with other account management activities and financial planning goals for comprehensive optimization.

Annual fee cost-benefit analysis requires comprehensive evaluation of account costs against benefits while considering alternative uses for fee payments and whether premium account features justify ongoing costs throughout changing financial circumstances.

Fee structure evaluation includes understanding total annual costs including annual fees, foreign transaction fees, balance transfer fees, and other charges while calculating true account cost for accurate cost-benefit comparison.

Benefit quantification for fee-based accounts includes calculating reward value, insurance benefits, travel perks, and other features while understanding how account benefits translate into monetary value and practical utility.

Alternative account comparison includes evaluating similar accounts with different fee structures while understanding how fee-free alternatives might provide comparable benefits without ongoing cost obligations.

Usage pattern analysis for fee justification includes understanding spending patterns and benefit utilization while determining whether account usage generates sufficient value to justify annual fee payments through reward optimization.

Relationship value assessment includes evaluating issuer relationship benefits, customer service quality, and potential future product access while considering how premium account relationships might provide intangible benefits.

Fee negotiation opportunities include understanding when issuers might waive or reduce annual fees while leveraging customer relationship value and account management excellence for fee reduction or elimination.

Timing considerations for fee evaluation include understanding optimal periods for fee assessment while coordinating evaluation with account anniversary dates and potential product changes that might affect fee structures.

Break-even calculation for fee-based accounts includes determining spending levels needed to justify annual fees through rewards while understanding how spending requirements affect overall financial management and budgeting.

Long-term cost projection includes calculating cumulative fee costs over expected account ownership periods while understanding how fee payments affect overall financial planning and alternative investment opportunities.

Integration with portfolio strategy ensures that fee decisions support overall account management objectives while maintaining strategic account positioning without excessive costs that don't provide proportional benefits.

Professional consultation for complex fee decisions includes understanding when expert assistance becomes valuable while evaluating sophisticated account portfolios that require specialized analysis and optimization expertise.

Credit limit optimization involves strategic approaches to maximizing available credit across account portfolios while understanding how credit limits affect utilization calculations, lending relationships, and overall creditworthiness demonstration.

Automatic limit increase opportunities with many issuers provide regular credit growth while demonstrating account management excellence and building available credit without requiring formal requests or credit inquiries.

Strategic limit increase timing includes understanding optimal periods for requests while coordinating with income increases, credit score improvements, and major financial milestones that support favorable consideration for credit line growth.

Income documentation for limit increases includes preparing current income verification while understanding how employment stability and income growth support larger credit limit requests and enhanced creditworthiness demonstration.

Multiple account limit coordination includes managing increase requests across different accounts while optimizing total available credit growth and ensuring that requests don't appear excessive or suggest financial overextension.

Soft pull versus hard pull implications for limit increases include prioritizing issuers that use soft credit inquiries while avoiding unnecessary hard inquiries that could temporarily impact credit scores during limit increase requests.

Relationship leverage for limit increases includes utilizing positive account management and customer relationships while demonstrating account value and creditworthiness that supports favorable consideration for credit line growth.

Utilization optimization through limit increases includes understanding how increased limits improve utilization ratios while supporting better credit scores without requiring spending changes or balance reduction efforts.

Business credit limit strategies include understanding how business credit cards might provide additional credit availability while maintaining optimal personal credit utilization through expanded credit access.

Alternative limit increase methods include product changes, account upgrades, and issuer-specific programs while exploring options beyond traditional increase requests that might provide credit line growth opportunities.

Limit decrease management includes understanding when to request lower limits for account management while recognizing situations where reduced limits might improve financial discipline without significantly harming credit scores.

Integration with credit building ensures that limit optimization supports broader credit improvement while coordinating with other account management activities for comprehensive credit portfolio development and optimization.

Account mix and diversity optimization involves maintaining optimal combinations of account types that demonstrate comprehensive creditworthiness while avoiding unnecessary complexity or accounts that don't contribute meaningfully to credit profiles.

Credit mix components include understanding how different account types contribute to credit scoring while maintaining appropriate balances between revolving credit, installment loans, and specialized credit products that demonstrate diverse credit management capability.

Revolving credit optimization includes maintaining appropriate numbers of credit cards while understanding how multiple revolving accounts contribute to credit mix without creating excessive inquiry activity or account management complexity.

Installment loan integration includes incorporating auto loans, personal loans, or credit builder loans while understanding how installment credit complements revolving credit for optimal credit mix demonstration and scoring benefits.

Mortgage credit impact includes understanding how home loans contribute to credit mix while recognizing that mortgage credit often provides substantial credit mix benefits due to loan size and payment complexity.

Store credit card considerations include evaluating retail credit cards for credit mix benefits while understanding how store cards contribute to account diversity without necessarily providing optimal utility or cost-effectiveness.

Specialized credit product evaluation includes understanding how unique account types such as charge cards, secured cards, and alternative credit products contribute to credit mix while providing practical benefits.

Account type redundancy assessment includes identifying unnecessary duplication while streamlining account portfolios to maintain optimal credit mix without excessive complexity or redundant account relationships.

Industry diversification through account mix includes maintaining accounts across different financial institutions while building diverse issuer relationships that provide enhanced financial service access and risk distribution.

Credit mix timing strategies include understanding optimal sequences for acquiring different account types while building comprehensive credit profiles through strategic account acquisition and relationship development.

Professional credit mix development includes understanding how sophisticated account portfolios demonstrate financial management capability while building relationships that support advanced financial planning and wealth building opportunities.

Integration with financial planning ensures that account mix optimization supports broader financial objectives while maintaining credit mix that enhances rather than complicates overall financial management and goal achievement.

Relationship banking through strategic account management involves building comprehensive financial service relationships that provide enhanced benefits, preferential treatment, and improved access to financial products through consolidated banking connections.

Institutional relationship development includes understanding how multiple account relationships with single institutions provide enhanced customer status while accessing relationship banking benefits and preferential treatment.

Cross-selling optimization includes leveraging existing account relationships for additional products while understanding how relationship depth affects account terms, fee structures, and customer service quality.

Banking tier achievement through relationship building includes understanding institutional customer classification systems while achieving preferred customer status that provides enhanced benefits and improved service access.

Private banking qualification through relationship development includes building account relationships that support private banking access while understanding how relationship value affects eligibility for exclusive financial services.

Customer service enhancement through relationship depth includes accessing dedicated support and relationship managers while building institutional connections that provide superior service and problem resolution assistance.

Product bundling benefits through relationship banking include understanding how multiple product relationships provide cost savings while accessing enhanced features and benefits that aren't available to single-product customers.

Geographic relationship considerations include understanding how branch access and local relationship banking might provide enhanced service while building community banking connections that support business and personal financial needs.

Digital relationship optimization includes leveraging online and mobile banking relationships while understanding how digital engagement affects customer classification and service access through technology-enhanced relationship management.

Business and personal relationship coordination includes understanding how business banking relationships affect personal account management while leveraging comprehensive relationships for enhanced financial service access.

Investment relationship integration includes understanding how investment accounts and wealth management services integrate with banking relationships while building comprehensive financial service access through institutional relationships.

Long-term relationship planning includes understanding how relationship development supports future financial needs while building institutional connections that provide ongoing value throughout changing financial circumstances and objectives.

Account management automation involves leveraging technology and systematic approaches to optimize account management effectiveness while reducing complexity and ensuring consistent execution of strategic account management principles.

Automated payment systems for account management include sophisticated autopay arrangements that optimize payment timing while ensuring perfect payment history across multiple accounts without manual management complexity.

Account monitoring automation includes real-time tracking systems that provide account performance updates while alerting to optimization opportunities and potential problems that require attention or intervention.

Credit limit monitoring automation includes systems that track limit changes and utilization impacts while providing optimization recommendations based on account performance and credit building objectives.

Fee tracking automation includes monitoring annual fees, interest charges, and other account costs while providing cost-benefit analysis and optimization recommendations for account portfolio management.

Reward optimization automation includes systems that maximize reward earning and redemption while ensuring optimal account usage patterns that support both reward generation and credit building objectives.

Balance management automation includes sophisticated utilization optimization systems while maintaining optimal ratios across multiple accounts through automated payment coordination and balance distribution.

Account security automation includes fraud monitoring, identity protection, and unauthorized activity detection while providing enhanced security for account portfolios without requiring constant manual oversight.

Communication automation with account issuers includes systematic interaction management while maintaining positive relationships and ensuring timely responses to issuer communications and account management opportunities.

Integration automation across multiple platforms includes coordinating account management with budgeting systems, credit monitoring, and financial planning tools while ensuring comprehensive financial management automation.

Performance analytics automation includes tracking account management effectiveness while providing optimization recommendations based on account performance data and credit building progress measurement.

Backup system automation includes redundant monitoring and management systems while ensuring account management continuation during technology failures or system outages that could compromise optimization effectiveness.

Account portfolio stress testing involves evaluating account management strategies under various economic scenarios and personal circumstances while ensuring portfolio resilience and optimization effectiveness throughout changing conditions.

Economic scenario planning for account management includes understanding how recession, inflation, and market volatility might affect account terms while developing strategies that maintain portfolio optimization during challenging economic periods.

Interest rate impact assessment includes understanding how rate changes affect account costs while developing strategies that optimize portfolio performance across different interest rate environments and market conditions.

Income volatility planning includes strategies for maintaining account management excellence during income fluctuations while ensuring that portfolio strategies remain viable throughout changing employment and financial circumstances.

Credit market stress testing includes understanding how lending environment changes affect account access while developing portfolio strategies that maintain optimization effectiveness during credit tightening or market disruption.

Issuer policy change adaptation includes understanding how banking industry changes affect account terms while developing strategies that maintain portfolio optimization despite changing issuer policies and relationship dynamics.

Regulatory impact assessment includes understanding how consumer protection changes affect account management while adapting strategies to leverage new protections and comply with changing regulatory requirements.

Personal circumstance stress testing includes evaluating portfolio strategies during major life events while ensuring that account management remains optimal during marriage, divorce, career changes, and other significant life transitions.

Emergency scenario planning includes strategies for maintaining account management during financial emergencies while ensuring that portfolio optimization supports rather than complicates financial recovery efforts.

Technology failure contingency planning includes backup account management strategies while ensuring portfolio optimization continuation during system outages and technology disruptions that could affect account management.

International stress testing includes understanding how global economic conditions affect domestic account management while developing strategies that maintain portfolio optimization during international financial instability.

Long-term sustainability assessment includes evaluating whether account management strategies remain viable throughout extended periods while ensuring that portfolio approaches support sustained financial success and optimization.

Professional account management consultation involves understanding when expert assistance becomes valuable while optimizing professional service utilization for sophisticated account portfolio management and strategic optimization.

Consultation timing assessment includes understanding optimal periods for seeking professional account management assistance while evaluating circumstances that justify professional investment and coordination with independent management efforts.

Professional credential evaluation for account management includes assessing consultant qualifications and specialization while understanding professional standards that ensure quality service and appropriate expertise for sophisticated portfolio management.

Service scope definition for account management consultation includes understanding professional service offerings while establishing clear expectations and deliverables that optimize professional assistance value and effectiveness.

Cost-benefit analysis for professional account management includes evaluating consultation costs against potential benefits while comparing professional assistance against independent management approaches for optimal resource allocation decisions.

Collaboration strategies with account management professionals include maintaining active participation while leveraging professional expertise effectively for optimal outcomes and skill development through professional guidance and mentorship.

Quality assessment for professional account management services includes evaluating service delivery and result achievement while ensuring that consultation provides intended value and supports account management objectives effectively.

Documentation coordination with professionals includes providing comprehensive portfolio information while understanding how professional assistance affects strategic planning and optimization for collaborative account management effectiveness.

Integration planning with professional services ensures that consultation supports broader financial planning objectives while coordinating effectively with other financial advisors and professional service providers for comprehensive assistance.

Performance monitoring for professional consultation includes tracking progress and evaluating effectiveness while ensuring accountability and maintaining clear communication throughout professional service relationships.

Termination planning for professional services includes understanding completion criteria and transition procedures while ensuring that professional assistance builds capabilities for independent account management and ongoing optimization.

Professional network development through consultation includes building relationships and ongoing connections while leveraging professional relationships for continued support and advanced financial planning assistance throughout changing circumstances.

Account management innovation involves developing creative approaches and optimization techniques that enhance account portfolio effectiveness while adapting to changing industry practices and emerging opportunities in credit management.

Innovation methodology for account management includes systematic approaches to developing novel strategies while understanding how creative thinking can enhance portfolio optimization and account relationship management effectiveness.

Technology innovation integration includes leveraging emerging tools and platforms while understanding how new technologies can enhance account management and provide competitive advantages in portfolio optimization.

Industry trend analysis for innovation includes understanding banking industry developments while identifying emerging opportunities that can enhance account management effectiveness and portfolio optimization capabilities.

Creative problem-solving for account challenges includes developing unique solutions for complex portfolio management issues while building innovation capabilities that support ongoing optimization and account management excellence.

Experimental approach development includes testing new account management strategies while understanding how systematic experimentation can improve portfolio optimization and discover enhanced management techniques.

Cross-industry learning for account management includes understanding how other industries approach relationship management while adapting successful strategies for credit account portfolio optimization and relationship building.

Innovation documentation and sharing includes recording successful innovations while contributing to broader account management knowledge and supporting community learning through strategy development and refinement.

Collaborative innovation through professional networks includes working with other sophisticated account managers while building collective knowledge and supporting innovation development through shared experience and expertise.

Innovation risk management includes understanding potential complications from novel strategies while implementing safeguards that protect portfolio optimization during innovation development and strategic experimentation.

Innovation integration with traditional strategies includes combining creative approaches with proven techniques while ensuring that innovation enhances rather than compromises established account management effectiveness.

Innovation sustainability assessment includes evaluating whether novel approaches provide lasting benefits while ensuring that innovative strategies remain viable throughout changing circumstances and market conditions.

Future innovation planning includes staying current with emerging opportunities while building capability for continued innovation development and strategic advancement in account management and portfolio optimization excellence.

Account management mastery development involves building comprehensive expertise across all aspects of strategic account management while developing capabilities that support advanced financial planning and professional excellence throughout changing circumstances.

Mastery characteristics for account management include deep understanding of credit systems while building systematic approaches to portfolio optimization that demonstrate sophisticated financial management capability and strategic thinking development.

Expertise integration across multiple account management approaches includes building comprehensive knowledge while understanding how different strategies interact and complement each other for optimal portfolio optimization and relationship management effectiveness.

Professional competency development through account management includes building skills that support consulting opportunities while developing expertise that enables assistance to others and contributes to broader financial literacy advancement.

Strategic thinking advancement through account management mastery includes developing analytical capabilities while building comprehensive understanding of financial systems that supports advanced planning and wealth building strategies.

Innovation capacity building through account management includes developing creativity and adaptation skills while building capability to develop novel approaches for unique circumstances and emerging opportunities in portfolio optimization.

Teaching and mentoring capability development includes building knowledge transfer skills while contributing to broader financial literacy and consumer protection through education and assistance provision to others seeking account management excellence.

Leadership development through account management excellence includes building influence and communication skills while contributing to broader financial inclusion and consumer protection efforts through expertise application and community assistance.

Comprehensive financial planning integration ensures that account management mastery supports broader wealth building while optimizing credit excellence within holistic financial management strategies and long-term security planning.

Quality maintenance for account management expertise includes systematic evaluation and skill refinement while ensuring that mastery remains current and effective throughout changing industry conditions and regulatory requirements.

Professional recognition opportunities through account management mastery include consulting possibilities and educational activities while leveraging expertise for career advancement and income enhancement through specialized knowledge application.

Legacy development through account management mastery includes building lasting impact while creating systems and relationships that extend expertise benefits beyond individual achievement through knowledge transfer and community contribution.

Impact optimization through account management excellence includes understanding how expertise creates value while contributing to broader financial empowerment and consumer protection through account management knowledge and strategic assistance.

Account management integration with comprehensive wealth building ensures that sophisticated account portfolio optimization supports broader financial objectives while enhancing wealth accumulation and long-term financial security through strategic credit management excellence.

Investment opportunity enhancement through account management includes leveraging optimal credit profiles for investment access while understanding how excellent credit management supports enhanced investment opportunities and portfolio development capabilities.

Business development support through account management excellence includes using personal credit optimization for business opportunities while building creditworthiness that supports entrepreneurial activities and business financing access through relationship development.

Real estate financing optimization through account management includes preparing credit profiles for real estate investment while understanding how account management excellence supports mortgage qualification and property financing opportunities.

Tax planning integration with account management includes understanding how credit optimization affects tax strategies while coordinating account management with comprehensive tax planning for optimal financial efficiency and wealth building effectiveness.

Estate planning coordination includes understanding how credit excellence affects wealth transfer while ensuring that account management supports legacy development and family financial security through comprehensive planning integration.

Risk management integration with account management includes coordinating credit strategies with comprehensive financial protection while ensuring that account management supports overall financial security and wealth preservation strategies.

Retirement planning enhancement through account management includes understanding how credit excellence supports retirement financing while ensuring that account management contributes to retirement security and financial independence achievement.

Professional development through account management expertise includes building consulting capabilities while leveraging account management knowledge for career advancement and income enhancement through specialized expertise application.

International financial planning integration includes understanding how account management supports global opportunities while adapting strategies for international investment and business development through comprehensive credit excellence.

Insurance optimization through account management includes understanding how credit excellence affects insurance costs while integrating account management with comprehensive risk management and financial protection planning.

Legacy creation through account management mastery includes building lasting financial expertise while contributing to financial literacy and consumer protection through account management knowledge and community assistance programs.

Wealth multiplication through account management excellence includes leveraging credit optimization for enhanced financial opportunities while building comprehensive wealth through optimal credit access and preferential lending relationships.

Account management performance measurement involves comprehensive evaluation methodologies that assess portfolio effectiveness while identifying optimization opportunities and ensuring that account management strategies produce maximum long-term value and financial benefit.

Performance metrics for account management include tracking credit score improvements, relationship value, cost optimization, and goal achievement while providing comprehensive evaluation of account management success and refinement opportunities.

Portfolio effectiveness analysis includes evaluating account coordination and synergy while understanding how account interactions contribute to overall portfolio performance and optimization effectiveness.

Cost-benefit measurement for account management includes analyzing account costs against benefits while ensuring optimal resource allocation and value achievement from account portfolio investments and management activities.

Relationship value assessment includes evaluating banking relationship benefits while understanding how institutional connections provide enhanced financial opportunities and preferential treatment that justify relationship investment.

Credit building contribution measurement includes tracking how account management supports credit improvement while evaluating account portfolio effectiveness for credit score optimization and creditworthiness enhancement.

Timeline effectiveness evaluation includes assessing account management efficiency while understanding factors that accelerate or delay portfolio optimization and strategic objective achievement through account management activities.

Technology utilization assessment includes evaluating digital tool effectiveness while optimizing technology integration for improved account management and reduced complexity through automation and monitoring enhancement.

Innovation measurement for account management includes evaluating novel approaches and creative strategies while identifying successful innovations that enhance portfolio optimization effectiveness and strategic account management capability.

Professional development assessment through account management includes evaluating skill advancement and expertise development while identifying opportunities for capability expansion and career enhancement through account management mastery.

Integration effectiveness analysis includes evaluating how account management coordinates with other financial activities while identifying optimization opportunities for enhanced coordination and comprehensive financial management improvement.

Long-term value assessment for account management includes comprehensive evaluation of portfolio benefits while understanding how account management excellence contributes to wealth building and financial opportunity enhancement throughout changing circumstances.

Success preservation strategies ensure that account management benefits continue supporting financial objectives while maintaining excellence and building sustainable account management practices for lifelong financial success and strategic optimization.

Advanced account management troubleshooting involves systematic approaches to identifying and resolving complex problems that arise during sophisticated portfolio management while maintaining optimization effectiveness and protecting account management investments.

Problem identification methodologies for account management include recognizing portfolio complications while understanding how multiple account relationships interact and affect each other during challenging situations and market changes.

Solution development for account management problems includes creating innovative approaches while maintaining portfolio optimization effectiveness and protecting progress achieved through strategic account management implementation.

Issuer relationship problem resolution includes addressing account policy changes and customer service issues while maintaining positive relationships and ensuring continued account access and optimization effectiveness.

Account closure management includes handling unexpected closures while adapting portfolio strategies to maintain optimization effectiveness despite changing account availability and relationship dynamics.

Credit limit reduction response includes addressing unexpected limit decreases while implementing strategies that maintain portfolio optimization and utilization management effectiveness despite reduced credit availability.

Fee increase management includes responding to annual fee changes while evaluating continued account value and implementing strategies that maintain portfolio cost-effectiveness and optimization benefits.

Technology integration problems include addressing automation failures while ensuring account management continuation and optimization effectiveness during system outages and platform integration difficulties.

Regulatory change adaptation includes responding to new consumer protection requirements while ensuring account management strategies remain compliant and effective throughout changing regulatory environments.

Economic stress response includes maintaining account management effectiveness during recession and market volatility while ensuring portfolio strategies support financial stability and optimization throughout challenging periods.

Professional assistance coordination for complex problems includes accessing specialized expertise while resolving complicated issues that exceed individual problem-solving capabilities and require expert intervention and guidance.

Recovery planning after account management problems includes restoring optimization effectiveness while implementing improvements that prevent similar issues and enhance portfolio resilience and management effectiveness.

Prevention strategies based on problem experience include implementing safeguards while building systems that reduce future problem likelihood and enhance account management reliability and optimization sustainability.

Account management education and skill development involve building comprehensive knowledge and capabilities that support advanced portfolio optimization while contributing to broader financial literacy and professional development through account management expertise.

Educational methodology for account management includes systematic learning approaches while building comprehensive understanding of credit systems and portfolio optimization that supports mastery development and professional competency achievement.

Skill progression for account management includes developing basic through advanced capabilities while building expertise that supports sophisticated portfolio optimization and strategic account relationship management excellence.

Knowledge integration across account management disciplines includes understanding connections between credit scoring, relationship banking, and portfolio optimization while building comprehensive expertise that supports advanced financial planning.

Practical application development includes implementing theoretical knowledge while building real-world account management experience that demonstrates expertise and supports professional development and mastery achievement.

Teaching capability development through account management expertise includes building knowledge transfer skills while contributing to broader financial literacy and consumer protection through education and assistance provision.

Professional certification consideration for account management includes evaluating credential programs while understanding how certifications might enhance expertise recognition and professional development opportunities.

Continuous learning commitment for account management includes staying current with industry developments while building adaptation capability for changing regulations, technologies, and market conditions affecting portfolio optimization.

Mentoring relationship development includes both seeking mentorship and providing guidance while building professional networks that support ongoing learning and expertise development throughout career advancement.

Research and analysis capability development includes building investigative skills while understanding how to evaluate account management strategies and industry developments for informed decision-making and optimization effectiveness.

Communication skill enhancement for account management includes building explanation and presentation capabilities while developing ability to share expertise and contribute to broader financial literacy advancement.

Innovation capacity building includes developing creativity and strategic thinking while building capability to develop novel approaches and optimize strategies for unique circumstances and emerging opportunities.

Professional network development through account management includes building relationships with industry professionals while accessing expertise and opportunities that support career advancement and knowledge enhancement throughout professional development.

Account management technology integration involves leveraging digital tools, platforms, and automation systems to enhance portfolio optimization effectiveness while reducing management complexity and ensuring consistent execution of strategic account management principles.

Comprehensive platform integration includes coordinating multiple technology solutions while ensuring seamless account management across different systems and tools that support portfolio optimization and strategic relationship management.

Artificial intelligence applications in account management include automated optimization recommendations while leveraging machine learning systems that adapt strategies based on portfolio performance and individual financial patterns.

Mobile technology optimization for account management includes smartphone and tablet integration while ensuring convenient access to portfolio monitoring and management capabilities that support real-time optimization and decision-making.

Data analytics integration includes sophisticated performance tracking while leveraging analytics tools that provide insights into account management effectiveness and optimization opportunities for strategic enhancement.

Security technology for account management includes protecting financial information while ensuring privacy and fraud protection throughout digital account management and portfolio optimization activities.

Automation system coordination includes managing multiple automated processes while ensuring coordination between different automation systems that support comprehensive account management and optimization effectiveness.

Integration challenges for account management technology include addressing system compatibility issues while optimizing technology utilization for enhanced portfolio management without creating excessive complexity or reliability problems.

Future technology planning for account management includes staying current with emerging tools while building capability to leverage new technologies for enhanced portfolio optimization and strategic account management excellence.

Technology cost-benefit analysis for account management includes evaluating digital tool investments while ensuring optimal resource allocation and technology utilization that supports portfolio optimization objectives effectively.

Backup system development for account management includes redundant technology solutions while ensuring account management continuation during system failures and technology disruptions that could compromise optimization effectiveness.

Professional technology consultation for account management includes accessing specialized expertise while optimizing technology integration for sophisticated portfolio management that exceeds individual technical capabilities.

Technology mastery development includes building comprehensive digital tool expertise while understanding how technology integration enhances account management effectiveness and supports advanced portfolio optimization throughout changing technological environments.

Account management risk assessment and mitigation involve understanding potential complications while implementing safeguards that protect portfolio optimization and financial interests throughout changing market conditions and personal circumstances.

Risk identification for account management includes recognizing potential problems while understanding how various factors might affect portfolio optimization and account relationship management effectiveness.

Credit risk assessment includes understanding how account management decisions affect creditworthiness while implementing strategies that maintain optimal credit profiles despite changing circumstances and market conditions.

Interest rate risk management includes understanding how rate changes affect account costs while developing strategies that optimize portfolio performance across different interest rate environments and economic conditions.

Issuer risk evaluation includes assessing banking relationship stability while understanding how institutional changes might affect account management and implementing diversification strategies that reduce dependence on single institutions.

Regulatory risk assessment includes understanding how policy changes affect account management while implementing strategies that maintain compliance and optimization effectiveness throughout changing regulatory environments.

Economic risk management includes understanding how market volatility affects account management while developing strategies that maintain portfolio optimization during recession and economic uncertainty.

Personal risk assessment includes understanding how life changes affect account management while implementing strategies that maintain optimization effectiveness during marriage, divorce, career changes, and other significant transitions.

Technology risk management includes understanding system failure implications while implementing backup procedures that ensure account management continuation during technology disruptions and platform failures.

Fraud risk mitigation includes protecting account portfolios while implementing security measures that prevent unauthorized access and identity theft without compromising account management effectiveness.

Liquidity risk management includes understanding cash flow implications while ensuring account management strategies support financial stability and emergency preparedness throughout changing circumstances.

Portfolio concentration risk includes understanding diversification benefits while implementing strategies that reduce dependence on single account relationships or issuer connections for portfolio optimization.

Comprehensive risk monitoring includes systematic risk assessment while implementing ongoing evaluation procedures that identify emerging risks and optimization opportunities for proactive risk management and portfolio protection.

Account management mastery integration with lifelong financial success involves building comprehensive expertise that supports sustained financial excellence while contributing to wealth building and financial empowerment throughout changing life circumstances and economic conditions.

Lifelong learning commitment for account management includes staying current with evolving industry practices while building adaptation capability that maintains expertise relevance and effectiveness throughout changing technological and regulatory environments.

Wealth building integration through account management includes leveraging credit excellence for enhanced financial opportunities while understanding how sophisticated account management supports investment access and business development throughout comprehensive wealth accumulation strategies.

Financial independence support through account management includes understanding how credit optimization contributes to financial freedom while building account management expertise that reduces financial costs and enhances opportunity access throughout independence achievement.

Legacy development through account management mastery includes building expertise that creates lasting value while contributing to family financial education and community financial literacy through knowledge transfer and assistance provision.

Professional impact through account management expertise includes developing consulting capabilities while contributing to broader consumer protection and financial empowerment through expertise application and educational assistance.

Innovation contribution through account management includes developing creative approaches while advancing industry best practices and supporting consumer protection enhancement through strategic innovation and knowledge sharing.

Community impact through account management expertise includes sharing knowledge while supporting financial inclusion and consumer empowerment through account management education and assistance programs that benefit underserved populations.

Mentoring capability development through account management mastery includes building guidance skills while supporting others' financial success through expertise transfer and personal development assistance throughout community engagement.

Industry influence through account management expertise includes contributing to policy development while supporting consumer protection advancement and industry improvement through expertise application and advocacy activities.

Educational contribution through account management mastery includes developing teaching capabilities while supporting financial literacy advancement and consumer education through account management expertise and instruction programs.

Sustainable impact through account management excellence includes creating lasting positive change while building systems and relationships that continue providing benefit beyond individual achievement through community building and institutional development.

Transformational impact through account management mastery includes creating significant positive change while contributing to systemic improvement in financial management and consumer protection through comprehensive expertise application and leadership development throughout lifelong contribution.

CHAPTER 18

RAPID CREDIT IMPROVEMENT TECHNIQUES

Rapid credit improvement techniques represent sophisticated strategies designed to achieve maximum credit score improvements in minimal timeframes while supporting urgent financial objectives and time-sensitive opportunities. These approaches leverage deep understanding of credit scoring algorithms, reporting mechanics, and strategic timing to produce substantial score increases within days or weeks rather than months or years.

The science of rapid credit improvement involves understanding specific scoring factors that provide immediate impact when optimized, particularly utilization ratios, account status corrections, and error removals that can produce score changes within single reporting cycles. Strategic manipulation of these factors creates opportunities for dramatic score improvements when properly executed.

Emergency credit repair situations require rapid improvement techniques when time-sensitive opportunities such as mortgage applications, business loans, or emergency financing needs demand immediate credit enhancement. Understanding how to prioritize and execute rapid improvement strategies becomes crucial for capitalizing on these opportunities.

The mathematical precision required for rapid improvement involves calculating exact changes needed to achieve specific score targets while understanding threshold effects and scoring model responses that enable precise optimization for desired outcomes within compressed timeframes.

Technology integration in rapid improvement includes real-time monitoring, automated optimization, and instant feedback systems that enable immediate strategy adjustment and outcome verification essential for time-sensitive credit improvement execution.

Rapid improvement risk management involves understanding potential negative consequences while implementing safeguards that protect long-term credit health during aggressive short-term optimization strategies that prioritize speed over gradual development.

The psychology of rapid improvement includes managing expectations while maintaining realistic goals and understanding that sustainable credit excellence requires both rapid intervention and long-term maintenance strategies for optimal outcomes.

Professional rapid improvement services have evolved to address urgent credit needs through specialized expertise and industry connections that can accelerate improvement timelines beyond what individual efforts might achieve independently.

Integration with comprehensive credit building ensures that rapid improvement techniques support rather than compromise long-term credit excellence while providing immediate benefits that enhance financial opportunities and wealth building potential.

Regulatory compliance in rapid improvement involves understanding consumer protection requirements while ensuring that aggressive optimization strategies remain legal and ethical throughout implementation and outcome achievement.

The 15/3 payment method represents one of the most effective rapid credit improvement techniques, involving strategic payment timing that can reduce reported credit card balances and improve credit scores within single reporting cycles through precise utilization optimization.

Payment timing mechanics for the 15/3 method involve making credit card payments 15 days before statement closing dates and again 3 days before closing dates to ensure optimal balance reporting while maintaining spending flexibility throughout monthly cycles.

Balance reduction calculation for 15/3 implementation includes determining exact payment amounts needed to achieve target utilization ratios while considering pending transactions and payment processing timing that affects reported balances.

Multiple account coordination for 15/3 strategies involves implementing the payment method across several credit cards simultaneously while optimizing overall utilization and individual account ratios for maximum score improvement effectiveness.

Cash flow management for 15/3 implementation includes coordinating payment timing with income schedules while ensuring adequate liquidity for double payment strategies without compromising other financial obligations or emergency preparedness.

Automation opportunities for 15/3 strategies include setting up systematic payment schedules while maintaining flexibility for manual adjustment based on spending patterns and optimization requirements throughout monthly cycles.

Score impact measurement for 15/3 implementation includes tracking credit score changes from payment timing optimization while understanding how utilization improvements translate into scoring benefits across different credit scoring models.

Statement date identification for 15/3 effectiveness requires understanding each credit card issuer's reporting schedule while coordinating payment timing with actual reporting dates rather than statement generation dates.

Emergency 15/3 implementation includes rapid deployment of payment strategies when urgent credit improvement is needed while understanding how to expedite payment processing and balance updates for time-sensitive applications.

Integration with other rapid techniques includes combining 15/3 payment methods with additional strategies while ensuring coordination between different improvement approaches for cumulative effectiveness and maximum score enhancement.

Monitoring and adjustment procedures for 15/3 strategies include tracking effectiveness while refining payment timing based on results and ensuring continued optimization throughout changing spending patterns and financial circumstances.

Long-term sustainability of 15/3 methods includes understanding how to maintain payment strategies while transitioning to sustainable credit management practices that support ongoing credit excellence beyond immediate improvement needs.

Rapid rescore services provide professional credit score updates that can reflect account changes and corrections within days rather than waiting for standard monthly reporting cycles, enabling immediate credit improvement for time-sensitive lending applications.

Rapid rescore mechanics involve mortgage lenders requesting expedited credit report updates from credit bureaus after consumers make account changes, providing updated scores within 24-72 hours for qualifying mortgage applications and refinancing decisions.

Qualifying changes for rapid rescore include credit card balance reductions, account closures, error corrections, and other modifications that affect credit scores while meeting lender requirements for rescore eligibility and processing.

Lender coordination for rapid rescore involves working with mortgage professionals who offer rescore services while understanding which lenders provide this option and how to access rapid rescore benefits for time-sensitive applications.

Cost considerations for rapid rescore include understanding service fees while evaluating costs against potential benefits from improved lending terms and mortgage qualification that result from enhanced credit scores.

Documentation requirements for rapid rescore include providing proof of account changes while ensuring lender access to updated account information that supports score improvement and rescore processing.

Timeline planning for rapid rescore includes coordinating account changes with application deadlines while ensuring adequate processing time for score updates and lender review throughout mortgage application processes.

Strategic account changes for rescore include optimizing modifications that provide maximum score improvement while focusing on changes that qualify for rapid rescore and produce meaningful lending benefits.

Multiple change coordination for rescore includes implementing several account modifications simultaneously while ensuring changes work together effectively for maximum score improvement and optimal lending qualification enhancement.

Alternative rescore options include understanding different rapid scoring services while evaluating options beyond traditional mortgage rescore for other lending applications and time-sensitive credit needs.

Integration with mortgage strategy includes coordinating rapid rescore with overall home financing plans while ensuring score improvements support optimal mortgage terms and qualification for preferred lending programs.

Success measurement for rapid rescore includes evaluating score improvements against costs while understanding how rescore benefits translate into improved lending terms and financial advantages throughout mortgage processes.

Statement date manipulation involves strategic timing of account changes relative to credit card reporting schedules to optimize reported information and achieve rapid credit score improvements through precise coordination with credit bureau reporting cycles.

Reporting schedule research includes identifying each credit card issuer's specific reporting dates while understanding how statement generation timing affects credit bureau reporting and score calculation updates.

Payment timing optimization for statement dates involves scheduling payments to post before reporting dates while ensuring optimal balance reporting regardless of actual spending patterns throughout monthly cycles.

Balance management through statement timing includes strategic spending and payment coordination while ensuring reported balances reflect optimal utilization ratios at statement generation rather than throughout entire monthly periods.

Multiple issuer coordination for statement manipulation involves managing different reporting schedules across various credit cards while optimizing timing across multiple accounts for cumulative score improvement effectiveness.

Emergency statement timing includes rapid implementation of balance changes before upcoming statement dates while understanding expedited payment processing and account update procedures for urgent score improvement needs.

Technology integration for statement timing includes automated monitoring of statement dates while using apps and systems that provide reporting date alerts and optimization recommendations for strategic account management.

Credit limit timing coordination includes requesting limit increases before statement dates while understanding how credit limit changes affect utilization calculations and reported ratios for score optimization.

Account closure timing relative to statements includes strategic closure scheduling while understanding how account closure affects utilization calculations and credit mix reporting for optimal score impact.

Purchase timing strategies include coordinating major expenses with statement cycles while ensuring spending patterns support rather than compromise optimal utilization reporting and score improvement objectives.

Dispute timing coordination includes aligning credit report disputes with statement reporting while understanding how dispute processing affects account reporting and score calculation during investigation periods.

Long-term statement strategy includes building sustainable timing practices while maintaining optimal reporting across multiple accounts throughout changing spending patterns and financial circumstances.

Multiple bureau optimization involves implementing rapid improvement strategies across all three major credit bureaus simultaneously while understanding scoring differences and reporting variations that require customized approaches for comprehensive score enhancement.

Bureau-specific strategies include understanding differences between Experian, Equifax, and TransUnion reporting while implementing targeted approaches that address each bureau's specific reporting characteristics and scoring model variations.

Reporting discrepancy leverage includes identifying differences in account reporting between bureaus while using discrepancies to support disputes and corrections that optimize scores across all three credit reporting agencies.

Simultaneous dispute coordination includes managing disputes across multiple bureaus while ensuring consistent messaging and documentation that supports favorable outcomes without creating conflicts or contradictions.

Score monitoring across bureaus includes tracking improvements on all three credit reports while understanding how different scoring models and bureau data affect various credit scores used by different lenders.

Lender bureau preference research includes understanding which credit bureaus specific lenders use while optimizing scores with preferred bureaus for target lending applications and financial objectives.

Alternative data integration includes leveraging services like Experian Boost while understanding how alternative data affects different bureaus and scoring models for comprehensive score improvement strategies.

Error correction across bureaus includes identifying and disputing inaccuracies while ensuring corrections are implemented consistently across all credit reporting agencies for comprehensive accuracy improvement.

Account optimization strategies include managing accounts to optimize reporting across all bureaus while understanding how different reporting practices affect multi-bureau scoring and creditworthiness assessment.

Professional consultation for multi-bureau optimization includes working with experts who understand bureau differences while implementing strategies that address complex multi-bureau scenarios and optimization requirements.

Integration challenges for multi-bureau strategies include coordinating different approaches while ensuring strategies work together effectively rather than creating conflicts or counterproductive effects across different credit reporting systems.

Success measurement for multi-bureau optimization includes tracking improvements across all scoring models while understanding how comprehensive score enhancement translates into improved lending opportunities and financial benefits.

Emergency credit repair strategies address urgent situations requiring immediate credit improvement for time-sensitive financial opportunities while implementing rapid response procedures that maximize score improvement within extremely compressed timeframes.

Crisis assessment for emergency repair includes identifying specific credit problems while understanding which issues can be resolved rapidly and which require longer-term strategies for comprehensive emergency response planning.

Triage approach to emergency repair involves prioritizing actions based on potential impact while focusing resources on strategies that provide maximum score improvement within available timeframes for urgent situations.

24-hour improvement strategies include actions that can be implemented immediately while understanding how expedited payments, rapid dispute submissions, and emergency corrections can produce next-day score improvements.

72-hour improvement plans include coordinated strategies requiring multiple days while implementing systematic approaches that build on immediate actions for substantial score enhancement within extended emergency timeframes.

Weekly improvement strategies include comprehensive approaches for urgent situations allowing longer implementation while coordinating multiple techniques for maximum score improvement within one-week timeframes.

Resource mobilization for emergency repair includes accessing available funds while implementing payment strategies that optimize credit utilization and account status for immediate score improvement benefits.

Professional emergency services include accessing specialized rapid credit repair assistance while understanding which professional services can provide emergency response capabilities and expedited improvement outcomes.

Documentation acceleration for emergency repair includes gathering required materials rapidly while ensuring proper evidence preparation for disputes and corrections that support emergency improvement strategies.

Communication strategies for emergency situations include contacting creditors and credit bureaus while implementing urgent communication protocols that support rapid response and expedited resolution of credit issues.

Monitoring intensification during emergencies includes real-time score tracking while implementing continuous monitoring that enables immediate strategy adjustment and outcome verification throughout emergency repair processes.

Risk management for emergency repair includes understanding potential complications while implementing safeguards that protect long-term credit health during aggressive rapid improvement strategies focused on immediate results.

Success preservation after emergency repair includes transitioning from crisis response to sustainable credit management while ensuring that emergency improvements are maintained and integrated into long-term credit excellence strategies.

Credit limit cycling involves strategic management of credit limits and available credit to optimize utilization ratios and credit scores through sophisticated understanding of credit reporting mechanics and payment processing timelines.

Cycling mechanics include understanding how payments restore available credit while using this credit restoration for continued spending without compromising optimal utilization ratios throughout monthly reporting cycles.

Payment processing timing for cycling includes understanding how long payments take to restore available credit while coordinating payment timing with spending needs and utilization optimization requirements.

Multiple card cycling strategies involve coordinating cycling across several credit cards while optimizing overall utilization and individual account management for maximum score improvement and practical spending flexibility.

Cash flow optimization for cycling includes managing payment timing with income schedules while ensuring adequate liquidity for cycling strategies without compromising other financial obligations or emergency fund requirements.

Utilization maintenance through cycling includes keeping optimal ratios while using available credit for necessary expenses throughout monthly cycles without creating suboptimal utilization reporting.

Emergency cycling procedures include rapid credit restoration when unexpected expenses threaten optimal utilization while implementing expedited payment processing and balance management for urgent situations.

Technology integration for cycling includes automated monitoring of available credit while using apps and systems that provide real-time utilization tracking and cycling optimization recommendations.

Risk management for cycling includes understanding potential complications while implementing safeguards that prevent overspending and ensure cycling strategies support rather than compromise financial stability.

Issuer policy compliance for cycling includes understanding credit card company terms while ensuring cycling activities remain within acceptable usage patterns and don't trigger adverse issuer actions.

Integration with budgeting systems includes coordinating cycling with overall financial management while ensuring cycling strategies support rather than complicate budget adherence and financial planning objectives.

Professional cycling strategies include advanced techniques for sophisticated credit management while understanding how cycling can support business credit building and comprehensive financial planning requirements.

Rapid dispute techniques involve accelerated approaches to credit report error correction that prioritize speed and immediate impact while maintaining effectiveness and compliance with credit reporting regulations and consumer protection requirements.

Expedited dispute submission includes using fastest available dispute methods while ensuring proper documentation and communication that supports rapid investigation and resolution of credit report inaccuracies.

Priority dispute identification includes focusing on errors with highest score impact while understanding which disputes can be resolved quickly and which provide maximum improvement for time-sensitive credit needs.

Documentation streamlining for rapid disputes includes organizing evidence efficiently while providing clear, compelling dispute packages that support rapid investigation and favorable resolution without unnecessary complexity.

Follow-up acceleration for rapid disputes includes intensive monitoring and communication while ensuring disputes receive prompt attention and investigation within required timeframes for urgent credit improvement needs.

Multiple dispute coordination includes managing several disputes simultaneously while ensuring consistency and avoiding conflicts that could compromise dispute effectiveness or create complications during investigation processes.

Professional dispute assistance includes accessing specialized rapid dispute services while understanding which professional services can provide expedited dispute resolution and enhanced success rates for urgent situations.

Regulatory leverage for rapid disputes includes understanding consumer protection requirements while using regulatory compliance obligations to support expedited investigation and resolution of credit report errors.

Technology utilization for rapid disputes includes online dispute systems and digital communication while understanding how technology can accelerate dispute processing and outcome verification for time-sensitive improvement needs.

Dispute escalation procedures include accessing supervisory review and regulatory assistance while implementing escalation strategies that support rapid resolution when standard dispute procedures prove inadequate.

Verification challenge strategies include advanced techniques for questioning inadequate investigations while implementing approaches that support rapid reinvestigation and correction of credit report inaccuracies.

Integration with other rapid techniques includes coordinating dispute activities with payment optimization and account management while ensuring comprehensive approach effectiveness for maximum score improvement within compressed timeframes.

Technology-enhanced rapid improvement involves leveraging digital tools, automated systems, and real-time monitoring to accelerate credit improvement timelines while maintaining precision and effectiveness throughout rapid optimization processes.

Real-time monitoring systems provide instant credit score updates while enabling immediate strategy adjustment and outcome verification essential for rapid improvement effectiveness and timing optimization.

Automated optimization systems include artificial intelligence applications while using machine learning to identify improvement opportunities and implement strategies for maximum score enhancement within minimal timeframes.

Mobile app integration for rapid improvement includes smartphone-based management while providing convenient access to optimization tools and monitoring capabilities that support real-time rapid improvement implementation.

Predictive analytics for rapid improvement include forecasting score changes while using data analysis to optimize strategy selection and implementation timing for maximum effectiveness within compressed timeframes.

Payment automation for rapid improvement includes sophisticated autopay systems while implementing strategic payment timing that optimizes utilization and account status for immediate score improvement benefits.

Alert systems for rapid improvement include real-time notifications while providing immediate awareness of optimization opportunities and required actions that support rapid improvement timing and effectiveness.

Data integration platforms include comprehensive financial data analysis while coordinating multiple improvement strategies through unified systems that enhance rapid improvement coordination and outcome optimization.

Digital communication tools for rapid improvement include secure messaging and document sharing while enabling efficient coordination with professional services and creditors that support rapid improvement objectives.

Cloud-based optimization includes access to sophisticated analysis tools while providing enhanced capability for rapid improvement strategy development and implementation through advanced technology platforms.

Security considerations for technology-enhanced improvement include protecting financial information while ensuring privacy and fraud protection throughout digital rapid improvement processes and system utilization.

Integration challenges for rapid improvement technology include coordinating multiple platforms while ensuring seamless operation and avoiding system conflicts that could compromise rapid improvement effectiveness.

Future technology trends for rapid improvement include emerging innovations while understanding how advancing technology capabilities will enhance rapid improvement opportunities and implementation effectiveness.

Professional rapid improvement services provide specialized expertise and industry connections that can accelerate credit improvement beyond individual capabilities while offering comprehensive approaches to urgent credit enhancement needs.

Service provider evaluation for rapid improvement includes assessing professional qualifications while understanding which services provide legitimate rapid improvement capabilities and appropriate expertise for urgent credit needs.

Service scope assessment includes understanding professional offerings while evaluating which services provide optimal value and effectiveness for specific rapid improvement objectives and timeline requirements.

Cost-benefit analysis for professional rapid improvement includes evaluating service costs against potential benefits while understanding how professional assistance can accelerate improvement timelines and enhance outcomes.

Professional consultation timing includes understanding optimal periods for seeking assistance while coordinating professional services with urgent credit needs and application deadlines for maximum effectiveness.

Service coordination includes working effectively with multiple professionals while ensuring comprehensive rapid improvement strategies that leverage different expertise areas and service capabilities.

Quality assessment for professional services includes evaluating effectiveness and outcome achievement while ensuring professional services provide intended value and support rapid improvement objectives appropriately.

Documentation coordination with professionals includes providing comprehensive information while understanding how professional assistance affects evidence development and strategy implementation for optimal collaboration.

Communication strategies with professional services include maintaining clear expectations while ensuring effective coordination and outcome achievement throughout professional service relationships and rapid improvement processes.

Integration planning with professional services ensures assistance supports broader financial objectives while coordinating with other financial planning activities and professional service providers for comprehensive assistance.

Performance monitoring for professional rapid improvement includes tracking progress while ensuring accountability and maintaining clear communication throughout professional service relationships and outcome achievement.

Termination planning for professional services includes understanding completion criteria while ensuring professional assistance builds capabilities for ongoing credit management and sustained improvement beyond immediate needs.

Professional network development through rapid improvement services includes building relationships while leveraging professional connections for continued support and advanced financial planning assistance throughout changing circumstances.

Rapid improvement timing strategies involve understanding optimal periods for implementing various techniques while coordinating rapid improvement activities with financial planning objectives and major life events that require enhanced credit profiles.

Application deadline coordination includes timing rapid improvement relative to credit application schedules while ensuring score improvements are reflected in credit reports when lenders evaluate creditworthiness for important financial decisions.

Reporting cycle optimization includes understanding credit bureau reporting schedules while timing improvement strategies to maximize impact within specific reporting periods for optimal score enhancement and application timing.

Seasonal timing considerations include understanding optimal periods for rapid improvement while considering economic cycles, lending environment changes, and personal financial patterns that affect improvement effectiveness.

Emergency timing protocols include immediate response procedures while implementing rapid improvement strategies when unexpected opportunities or crises require urgent credit enhancement within extremely compressed timeframes.

Life event coordination includes timing rapid improvement around major transitions while ensuring credit optimization supports important life changes such as marriage, career changes, or major purchases requiring financing.

Market timing considerations include understanding economic conditions while implementing rapid improvement strategies during optimal lending environments and market conditions that enhance financial opportunity access.

Holiday and weekend timing includes understanding processing limitations while coordinating rapid improvement activities with business schedules and payment processing availability for optimal timing effectiveness.

Multiple application timing includes coordinating rapid improvement with various credit applications while understanding how multiple inquiries and applications affect timing strategies and improvement effectiveness.

Long-term timing integration includes understanding how rapid improvement fits into broader credit building while ensuring short-term strategies support rather than compromise long-term credit excellence and financial planning.

International timing considerations include understanding global economic factors while implementing rapid improvement strategies that account for international market conditions and cross-border financial implications.

Professional timing coordination includes aligning rapid improvement with professional service availability while ensuring optimal timing for accessing expert assistance and maximizing professional service effectiveness.

Rapid improvement measurement and evaluation involve comprehensive assessment methodologies that track effectiveness while identifying optimization opportunities and ensuring rapid improvement strategies produce maximum value within compressed timeframes.

Performance metrics for rapid improvement include tracking score changes, timeline effectiveness, cost efficiency, and goal achievement while providing comprehensive evaluation of rapid improvement success and refinement opportunities.

Score impact correlation includes analyzing which techniques produce optimal results while understanding specific strategies that contribute most significantly to rapid score improvement and effectiveness optimization.

Timeline analysis for rapid improvement includes measuring strategy implementation speed while identifying factors that accelerate or delay improvement outcomes and optimizing timing for maximum effectiveness.

Cost-effectiveness evaluation for rapid improvement includes analyzing resource investments against achieved outcomes while ensuring optimal resource allocation and strategy selection for maximum return on rapid improvement investments.

Success factor identification includes understanding which approaches produce optimal results while recognizing timing factors, technique combinations, and implementation methods that contribute most to rapid improvement success.

Comparison analysis between rapid techniques includes evaluating different strategy effectiveness while understanding how various approaches compare in terms of speed, impact, and resource requirements for optimal selection.

Technology effectiveness measurement includes assessing digital tool contribution while understanding how technology integration enhances rapid improvement outcomes and supports implementation effectiveness.

Professional service evaluation includes measuring assistance value while understanding how professional services contribute to rapid improvement outcomes and justify investment in expert assistance.

Integration effectiveness assessment includes evaluating how rapid techniques coordinate with other strategies while identifying optimization opportunities for enhanced coordination and comprehensive improvement.

Risk assessment for rapid improvement includes understanding potential complications while evaluating how aggressive strategies affect long-term credit health and ensuring sustainable improvement approaches.

Long-term impact measurement includes tracking sustained benefits while understanding how rapid improvement strategies affect ongoing credit management and long-term financial success achievement.

Continuous improvement for rapid techniques includes refining strategies based on results while building expertise and capability for enhanced rapid improvement effectiveness throughout changing circumstances and objectives.

Rapid improvement risk management involves understanding potential complications while implementing safeguards that protect long-term credit health during aggressive optimization strategies that prioritize speed over gradual development.

Short-term versus long-term balance includes understanding how aggressive rapid improvement might affect sustained credit health while implementing strategies that achieve immediate objectives without compromising long-term credit excellence.

Credit profile volatility management includes understanding how rapid changes might affect credit stability while implementing approaches that provide improvement without creating score volatility that could concern lenders.

Relationship preservation during rapid improvement includes maintaining positive creditor relationships while implementing aggressive optimization strategies that don't trigger adverse issuer actions or relationship damage.

Financial stability protection includes ensuring rapid improvement strategies don't compromise overall financial health while maintaining emergency preparedness and budget stability throughout aggressive optimization periods.

Regulatory compliance during rapid improvement includes understanding consumer protection requirements while ensuring rapid strategies remain legal and ethical throughout implementation and outcome achievement.

Documentation preservation during rapid improvement includes maintaining comprehensive records while ensuring rapid improvement activities create appropriate evidence and support continued credit management effectiveness.

Professional consultation for risk management includes accessing specialized expertise while understanding when professional assistance becomes necessary for complex rapid improvement situations requiring expert guidance.

Monitoring intensification during rapid improvement includes enhanced tracking of outcomes while implementing continuous oversight that enables immediate strategy adjustment when complications arise or risks emerge.

Contingency planning for rapid improvement includes backup strategies while ensuring alternative approaches are available when primary rapid improvement strategies encounter obstacles or prove less effective than anticipated.

Recovery planning after rapid improvement includes transitioning from aggressive strategies to sustainable practices while ensuring rapid improvements are maintained and integrated into long-term credit management excellence.

Quality control for rapid improvement includes ensuring strategies maintain effectiveness standards while avoiding approaches that might provide temporary benefits but compromise long-term credit health and optimization.

Industry-specific rapid improvement applications recognize that different lending contexts require adapted rapid improvement approaches while optimizing strategies for specific financial goals and lending environments.

Mortgage application rapid improvement includes strategies specifically designed for home loan qualification while understanding how mortgage underwriting evaluates credit and implementing techniques that optimize mortgage approval and terms.

Auto loan rapid improvement includes techniques for vehicle financing while understanding how automotive lending evaluates creditworthiness and implementing strategies that support optimal auto loan qualification and rates.

Business loan rapid improvement includes personal credit optimization for business financing while understanding how business lenders evaluate personal creditworthiness and implementing strategies that support entrepreneurial financing access.

Credit card application rapid improvement includes strategies for optimal credit card approval while understanding how card issuers evaluate applications and implementing techniques that support approval for preferred credit products.

Personal loan rapid improvement includes techniques for personal financing while understanding how personal loan underwriting works and implementing strategies that support qualification for optimal personal loan terms and conditions.

Student loan rapid improvement includes credit enhancement for educational financing while understanding how student loan programs evaluate creditworthiness and implementing techniques that support educational investment opportunities.

Insurance rapid improvement includes credit optimization for insurance qualification while understanding how insurance companies use credit information and implementing strategies that support optimal insurance rates and coverage.

Employment rapid improvement includes credit enhancement for job applications while understanding how employers use credit information and implementing strategies that support career opportunities requiring credit evaluation.

Rental application rapid improvement includes credit optimization for housing applications while understanding how property managers evaluate credit and implementing strategies that support optimal rental qualification and terms.

Investment account rapid improvement includes credit enhancement for investment opportunities while understanding how investment firms evaluate creditworthiness and implementing strategies that support enhanced investment access.

Professional licensing rapid improvement includes credit optimization for professional requirements while understanding how licensing boards evaluate credit and implementing strategies that support professional development and licensing.

International rapid improvement includes credit enhancement for global opportunities while understanding how international financial institutions evaluate credit and implementing strategies that support cross-border financial access.

Rapid improvement integration with emergency financial planning involves coordinating credit enhancement with crisis management while ensuring rapid improvement supports rather than complicates financial emergency response and recovery.

Emergency fund coordination with rapid improvement includes managing liquidity while implementing credit strategies that don't compromise emergency preparedness or financial stability during rapid optimization periods.

Debt crisis management through rapid improvement includes using credit enhancement to address financial emergencies while understanding how rapid improvement can support debt consolidation and financial recovery strategies.

Income loss response through rapid improvement includes credit optimization during unemployment while implementing strategies that maintain creditworthiness and support financial stability during income disruption periods.

Medical emergency coordination includes rapid improvement strategies that support healthcare financing while understanding how credit enhancement can improve access to medical financing and payment arrangements.

Divorce and separation rapid improvement includes credit optimization during relationship changes while implementing strategies that protect individual creditworthiness and support financial independence achievement.

Job transition rapid improvement includes credit enhancement during career changes while understanding how credit optimization supports professional transitions and new employment opportunity access.

Foreclosure prevention through rapid improvement includes credit strategies that support mortgage modification while implementing techniques that enhance qualification for foreclosure prevention programs and alternatives.

Bankruptcy consideration and rapid improvement includes understanding how credit enhancement might affect bankruptcy decisions while implementing strategies that preserve options and support optimal financial recovery planning.

Natural disaster recovery through rapid improvement includes credit optimization following emergencies while implementing strategies that support financial recovery and access to disaster relief financing and assistance.

Identity theft recovery coordination includes rapid improvement strategies for fraud victims while understanding how credit enhancement supports identity theft recovery and creditworthiness restoration processes.

Legal issue coordination includes rapid improvement during legal proceedings while understanding how credit enhancement supports legal representation financing and maintains creditworthiness during legal challenges.

Crisis communication strategies include working with creditors during emergencies while implementing communication approaches that support both crisis management and rapid credit improvement objectives throughout emergency situations.

Advanced rapid improvement techniques involve sophisticated strategies that leverage deep understanding of credit scoring algorithms and industry practices while implementing cutting-edge approaches for maximum score enhancement within minimal timeframes.

Algorithm exploitation for rapid improvement includes understanding scoring model mechanics while implementing strategic changes that trigger maximum score responses within credit scoring system calculations and optimization parameters.

Credit score threshold targeting includes identifying specific score ranges while implementing precise strategies that achieve target scores for particular lending requirements and financial objectives within compressed timeframes.

Multiple scoring model optimization includes addressing different credit scores simultaneously while understanding how various scoring models respond to changes and implementing strategies that optimize across multiple scoring systems.

Advanced utilization strategies include sophisticated balance management while implementing complex timing and distribution techniques that maximize utilization optimization benefits within rapid improvement timeframes.

Professional credit profile engineering includes systematic approach to credit profile design while implementing comprehensive strategies that create optimal creditworthiness demonstration for specific lending contexts and requirements.

Relationship leverage for rapid improvement includes utilizing banking relationships while implementing strategies that access preferential treatment and expedited services that support rapid improvement objectives and timeline achievement.

Industry connection utilization includes accessing professional networks while leveraging industry relationships and expertise that can accelerate improvement timelines beyond individual capability and resource limitations.

Technology innovation for rapid improvement includes cutting-edge digital tools while implementing advanced platforms and systems that provide competitive advantages in rapid improvement implementation and outcome optimization.

Legal strategy integration includes understanding consumer protection rights while implementing approaches that leverage legal protections and regulatory requirements to support rapid improvement objectives and dispute resolution.

Regulatory insight application includes understanding industry oversight while implementing strategies that leverage regulatory pressure and compliance requirements to support rapid improvement objectives and creditor cooperation.

Market timing sophistication includes understanding economic cycles while implementing strategies that leverage market conditions and lending environment factors for optimal rapid improvement effectiveness and opportunity access.

Innovation development for rapid improvement includes creating novel approaches while implementing cutting-edge strategies that advance rapid improvement capabilities and provide competitive advantages in urgent credit enhancement situations.

Rapid improvement psychology involves understanding the mental and emotional aspects of urgent credit enhancement while developing sustainable approaches that support both immediate objectives and long-term financial well-being.

Stress management during rapid improvement includes maintaining psychological balance while implementing aggressive strategies that can create anxiety and pressure throughout urgent credit enhancement processes and timeline pressure.

Motivation maintenance for rapid improvement includes sustaining commitment while building psychological resilience that supports continued effort despite challenges and setbacks during compressed improvement timelines.

Expectation management for rapid improvement includes setting realistic goals while understanding limitations and possibilities that help maintain appropriate perspective during urgent credit enhancement activities.

Decision-making under pressure includes maintaining quality judgment while implementing rapid improvement strategies that require quick decisions and strategic thinking under compressed timeframes and high stakes.

Emotional regulation during rapid improvement includes managing anxiety and impatience while maintaining psychological health throughout urgent credit enhancement processes that can create significant emotional stress.

Confidence building through rapid improvement includes developing self-efficacy while building belief in ability to achieve credit objectives and manage complex financial challenges throughout rapid improvement implementation.

Habit formation for sustainable improvement includes building long-term practices while ensuring rapid improvement strategies support rather than compromise ongoing credit management excellence and financial discipline.

Social support during rapid improvement includes accessing encouragement and assistance while building relationships that support both immediate improvement objectives and long-term financial success achievement.

Professional psychological consultation includes understanding when mental health support becomes valuable while managing stress and emotional challenges that can arise during urgent financial situations requiring rapid credit improvement.

Mindfulness applications for rapid improvement include conscious awareness techniques while developing present-moment focus that enhances decision-making and reduces reactive behavior during urgent credit enhancement activities.

Success psychology for rapid improvement includes building achievement mindset while developing psychological frameworks that support both immediate goal achievement and long-term financial success throughout changing circumstances.

Recovery psychology after rapid improvement includes transitioning from crisis mode while building sustainable psychological approaches that support ongoing credit management and financial well-being beyond immediate improvement needs.

Rapid improvement case studies demonstrate real-world applications of sophisticated techniques while providing practical examples of successful rapid credit enhancement across different scenarios and financial objectives.

Mortgage qualification case study includes comprehensive rapid improvement for home loan approval while demonstrating coordinated strategies that achieved qualifying credit scores within 30-day timeframes for time-sensitive real estate transactions.

Business loan approval case study includes personal credit optimization for business financing while showing how rapid improvement supported entrepreneurial objectives and business loan qualification within compressed application deadlines.

Emergency refinancing case study includes rapid improvement for urgent refinancing needs while demonstrating strategies that achieved improved credit scores for better refinancing terms during financial crisis situations.

Credit card approval case study includes rapid optimization for premium card applications while showing how strategic improvement supported qualification for preferred credit products with enhanced benefits and optimal terms.

Auto loan optimization case study includes rapid improvement for vehicle financing while demonstrating techniques that achieved improved lending terms and qualification for preferred automotive financing programs.

Student loan qualification case study includes rapid credit enhancement for educational financing while showing how improvement strategies supported access to optimal student loan programs and terms for educational investment.

Insurance rate improvement case study includes rapid optimization for insurance qualification while demonstrating how credit enhancement reduced insurance costs and improved coverage access through better credit profiles.

Employment opportunity case study includes rapid improvement for job applications while showing how credit enhancement supported career opportunities requiring credit evaluation and professional advancement objectives.

Rental qualification case study includes rapid optimization for housing applications while demonstrating strategies that achieved rental approval and optimal terms through strategic credit enhancement within tight timelines.

Investment access case study includes rapid improvement for investment opportunities while showing how credit enhancement supported access to margin accounts and investment financing for wealth building objectives.

Divorce recovery case study includes rapid credit rebuilding following relationship dissolution while demonstrating comprehensive strategies that restored individual creditworthiness and financial independence within accelerated timelines.

Identity theft recovery case study includes rapid improvement following fraud while showing how victims restored creditworthiness and financial standing through coordinated rapid improvement strategies and professional assistance.

Rapid improvement technology platforms represent the cutting edge of credit enhancement tools while providing sophisticated automation and optimization capabilities that accelerate improvement timelines and enhance outcome effectiveness.

Artificial intelligence platforms for rapid improvement include machine learning systems while providing personalized optimization recommendations and automated strategy implementation that maximizes improvement effectiveness within compressed timeframes.

Real-time optimization systems include instant feedback and adjustment capabilities while providing continuous monitoring and strategy refinement that ensures optimal rapid improvement implementation and outcome achievement.

Mobile application integration for rapid improvement includes smartphone-based management while providing convenient access to sophisticated optimization tools and monitoring capabilities that support real-time rapid improvement coordination.

Cloud computing applications for rapid improvement include advanced analytics and processing power while providing enhanced capability for complex strategy development and implementation through distributed computing resources.

Blockchain applications for rapid improvement include emerging verification and security technologies while providing potential enhancements to credit reporting accuracy and rapid improvement implementation through innovative technological solutions.

Data analytics platforms for rapid improvement include sophisticated analysis capabilities while providing insights into optimization opportunities and strategy effectiveness that enhance rapid improvement decision-making and outcome achievement.

Integration platforms for rapid improvement include comprehensive system coordination while providing unified access to multiple optimization tools and services that streamline rapid improvement implementation and management.

Security technology for rapid improvement includes advanced protection systems while ensuring financial information safety and fraud prevention throughout digital rapid improvement processes and platform utilization.

Predictive modeling for rapid improvement includes forecasting capabilities while providing strategic guidance and outcome prediction that optimizes rapid improvement strategy selection and implementation timing.

Communication platforms for rapid improvement include secure messaging and collaboration tools while providing efficient coordination with professional services and creditors that support rapid improvement objectives and timeline achievement.

Monitoring technology for rapid improvement includes comprehensive tracking systems while providing real-time awareness of progress and optimization opportunities that enable immediate strategy adjustment and effectiveness enhancement.

Future technology trends for rapid improvement include emerging innovations while understanding how advancing technology capabilities will continue enhancing rapid improvement opportunities and implementation effectiveness throughout evolving technological environments.

Rapid improvement mastery development involves building comprehensive expertise across all sophisticated techniques while developing capabilities that support both emergency credit enhancement and advanced financial planning throughout changing circumstances.

Mastery characteristics for rapid improvement include deep understanding of credit systems while building systematic approaches to urgent optimization that demonstrate sophisticated financial management capability and strategic thinking development.

Expertise integration across multiple rapid techniques includes building comprehensive knowledge while understanding how different strategies interact and complement each other for optimal rapid improvement effectiveness and outcome achievement.

Professional competency development through rapid improvement includes building skills that support consulting opportunities while developing expertise that enables assistance to others facing urgent credit enhancement needs and time-sensitive financial objectives.

Strategic thinking advancement through rapid improvement mastery includes developing analytical capabilities while building comprehensive understanding of financial systems that supports advanced planning and wealth building strategies.

Innovation capacity building through rapid improvement includes developing creativity and adaptation skills while building capability to develop novel approaches for unique circumstances and emerging opportunities in urgent credit enhancement.

Teaching capability development through rapid improvement expertise includes building knowledge transfer skills while contributing to broader financial literacy and consumer protection through education and assistance provision to others.

Leadership development through rapid improvement excellence includes building influence and communication skills while contributing to broader financial inclusion and consumer protection efforts through expertise application and community assistance.

Crisis management capability through rapid improvement mastery includes building skills for handling financial emergencies while developing expertise that supports both individual crisis response and assistance to others facing urgent financial challenges.

Quality maintenance for rapid improvement expertise includes systematic evaluation and skill refinement while ensuring mastery remains current and effective throughout changing industry conditions and regulatory requirements.

Professional recognition opportunities through rapid improvement mastery include consulting possibilities and educational activities while leveraging expertise for career advancement and income enhancement through specialized knowledge application.

Impact optimization through rapid improvement excellence includes understanding how expertise creates value while contributing to broader financial empowerment and consumer protection through rapid improvement knowledge and strategic assistance.

Legacy development through rapid improvement mastery includes building lasting impact while creating systems and relationships that extend expertise benefits beyond individual achievement through knowledge transfer and community contribution throughout lifelong financial success.

CHAPTER 19

BANKRUPTCY, DIVORCE, AND LIFE CHANGES

Life-altering events such as bankruptcy, divorce, career transitions, and major health crises create unique credit challenges that require specialized strategies and deep understanding of how these circumstances affect creditworthiness, credit reporting, and financial recovery. These situations demand comprehensive approaches that address both immediate credit protection and long-term rebuilding while navigating complex legal and financial frameworks.

The intersection of major life changes with credit management creates both challenges and opportunities that require sophisticated understanding of how personal circumstances affect credit reporting, scoring, and lender evaluation. Each type of life change involves specific legal protections, reporting requirements, and recovery strategies that must be understood for optimal outcomes.

Bankruptcy represents one of the most significant credit events, yet proper understanding of bankruptcy law and post-discharge credit building can accelerate recovery beyond what many consumers expect. The key lies in understanding how bankruptcy affects different aspects of credit reporting and leveraging legal protections for maximum recovery benefit.

Divorce proceedings create complex credit situations involving joint account management, responsibility allocation, and individual credit establishment that require careful coordination between legal strategy and credit protection. Understanding how marital dissolution affects credit helps optimize both legal outcomes and financial recovery.

Medical emergencies and chronic health conditions create unique financial stresses that can devastate credit profiles while requiring specialized approaches that address both healthcare financing and credit protection during extended illness or disability periods.

Job loss and career transitions affect credit through income disruption and potential payment difficulties while creating opportunities for strategic credit management during transition periods that can support career advancement and financial stability.

Educational transitions, whether returning to school or supporting family education, create financial pressures and opportunities that require strategic credit management to optimize educational financing while protecting and building creditworthiness.

Geographic relocation involves complex financial considerations including housing transitions, employment changes, and cost-of-living adjustments that affect credit management and require strategic planning for optimal financial outcomes.

Identity theft recovery represents a specialized area requiring understanding of legal protections, credit restoration procedures, and prevention strategies that protect against ongoing fraud while rebuilding damaged credit profiles.

Estate and inheritance situations create unique credit considerations for both deceased persons' estates and surviving family members while requiring understanding of how death affects credit reporting and responsibility allocation.

Post-bankruptcy credit building involves leveraging the fresh start provided by bankruptcy discharge while implementing strategic approaches that accelerate credit recovery and position consumers for optimal long-term financial success through systematic credit rebuilding.

Bankruptcy discharge benefits include elimination of most unsecured debts while providing opportunities for immediate credit building without the burden of overwhelming debt obligations that previously prevented credit improvement and financial stability.

Timeline expectations for post-bankruptcy credit building include understanding realistic recovery periods while implementing strategies that accelerate improvement beyond typical expectations through sophisticated credit building and relationship management.

Credit score recovery patterns after bankruptcy show that consumers can achieve good credit scores within 12-24 months post-discharge while implementing strategic approaches that optimize scoring factors and demonstrate creditworthiness improvement.

Secured credit card strategies for bankruptcy recovery include selecting optimal products while implementing usage patterns that demonstrate responsible credit management and build positive payment history essential for credit score improvement.

Credit builder loan integration with post-bankruptcy planning includes incorporating installment credit while building diverse credit mix and payment history that supports comprehensive credit profile development beyond revolving credit alone.

Authorized user opportunities for bankruptcy recovery include accessing family relationships while building credit through established accounts that provide immediate positive history and scoring benefits during early recovery periods.

Employment considerations after bankruptcy include understanding potential employment impacts while building credit profiles that support career advancement and access to employment opportunities requiring credit evaluation.

Housing strategies post-bankruptcy include preparing for rental and homeownership opportunities while building credit profiles that support housing access and optimal financing terms for residential stability and wealth building.

Banking relationship establishment after bankruptcy includes building financial service access while demonstrating stability and creditworthiness that supports expanded financial product access and relationship development.

Business credit development after personal bankruptcy includes establishing business credit while leveraging personal credit recovery to support entrepreneurial activities and business financing access for income generation and wealth building.

Insurance considerations after bankruptcy include understanding how bankruptcy affects insurance rates while building credit profiles that support optimal insurance terms and comprehensive risk management planning.

Long-term planning integration ensures that post-bankruptcy credit building supports broader financial goals while building sustainable credit management practices that prevent future financial difficulties and support ongoing prosperity.

Divorce and credit considerations involve understanding how marital dissolution affects joint accounts, individual creditworthiness, and financial responsibility while implementing strategies that protect credit profiles and support independent financial stability.

Joint account management during divorce includes understanding legal responsibility while implementing strategies that protect individual credit during account closure, responsibility transfer, and debt allocation throughout divorce proceedings.

Credit report separation strategies include removing authorized user accounts while establishing individual credit profiles that reflect personal creditworthiness rather than joint financial management and marital credit relationships.

Debt allocation considerations include understanding how divorce decrees affect credit reporting while implementing strategies that ensure debt responsibility allocation aligns with credit reporting and individual financial capability.

Individual credit establishment during divorce includes building independent credit while demonstrating individual creditworthiness that supports post-divorce financial stability and access to financial products and services.

Asset protection through credit management includes preserving creditworthiness while protecting financial assets during divorce proceedings and ensuring optimal financial positioning for post-divorce wealth building and financial security.

Spousal support and credit implications include understanding how support obligations affect creditworthiness while managing payment responsibilities that support both compliance and individual credit health.

Housing transition credit planning includes preparing for residential changes while building credit profiles that support rental qualification, mortgage access, and housing stability during and after divorce proceedings.

Employment and income documentation includes establishing individual income verification while building employment stability that supports credit applications and demonstrates individual financial capability and creditworthiness.

Legal coordination with credit strategy includes working with divorce attorneys while ensuring legal strategy supports credit protection and optimal financial outcomes throughout divorce proceedings and post-divorce recovery.

Timeline planning for divorce and credit includes coordinating credit building with divorce proceedings while ensuring credit strategies support legal objectives and post-divorce financial independence achievement.

Professional assistance coordination includes working with financial advisors while ensuring a comprehensive approach to divorce planning that addresses both legal objectives and credit protection throughout transition periods.

Recovery planning post-divorce includes building individual financial stability while implementing credit strategies that support long-term financial success and independence following marital dissolution and life transition.

Medical debt and credit impact require specialized understanding of healthcare financing, insurance coordination, and credit protection strategies that address both medical treatment needs and financial stability during health crises and chronic conditions.

Medical debt prevention includes understanding healthcare financing options while implementing strategies that minimize credit impact from medical expenses through insurance optimization, payment planning, and provider negotiation.

Insurance coordination for credit protection includes maximizing insurance benefits while understanding how insurance disputes and payment delays affect medical debt and credit reporting during healthcare treatment and recovery.

Hospital and provider negotiation includes payment plan establishment while implementing strategies that prevent negative credit reporting through provider cooperation and financial assistance program utilization.

Medical bill dispute strategies include understanding billing errors while implementing correction procedures that address inappropriate charges, insurance coordination failures, and billing system mistakes that affect financial responsibility.

Charity care and financial assistance programs include accessing hospital assistance while understanding eligibility requirements and application procedures that can eliminate medical debt and prevent negative credit impact.

Medical bankruptcy considerations include understanding when bankruptcy might be appropriate while evaluating alternatives that address medical debt without bankruptcy filing and long-term credit impact.

Chronic condition financial planning includes long-term healthcare cost management while building financial strategies that support ongoing medical care without compromising credit health and financial stability.

Disability and credit management include understanding how disability affects income while implementing credit protection strategies that maintain financial stability during disability periods and income reduction.

Medicare and insurance transition planning includes understanding coverage changes while preparing for healthcare cost variations that affect financial planning and credit management during insurance transition periods.

Medical identity theft protection includes understanding healthcare fraud while implementing prevention and recovery strategies that protect both medical records and financial information from fraudulent healthcare activity.

Estate planning for medical expenses includes understanding how medical debt affects estate settlement while implementing planning strategies that protect family members from medical debt responsibility and credit impact.

Recovery planning after a medical crisis includes rebuilding financial stability while implementing credit recovery strategies that address medical debt impact and support long-term financial health following healthcare emergencies.

Student loan defaults and rehabilitation present unique opportunities for credit repair that don't exist for other debt types, involving federal programs that can completely remove default status and restore positive credit reporting through systematic rehabilitation processes.

Default impact understanding includes recognizing how student loan defaults affect credit while understanding the comprehensive credit damage that extends beyond credit scores to include employment, professional licensing, and housing implications.

Rehabilitation program mechanics include understanding federal rehabilitation requirements while implementing strategic approaches that complete rehabilitation efficiently and restore positive credit reporting through consistent payment demonstration.

Payment calculation for rehabilitation includes understanding affordable payment determination while ensuring rehabilitation payments fit within overall financial planning and don't compromise other financial obligations during rehabilitation periods.

Timeline planning for rehabilitation includes understanding program duration while coordinating rehabilitation with other financial objectives and ensuring completion supports broader credit building and financial recovery goals.

Consolidation alternatives to rehabilitation include understanding direct consolidation options while evaluating whether consolidation or rehabilitation provides better outcomes for individual circumstances and financial objectives.

Credit reporting during rehabilitation includes understanding how rehabilitation affects credit reports while monitoring progress and ensuring proper reporting of rehabilitation status and payment history throughout program participation.

Employment protection during default includes understanding federal employment rights while implementing strategies that protect employment and professional opportunities during default resolution and credit recovery processes.

Tax refund and wage garnishment relief includes understanding collection suspension during rehabilitation while implementing strategies that restore normal income access and financial stability throughout rehabilitation participation.

Post-rehabilitation credit building includes leveraging rehabilitation completion while implementing comprehensive credit building strategies that maximize credit recovery and position for optimal long-term financial success.

Professional licensing considerations include understanding how student loan default affects professional credentials while implementing resolution strategies that protect professional opportunities and career advancement.

Borrower defense applications include understanding loan forgiveness opportunities while evaluating whether borrower defense provides better outcomes than rehabilitation for specific circumstances involving school closure or fraud.

Long-term planning integration ensures that student loan resolution supports broader financial objectives while building sustainable approaches that prevent future default and support ongoing financial prosperity and educational investment.

Identity theft recovery involves comprehensive strategies that address both immediate fraud resolution and long-term credit restoration while implementing prevention measures that protect against ongoing fraudulent activity and financial damage.

Immediate response procedures for identity theft include rapid fraud reporting while implementing containment strategies that minimize ongoing damage and begin recovery processes through systematic fraud documentation and creditor notification.

Credit report correction for identity theft includes disputing fraudulent accounts while implementing specialized procedures that leverage identity theft protections for enhanced dispute resolution and account removal effectiveness.

Account closure and replacement includes securing compromised financial accounts while establishing new account relationships that restore financial access and functionality without ongoing fraud exposure and security risks.

Documentation requirements for identity theft include comprehensive record keeping while maintaining evidence that supports fraud claims and provides protection against ongoing fraudulent activity and credit report errors.

Law enforcement coordination includes filing police reports while understanding how criminal reports support civil fraud resolution and provide enhanced protection under consumer protection laws and identity theft statutes.

Credit monitoring enhancement after identity theft includes implementing comprehensive monitoring while building surveillance systems that provide early detection of ongoing fraudulent activity and protection against future identity theft.

Professional assistance for complex identity theft includes accessing specialized services while understanding when expert assistance becomes necessary for comprehensive fraud resolution and credit restoration that exceeds individual capabilities.

Prevention strategies for ongoing protection include implementing security measures while building practices that reduce future identity theft risk and protect personal information from unauthorized access and fraudulent use.

Financial account security enhancement includes strengthening authentication while implementing security measures that protect banking, investment, and credit accounts from ongoing fraud attempts and unauthorized access.

Insurance considerations for identity theft include understanding coverage options while evaluating identity theft insurance that provides financial protection and professional assistance for future fraud incidents and recovery costs.

Employment and professional implications include understanding how identity theft affects employment while implementing protection strategies that preserve professional reputation and career opportunities during fraud resolution and recovery.

Long-term monitoring and maintenance includes building sustainable protection practices while implementing ongoing surveillance and security measures that provide continued protection against future identity theft and financial fraud.

Job loss and career transition credit management involve strategies that protect creditworthiness during income disruption while positioning for enhanced financial opportunities through strategic credit management and career advancement planning.

Immediate protection strategies for job loss include implementing emergency financial measures while protecting credit accounts and payment history during income transition periods and employment search activities.

Unemployment benefit optimization includes maximizing available assistance while understanding how unemployment compensation affects creditworthiness and financial planning during employment transition periods.

Credit account management during unemployment includes maintaining optimal account status while implementing strategies that preserve credit health without compromising limited financial resources during income disruption.

Emergency fund utilization for credit protection includes strategic use of savings while prioritizing credit protection that supports employment search and career transition activities through maintained creditworthiness.

Creditor communication during job loss includes proactive relationship management while implementing communication strategies that preserve positive relationships and access payment accommodations when necessary during employment transitions.

Career advancement credit preparation includes building credit profiles while positioning for enhanced employment opportunities that require credit evaluation and support professional advancement and income improvement.

Professional development financing includes strategic credit utilization while accessing educational and training opportunities that support career transition and advancement through optimal credit management and educational investment.

Business development opportunities during career transition include entrepreneurial credit preparation while building credit profiles that support business financing and self-employment opportunities during career changes and professional transitions.

Income documentation and credit applications include managing credit access while building employment stability that supports credit qualification and demonstrates financial capability during career transition periods.

Industry-specific credit considerations include understanding professional requirements while building credit profiles that support specific career paths and professional licensing requirements that affect employment opportunities.

Geographic relocation credit planning includes preparing for location changes while building credit profiles that support housing, employment, and financial service access in new geographic areas during career transitions.

Long-term career planning integration ensures that credit management supports professional objectives while building sustainable approaches that enhance career advancement and financial prosperity throughout changing employment circumstances.

Educational financing and credit management involve strategic approaches that optimize educational investment while protecting and building creditworthiness through sophisticated understanding of educational financing options and credit implications.

Student loan optimization includes understanding federal and private loan options while implementing strategies that minimize educational debt burden and optimize credit impact through strategic loan selection and management.

Educational credit building includes leveraging student status while implementing credit building strategies that take advantage of student credit opportunities and build creditworthiness during educational periods.

Family education financing includes managing household educational expenses while implementing strategies that support family educational investment without compromising household financial stability and credit health.

Career transition education includes financing professional development while understanding how educational investment affects credit and implementing strategies that support career advancement through optimal educational financing.

Adult education and credit considerations include understanding how returning to school affects credit while implementing strategies that manage education costs and credit protection during educational transitions and career development.

Graduate school financing includes understanding advanced degree costs while implementing strategies that optimize graduate education financing through credit management and educational investment planning.

Professional certification and licensing education includes financing specialized training while understanding how professional development affects credit and implementing strategies that support professional advancement through educational investment.

International education financing includes understanding study abroad costs while implementing strategies that support international educational opportunities through optimal credit management and international financial planning.

Educational emergency planning includes preparing for educational cost changes while implementing strategies that protect educational investment and credit health during financial emergencies affecting educational planning.

Scholarship and grant maximization includes accessing non-debt educational financing while understanding how educational assistance affects overall financial planning and credit management during educational periods.

Educational debt consolidation and management includes understanding repayment options while implementing strategies that optimize educational debt management and credit impact through strategic repayment planning and consolidation evaluation.

Long-term educational planning integration ensures that educational financing supports career objectives while building sustainable approaches that enhance professional development and financial prosperity through strategic educational investment and credit management.

Geographic relocation and credit management involve understanding how location changes affect credit while implementing strategies that support successful relocation through optimal financial planning and credit preparation.

Pre-relocation credit preparation includes building credit profiles while preparing for geographic transition that supports housing, employment, and financial service access in new locations through strategic credit optimization.

Housing transition credit planning includes preparing for residential changes while building credit profiles that support rental qualification, mortgage access, and housing stability during geographic relocation and community transition.

Employment transition credit considerations include understanding how relocation affects employment while building credit profiles that support job search and employment opportunities in new geographic areas and professional markets.

Cost-of-living adjustment planning includes understanding geographic cost differences while implementing financial strategies that address cost-of-living changes and their impact on credit management and financial stability.

Banking relationship establishment in new locations includes building financial service access while establishing local banking relationships that support comprehensive financial service access and community integration.

State law variation understanding includes recognizing different consumer protection requirements while adapting credit strategies to new state regulations and protections that affect credit management and financial planning.

Credit report address updates include ensuring accurate location reporting while implementing procedures that maintain credit report accuracy and prevent complications from geographic transition and address changes.

Insurance transition planning includes understanding coverage changes while preparing for insurance cost and availability variations that affect financial planning and credit management during geographic relocation.

Tax implication management includes understanding state tax differences while implementing strategies that address tax changes and their impact on financial planning and credit management during geographic transition.

Emergency planning for relocation includes preparing for unexpected relocation costs while implementing strategies that protect credit health and financial stability during emergency geographic transitions and crisis situations.

Professional licensing transfer includes understanding credential requirements while implementing strategies that support professional licensing transfer and career continuity during geographic relocation and professional transition.

Community integration financial planning includes understanding local financial service options while building relationships and accessing services that support successful community integration and long-term financial stability in new locations.

Chronic illness and disability credit management require specialized approaches that address ongoing healthcare costs, income changes, and financial stability while protecting creditworthiness during extended health challenges and disability periods.

Disability income transition includes understanding benefit systems while implementing strategies that maintain financial stability and credit health during income changes from disability benefits and work capacity limitations.

Healthcare cost management includes understanding insurance and assistance programs while implementing strategies that minimize credit impact from ongoing medical expenses and treatment costs during chronic illness management.

Medication and treatment financing includes managing ongoing healthcare costs while implementing strategies that address prescription and treatment expenses without compromising credit health and financial stability.

Insurance coordination for chronic conditions includes optimizing coverage while understanding how insurance changes affect financial planning and credit management during ongoing healthcare needs and treatment requirements.

Accessibility modification financing includes managing home and vehicle modifications while implementing strategies that address accessibility needs through optimal financing and credit management during disability adaptation.

Employment accommodation and credit includes understanding workplace rights while implementing strategies that maintain employment and income stability during disability accommodation and workplace adaptation.

Social Security and disability benefits optimization includes maximizing available assistance while understanding how benefit programs affect creditworthiness and financial planning during disability and chronic illness management.

Estate planning for disability includes understanding long-term care costs while implementing planning strategies that protect assets and credit health during extended disability and potential incapacitation periods.

Caregiver financial planning includes understanding family impact while implementing strategies that address caregiver financial needs and credit protection during family illness and disability situations.

Emergency healthcare financing includes preparing for crisis medical expenses while implementing strategies that protect credit health during medical emergencies and unexpected healthcare costs.

Long-term care planning includes understanding care costs while implementing strategies that address long-term care financing through optimal credit management and financial planning for extended care needs.

Recovery and rehabilitation financial planning includes managing comeback costs while implementing strategies that support health recovery and financial stability through optimal credit management during rehabilitation and recovery periods.

Elder financial management and credit protection involve specialized strategies that address aging-related financial challenges while protecting creditworthiness and implementing safeguards against financial exploitation and age-related financial difficulties.

Retirement transition credit management includes understanding income changes while implementing strategies that maintain credit health during retirement transition and fixed income adjustment periods.

Medicare and healthcare transition planning includes understanding coverage changes while preparing for healthcare cost variations that affect financial planning and credit management during insurance transition and aging-related healthcare needs.

Social Security optimization includes maximizing retirement benefits while understanding how benefit timing affects financial planning and credit management during retirement transition and income adjustment.

Estate planning integration includes understanding how credit management affects estate planning while implementing strategies that support wealth transfer and family financial protection through optimal credit and estate coordination.

Financial exploitation protection includes understanding elder fraud risks while implementing safeguards that protect against financial exploitation and maintain credit health during vulnerable aging periods and cognitive changes.

Long-term care financing includes understanding care costs while implementing strategies that address long-term care expenses through optimal credit management and insurance planning for extended care needs and facility costs.

Family financial coordination includes managing intergenerational financial relationships while implementing strategies that support family financial planning and credit protection across multiple generations and family circumstances.

Professional assistance for elder financial management includes accessing specialized services while understanding when expert assistance becomes necessary for complex financial management during aging and potential cognitive decline.

Technology adaptation for financial management includes understanding digital financial services while implementing strategies that maintain financial access and credit management capabilities during technology transition and adaptation needs.

Housing transition planning for aging includes understanding senior housing options while implementing strategies that support housing transition and maintain credit health during residential changes and aging-related moves.

Healthcare directive and financial planning includes understanding medical decision-making while implementing strategies that protect financial interests and credit health during potential incapacitation and medical decision-making periods.

Legacy planning through credit management includes understanding how credit excellence affects wealth transfer while implementing strategies that support family financial security and intergenerational wealth building through optimal credit management.

Military service and credit management involve understanding unique financial challenges and opportunities that affect service members while implementing strategies that leverage military benefits and protect creditworthiness during service and transition periods.

Deployment financial management includes understanding deployment income while implementing strategies that optimize deployment earnings and maintain credit health during extended deployment periods and family separation.

Military lending protection includes understanding Service members Civil Relief Act (SCRA) benefits while implementing strategies that leverage military protections for optimal credit management and financial security during service periods.

PCS move financial planning includes understanding relocation costs while implementing strategies that address frequent geographic transitions and their impact on credit management and financial stability during military career progression.

Military family financial coordination includes managing dual military careers while implementing strategies that address family financial planning and credit management during military service and potential separation periods.

VA loan preparation and credit building includes understanding VA loan benefits while building credit profiles that optimize VA loan qualification and leverage military homeownership benefits for wealth building and financial stability.

Military retirement transition planning includes understanding retirement benefits while implementing strategies that address transition to civilian financial management and credit optimization during military retirement and career transition.

Security clearance and credit requirements include understanding clearance standards while implementing strategies that maintain credit profiles supporting security clearance qualification and career advancement in security-related positions.

Emergency leave financial planning includes understanding family emergency costs while implementing strategies that address unexpected travel and family emergency expenses during military service and family crisis situations.

Education benefits optimization includes maximizing GI Bill benefits while implementing strategies that address educational financing and credit management during military education and post-service educational transitions.

Business development for military families includes understanding entrepreneur support while implementing strategies that support military family business development through optimal credit management and military entrepreneur resources.

International assignment financial planning includes understanding overseas cost differences while implementing strategies that address international financial management and credit protection during overseas military assignments.

Veteran transition financial planning includes understanding veteran benefits while implementing comprehensive strategies that address military to civilian financial transition and optimize veteran benefits for long-term financial prosperity and credit excellence.

Death and estate credit issues involve understanding how death affects credit reporting and responsibility while implementing strategies that protect surviving family members and properly settle estate financial obligations.

Immediate post-death procedures include understanding creditor notification while implementing strategies that protect surviving family members from inappropriate debt collection and credit reporting during estate settlement and grief periods.

Estate debt responsibility includes understanding survivor liability while implementing strategies that protect family members from inappropriate debt collection on estate obligations and ensure proper debt settlement procedures.

Credit report correction after death includes understanding deceased reporting while implementing procedures that correct credit reports and prevent ongoing credit activity on deceased person accounts and credit profiles.

Probate and credit considerations include understanding court procedures while implementing strategies that address credit obligations during probate and ensure proper estate debt settlement through legal processes and court oversight.

Survivor credit protection includes understanding joint account impacts while implementing strategies that protect surviving spouse creditworthiness and maintain financial access during estate settlement and financial transition.

Business succession and credit includes understanding business debt responsibility while implementing strategies that address business credit obligations and protect personal credit during business succession and ownership transition.

Life insurance and debt settlement includes understanding policy benefits while implementing strategies that optimize life insurance proceeds for debt settlement and survivor financial security during estate settlement.

Identity theft prevention for deceased includes understanding posthumous fraud risks while implementing strategies that protect deceased person identity and prevent fraudulent account opening and credit activity.

Family financial transition includes understanding survivor financial needs while implementing strategies that support family financial stability and credit protection during grief periods and financial adjustment.

Legal assistance for estate credit issues includes understanding when professional help becomes necessary while accessing estate planning and credit expertise for complex estate settlement and credit management situations.

Memorial and funeral financing includes understanding final expense costs while implementing strategies that address memorial expenses without compromising survivor financial stability and credit health during grief periods.

Legacy planning through estate credit management includes understanding how proper estate planning affects family credit while implementing strategies that protect family financial security and support intergenerational wealth transfer through optimal estate management.

Addiction recovery and financial rehabilitation involve understanding how substance abuse affects financial stability while implementing comprehensive strategies that support recovery and rebuild creditworthiness during rehabilitation and ongoing recovery processes.

Financial damage assessment from addiction includes understanding credit impact while implementing strategies that evaluate financial damage and develop comprehensive recovery plans that address both substance abuse recovery and financial rehabilitation.

Treatment financing and credit protection includes understanding healthcare costs while implementing strategies that address addiction treatment expenses without compromising long-term financial stability and credit health during recovery processes.

Income stability during recovery includes understanding employment challenges while implementing strategies that maintain financial stability and credit health during addiction recovery and employment rebuilding periods.

Family financial impact includes understanding addiction effects on family finances while implementing strategies that protect family creditworthiness and financial stability during addiction recovery and family healing processes.

Legal financial implications include understanding court-ordered obligations while implementing strategies that address legal costs and compliance requirements during addiction recovery and legal consequence management.

Insurance and recovery benefits includes understanding coverage options while implementing strategies that maximize insurance benefits for addiction treatment and recovery support services during rehabilitation periods.

Emergency financial planning for recovery includes understanding crisis prevention while implementing strategies that address financial emergencies without compromising recovery progress and sobriety maintenance during challenging periods.

Professional assistance for financial recovery includes understanding specialized services while accessing financial counseling and credit repair expertise that addresses addiction-related financial damage and supports comprehensive recovery planning.

Employment and credit rebuilding includes understanding career rebuilding while implementing strategies that support employment stability and career advancement during addiction recovery and professional rehabilitation.

Housing stability during recovery includes understanding residential needs while implementing strategies that support stable housing and credit rebuilding during addiction recovery and life rebuilding processes.

Long-term financial planning for sobriety includes understanding ongoing recovery costs while implementing strategies that support sustained sobriety and financial prosperity through comprehensive financial planning and credit management excellence.

Support system financial coordination includes understanding family and community support while implementing strategies that leverage support networks for financial recovery and maintain accountability during addiction recovery and financial rehabilitation.

Mental health and credit management involve understanding how mental health challenges affect financial decision-making while implementing strategies that protect creditworthiness and support financial stability during mental health treatment and recovery.

Depression and financial management includes understanding motivation challenges while implementing automated systems and support strategies that maintain credit health during depression treatment and emotional recovery periods.

Anxiety and credit decisions includes understanding decision-making impacts while implementing strategies that address anxiety-related financial avoidance and support healthy credit management during anxiety treatment and management.

Bipolar disorder and financial stability includes understanding mood-related financial decisions while implementing strategies that protect against manic spending and maintain credit health during mood stabilization and treatment periods.

Mental health treatment financing includes understanding healthcare costs while implementing strategies that address therapy and medication expenses without compromising financial stability and credit health during mental health treatment.

Disability benefits for mental health includes understanding benefit systems while implementing strategies that maximize available assistance and maintain financial stability during mental health disability and treatment periods.

Emergency mental health planning includes understanding crisis costs while implementing strategies that address mental health emergencies and hospitalization expenses without compromising long-term financial stability and credit health.

Professional support coordination includes understanding mental health and financial assistance while implementing strategies that coordinate mental health treatment with financial counseling and credit management support during recovery.

Family support and financial management includes understanding caregiver roles while implementing strategies that address family financial impact and support during mental health treatment and recovery processes.

Employment accommodation and mental health includes understanding workplace rights while implementing strategies that maintain employment stability and income during mental health treatment and workplace accommodation.

Insurance optimization for mental health includes understanding coverage benefits while implementing strategies that maximize mental health insurance benefits and minimize out-of-pocket costs during treatment and recovery periods.

Medication management and financial planning includes understanding prescription costs while implementing strategies that address ongoing medication expenses and maintain access to necessary mental health medications without compromising financial stability.

Long-term planning for mental health management includes understanding ongoing treatment needs while implementing strategies that support sustained mental health and financial prosperity through comprehensive treatment and financial planning integration.

Legal issues and credit protection involve understanding how legal proceedings affect creditworthiness while implementing strategies that protect financial interests and maintain credit health during litigation, legal settlements, and criminal proceedings.

Lawsuit and credit implications include understanding litigation costs while implementing strategies that address legal expenses and potential settlements without compromising long-term financial stability and credit health during legal proceedings.

Criminal charges and financial consequences include understanding legal costs while implementing strategies that address defense expenses, fines, and restitution without destroying creditworthiness and financial stability during criminal proceedings.

Civil litigation and asset protection includes understanding judgment risks while implementing strategies that protect assets and credit health during civil litigation and potential adverse judgments or settlement obligations.

Divorce litigation and credit management includes understanding legal costs while implementing strategies that address divorce legal expenses and protect individual creditworthiness during contested divorce proceedings and asset division.

Business litigation and personal credit includes understanding liability exposure while implementing strategies that protect personal credit during

business litigation and potential business debt personal guarantee enforcement.

Professional licensing defense includes understanding career protection costs while implementing strategies that address professional license defense expenses and maintain career stability during professional regulatory proceedings.

Legal settlement financing includes understanding payment obligations while implementing strategies that address settlement payment requirements without compromising ongoing financial stability and credit health after legal resolution.

Bankruptcy alternatives during legal proceedings include understanding debt relief options while implementing strategies that address legal debt and financial obligations through alternatives to bankruptcy filing during legal difficulties.

Insurance coordination for legal protection includes understanding coverage benefits while implementing strategies that maximize insurance protection and minimize out-of-pocket legal costs during litigation and legal proceedings.

Emergency legal financing includes understanding crisis legal needs while implementing strategies that address urgent legal expenses and maintain financial stability during emergency legal situations and crisis proceedings.

Professional assistance coordination includes understanding legal and financial expertise while implementing strategies that coordinate legal representation with financial planning and credit protection during complex legal situations.

Recovery planning after legal resolution includes understanding post-legal financial rebuilding while implementing strategies that address legal aftermath and rebuild financial stability and credit health following legal proceedings and resolution.

Natural disaster recovery and credit management involve understanding how disasters affect financial stability while implementing strategies that protect creditworthiness and support financial recovery during emergency response and community rebuilding.

Immediate disaster response financial planning includes understanding emergency costs while implementing strategies that address immediate disaster expenses and maintain credit health during crisis response and emergency evacuation periods.

Insurance claim management and credit protection includes understanding coverage benefits while implementing strategies that maximize insurance recovery and minimize credit impact during insurance claim processing and settlement periods.

Federal disaster assistance optimization includes understanding available aid while implementing strategies that access disaster relief programs and maintain financial stability during disaster recovery and community rebuilding periods.

Emergency relocation financing includes understanding temporary housing costs while implementing strategies that address relocation expenses and maintain credit health during emergency housing and temporary displacement periods.

Property repair and reconstruction financing includes understanding rebuilding costs while implementing strategies that address property restoration expenses through optimal financing and credit management during reconstruction periods.

Employment disruption during disasters includes understanding income loss while implementing strategies that maintain financial stability and credit health during employment interruption and economic recovery following natural disasters.

Business recovery and credit management includes understanding business interruption while implementing strategies that address business recovery costs and maintain personal credit health during business rebuilding and economic recovery.

Community resource coordination includes understanding local assistance while implementing strategies that access community aid and support during disaster recovery and coordinate assistance with personal financial management.

Long-term recovery planning includes understanding extended rebuilding while implementing strategies that support sustained recovery and financial stability through comprehensive disaster recovery and community rebuilding processes.

Disaster prevention financial planning includes understanding future risk management while implementing strategies that prepare for potential future disasters and maintain financial resilience during ongoing disaster risk and preparedness.

Insurance optimization for disaster protection includes understanding coverage adequacy while implementing strategies that maximize disaster insurance protection and minimize financial vulnerability during future disaster risks.

Resilience building through financial planning includes understanding community stability while implementing strategies that support both personal financial security and community resilience during ongoing disaster recovery and preparedness.

Immigration and credit establishment involve understanding how immigration status affects credit access while implementing strategies that build creditworthiness and establish financial stability in the United States through systematic credit building and relationship development.

Initial credit establishment for immigrants includes understanding credit system basics while implementing strategies that build credit history from zero through secured cards, credit builder loans, and alternative credit building methods.

Documentation requirements for immigrant credit building include understanding identification needs while implementing strategies that meet creditor requirements and establish financial identity through proper documentation and verification procedures.

Banking relationship establishment includes understanding account requirements while implementing strategies that establish banking relationships and access financial services through immigrant-friendly banking programs and community resources.

Employment documentation and credit includes understanding work authorization while implementing strategies that demonstrate employment stability and income for credit applications and financial service access during immigration status transitions.

Student visa and credit building includes understanding international student needs while implementing strategies that build credit during educational periods and establish financial foundation for post-graduation opportunities.

Family sponsorship and credit implications include understanding sponsor responsibilities while implementing strategies that address family financial obligations and build individual creditworthiness during family immigration and sponsorship periods.

Professional licensing and credit requirements include understanding career development needs while implementing strategies that build credit profiles supporting professional licensing and career advancement during immigration and professional development.

Housing access and credit building includes understanding rental and homeownership barriers while implementing strategies that demonstrate creditworthiness and access housing opportunities during immigration settlement and community integration.

Business development for immigrants includes understanding entrepreneur opportunities while implementing strategies that build credit for business financing and support immigrant entrepreneur success through optimal credit and business development.

Cultural adaptation and financial services includes understanding American financial systems while implementing strategies that leverage cultural background and adapt to American credit and financial service practices.

Language barrier management includes understanding communication challenges while implementing strategies that access financial services and build credit despite language limitations through community resources and assistance programs.

Long-term planning for immigrant credit excellence includes understanding pathway to citizenship while implementing strategies that support comprehensive financial planning and credit excellence throughout immigration status progression and American financial integration.

Domestic violence and financial recovery involve understanding how abuse affects financial stability while implementing strategies that protect creditworthiness and support financial independence during abuse recovery and safety planning.

Financial abuse recognition includes understanding economic control tactics while implementing strategies that identify financial abuse and develop safety plans that address both physical safety and financial security during abuse situations.

Emergency safety and credit protection includes understanding immediate financial needs while implementing strategies that protect credit access and financial resources during emergency safety planning and domestic violence escape.

Legal protection and financial rights includes understanding domestic violence legal protections while implementing strategies that leverage legal protections for financial security and credit protection during abuse recovery and legal proceedings.

Housing safety and credit requirements includes understanding safe housing needs while implementing strategies that access safe housing and maintain credit health during domestic violence recovery and housing transition periods.

Employment protection and financial stability includes understanding workplace safety while implementing strategies that maintain employment and income stability during domestic violence recovery and safety planning.

Children and family financial security includes understanding family protection needs while implementing strategies that address children's financial security and education during domestic violence recovery and family safety planning.

Professional assistance for domestic violence recovery includes understanding specialized services while accessing domestic violence and financial counseling expertise that addresses abuse-related financial damage and supports comprehensive recovery planning.

Credit report correction for financial abuse includes understanding abuse-related credit damage while implementing procedures that correct credit reports and address fraudulent accounts opened through domestic violence and financial abuse.

Identity protection from abusers includes understanding ongoing safety risks while implementing strategies that protect personal information and prevent ongoing financial abuse and stalking through financial account access.

Support system financial coordination includes understanding community resources while implementing strategies that leverage support networks for financial recovery and maintain safety during domestic violence recovery and independence building.

Legal financial assistance includes understanding available aid while implementing strategies that access legal assistance and address legal costs during domestic violence proceedings and protection order enforcement.

Long-term financial independence planning includes understanding abuse recovery timeline while implementing strategies that support sustained financial independence and security through comprehensive financial planning and credit management excellence during ongoing recovery and safety maintenance.

Life change integration and comprehensive planning involve understanding how major life transitions affect financial management while implementing strategies that coordinate credit management with life planning and ensure financial stability throughout changing circumstances.

Life stage financial planning includes understanding age-related financial needs while implementing strategies that address changing financial priorities and credit requirements throughout life transitions and developmental stages.

Family planning and credit management includes understanding household financial changes while implementing strategies that address family growth, education costs, and changing financial needs through optimal credit management and financial planning.

Career development and credit optimization includes understanding professional advancement needs while implementing strategies that support career growth and maintain credit excellence throughout professional development and advancement opportunities.

Health and financial planning integration includes understanding wellness costs while implementing strategies that address healthcare needs and maintain financial stability through comprehensive health and financial planning coordination.

Housing lifecycle and credit management includes understanding residential transitions while implementing strategies that address changing housing needs and maintain credit health throughout homeownership advancement and geographic transitions.

Education investment and credit planning includes understanding learning costs while implementing strategies that support educational investment and maintain financial stability through educational financing and career development planning.

Retirement transition and credit management includes understanding retirement financial needs while implementing strategies that address retirement income changes and maintain credit health during retirement transition and fixed income periods.

Estate planning and credit legacy includes understanding wealth transfer implications while implementing strategies that address estate planning needs and maintain credit excellence for family financial security and intergenerational wealth building.

Emergency preparedness and credit protection includes understanding crisis planning while implementing strategies that address emergency financial needs and maintain credit health during unexpected life challenges and crisis situations.

Technology adaptation and financial management includes understanding digital financial services while implementing strategies that leverage technology for financial management and maintain credit excellence through technological adaptation and digital financial service integration.

Community involvement and financial stability includes understanding civic engagement costs while implementing strategies that support community participation and maintain financial health through volunteer work, charitable giving, and community leadership activities.

Spiritual and values-based financial planning includes understanding personal values while implementing strategies that align financial management with spiritual beliefs and personal values throughout life transitions and value development.

Cultural tradition and financial management includes understanding heritage financial practices while implementing strategies that honor cultural traditions and maintain credit excellence through culturally sensitive financial planning and management approaches.

Global perspective and financial planning includes understanding international influences while implementing strategies that address global economic factors and maintain financial stability through international awareness and cross-cultural financial management.

Innovation and financial adaptation includes understanding changing economic conditions while implementing strategies that adapt to economic evolution and maintain credit excellence through innovative financial management and strategic adaptation throughout changing economic environments.

Personal growth and financial maturity includes understanding developmental changes while implementing strategies that support personal development and maintain financial responsibility through psychological growth and maturity advancement throughout lifelong learning and development.

Legacy creation through life change mastery includes understanding long-term impact while implementing strategies that create lasting positive change and contribute to family and community financial well-being through expertise application and knowledge transfer throughout lifelong contribution and service.

CHAPTER 20

THE PATH TO PERFECT CREDIT

The path to perfect credit represents the culmination of sophisticated credit management expertise, systematic optimization, and strategic planning that achieves the highest possible credit scores while demonstrating absolute creditworthiness to lenders and financial institutions. Perfect credit, typically defined as scores of 800-850 across major scoring models, requires understanding the precise mathematical relationships between scoring factors and implementing flawless execution of credit management principles.

Perfect credit extends beyond mere score achievement to encompass comprehensive creditworthiness that includes optimal account management, diverse credit relationships, and strategic financial positioning that maximizes opportunities while minimizing costs throughout all financial endeavors. This level of credit excellence creates access to the most favorable lending terms, exclusive financial products, and preferential treatment that compound financial advantages over time.

The mathematics of perfect credit involve understanding exact scoring thresholds and optimization targets that distinguish excellent credit from truly perfect credit. While scores above 740 generally qualify for the best lending terms, perfect credit provides psychological advantages, negotiation leverage, and access to exclusive opportunities that justify the additional effort required for score optimization.

Scoring model variations affect perfect credit achievement since different scoring versions weight factors differently and may require specific optimization strategies. Understanding FICO 8, FICO 9, VantageScore, and industry-specific scoring models helps develop comprehensive strategies that achieve perfection across multiple scoring systems used by different lenders.

The timeline for perfect credit achievement varies significantly based on starting points, but consumers with good credit can typically achieve perfect scores within 12-24 months through strategic optimization, while those rebuilding from poor credit may require 3-5 years of systematic credit building and management excellence.

Perfect credit maintenance requires ongoing attention and systematic management that preserves optimal scoring while adapting to changing financial circumstances, regulatory requirements, and scoring model evolution. Maintenance strategies ensure that perfect credit provides sustained benefits rather than temporary achievement.

The business value of perfect credit extends beyond personal financial benefits to include professional opportunities, business financing access, and comprehensive financial planning advantages that support wealth building and entrepreneurial activities throughout changing economic conditions.

Technology integration in perfect credit pursuit includes sophisticated monitoring, automation, and optimization tools that maintain precision while reducing management complexity and ensuring consistent execution of perfect credit strategies and maintenance procedures.

Risk management for perfect credit involves understanding potential threats to score optimization while implementing safeguards that protect perfect credit status during financial emergencies, life changes, and market volatility that could compromise credit excellence.

Professional recognition of perfect credit demonstrates financial sophistication that enhances lending relationships, business opportunities, and comprehensive financial planning while building credibility that supports advanced financial objectives and wealth building strategies.

Understanding the 850 score involves recognizing the specific requirements and optimization strategies that distinguish perfect credit from merely excellent credit while implementing systematic approaches that achieve and maintain the highest possible credit score levels across all major scoring models.

Mathematical precision for perfect credit requires exact optimization of all scoring factors including payment history perfection, utilization precision, account age maximization, credit mix optimization, and inquiry minimization that collectively create the mathematical combinations necessary for perfect score achievement.

Payment history perfection for 850 scores demands absolute payment compliance with zero late payments, zero delinquencies, and zero negative payment reporting across all credit accounts throughout the entire credit history period visible to scoring models and credit reporting systems.

Utilization optimization for perfect credit typically requires aggregate utilization below 5% and individual account utilization below 10% across all revolving credit accounts, with many perfect credit achievers maintaining utilization below 1% to ensure optimal scoring across all utilization calculation methods.

Account age requirements for perfect credit generally include average account age above 7-10 years with oldest accounts exceeding 15-20 years, demonstrating long-term credit management capability and stability that scoring models reward with maximum points for credit history length factors.

Credit mix optimization for perfect credit includes diverse account types such as revolving credit, installment loans, and potentially mortgage credit that demonstrate comprehensive credit management capability across different credit categories and lending relationships.

Inquiry management for perfect credit involves minimizing hard credit inquiries while strategic timing ensures that necessary credit applications don't compromise perfect scoring through excessive inquiry activity or poor inquiry spacing that might suggest credit seeking behavior.

Account management precision for perfect credit requires optimal management of all credit accounts including active accounts, closed accounts, and authorized user accounts that contribute to perfect scoring through strategic account portfolio optimization and relationship management.

Scoring model comprehensive optimization includes achieving perfect scores across multiple scoring versions including FICO 8, FICO 9, VantageScore 3.0, and industry-specific scoring models that different lenders use for various credit decisions and financial product evaluations.

Threshold understanding for perfect credit includes recognizing specific score ranges that different lenders consider perfect while understanding how scoring model variations affect perfect credit recognition and lending decision-making processes.

Maintenance precision for perfect credit involves ongoing optimization that preserves perfect scoring while adapting to changing account relationships, credit needs, and financial circumstances that could affect perfect credit maintenance and score preservation.

Strategic patience for perfect credit achievement includes understanding realistic timelines while maintaining systematic optimization approaches that build toward perfect credit through consistent execution and strategic account management over extended periods.

Requirements for perfect credit encompass comprehensive creditworthiness demonstration that extends beyond scoring factors to include account relationships, financial stability, and strategic positioning that creates optimal lending profiles and maximum financial opportunity access.

Comprehensive payment history excellence requires perfect payment compliance across all credit obligations including credit cards, installment loans, mortgage payments, and any other credit arrangements that report to credit bureaus and affect creditworthiness calculations and lender evaluation.

Sophisticated utilization management for perfect credit involves maintaining optimal ratios across all accounts while demonstrating credit usage that proves creditworthiness without suggesting financial stress or overextension that might concern lenders or scoring algorithms.

Advanced account age strategies include building and preserving long-term account relationships while optimizing account opening timing and closure decisions that maximize credit history length benefits and demonstrate financial stability over extended periods.

Strategic credit mix development includes acquiring and managing diverse credit types that demonstrate comprehensive credit management capability while avoiding unnecessary complexity or accounts that don't contribute meaningfully to credit profiles or perfect scoring achievement.

Professional inquiry management includes strategic timing of credit applications while minimizing unnecessary inquiries and optimizing inquiry spacing that demonstrates strategic credit management rather than credit seeking behavior that might concern lenders.

Optimal account portfolio management includes maintaining appropriate numbers of accounts while ensuring account diversity, relationship value, and ongoing utility that support perfect credit maintenance and comprehensive financial service access.

Geographic and demographic optimization includes understanding how location, income, and demographic factors might affect credit decisions while positioning credit profiles for optimal recognition and treatment across diverse lending environments and geographic markets.

Banking relationship excellence includes building comprehensive financial service relationships while demonstrating customer value and financial sophistication that supports preferential treatment and enhanced access to financial products and services.

Professional financial management demonstration includes sophisticated account management that proves financial competency while building relationships and credibility that support advanced financial opportunities and wealth building throughout changing circumstances.

Insurance and risk management integration includes optimal insurance coordination while understanding how insurance decisions affect credit and financial planning while supporting comprehensive risk management that protects perfect credit and financial stability.

Estate and legacy planning integration includes understanding how perfect credit affects wealth transfer while implementing strategies that support family financial security and intergenerational wealth building through credit excellence and financial sophistication.

Maintaining excellent credit long-term requires systematic approaches that preserve perfect credit through changing life circumstances, economic conditions, and regulatory environments while adapting strategies to maintain optimization effectiveness throughout evolving financial landscapes.

Systematic monitoring for credit maintenance includes comprehensive oversight systems that track account performance, score changes, and optimization opportunities while ensuring perfect credit preservation through continuous attention and strategic adjustment.

Life change adaptation for credit maintenance includes strategies for preserving perfect credit during major transitions such as marriage, divorce, career changes, geographic relocation, and family changes that could affect credit management and optimization effectiveness.

Economic cycle management for perfect credit includes understanding how recession, inflation, and market volatility affect credit while implementing strategies that maintain perfect credit during challenging economic periods and market uncertainty.

Regulatory adaptation for credit maintenance includes staying current with credit reporting changes while adapting strategies to leverage new consumer protections and optimize perfect credit under evolving regulatory requirements and industry standards.

Technology integration for credit maintenance includes leveraging digital tools while implementing automation systems that maintain perfect credit with minimal manual management complexity and maximum optimization effectiveness throughout changing technological environments.

Account relationship maintenance includes preserving valuable banking relationships while adapting account portfolios to changing needs and ensuring continued access to optimal financial products and services that support perfect credit maintenance.

Strategic account management evolution includes adapting account strategies while maintaining perfect credit through changing financial needs, credit requirements, and account availability that might affect credit portfolio optimization and maintenance effectiveness.

Emergency planning for credit protection includes procedures for maintaining perfect credit during financial crises while implementing safeguards that protect credit excellence during unexpected challenges and emergency situations.

Professional consultation for credit maintenance includes understanding when expert assistance becomes valuable while accessing specialized knowledge that supports perfect credit preservation throughout complex situations requiring professional expertise.

Family coordination for credit maintenance includes household financial management while ensuring family financial decisions support rather than compromise perfect credit maintenance and optimization throughout changing family circumstances and financial objectives.

Innovation adaptation for credit maintenance includes leveraging new credit building opportunities while adapting to emerging financial products and services that might enhance perfect credit maintenance and optimization effectiveness.

Legacy planning for credit excellence includes understanding how perfect credit contributes to long-term financial success while implementing strategies that support sustained financial prosperity and family financial security throughout changing economic and personal circumstances.

Advanced optimization strategies for perfect credit involve sophisticated techniques that achieve maximum scoring while positioning credit profiles for optimal recognition and treatment across all lending contexts and financial service relationships.

Micro-optimization techniques for perfect credit include precise balance management, strategic payment timing, and account utilization coordination that achieves exact optimization targets while maintaining practical account usage and financial management convenience.

Multi-bureau optimization for perfect credit includes achieving optimal scores across all three major credit bureaus while understanding reporting differences and implementing strategies that optimize comprehensive credit excellence across diverse credit reporting and scoring systems.

Scoring model arbitrage includes leveraging differences between scoring versions while optimizing for specific scoring models used by target lenders and financial institutions that affect important financial decisions and opportunity access.

Professional credit portfolio engineering includes systematic design of credit profiles while implementing comprehensive strategies that create optimal creditworthiness demonstration across diverse lending contexts and financial service relationships.

Advanced utilization strategies for perfect credit include sophisticated balance distribution, payment timing coordination, and credit limit optimization that maintains perfect utilization ratios while supporting practical spending needs and financial management.

Strategic account acquisition for perfect credit includes identifying optimal credit products while building account relationships that enhance credit profiles and provide valuable financial services that support comprehensive financial planning and wealth building.

Relationship banking optimization for perfect credit includes building institutional relationships while accessing preferential treatment and enhanced financial services that support perfect credit maintenance and comprehensive financial opportunity access.

Professional recognition strategies include demonstrating credit excellence while building credibility and institutional relationships that support advanced financial opportunities and preferential treatment throughout financial service interactions.

Industry-specific optimization includes understanding how different lending contexts evaluate perfect credit while adapting strategies for mortgage lending, business financing, investment account access, and specialized financial products requiring optimal creditworthiness.

International credit optimization includes understanding global credit systems while building international financial relationships and creditworthiness that supports global financial opportunities and cross-border financial management.

Innovation integration for perfect credit includes leveraging emerging credit building opportunities while adapting to new financial products and services that might enhance perfect credit achievement and maintenance effectiveness.

Comprehensive optimization measurement includes tracking perfect credit achievement across multiple metrics while evaluating optimization effectiveness and identifying refinement opportunities that support continued perfect credit excellence and financial opportunity maximization.

Common mistakes at high scores involve understanding pitfalls that can compromise perfect credit achievement while implementing safeguards that protect excellent credit from errors and oversights that might prevent perfect credit attainment or maintenance.

Complacency risks for excellent credit include neglecting optimization opportunities while assuming excellent credit requires no further improvement or maintenance attention that could lead to gradual score degradation or missed perfect credit achievement opportunities.

Over-optimization dangers include excessive focus on credit scoring while neglecting practical financial management or implementing strategies that optimize scores at the expense of financial utility or comprehensive financial planning effectiveness.

Account management errors at high credit levels include closing valuable accounts, reducing credit utilization too aggressively, or making strategic errors that compromise credit mix or account age benefits that support perfect credit achievement.

Utilization mistakes for excellent credit include maintaining zero utilization that might reduce scoring or allowing utilization to exceed optimal thresholds that prevent perfect credit achievement despite otherwise excellent credit management.

Inquiry management errors include unnecessary credit applications while failing to coordinate inquiry timing strategically or allowing inquiry accumulation that prevents perfect credit achievement despite excellent payment history and account management.

Credit mix imbalances include inadequate account diversity while maintaining too many similar account types or lacking account categories that demonstrate comprehensive credit management capability necessary for perfect credit achievement.

Professional service over-reliance includes depending too heavily on credit repair services while neglecting personal credit management skill development or maintaining dependency relationships that compromise financial independence and expertise development.

Technology dependence risks include over-relying on automated systems while neglecting strategic thinking and personal oversight that ensures technology enhances rather than replaces sophisticated credit management and strategic decision-making.

Perfectionism paralysis includes excessive analysis while avoiding necessary credit decisions or implementing strategies that might temporarily affect scores but support long-term perfect credit achievement and financial optimization.

Relationship neglect includes failing to maintain banking relationships while missing opportunities for enhanced financial services and institutional recognition that support perfect credit maintenance and financial opportunity access.

Strategic inflexibility includes rigid adherence to optimization strategies while failing to adapt to changing circumstances or new opportunities that might enhance perfect credit achievement through strategic evolution and improvement.

Maintenance oversight includes neglecting ongoing optimization while assuming perfect credit achievement requires no continued attention or strategic management that could lead to gradual score degradation or lost perfect credit status.

Credit as a financial tool involves understanding how perfect credit becomes a strategic asset that enhances all financial opportunities while providing leverage for wealth building, business development, and comprehensive financial planning throughout changing economic conditions.

Investment opportunity enhancement through perfect credit includes access to margin accounts, favorable investment financing, and enhanced investment opportunities that leverage creditworthiness for wealth building and portfolio development beyond traditional investment approaches.

Business development leverage through perfect credit includes optimal business financing access while building business credit that supports entrepreneurial activities and business growth through enhanced financing terms and expanded business opportunity access.

Real estate investment advantages through perfect credit include optimal mortgage terms while accessing investment property financing and real estate development opportunities that leverage creditworthiness for property investment and wealth building.

Tax optimization through credit excellence includes understanding how credit decisions affect tax planning while leveraging optimal credit for tax-advantaged financing and investment strategies that enhance after-tax wealth building and financial efficiency.

Insurance benefits from perfect credit include optimal insurance rates while accessing enhanced coverage options and specialized insurance products that provide comprehensive risk management at reduced costs through credit-based insurance pricing.

Employment and professional advantages through perfect credit include enhanced employment opportunities while accessing professional positions requiring credit evaluation and building professional credibility that supports career advancement and income enhancement.

Negotiation leverage through perfect credit includes enhanced bargaining power while accessing preferential treatment and exclusive opportunities that perfect credit provides in various financial and business contexts throughout economic transactions.

Emergency financial access through perfect credit includes optimal emergency financing while accessing credit lines and emergency funding that provides financial security and flexibility during unexpected circumstances and crisis situations.

International financial opportunities through perfect credit include global banking access while building international financial relationships and creditworthiness that supports international business and investment opportunities throughout global economic participation.

Estate planning enhancement through perfect credit includes wealth transfer optimization while building credit excellence that supports family financial security and intergenerational wealth building through optimal credit management and financial planning.

Professional development through credit expertise includes consulting opportunities while leveraging credit knowledge for career advancement and income enhancement through specialized expertise and professional service provision.

Legacy creation through perfect credit includes building lasting financial advantages while contributing to family and community financial education and empowerment through credit excellence demonstration and knowledge transfer.

Perfect credit psychology involves understanding the mental and emotional aspects of credit excellence while developing sustainable approaches that support both perfect credit achievement and comprehensive financial well-being throughout lifelong financial management.

Achievement mindset for perfect credit includes developing persistence while building confidence and strategic thinking that supports perfect credit pursuit through systematic effort and strategic optimization over extended periods.

Perfectionist balance includes healthy pursuit of credit excellence while avoiding obsessive behavior that might compromise overall financial well-being or life satisfaction in pursuit of perfect credit achievement.

Long-term perspective for perfect credit includes understanding achievement timelines while maintaining motivation and strategic focus throughout extended improvement periods and optimization processes that require sustained effort and patience.

Financial discipline integration includes building credit excellence within comprehensive financial management while ensuring perfect credit pursuit supports rather than compromises overall financial health and life objectives.

Stress management during perfect credit pursuit includes maintaining psychological balance while managing the complexity and precision required for perfect credit achievement without creating excessive anxiety or life disruption.

Success celebration and motivation maintenance includes recognizing achievement while building psychological resilience that supports continued perfect credit maintenance and ongoing financial excellence throughout changing circumstances.

Social considerations for perfect credit include managing family and relationship dynamics while implementing credit excellence strategies that coordinate with household financial management and social responsibilities.

Professional confidence building through credit excellence includes developing financial sophistication while building credibility and expertise that supports professional advancement and financial opportunity access through credit excellence demonstration.

Sustainable habits for perfect credit include building automatic behaviors while creating systems that support perfect credit maintenance without requiring constant conscious attention and decision-making energy that could create burnout.

Educational psychology for perfect credit includes optimal learning approaches while building credit expertise through systematic knowledge development and skill building that supports perfect credit achievement and financial mastery.

Community contribution through perfect credit includes sharing knowledge while contributing to broader financial literacy and consumer protection through credit excellence expertise and educational assistance to others.

Therapeutic applications of perfect credit include understanding how credit excellence supports psychological well-being while building financial confidence and security that enhances overall life satisfaction and mental health throughout financial stability achievement.

Technology and perfect credit involve leveraging advanced digital tools, monitoring systems, and optimization platforms to achieve and maintain perfect credit while reducing management complexity and ensuring consistent execution of sophisticated credit management strategies.

Artificial intelligence applications for perfect credit include machine learning systems that optimize credit management while providing personalized recommendations and automated strategy adjustment that maintains perfect credit with minimal manual oversight.

Real-time monitoring systems for perfect credit include instant score tracking while providing immediate feedback and optimization alerts that enable rapid strategy adjustment and perfect credit maintenance through continuous oversight and management.

Predictive analytics for perfect credit include forecasting systems that anticipate optimization opportunities while providing strategic guidance and outcome prediction that optimizes perfect credit strategy selection and implementation timing.

Mobile optimization for perfect credit includes smartphone-based management while providing convenient access to sophisticated optimization tools and monitoring capabilities that support perfect credit maintenance regardless of location or schedule constraints.

Automation systems for perfect credit include sophisticated payment timing while implementing strategic balance management and account coordination that maintains perfect credit through automated execution of complex optimization strategies.

Data integration platforms for perfect credit include comprehensive financial analysis while coordinating multiple optimization strategies through unified systems that enhance perfect credit coordination and outcome optimization.

Security technology for perfect credit includes advanced protection systems while ensuring financial information safety and fraud prevention throughout digital perfect credit management and platform utilization.

Cloud computing applications for perfect credit include enhanced processing capabilities while providing advanced analytics and optimization tools that support sophisticated perfect credit strategies through distributed computing resources.

Blockchain applications for perfect credit include emerging verification technologies while providing potential enhancements to credit reporting accuracy and perfect credit achievement through innovative technological solutions.

Communication platforms for perfect credit include secure coordination tools while enabling efficient collaboration with professional services and financial institutions that support perfect credit objectives and optimization assistance.

Future technology trends for perfect credit include emerging innovations while understanding how advancing technology capabilities will continue enhancing perfect credit opportunities and management effectiveness throughout evolving technological environments.

Professional technology consultation for perfect credit includes accessing specialized expertise while optimizing technology integration for sophisticated perfect credit management that exceeds individual technical capabilities and provides competitive advantages.

Perfect credit and wealth building integration involves understanding how credit excellence enhances wealth accumulation while implementing strategies that leverage perfect credit for optimal investment opportunities, business development, and comprehensive financial planning throughout lifelong prosperity building.

Investment leverage through perfect credit includes optimal margin account access while utilizing creditworthiness for enhanced investment opportunities and portfolio development that multiplies wealth building potential through strategic credit utilization.

Business financing optimization through perfect credit includes superior business loan terms while accessing business credit that supports entrepreneurial activities and business growth through enhanced financing costs and expanded opportunity access.

Real estate wealth building through perfect credit includes optimal mortgage terms while accessing investment property financing and real estate development opportunities that leverage creditworthiness for property investment and appreciation benefits.

Tax-advantaged financing through perfect credit includes strategic debt utilization while leveraging optimal credit terms for tax-deductible financing that enhances after-tax wealth building and financial efficiency through sophisticated financial planning.

Cash flow optimization through perfect credit includes strategic credit utilization while maintaining liquidity and financial flexibility that supports wealth building activities and investment opportunities throughout optimal resource allocation and financial management.

Risk management integration through perfect credit includes comprehensive insurance optimization while building financial security that protects wealth accumulation and supports risk-adjusted wealth building throughout changing economic conditions.

Estate planning enhancement through perfect credit includes wealth transfer optimization while building credit excellence that supports family financial security and intergenerational wealth building through optimal financial planning and legacy development.

International wealth building through perfect credit includes global financial access while building international investment opportunities and business development that leverages creditworthiness for worldwide wealth accumulation and financial opportunity access.

Professional development through perfect credit includes career enhancement while leveraging credit excellence for professional advancement and income enhancement that supports wealth building through professional success and expertise development.

Retirement planning optimization through perfect credit includes retirement financing enhancement while building financial security that supports retirement wealth and financial independence through optimal credit management and retirement planning integration.

Charitable giving optimization through perfect credit includes strategic philanthropy while leveraging credit excellence for charitable giving strategies that support community contribution and tax optimization throughout wealth building and legacy development.

Legacy wealth creation through perfect credit includes multi-generational financial planning while building credit excellence that supports family wealth building and financial education throughout intergenerational prosperity and knowledge transfer.

Perfect credit in different life stages involves understanding how credit excellence requirements and opportunities change throughout life while adapting strategies to maintain perfect credit and optimize financial benefits across different ages and life circumstances.

Young adult perfect credit includes early credit establishment while building foundation strategies that support perfect credit achievement during college, early career, and initial financial independence development throughout young adult financial development.

Early career perfect credit includes income growth coordination while building credit excellence that supports career advancement and major financial decisions such as home purchases and business development during professional establishment periods.

Mid-career perfect credit includes wealth building integration while maintaining credit excellence that supports peak earning period optimization and major financial goals including investment property, business development, and family financial planning.

Family planning and perfect credit includes household financial coordination while maintaining credit excellence that supports family financial objectives including education financing, housing needs, and comprehensive family financial security planning.

Peak career perfect credit includes wealth accumulation optimization while leveraging credit excellence for sophisticated financial strategies including business development, investment opportunities, and advanced financial planning throughout peak earning periods.

Pre-retirement perfect credit includes retirement preparation while maintaining credit excellence that supports retirement financing and estate planning throughout the transition from active earning to retirement financial management.

Retirement perfect credit includes fixed income coordination while maintaining credit excellence that supports retirement financial security and estate planning throughout retirement financial management and legacy development.

Senior perfect credit includes estate planning integration while maintaining credit excellence that supports family financial security and wealth transfer throughout elder financial management and legacy completion.

Life transition perfect credit includes maintaining credit excellence during major changes while adapting strategies to support different life circumstances including marriage, divorce, career changes, and geographic relocation throughout life transition management.

Health consideration perfect credit includes maintaining credit excellence during health challenges while adapting strategies to support medical financing and healthcare cost management throughout health-related financial planning.

Emergency planning perfect credit includes maintaining credit excellence during crisis while implementing strategies that support emergency financial management and recovery throughout unexpected challenge management and crisis response.

Legacy perfect credit includes maintaining credit excellence for family benefit while implementing strategies that support intergenerational wealth transfer and family financial education throughout legacy development and knowledge transfer.

Perfect credit maintenance automation involves implementing sophisticated systems that preserve credit excellence with minimal manual oversight while ensuring consistent execution of complex optimization strategies throughout changing circumstances and evolving financial needs.

Automated monitoring systems for perfect credit include real-time tracking while providing continuous oversight that maintains perfect credit through systematic attention and immediate response to optimization opportunities and potential threats.

Payment automation for perfect credit includes strategic timing systems while implementing sophisticated payment coordination that maintains optimal utilization and payment history through automated execution of complex timing strategies.

Account management automation for perfect credit includes systematic oversight while implementing automated account monitoring and optimization that maintains perfect credit portfolio management through technology-enhanced systematic attention.

Alert systems for perfect credit include comprehensive notification while providing immediate awareness of optimization opportunities and potential threats that require attention or strategic adjustment throughout perfect credit maintenance.

Balance optimization automation includes sophisticated utilization management while implementing automated systems that maintain optimal ratios through strategic balance coordination and payment timing throughout complex optimization requirements.

Credit monitoring integration includes automated score tracking while providing comprehensive oversight that maintains perfect credit through systematic monitoring and optimization adjustment throughout changing credit reporting and scoring.

Professional service automation includes systematic coordination while implementing automated communication and management that maintains professional assistance effectiveness throughout ongoing perfect credit maintenance and optimization.

Technology platform integration includes comprehensive system coordination while implementing unified automation that maintains perfect credit through coordinated technology utilization and systematic optimization management.

Security automation for perfect credit includes fraud protection while implementing automated security systems that protect perfect credit from identity theft and unauthorized activity throughout ongoing security maintenance and protection.

Performance analytics automation includes systematic tracking while implementing automated measurement and optimization that maintains perfect credit effectiveness through data-driven strategy adjustment and continuous improvement.

Backup system automation includes redundant protection while implementing automated failsafe systems that maintain perfect credit during technology failures and system outages throughout reliability maintenance and system protection.

Future automation planning for perfect credit includes emerging technology integration while building capability to leverage advancing automation for enhanced perfect credit maintenance throughout evolving technological environments and optimization opportunities.

Perfect credit troubleshooting involves systematic approaches to identifying and resolving problems that threaten credit excellence while implementing solutions that restore and protect perfect credit through comprehensive problem-solving and prevention strategies.

Score decline identification for perfect credit includes recognizing threats while understanding factors that might compromise perfect credit and implementing rapid response procedures that restore credit excellence through systematic problem resolution.

Account problem resolution for perfect credit includes addressing account issues while implementing solutions that maintain credit excellence and prevent score decline through effective account management and relationship preservation.

Reporting error correction for perfect credit includes dispute procedures while implementing systematic approaches that correct credit report inaccuracies and maintain perfect credit through comprehensive error resolution and prevention.

Identity theft response for perfect credit includes fraud resolution while implementing recovery procedures that restore credit excellence and prevent ongoing fraud through comprehensive identity protection and recovery management.

Emergency financial management for perfect credit includes crisis response while implementing strategies that maintain credit excellence during financial emergencies and unexpected challenges through crisis management and credit protection.

Professional assistance coordination for complex perfect credit problems includes accessing specialized expertise while resolving complicated issues that exceed individual problem-solving capabilities and require expert intervention and guidance.

Technology failure management for perfect credit includes backup procedures while implementing alternative management systems that maintain credit excellence during system outages and technology failures through redundant oversight and management.

Relationship problem resolution for perfect credit includes addressing creditor issues while maintaining positive relationships and account access that support perfect credit maintenance through effective communication and relationship management.

Legal issue coordination for perfect credit includes protecting credit during legal proceedings while implementing strategies that maintain credit excellence despite legal challenges and potential adverse outcomes through legal protection and credit management.

Regulatory change adaptation for perfect credit includes staying current with credit requirements while implementing strategies that maintain perfect credit under evolving regulatory environments and industry standards throughout regulatory adaptation.

Recovery planning after perfect credit problems includes restoring credit excellence while implementing improvements that prevent similar issues and enhance perfect credit resilience throughout problem recovery and prevention planning.

Prevention strategies for perfect credit include implementing safeguards while building systems that reduce future problem likelihood and maintain perfect credit reliability throughout ongoing protection and maintenance planning.

Perfect credit education and mastery development involve building comprehensive expertise that supports perfect credit achievement while developing capabilities for ongoing credit excellence and professional development throughout lifelong financial management and expertise advancement.

Educational methodology for perfect credit includes systematic learning approaches while building a comprehensive understanding of credit systems and optimization that supports perfect credit achievement and financial mastery development.

Skill progression for perfect credit includes developing basic through advanced capabilities while building expertise that supports sophisticated credit management and perfect credit optimization throughout capability development and mastery achievement.

Knowledge integration across perfect credit disciplines includes understanding connections between scoring, optimization, and financial planning while building comprehensive expertise that supports advanced financial planning and perfect credit excellence.

Practical application development includes implementing theoretical knowledge while building real-world perfect credit experience that demonstrates expertise and supports professional development and mastery achievement throughout hands-on learning.

Teaching capability development through perfect credit expertise includes building knowledge transfer skills while contributing to broader financial literacy and consumer protection through education and assistance provision throughout expertise sharing.

Professional certification consideration for perfect credit includes evaluating credential programs while understanding how certifications might enhance expertise recognition and professional development opportunities throughout career advancement.

Continuous learning commitment for perfect credit includes staying current with industry developments while building adaptation capability for changing regulations, technologies, and market conditions affecting perfect credit throughout ongoing education.

Mentoring relationship development includes both seeking mentorship and providing guidance while building professional networks that support ongoing learning and expertise development throughout career advancement and knowledge sharing.

Research and analysis capability development includes building investigative skills while understanding how to evaluate perfect credit strategies and industry developments for informed decision-making and optimization effectiveness throughout expertise development.

Innovation capacity building includes developing creativity and strategic thinking while building capability to develop novel approaches and optimize strategies for unique circumstances and emerging opportunities throughout innovation development.

Professional network development through perfect credit includes building relationships with industry professionals while accessing expertise and opportunities that support career advancement and knowledge enhancement throughout professional development.

Legacy development through perfect credit mastery includes building lasting impact while creating systems and relationships that extend expertise benefits beyond individual achievement through knowledge transfer and community contribution throughout lifelong contribution.

Perfect credit and professional development involve understanding how credit excellence enhances career opportunities while building professional capabilities that leverage credit expertise for career advancement and income enhancement throughout professional growth and development.

Career enhancement through perfect credit includes understanding professional opportunities while building credit excellence that supports career advancement and access to positions requiring financial responsibility and credit evaluation throughout professional development.

Professional credibility through credit excellence includes demonstrating financial sophistication while building credibility and expertise that supports professional advancement and enhanced professional relationships throughout career development.

Consulting opportunities through perfect credit expertise include building specialized knowledge while developing consulting capabilities that provide income enhancement and professional recognition through credit expertise and assistance provision.

Educational opportunities through perfect credit mastery include teaching and training capabilities while contributing to professional education and financial literacy advancement through expertise sharing and educational service provision.

Industry involvement through credit expertise includes professional organization participation while contributing to industry development and standards advancement through expertise application and professional contribution throughout industry engagement.

Professional networking through credit excellence includes building relationships while accessing opportunities and expertise that support career advancement and professional development through credit excellence demonstration and expertise sharing.

Speaking and presentation opportunities through perfect credit expertise include professional recognition while building public speaking capabilities that support career advancement and professional recognition through expertise demonstration and knowledge sharing.

Writing and publication opportunities through credit expertise include content creation while building professional recognition and expertise demonstration through written communication and knowledge sharing throughout professional contribution.

Professional certification and licensing enhancement through credit excellence includes understanding credential requirements while building credit profiles that support professional licensing and certification achievement throughout professional development.

Business development through credit expertise includes entrepreneurial opportunities while leveraging credit knowledge for business development and income enhancement through specialized expertise and service provision throughout business growth.

Income enhancement through credit expertise includes multiple revenue streams while building financial opportunities that leverage credit knowledge for increased income and financial security throughout professional and financial development.

Legacy creation through professional credit excellence includes building lasting professional impact while contributing to industry advancement and professional development through expertise application and knowledge transfer throughout career contribution.

Perfect credit lifestyle integration involves understanding how credit excellence fits into comprehensive life planning while building sustainable approaches that support both credit perfection and overall life satisfaction throughout balanced living and financial management.

Lifestyle design with perfect credit includes understanding how credit excellence supports life objectives while building financial capability that enables lifestyle choices and life satisfaction throughout comprehensive life planning and goal achievement.

Financial freedom through perfect credit includes understanding how credit excellence supports financial independence while building wealth and financial security that enables lifestyle freedom and choice throughout financial independence achievement.

Stress reduction through credit excellence includes understanding how perfect credit reduces financial anxiety while building financial security and confidence that enhances overall life satisfaction and psychological well-being throughout stress management.

Relationship benefits from perfect credit include understanding how credit excellence affects family and social relationships while building financial security that supports relationship stability and family financial security throughout relationship development.

Housing optimization through perfect credit includes understanding how credit excellence affects housing opportunities while building access to optimal housing and real estate investment that supports lifestyle and wealth building throughout housing advancement.

Travel and leisure enhancement through perfect credit includes understanding how credit excellence supports travel and lifestyle experiences while building financial capability that enables enhanced life experiences and personal fulfillment throughout lifestyle enhancement.

Health and wellness support through perfect credit includes understanding how financial security affects health while building credit excellence that supports healthcare access and wellness investment throughout health optimization and life quality enhancement.

Education and personal development support through perfect credit includes understanding how credit excellence enables learning and growth while building financial capability that supports educational investment and personal development throughout lifelong learning.

Charitable giving and community contribution through perfect credit includes understanding how financial security enables giving while building credit excellence that supports charitable activities and community contribution throughout social responsibility and legacy development.

Family legacy development through perfect credit includes understanding how credit excellence supports family financial security while building intergenerational wealth and financial education that benefits family members throughout legacy creation and family development.

Personal fulfillment through financial excellence includes understanding how perfect credit contributes to life satisfaction while building financial security that enables personal goal achievement and life fulfillment throughout comprehensive life satisfaction.

Balanced living with perfect credit includes understanding how to maintain credit excellence without compromising other life priorities while building sustainable approaches that support both financial excellence and overall life satisfaction throughout balanced lifestyle management.

Perfect credit innovation and future trends involve understanding emerging developments that will affect credit excellence while building adaptability that maintains perfect credit effectiveness throughout changing credit industry environments and technological advancement.

Artificial intelligence impact on perfect credit includes understanding how machine learning affects credit scoring while adapting strategies to leverage AI development for enhanced credit management and perfect credit achievement throughout technological advancement.

Blockchain technology impact on credit includes understanding distributed ledger applications while preparing for potential credit reporting changes that might affect perfect credit strategies and optimization techniques throughout technology evolution.

Alternative data integration in perfect credit includes understanding how new data sources affect scoring while leveraging emerging credit building opportunities that might enhance perfect credit achievement and maintenance throughout data evolution.

Regulatory evolution affecting perfect credit includes understanding policy changes while adapting strategies to leverage new consumer protections and maintain perfect credit under evolving regulatory requirements throughout regulatory development.

Global credit standardization impact includes understanding international credit development while preparing for potential global credit reporting standards that might affect perfect credit strategies and international financial opportunities throughout globalization.

Financial technology innovation affecting perfect credit includes understanding fintech development while leveraging new financial products and services that might enhance perfect credit achievement and maintenance throughout technological innovation.

Consumer education advancement for perfect credit includes understanding improved financial literacy while contributing to broader perfect credit education and achievement that benefits multiple consumers throughout educational advancement.

Industry consolidation impact on perfect credit includes understanding banking industry changes while adapting strategies to changing issuer relationships and credit product availability throughout industry evolution.

Economic cycle adaptation for perfect credit includes understanding how economic changes affect credit while building resilience that maintains perfect credit throughout recession, inflation, and economic uncertainty throughout economic adaptation.

Professional service evolution for perfect credit includes understanding changing expert assistance while accessing emerging professional services that support perfect credit achievement and maintenance throughout service development.

Innovation opportunities in perfect credit include emerging strategies while developing novel approaches that enhance perfect credit achievement and create competitive advantages throughout innovation development and strategic advancement.

Future preparation for perfect credit includes building adaptability while maintaining capability to leverage emerging opportunities and adapt to changing requirements throughout evolving credit industry conditions and technological advancement.

Perfect credit measurement and evaluation involve comprehensive assessment methodologies that track credit excellence while identifying optimization opportunities and ensuring that perfect credit strategies produce maximum long-term value and financial benefit throughout achievement and maintenance.

Performance metrics for perfect credit include comprehensive tracking while monitoring score achievement, maintenance consistency, cost-effectiveness, and goal attainment that provide complete evaluation of perfect credit success and optimization opportunities.

Score achievement correlation includes analyzing which strategies produce optimal results while understanding specific techniques that contribute most significantly to perfect credit achievement and maintenance effectiveness throughout strategy optimization.

Timeline effectiveness evaluation includes measuring achievement speed while identifying factors that accelerate or delay perfect credit attainment and optimizing strategy timing for maximum effectiveness throughout achievement planning.

Cost-benefit analysis for perfect credit includes evaluating resource investments against achieved benefits while ensuring optimal resource allocation and strategy selection for maximum return on perfect credit investments throughout cost optimization.

Maintenance effectiveness assessment includes tracking long-term credit excellence while understanding factors that support sustained perfect credit and identifying optimization opportunities for ongoing maintenance effectiveness throughout preservation planning.

Integration effectiveness analysis includes evaluating how perfect credit coordinates with other financial activities while identifying optimization opportunities for enhanced coordination and comprehensive financial improvement throughout integration planning.

Technology utilization effectiveness includes assessing digital tool contribution while understanding how technology integration enhances perfect credit outcomes and supports optimization effectiveness throughout technology optimization.

Professional service effectiveness includes measuring assistance value while understanding how professional services contribute to perfect credit achievement and justify investment in expert assistance throughout service evaluation.

Risk management effectiveness includes understanding how well protection strategies safeguard perfect credit while identifying additional safeguards that enhance perfect credit security and resilience throughout protection planning.

Innovation assessment for perfect credit includes evaluating novel approaches while identifying creative solutions that enhance perfect credit effectiveness and provide competitive advantages throughout innovation development.

Long-term value assessment for perfect credit includes comprehensive evaluation of credit excellence benefits while understanding how perfect credit contributes to wealth building and financial opportunity enhancement throughout value optimization.

Success preservation strategies ensure that perfect credit benefits continue supporting financial objectives while maintaining excellence and building sustainable credit management practices for lifelong financial success throughout achievement maintenance.

Perfect credit mastery integration with comprehensive financial planning ensures that credit excellence supports broader wealth building while optimizing credit perfection within holistic financial management and long-term security planning throughout integrated financial development.

Financial integration through perfect credit includes understanding how credit excellence enhances investment opportunities while leveraging creditworthiness for optimal investment access and portfolio development that multiplies wealth building potential through strategic credit utilization and financial leverage.

Risk management coordination includes integrating perfect credit with comprehensive financial protection while ensuring credit excellence supports overall financial security and wealth preservation through optimal credit management and comprehensive risk planning throughout changing economic conditions.

Tax planning integration with perfect credit includes understanding how credit optimization affects tax strategies while coordinating credit excellence with comprehensive tax planning for optimal financial efficiency and wealth building throughout tax-advantaged financial management.

Estate planning coordination includes understanding how perfect credit affects wealth transfer while ensuring credit excellence supports legacy development and family financial security through comprehensive planning integration throughout intergenerational wealth building.

Business development support through perfect credit includes leveraging credit excellence for entrepreneurial opportunities while building creditworthiness that supports business financing and professional advancement through optimal credit management and business development.

Investment opportunity enhancement through perfect credit includes understanding how credit excellence affects investment access while leveraging improved creditworthiness for enhanced investment opportunities and portfolio development throughout wealth building acceleration.

International financial planning integration includes understanding how perfect credit supports global opportunities while adapting credit strategies for international investment and business development through comprehensive global financial management.

Retirement planning enhancement through perfect credit includes understanding how credit excellence supports retirement financing while ensuring credit management excellence enhances retirement security and financial independence throughout retirement planning.

Insurance optimization through perfect credit includes understanding how credit excellence affects insurance costs while integrating credit management with comprehensive risk management and financial protection planning throughout insurance coordination.

Professional development through perfect credit expertise includes building consulting capabilities while leveraging credit knowledge for career advancement and income enhancement through specialized expertise and professional service provision.

Educational contribution through perfect credit mastery includes developing teaching capabilities while supporting financial literacy advancement and consumer education through credit expertise and instruction throughout educational contribution.

Legacy creation through perfect credit excellence includes building lasting financial expertise while contributing to financial literacy and consumer protection through credit knowledge and community assistance throughout lifelong contribution and impact creation.

Perfect credit legacy and impact involve understanding how credit excellence creates lasting value while contributing to broader financial empowerment and consumer protection through expertise development and knowledge sharing throughout lifelong contribution and community benefit.

Personal legacy development through perfect credit includes building lasting financial capabilities while creating foundation skills that support lifelong financial success and provide resilience through changing economic conditions throughout personal development and achievement.

Family impact through perfect credit mastery includes teaching family members while building household financial management excellence that supports multi-generational wealth building and financial security through credit optimization knowledge and family education.

Professional legacy creation includes developing consulting capabilities while contributing to broader financial literacy and consumer protection through perfect credit expertise and educational assistance throughout professional contribution and industry advancement.

Community contribution through perfect credit expertise includes sharing knowledge while supporting broader financial inclusion and consumer empowerment through credit optimization education and assistance programs throughout community service and impact.

Industry impact through perfect credit innovation includes contributing to best practices while advancing credit optimization techniques and supporting industry improvement through expertise development and knowledge sharing throughout industry advancement.

Educational contribution through perfect credit mastery includes developing teaching capabilities while supporting financial literacy advancement and consumer education through credit expertise and instruction throughout educational service and knowledge transfer.

Research contribution through perfect credit expertise includes documenting best practices while advancing understanding of credit optimization through systematic analysis and knowledge development that benefits broader consumer education throughout research advancement.

Policy influence through perfect credit mastery includes understanding regulatory implications while contributing to consumer protection advancement and credit reporting improvement through expertise application and advocacy activities throughout policy development.

Innovation legacy through perfect credit mastery includes developing creative approaches while contributing to credit optimization advancement and financial management innovation through practical expertise and strategic thinking development throughout innovation contribution.

Mentoring capability development through perfect credit excellence includes building guidance skills while supporting others' financial success through credit optimization knowledge transfer and personal development assistance throughout mentoring contribution and impact.

Knowledge preservation through perfect credit expertise includes documenting effective strategies while ensuring credit optimization knowledge continues benefiting future generations through systematic knowledge transfer and educational resource development throughout knowledge legacy.

Transformational impact through perfect credit excellence includes creating significant positive change while contributing to systemic improvement in financial management and consumer protection through comprehensive expertise application and leadership development throughout lifelong contribution and transformational legacy creation.

Perfect credit represents not merely a score achievement but a comprehensive demonstration of financial mastery that opens doors to unlimited financial opportunities while providing the foundation for lifelong prosperity, professional success, and meaningful contribution to others' financial empowerment and success throughout sustained excellence and community impact.

APPENDIX A

SAMPLE LETTERS AND TEMPLATES

CREDIT BUREAU DISPUTE LETTER TEMPLATE

[Your Name]

[Your Address]

[City, State, ZIP Code]

[Date]

[Credit Bureau Name]

[Dispute Department Address]

[City, State, ZIP Code]

Re: Request for Investigation of Credit Report Information

Social Security Number: XXX-XX-XXXX

Date of Birth: [Your DOB]

Dear Sir or Madam:

I am writing to dispute inaccurate information on my credit report. I have enclosed a copy of my credit report with the disputed items circled for your reference.

Item 1: [Account Name/Number]

Dispute Reason: This account shows a late payment on [date], but my records indicate the payment was made on time. I have enclosed a copy of my bank statement showing the payment was processed on [date], which was before the due date.

Item 2: [Account Name/Number]

Dispute Reason: This account is not mine. I have never had an account with this company, and this appears to be the result of mixed files or identity theft.

Item 3: [Account Name/Number]

Dispute Reason: This account shows an incorrect balance of $[amount]. The correct balance should be $[amount] as verified by my recent statement from the creditor.

I am requesting that these items be investigated and corrected or removed from my credit report. Please conduct a reasonable investigation as required by the Fair Credit Reporting Act and provide me with the results of your investigation.

Enclosed you will find:

- Copy of credit report with disputed items marked

- Copy of bank statement (for Item 1)

- Copy of account statement (for Item 3)

- Copy of driver's license for identification

Please send me a corrected copy of my credit report to the address listed above. Thank you for your prompt attention to this matter.

Sincerely,

[Your Signature]

[Your Printed Name]

DEBT VALIDATION LETTER TEMPLATE

[Your Name]

[Your Address]

[City, State, ZIP Code]

[Date]

[Collection Agency Name]

[Address]

[City, State, ZIP Code]

Re: Account Number: [Account Number]

Amount: $[Amount]

Dear Sir or Madam:

This letter is sent in response to a notice I received from your company on [date]. Be advised that this is not a refusal to pay, but a notice that your claim is disputed and validation is requested.

Under the Fair Debt Collection Practices Act, I have the right to request validation of the debt you are attempting to collect. I am requesting that you provide me with competent evidence that I have any legal obligation to pay you.

Please provide me with the following information:

1. What the money you say I owe is for

2. Explain and show me how you calculated what you say I owe

3. Provide me with copies of any papers that show I agreed to pay what you say I owe

4. Prove the Statute of Limitations has not expired on this account

5. Show me that you are licensed to collect in my state

6. Provide documentation that you own this debt or have been assigned this debt

If you cannot validate this debt, then it must be removed from my credit report and I must be notified of such removal. Also, if you cannot validate then you must cease collection efforts.

If you do validate the debt, then I will require proof that you are authorized to collect in my state and proof that the original creditor had the right to assign this debt to you.

This is a formal request for validation made under the FDCPA. Please be governed accordingly.

Sincerely,

[Your Signature]

[Your Printed Name]

GOODWILL LETTER TEMPLATE

[Your Name]

[Your Address]

[City, State, ZIP Code]

[Date]

[Creditor Name]

[Customer Service Department]

[Address]

[City, State, ZIP Code]

Re: Account Number: [Account Number]

Request for Goodwill Adjustment

Dear [Customer Service Manager/Executive],

I hope this letter finds you well. I am writing as a long-standing customer to request your consideration for a goodwill adjustment to my credit report regarding my account with your company.

I have been a loyal customer of [Company Name] for [time period] and have generally maintained a positive payment history with your organization. Unfortunately, due to [brief explanation of circumstances - job loss, medical emergency, family crisis, etc.], I experienced financial difficulties that resulted in [specific issue - late payment, missed payment, etc.] on [date(s)].

Since that time, I have taken the following steps to improve my financial situation:

- [Specific action taken]

- [Another specific action]

- [Additional improvements made]

My account is now current, and I have maintained consistent, on-time payments for the past [time period]. I have learned from this experience and have implemented better financial management practices to ensure this situation does not occur again.

I am respectfully requesting that you consider removing the negative reporting from [date] as a gesture of goodwill. This adjustment would significantly help my credit score and would be deeply appreciated. I value my relationship with [Company Name] and hope to continue as a customer for many years to come.

I understand that this is an extraordinary request, and I genuinely appreciate your time and consideration. If you need any additional information or documentation, please don't hesitate to contact me at [phone number] or [email address].

Thank you for your understanding and for the opportunity to explain my situation.

Sincerely,

[Your Signature]

[Your Printed Name]

PAY-FOR-DELETE LETTER TEMPLATE

[Your Name]

[Your Address]

[City, State, ZIP Code]

[Date]

[Collection Agency Name]

[Address]

[City, State, ZIP Code]

Re: Account Number: [Account Number]

Original Creditor: [Original Creditor Name]

Settlement Proposal

Dear Collection Manager:

I am writing regarding the above-referenced account to propose a settlement arrangement that would be mutually beneficial.

I acknowledge that your company is reporting this account to the credit bureaus, and I am prepared to resolve this matter. I am willing to pay $[settlement amount] as payment in full for this account, provided you agree to the following terms:

1. Upon receipt of payment, you will remove all references to this account from my credit reports with Experian, Equifax, and TransUnion

2. You will provide me with a letter confirming the deletion within 30 days of payment

3. This account will be considered paid in full and closed

4. You agree not to resell or transfer this account to another collection agency

This offer is contingent upon your written agreement to remove all negative reporting associated with this account. I am not able to proceed with payment unless you confirm in writing that the account will be deleted from my credit reports.

If these terms are acceptable, please send me a written agreement outlining these conditions before I submit payment. Payment will be made via [payment method] within 10 days of receiving your written confirmation.

This letter is not an admission of liability, and I reserve all rights under state and federal law. Please consider this offer carefully, as it represents my best and final offer for resolution of this matter.

I look forward to your response and to resolving this matter quickly and amicably.

Sincerely,

[Your Signature]

[Your Printed Name]

CEASE AND DESIST LETTER TEMPLATE

[Your Name]

[Your Address]

[City, State, ZIP Code]

[Date]

[Collection Agency Name]

[Address]

[City, State, ZIP Code]

Re: Account Number: [Account Number]

Cease and Desist Communication

Dear Sir or Madam:

You are hereby notified under provisions of Public Law 95-109, Section 805-C of the Fair Debt Collection Practices Act that your services are no longer desired.

You and your company are instructed to CEASE AND DESIST all attempts to collect the above debt. This includes but is not limited to:

- Telephone calls to my home, cell phone, or place of employment

- Mailing letters or notices to my home or place of employment

- Contacting third parties regarding this alleged debt

- Reporting or threatening to report adverse information to credit bureaus

- Any other form of communication regarding this matter

Please be advised that I am aware of my rights under the Fair Debt Collection Practices Act and will not hesitate to report violations to the appropriate authorities including:

- The Consumer Financial Protection Bureau

- My state's Attorney General

- The Federal Trade Commission

This is a formal cease and desist notice. Your compliance is required by law.

The only contact I will accept from this point forward is:

1. To advise me that your debt collection efforts are being terminated, or

2. To notify me that you or the debt collector intends to invoke a specific remedy which you ordinarily invoke

Be governed accordingly.

Sincerely,

[Your Signature]

[Your Printed Name]

IDENTITY THEFT AFFIDAVIT TEMPLATE

[Your Name]

[Your Address]

[City, State, ZIP Code]

[Date]

[Creditor/Credit Bureau Name]

[Address]

[City, State, ZIP Code]

Re: Identity Theft Affidavit

Account Number: [Account Number if applicable]

SSN: XXX-XX-XXXX

Dear Sir or Madam:

I am writing to report that I have been a victim of identity theft. Fraudulent accounts have been opened in my name without my knowledge or authorization.

Details of Identity Theft:

- Date discovered: [Date]

- Estimated date of theft: [Date range]

- How discovered: [How you found out]

Fraudulent Accounts Identified:

1. [Account/Company Name] - Account [Number] - Amount: $[Amount]

2. [Account/Company Name] - Account [Number] - Amount: $[Amount]

I did not open these accounts, authorize anyone to open them, or make any charges on these accounts. I am requesting that:

1. These accounts be closed immediately

2. All fraudulent charges be removed

3. This information be removed from my credit reports

4. You provide me with documentation confirming these actions

Enclosed please find:

- Copy of police report (Report [Number])

- Copy of FTC Identity Theft Report

- Copy of driver's license

- Signed affidavit under penalty of perjury

I declare under penalty of perjury that the information I have provided is true and correct to the best of my knowledge.

Affidavit:

I swear or affirm that:

- I am [Your Name] and I am [age] years old

- The above information is true and accurate

- I did not authorize anyone to use my personal information to open accounts or make charges

- I did not receive any benefit from the fraudulent activities

- I am willing to cooperate in the prosecution of the person(s) who committed this fraud

Signature: ____________________________ Date: ___________

[Your Printed Name]

Notarized: ____________________________

[Notary Signature and Seal]

Please contact me at [phone number] if you need any additional information.

Sincerely,

[Your Signature]

[Your Printed Name]

FURNISHER DISPUTE LETTER TEMPLATE

[Your Name]

[Your Address]

[City, State, ZIP Code]

[Date]

[Original Creditor Name]

[Address]

[City, State, ZIP Code]

Re: Account Number: [Account Number]

Direct Dispute Under FCRA Section 623

Dear Sir or Madam:

I am writing to dispute inaccurate information that your company is furnishing to credit reporting agencies regarding my account. I recently disputed this information with [Credit Bureau Name], and they have indicated that they verified the information with your company. However, the information remains inaccurate.

Disputed Information:

Account shows: [Incorrect information]

Should show: [Correct information]

Supporting Documentation:

I have enclosed copies of documentation that supports my position:

- [List of enclosed documents]

Under Section 623 of the Fair Credit Reporting Act, you are required to:

1. Investigate disputes about the accuracy of information you furnish
2. Review all relevant information provided by me
3. Report the results of your investigation to the credit reporting agency

4. If the information is found to be inaccurate, report the correct information to all credit reporting agencies to which you furnished the incorrect information

I am requesting that you:

1. Conduct a reasonable investigation of this dispute

2. Correct the inaccurate information with all credit reporting agencies

3. Provide me with written confirmation of the corrections made

4. Ensure that future reporting is accurate

Please be advised that I am aware of my rights under the Fair Credit Reporting Act, and I will pursue all available remedies if this matter is not resolved appropriately.

I expect to hear from you within 30 days regarding the resolution of this matter. Please send your response to the address listed above.

Thank you for your prompt attention to this important matter.

Sincerely,

[Your Signature]

[Your Printed Name]

CREDIT LIMIT INCREASE REQUEST LETTER

[Your Name]

[Your Address]

[City, State, ZIP Code]

[Date]

[Credit Card Company Name]

[Customer Service Department]

[Address]

[City, State, ZIP Code]

Re: Account Number: [Account Number]
Request for Credit Limit Increase

Dear Credit Review Department:

I am writing to request an increase in the credit limit on my account. I have been a valued customer of [Company Name] for [time period] and believe that my account management and financial improvements warrant consideration for a credit limit increase.

Current Account Information:

- Current credit limit: $[amount]

- Account opening date: [date]

- Average monthly usage: $[amount]

- Payment history: Excellent (no late payments)

Requested Increase:

I am requesting an increase to $[amount], which represents an increase of $[amount].

Justification for Increase:

- Income increase: My annual income has increased from $[old amount] to $[new amount]

- Improved credit score: My credit score has improved to [score] from [previous score]

- Responsible usage: I maintain low utilization and pay my balance in full each month

- Increased spending needs: [Brief explanation of why you need the increase]

Supporting Documentation:

I have enclosed the following documentation to support my request:

- Recent pay stubs showing current income

- Recent credit report showing improved score

- Bank statements showing financial stability

I have been very satisfied with your company's service and would like to continue our relationship with an increased credit limit. I believe this increase would be mutually beneficial as it would allow me to use your card for more of my spending while maintaining the low utilization ratio that we both value.

Please let me know if you need any additional information to process this request. I can be reached at [phone number] or [email address].

Thank you for considering my request. I look forward to your favorable response.

Sincerely,

[Your Signature]

[Your Printed Name]

AUTHORIZED USER REMOVAL REQUEST LETTER

[Your Name]

[Your Address]

[City, State, ZIP Code]

[Date]

[Credit Card Company Name]

[Customer Service Department]

[Address]

[City, State, ZIP Code]

Re: Account Number: [Account Number]

Primary Cardholder: [Primary Cardholder Name]

Request for Authorized User Removal

Dear Customer Service:

I am writing to request that I be removed as an authorized user from the above-referenced credit card account. I was added as an authorized user on [date] but now wish to be removed from this account.

Account Details:

- Primary Account Holder: [Name]

- Authorized User to Remove: [Your Name]

- Date Added as Authorized User: [Date]

- Relationship to Primary: [Relationship]

Reason for Removal:

[Brief explanation - building independent credit, changed relationship status, etc.]

Please ensure that:

1. My name is completely removed from the account

2. I no longer have any access to the account

3. The account will no longer appear on my credit reports

4. You update the credit bureaus about this removal

5. Any cards issued in my name are deactivated

I understand that this removal is permanent and that I would need the primary account holder's authorization to be added again in the future.

Please send me written confirmation once this removal has been completed. If you need verification from the primary account holder, please contact them at [primary holder's phone number].

Contact Information:

Please send confirmation to:

[Your Name]

[Your Address]

[City, State, ZIP Code]

Phone: [Your Phone Number]

Email: [Your Email]

Thank you for processing this request promptly. Please let me know if you need any additional information.

Sincerely,

[Your Signature]

[Your Printed Name]

MORTGAGE RAPID RESCORE REQUEST LETTER

[Your Name]

[Your Address]

[City, State, ZIP Code]

[Date]

[Mortgage Lender Name]

[Loan Officer Name]

[Address]

[City, State, ZIP Code]

Re: Loan Application Number: [Number]

Request for Rapid Rescore

Dear [Loan Officer Name]:

Thank you for working with me on my mortgage application. As discussed, I have made several changes to my credit accounts that should improve my credit scores and potentially qualify me for better loan terms.

Changes Made:

1. Paid down credit card balances from $[old amount] to $[new amount]

   - [Card Name]: Reduced from $[amount] to $[amount]

   - [Card Name]: Reduced from $[amount] to $[amount]

2. Paid off loan: [Loan Name] - $[amount] paid in full

3. Disputed and corrected error: [Description of correction]

Documentation Provided:

I have enclosed the following documentation to support the rapid rescore:

- Updated credit card statements showing new balances

- Payment confirmations for balance reductions

- Loan payoff confirmation

- Credit bureau confirmation of dispute resolution

Request:

I am requesting a rapid rescore to reflect these improvements in my credit profile. Based on these changes, I believe my credit scores should improve by approximately [estimated points], which should qualify me for:

- Better interest rate: [current rate] to [expected rate]

- Improved loan terms

- Reduced PMI requirements

Timeline:

I understand that rapid rescoring typically takes 2-3 business days. Please let me know:

- If any additional documentation is needed

- The timeline for completion

- When new loan terms will be available

I am committed to closing on [property address] and appreciate your assistance in optimizing my loan terms through this rapid rescore process.

Please contact me at [phone number] if you have any questions or need additional information.

Thank you for your continued assistance.

Sincerely,

[Your Signature]

[Your Printed Name]

MEDICAL DEBT DISPUTE LETTER

[Your Name]

[Your Address]

[City, State, ZIP Code]

[Date]

[Medical Provider/Collection Agency Name]

[Address]

[City, State, ZIP Code]

Re: Account Number: [Account Number]

Date of Service: [Date]

Dispute of Medical Debt

Dear Sir or Madam:

I am writing to dispute the medical debt you are attempting to collect. I believe this debt is either incorrect or has been resolved through insurance coverage.

Dispute Details:

- Patient Name: [Your Name]

- Date of Birth: [DOB]

- Date of Service: [Date]

- Provider: [Medical Provider Name]

- Amount in Question: $[Amount]

Reason for Dispute:

[Select appropriate reason]

□ This bill was covered by insurance and should have been paid

□ This amount exceeds what I owe after insurance adjustments

□ I never received these services

□ This bill contains errors in the services provided

□ This debt was already paid

□ Other: [Explanation]

Insurance Information:

- Insurance Company: [Insurance Name]
- Policy Number: [Policy Number]
- Group Number: [Group Number]
- Claim Number: [Claim Number if available]

Supporting Documentation Enclosed:

□ Insurance card copy

□ Explanation of Benefits (EOB)

□ Payment records

□ Medical records

□ Previous correspondence

Requests:

1. Please investigate this matter thoroughly
2. Provide me with itemized billing for all services
3. Provide documentation of insurance billing and response
4. If debt is verified as accurate, provide payment plan options
5. Remove any negative credit reporting until this is resolved

Under the Fair Debt Collection Practices Act, you must cease collection activities until you have validated this debt. Please do not report this to credit bureaus while the dispute is being investigated.

HIPAA Authorization:

I hereby authorize [Medical Provider] to release medical information necessary to resolve this billing dispute to my insurance company and their authorized representatives.

Patient Signature: ______________________ Date: ________

Please respond in writing within 30 days with the results of your investigation.

Sincerely,

[Your Signature]

[Your Printed Name]

STUDENT LOAN REHABILITATION REQUEST LETTER

[Your Name]

[Your Address]

[City, State, ZIP Code]

[Date]

[Loan Servicer Name]

[Address]

[City, State, ZIP Code]

Re: Student Loan Rehabilitation Request

Borrower Name: [Your Name]

SSN: XXX-XX-XXXX

Dear Student Loan Rehabilitation Department:

I am writing to request rehabilitation of my defaulted federal student loans. I understand that loan rehabilitation is a process that can remove the default status from my credit report and restore my loans to good standing.

Loan Information:

- Borrower: [Your Name]

- Social Security Number: XXX-XX-XXXX

- Approximate loan balance: $[Amount]

- Default date: [Date if known]

Financial Information:

- Current monthly income: $[Amount]

- Source of income: [Employment/Benefits/etc.]

- Dependents: [Number]

- Other monthly obligations: $[Amount]

Rehabilitation Request:

I am requesting to enter into a loan rehabilitation agreement. I understand that:

- I must make 9 consecutive, voluntary, on-time monthly payments

- Payment amount will be based on my income and expenses

- Upon completion, the default status will be removed from my credit report

- My loans will be eligible for benefits like deferment and forbearance again

Proposed Payment Amount:

Based on my financial situation, I believe I can afford $[Amount] per month. I have enclosed financial documentation to support this payment amount:

□ Pay stubs

□ Tax returns

□ Bank statements

□ Benefits statements

□ Expense documentation

Commitment:

I am committed to making all required payments on time and completing the rehabilitation process. I understand the importance of this opportunity and will not miss any payments.

Please send me the rehabilitation agreement and let me know:

- The exact payment amount based on my financial information

- Payment due dates

- Payment methods accepted

- Contact information for questions

I am eager to begin this process and restore my loans to good standing. Please contact me at [phone number] if you need any additional information.

Thank you for your assistance.

Sincerely,

[Your Signature]

[Your Printed Name]

BUSINESS CREDIT DISPUTE LETTER

[Your Name/Business Name]

[Business Address]

[City, State, ZIP Code]

[Date]

[Business Credit Bureau Name]

[Dispute Department]

[Address]

[City, State, ZIP Code]

Re: Business Credit Report Dispute

Business Name: [Business Name]

EIN: XX-XXXXXXX

DUNS Number: [Number if applicable]

Dear Sir or Madam:

I am writing to dispute inaccurate information appearing on my business credit report. The following items are incorrect and need to be investigated and corrected.

Business Information:

- Legal Business Name: [Name]

- DBA Name: [Name if different]

- Business Address: [Address]

- EIN: XX-XXXXXXX

- Business Type: [Corporation/LLC/Partnership/etc.]

- Years in Business: [Number]

Disputed Items:

Item 1: [Trade Line/Public Record]

- Creditor: [Name]

- Account Number: [Number]

- Reported Information: [What is currently showing]

- Correct Information: [What it should show]

- Reason for Dispute: [Explanation]

Item 2: [Trade Line/Public Record]

- Creditor: [Name]

- Account Number: [Number]

- Reported Information: [What is currently showing]

- Correct Information: [What it should show]

- Reason for Dispute: [Explanation]

Supporting Documentation:

I have enclosed the following documentation to support my disputes:

□ Business license

□ Articles of incorporation

□ Tax ID documentation

□ Payment records

□ Contracts/agreements

□ Bank statements

□ Other: [Specify]

Requested Actions:

1. Investigate the disputed items listed above

2. Correct any inaccurate information

3. Remove any information that cannot be verified

4. Provide me with an updated business credit report

5. Notify all parties who have received reports in the past 6 months of any changes

Please conduct a thorough investigation as required by the Fair Credit Reporting Act and provide me with written results of your investigation within 30 days.

If you need any additional information, please contact me at [phone number] or [email address].

Sincerely,

[Your Signature]

[Your Printed Name]

[Title]

EMPLOYMENT CREDIT REPORT DISPUTE LETTER

[Your Name]

[Your Address]

[City, State, ZIP Code]

[Date]

[Employer Name]

[Human Resources Department]

[Address]

[City, State, ZIP Code]

Re: Dispute of Employment Credit Report Decision

Application for: [Position Title]

Application Date: [Date]

Dear Human Resources Manager:

I am writing regarding the adverse employment action taken based on information in my consumer credit report. I received your pre-adverse action notice on [date] and wish to dispute the accuracy of the credit information used in your employment decision.

Credit Report Information in Dispute:

1. [Specific item from credit report]

   - This information is inaccurate because: [Explanation]

   - Supporting documentation: [What you're providing]

2. [Specific item from credit report]

   - This information is inaccurate because: [Explanation]

   - Supporting documentation: [What you're providing]

Corrected Information:

I have enclosed documentation that corrects the inaccurate information:

□ Updated credit report showing corrections

□ Payment records

□ Account statements

□ Court documents

□ Other: [Specify]

Request for Reconsideration:

I am requesting that you reconsider your employment decision based on this corrected information. The inaccurate credit information does not reflect my true creditworthiness or character, and I believe the corrected information demonstrates my suitability for the position.

Additional Context:

[If appropriate, provide brief context about any legitimate credit issues]

- [Explanation of circumstances]

- [Steps taken to resolve issues]

- [Current financial stability]

I am very interested in this position and believe I would be a valuable addition to your team. The credit issues that appeared on the report do not accurately reflect my current financial responsibility or my ability to perform the job duties.

Please let me know if you need any additional information. I can be reached at [phone number] or [email address].

I look forward to your reconsideration and the opportunity to discuss this position further.

Sincerely,

[Your Signature]

[Your Printed Name]

RENTAL APPLICATION CREDIT EXPLANATION LETTER

[Your Name]

[Current Address]

[City, State, ZIP Code]

[Date]

[Property Manager/Landlord Name]

[Property Management Company]

[Address]

[City, State, ZIP Code]

Re: Rental Application for [Property Address]

Credit Report Explanation

Dear [Property Manager/Landlord Name]:

Thank you for considering my rental application for [property address]. I understand that my credit report shows some negative information, and I wanted to provide you with an explanation and context for these items.

Application Information:

- Applicant Name: [Your Name]

- Desired Move-in Date: [Date]

- Monthly Rent: $[Amount]

- Security Deposit: $[Amount]

Credit Issues Explanation:

Issue 1: [Description of credit problem]

- When it occurred: [Time period]

- Circumstances: [Brief explanation of what happened]

- Resolution: [What you did to resolve it]

- Current status: [Current situation]

Issue 2: [Description of credit problem]

- When it occurred: [Time period]
- Circumstances: [Brief explanation of what happened]
- Resolution: [What you did to resolve it]
- Current status: [Current situation]

Financial Stability Evidence:

Despite past credit challenges, I can demonstrate current financial stability:

- Current monthly income: $[Amount]
- Employment: [Job title] at [Company] for [time period]
- Rental history: [Previous rental history]
- Savings: $[Amount] in savings for emergencies

Supporting Documentation:

I have provided the following documentation with my application:

□ Recent pay stubs

□ Bank statements

□ Employment verification letter

□ Previous landlord references

□ Personal references

Additional Considerations:

- I am willing to provide an additional security deposit if needed
- I can provide a co-signer if required
- I am available for additional income verification
- I can provide proof of renters insurance

Character References:

[List 2-3 references who can speak to your character and reliability]

1. [Name], [Relationship], [Phone Number]

2. [Name], [Relationship], [Phone Number]

3. [Name], [Relationship], [Phone Number]

I understand that credit history is important, but I hope you will consider the context of my situation and my current financial stability. I am committed to being a responsible tenant and taking excellent care of your property.

Please let me know if you need any additional information or documentation. I can be reached at [phone number] or [email address].

Thank you for your consideration.

Sincerely,

[Your Signature]

[Your Printed Name]

INSURANCE CREDIT SCORE DISPUTE LETTER

[Your Name]

[Your Address]

[City, State, ZIP Code]

[Date]

[Insurance Company Name]

[Underwriting Department]

[Address]

[City, State, ZIP Code]

Re: Policy Number: [Policy Number]

Credit Score Rating Dispute

Dear Underwriting Department:

I am writing to dispute the credit-based insurance score that was used to determine my insurance rates. I believe the credit information used contains errors that have resulted in higher premiums than I should be paying.

Policy Information:

- Policyholder: [Your Name]

- Policy Number: [Number]

- Policy Type: [Auto/Home/etc.]

- Current Premium: $[Amount]

- Effective Date: [Date]

Credit Score Issues:

I have recently obtained a copy of my credit report and identified the following errors that likely affected my insurance credit score:

1. [Specific error]

   - Impact: [How this affects credit score]

- Resolution: [What you've done to correct it]

2. [Specific error]

   - Impact: [How this affects credit score]

   - Resolution: [What you've done to correct it]

Updated Credit Information:

I have enclosed:

□ Updated credit report showing corrections

□ Credit score improvement documentation

□ Dispute resolution letters from credit bureaus

□ Payment history documentation

Request for Rate Adjustment:

Based on the corrected credit information, I am requesting:

1. Re-evaluation of my insurance credit score

2. Adjustment of my premium rates to reflect accurate credit information

3. Refund of overpaid premiums if applicable

4. Updated policy documents reflecting new rates

Current Credit Status:

- Updated credit score: [Score]

- Credit report date: [Date]

- Significant improvements: [List key improvements]

I understand that insurance companies use credit information as one factor in determining rates, and I want to ensure that accurate information is being used for my policy.

Please let me know what additional documentation you need and when I can expect a response regarding the rate adjustment.

You can reach me at [phone number] or [email address] if you have any questions.

Thank you for your prompt attention to this matter.

Sincerely,

[Your Signature]

[Your Printed Name]

DIVORCE CREDIT PROTECTION LETTER

[Your Name]

[Your Address]

[City, State, ZIP Code]

[Date]

[Creditor Name]

[Customer Service Department]

[Address]

[City, State, ZIP Code]

Re: Account Number: [Account Number]

Divorce Proceedings - Account Responsibility

Dear Customer Service:

I am writing to inform you that I am currently involved in divorce proceedings and to clarify responsibility for the above-referenced account during this process.

Account Information:

- Primary Account Holder: [Name]

- Joint Account Holder: [Spouse Name]

- Account Type: [Credit Card/Loan/etc.]

- Current Balance: $[Amount]

Divorce Status:

- Divorce filed: [Date]

- Expected completion: [Date]

- Case Number: [Number]

- Attorney: [Attorney Name and Contact]

Account Responsibility:

According to the divorce proceedings:

□ I will be responsible for this account

□ My spouse will be responsible for this account

□ The account will be closed and balance split

□ The account responsibility is still being determined

Immediate Requests:

1. Please flag this account due to ongoing divorce proceedings
2. Do not allow any new charges without my explicit written consent
3. Send all correspondence to my current address only
4. Do not discuss account information with my spouse
5. Require written authorization from me for any account changes

Documentation:

I have enclosed:

□ Copy of divorce filing

□ Copy of temporary court orders

□ Change of address form

□ Authorization for account restrictions

Contact Information:

Please update your records with my current contact information:

- Address: [Your New Address]
- Phone: [Your Phone Number]
- Email: [Your Email]

Future Changes:

I will provide you with copies of the final divorce decree once it is finalized, which will specify the final responsibility for this account.

Until the divorce is finalized, please:

- Continue sending statements to my address

- Require my written authorization for any account modifications

- Maintainthe account in good standing according to current terms

- Contact me immediately if there are any issues or unauthorized changes

Legal Notice:

Please be advised that any actions taken on this account without proper authorization during the divorce proceedings may be subject to review by the court. I am committed to meeting my legal obligations while protecting my financial interests during this transition.

If you have any questions or need clarification about these requests, please contact me at [phone number] or my attorney at [attorney phone number].

Thank you for your cooperation during this difficult time.

Sincerely,

[Your Signature]

[Your Printed Name]

MILITARY SCRA BENEFITS REQUEST LETTER

[Your Name]

[Military Address]

[City, State, ZIP Code]

[Date]

[Creditor Name]

[Customer Service Department]

[Address]

[City, State, ZIP Code]

Re: Account Number: [Account Number]

Request for SCRA Benefits

Dear Sir or Madam:

I am writing to request benefits under the Servicemembers Civil Relief Act (SCRA) for the above-referenced account. I am an active duty service member and am entitled to certain protections and benefits under federal law.

Military Service Information:

- Name: [Your Name]

- Rank: [Your Rank]

- Service Number: [Service Number]

- Branch: [Army/Navy/Air Force/Marines/Coast Guard]

- Unit: [Unit Designation]

- Duty Station: [Current Assignment]

Service Dates:

- Active Duty Start Date: [Date]

- Expected End of Service: [Date]

- Deployment Status: [If applicable]

Account Information:

- Account Number: [Number]
- Account Type: [Credit Card/Auto Loan/Mortgage/etc.]
- Current Balance: $[Amount]
- Current Interest Rate: [Rate]%
- Monthly Payment: $[Amount]

SCRA Benefits Requested:

□ Interest rate reduction to 6% (for pre-service debt)

□ Stay or postponement of proceedings

□ Protection against default judgment

□ Lease termination rights

□ Foreclosure protection

□ Other: [Specify]

Pre-Service Debt Verification:

This account was opened on [date], which was [before/during] my active duty service. Under SCRA Section 207, interest rates on debts incurred before military service should be reduced to 6% upon written request.

Financial Impact of Military Service:

My military service has affected my ability to meet financial obligations due to:

□ Reduced income compared to civilian employment

□ Deployment to combat zone

□ Permanent change of station (PCS) orders

□ Family separation costs

□ Other military-related financial impacts

Documentation Provided:

I have enclosed the following documentation:

□ Copy of military orders

□ Letter from commanding officer

□ Military ID copy

□ Current Leave and Earnings Statement (LES)

Contact Information:

Military Address: [Address]

Civilian Phone: [Phone Number]

Military Email: [Email]

Emergency Contact: [Name and Phone]

Request for Response:

Please confirm receipt of this request and provide:

1. Written acknowledgment of SCRA benefits application
2. Adjusted payment terms if applicable
3. New account statements reflecting changes
4. Timeline for implementation of benefits

I understand my rights under the SCRA and request that you apply all applicable protections to my account immediately.

Thank you for supporting our military personnel. Please contact me if you need any additional documentation.

Sincerely,

[Your Signature]

[Your Printed Name]

[Rank and Service Branch]

SENIOR CITIZEN FINANCIAL PROTECTION LETTER

[Your Name]

[Your Address]

[City, State, ZIP Code]

[Date]

[Financial Institution Name]

[Customer Service Department]

[Address]

[City, State, ZIP Code]

Re: Account Number: [Account Number]

Senior Citizen Protection Request

Dear Customer Service Manager:

I am writing as a senior citizen (age [age]) to request additional protections and considerations for my account based on my age and potential vulnerability to financial exploitation.

Account Holder Information:

- Name: [Your Name]

- Date of Birth: [DOB]

- Age: [Age]

- Account Numbers: [List all accounts]

- Relationship with Institution: [Years as customer]

Requested Protections:

1. Transaction Monitoring: Please flag unusual or large transactions for verification

2. Third-Party Contact: I authorize you to contact [trusted person name] at [phone number] if suspicious activity is detected

3. Hold Periods: Please implement longer hold periods on large withdrawals to allow verification

4. In-Person Requirements: Require in-person verification for account changes over $[amount]

5. Trusted Person Access: I designate [name] as a trusted contact for account verification purposes

Trusted Contact Information:

- Name: [Trusted Person Name]

- Relationship: [Son/Daughter/etc.]

- Phone: [Phone Number]

- Address: [Address]

- Email: [Email]

Specific Concerns:

I am requesting these protections because:

□ I have been targeted by scammers in the past

□ I want to protect against potential cognitive decline

□ Family member has expressed concerns about exploitation

□ I live alone and want additional security

□ Other: [Specify]

Account Management Preferences:

- Preferred contact method: [Phone/Mail/Email]

- Best time to contact: [Time period]

- Language preference: [English/Other]

- Communication needs: [Large print/etc.]

Medical Considerations:

□ I have no medical issues affecting financial decisions

□ I have [condition] that may affect my judgment

□ I take medications that may affect cognitive function

□ I have appointed a power of attorney: [Name and contact]

Documentation Enclosed:

□ Copy of ID

□ Power of attorney documents (if applicable)

□ Medical documentation (if relevant)

□ Emergency contact information

Family Notification:

□ I consent to sharing account information with trusted contacts in emergencies

□ I do not consent to sharing information with anyone

□ I consent only under specific circumstances: [Specify]

Regular Review:

I request that these protections be reviewed annually or if my circumstances change. Please contact me on [date] each year to confirm these arrangements.

Emergency Procedures:

In case of emergency, please contact:

1. [Name], [Relationship], [Phone]

2. [Name], [Relationship], [Phone]

3. Local Adult Protective Services: [Phone if known]

Please confirm in writing that these protections have been implemented and provide me with documentation of the safeguards in place.

Thank you for helping to protect senior customers from financial exploitation.

Sincerely,

[Your Signature]

[Your Printed Name]

Witness Signature (if applicable):

____

[Witness Name and Date]

ESTATE CREDIT ACCOUNT NOTIFICATION LETTER

[Your Name/Estate Representative]

[Your Address]

[City, State, ZIP Code]

[Date]

[Creditor Name]

[Customer Service Department]

[Address]

[City, State, ZIP Code]

Re: Account Number: [Account Number]

Notification of Account Holder Death

Dear Customer Service:

I am writing to notify you of the death of [Deceased Name], who held the above-referenced account with your company.

Deceased Information:

- Full Name: [Deceased Full Name]
- Date of Birth: [DOB]
- Date of Death: [Date of Death]
- Social Security Number: XXX-XX-XXXX
- Account Number: [Account Number]

Estate Representative Information:

- Name: [Your Name]
- Relationship: [Executor/Administrator/Spouse/etc.]
- Address: [Your Address]
- Phone: [Your Phone Number]

- Email: [Your Email]

Legal Documentation:

I have enclosed the following documentation:

□ Certified copy of death certificate

□ Letters of administration/testamentary

□ Court appointment documents

□ Power of attorney (if applicable)

□ Marriage certificate (if spouse)

Account Status Requests:

Please take the following actions immediately:

1. Close the account to prevent new charges
2. Stop all automatic payments and transfers
3. Provide final account statement
4. Calculate final balance owed or refund due
5. Remove authorized users if applicable
6. Stop all collection activities if account is delinquent

Estate Settlement:

Please provide the following information:

- Final account balance as of date of death
- List of all transactions since date of death
- Payoff amount if applicable
- Instructions for estate payment
- Timeline for estate settlement

Authorized Users:

The following authorized users should be removed:

- [Name], [Relationship]

- [Name], [Relationship]

Joint Account Holders:

□ This was an individual account

□ This was a joint account with: [Name]

□ Joint account holder wishes to: [Continue/Close]

Contact Information:

Please update your records to send all correspondence to:

[Your Name]

[Your Address]

[City, State, ZIP Code]

Phone: [Your Phone Number]

Email: [Your Email]

Legal Notice:

Please be advised that any collection activities against the estate must comply with applicable state and federal laws regarding deceased debtors. Do not contact family members who are not responsible for the debt.

Credit Reporting:

Please ensure that the account is properly reported to credit bureaus as "deceased" and remove any negative reporting that may affect surviving family members who were not responsible for this debt.

If you have any questions or need additional documentation, please contact me at [phone number] or my attorney at [attorney phone number].

Thank you for your assistance during this difficult time.

Sincerely,

[Your Signature]

[Your Printed Name]

[Title - Executor/Administrator/etc.]

Appendix B: Credit Score Simulators and Calculators

CREDIT SCORE IMPACT CALCULATOR

Use this calculator to estimate how various credit changes might affect your credit score. Remember that actual score changes depend on your complete credit profile and the specific scoring model used.

Current Credit Profile:

- Current Credit Score: _______

- Number of Credit Cards: _______

- Total Credit Limits: $_______

- Total Balances: $_______

- Current Utilization: _______%

- Number of Late Payments (24 months): _______

- Oldest Account Age: _______ years

- Average Account Age: _______ years

- Number of Hard Inquiries (12 months): _______

UTILIZATION IMPACT CALCULATOR

Current Situation:

- Total Credit Limits: $_______

- Total Current Balances: $_______

- Current Utilization: _______%

Proposed Changes:

- New Total Balances: $_______

- New Utilization: _______%

Estimated Score Impact:

- Utilization 30%+: Potentially -50 to -100 points

- Utilization 10-29%: Potentially -10 to -30 points

- Utilization 1-9%: Optimal range (0 to +20 points)

- Utilization 0%: May reduce score by -5 to -15 points

Your Estimated Change: _______points

PAYMENT HISTORY IMPACT CALCULATOR

Current Late Payments:

- 30 days late: _______ (within 24 months)

- 60 days late: _______ (within 24 months)

- 90+ days late: _______ (within 24 months)

Estimated Score Impact of Late Payments:

- One 30-day late: -60 to -110 points

- One 60-day late: -70 to -130 points

- One 90+ day late: -80 to -150 points

- Multiple recent lates: -100 to -200 points

Recovery Timeline:

- 30-day late: 3-9 months for significant recovery

- 60-day late: 6-12 months for significant recovery

- 90+ day late: 12-24 months for significant recovery

ACCOUNT AGE IMPACT CALCULATOR

Current Account Ages:

1. Account 1: _______ years
2. Account 2: _______ years
3. Account 3: _______ years
4. Account 4: _______ years
5. Account 5: _______ years

Calculations:

- Average Account Age: _______ years

- Oldest Account: _______ years

Estimated Impact of Closing Oldest Account:

- If oldest account closed: New average age = _______ years

- Potential score impact: -5 to -25 points

NEW ACCOUNT IMPACT CALCULATOR

Proposed New Account:

- Type: Credit Card / Auto Loan / Personal Loan / Other

- Credit Limit (if credit card): $_______

Impact Calculations:

Current average age: _______ years

With new account: _______ years

Age reduction: _______ years

Estimated Score Impact:

- New account inquiry: -3 to -7 points (temporary)

- Average age reduction: -2 to -10 points

- Utilization improvement (if credit card): +5 to +20 points

- Net estimated impact: _______ points

CREDIT MIX EVALUATION TOOL

Current Credit Mix:

□ Credit Cards: _______ accounts

□ Auto Loans: _______ accounts

□ Personal Loans: _______ accounts

□ Mortgage: _______ accounts

□ Student Loans: _______ accounts

□ Other Installment: _______ accounts

Credit Mix Scoring:

- Credit cards only: Suboptimal (-5 to -15 points potential)

- Cards + 1 installment type: Good (baseline)

- Cards + 2+ installment types: Excellent (+5 to +15 points potential)

Your Current Mix Score: _______

Recommendations:

□ Add installment loan for better mix

□ Current mix is optimal

□ Consider mortgage for major mix improvement

INQUIRY IMPACT CALCULATOR

Current Inquiries (12 months):

1. _______ (Date: _______)

2. _______ (Date: _______)

3. _______ (Date: _______)

4. _______ (Date: _______)

5. _______ (Date: _______)

Total Recent Inquiries: _______

Estimated Score Impact:

- 0-1 inquiries: Minimal impact (0 to -3 points)

- 2-4 inquiries: Moderate impact (-5 to -15 points)

- 5-10 inquiries: Significant impact (-15 to -40 points)

- 10+ inquiries: Severe impact (-40 to -80 points)

Your Estimated Impact: _______ points

Recovery Timeline:

- Impact decreases after 12 months

- Inquiries fall off report after 24 months

DEBT-TO-INCOME CALCULATOR

Monthly Income:

- Gross monthly income: $_______
- Net monthly income: $_______

Monthly Debt Payments:

- Credit card minimums: $_______
- Auto loan payment: $_______
- Student loan payment: $_______
- Personal loan payment: $_______
- Mortgage payment: $_______
- Other debt payments: $_______

Total Monthly Debt: $_______

Debt-to-Income Ratios:

- DTI Ratio (gross): _______%
- DTI Ratio (net): _______%

DTI Guidelines:

- Under 20%: Excellent
- 20-36%: Good
- 36-50%: Fair (may affect loan approval)
- Over 50%: Poor (likely loan denials)

CREDIT UTILIZATION OPTIMIZER

Individual Card Analysis:

Card 1:

- Limit: $_______

- Balance: $_______
- Utilization: _______%
- Target balance for 10% utilization: $_______
- Target balance for 5% utilization: $_______

Card 2:

- Limit: $_______
- Balance: $_______
- Utilization: _______%
- Target balance for 10% utilization: $_______
- Target balance for 5% utilization: $_______

Card 3:

- Limit: $_______
- Balance: $_______
- Utilization: _______%
- Target balance for 10% utilization: $_______
- Target balance for 5% utilization: $_______

Overall Optimization:

- Current total utilization: _______%
- Target total balance for 10%: $_______
- Target total balance for 5%: $_______
- Amount to pay down: $_______

PERFECT CREDIT TIMELINE CALCULATOR

Starting Point Assessment:

Current credit score: _______

Timeline Estimates by Starting Score:

From 500-579 (Poor):

- To 580-669 (Fair): 6-12 months
- To 670-739 (Good): 12-24 months
- To 740-799 (Very Good): 24-36 months
- To 800-850 (Excellent): 36-48 months

From 580-669 (Fair):

- To 670-739 (Good): 6-12 months
- To 740-799 (Very Good): 12-24 months
- To 800-850 (Excellent): 18-30 months

From 670-739 (Good):

- To 740-799 (Very Good): 3-12 months
- To 800-850 (Excellent): 6-18 months

From 740-799 (Very Good):

- To 800-850 (Excellent): 3-12 months

Your Estimated Timeline:

- Target score: _______
- Estimated time: _______ months
- Target achievement date: _______

Action Items for Faster Improvement:

□ Pay down high utilization cards

- □ Set up automatic payments
- □ Dispute credit report errors
- □ Become authorized user on old account
- □ Consider credit builder loan
- □ Request credit limit increases

BANKRUPTCY RECOVERY CALCULATOR

Bankruptcy Information:

- Bankruptcy type: Chapter 7 / Chapter 13

- Discharge date: _______

- Years since discharge: _______

Recovery Timeline:

Chapter 7 Recovery:

- Year 1: 500-550 score range typical

- Year 2: 550-600 score range typical

- Year 3-4: 600-650 score range typical

- Year 5-7: 650-700+ possible

- After 10 years: Bankruptcy removed from report

Chapter 13 Recovery:

- Year 1: 550-600 score range typical

- Year 2-3: 600-650 score range typical

- Year 4-5: 650-700+ possible

- After 7 years: Bankruptcy removed from report

Your Expected Score Range: _______

CREDIT BUILDING STRATEGY SELECTOR

Your Situation: (Check all that apply)

□ No credit history

□ Poor credit (under 580)

□ Fair credit (580-669)

□ Good credit (670-739)

□ Very good credit (740-799)

□ Excellent credit (800+)

□ Recent bankruptcy

□ Collections accounts

□ High utilization

□ Limited credit mix

Recommended Strategies:

For No Credit History:

1. Secured credit card
2. Credit builder loan
3. Authorized user on family member's account
4. Student credit card (if student)

For Poor Credit:

1. Secured credit card
2. Pay down existing debts
3. Dispute credit report errors
4. Consider debt consolidation

For Fair Credit:

1. Optimize utilization below 10%
2. Request credit limit increases
3. Add installment loan for mix
4. Dispute any remaining errors

For Good Credit and Above:

1. Fine-tune utilization to 1-5%
2. Strategic account management
3. Monitor for errors monthly
4. Consider premium credit cards

Priority Action Items:

1. ______________________
2. ______________________
3. ______________________

CREDIT CARD PAYOFF CALCULATOR

Credit Card Details:

Card 1:

- Balance: $_______

- Interest Rate: _______%

- Minimum Payment: $_______

Card 2:

- Balance: $_______

- Interest Rate: _______%

- Minimum Payment: $_______

Card 3:

- Balance: $_______

- Interest Rate: _______%

- Minimum Payment: $_______

Payoff Strategies:

Minimum Payments Only:

Total monthly minimum: $_______

Estimated payoff time: _______ months

Total interest paid: $_______

Debt Avalanche (Highest Interest First):

Extra payment available: $_______

Order of payoff:

1. Card ___: _______ months

2. Card ___: _______ months

3. Card ___: _______ months

Total time: _______ months

Total interest saved: $_______

Debt Snowball (Lowest Balance First):

Order of payoff:

1. Card ___: _______ months

2. Card ___: _______ months

3. Card ___: _______ months

Total time: _______ months

Psychological benefit: Faster early wins

Utilization Impact of Payoff:

Current utilization: _______%

After paying off Card 1:

New utilization: _______%

Estimated score increase: _______ points

After paying off Card 2:

New utilization: _______%

Estimated score increase: _______ points

After paying off all cards:

New utilization: 0%

Estimated score increase: _______ points

CREDIT LIMIT INCREASE IMPACT

Current Situation:

Total credit limits: $_______

Total balances: $_______

Current utilization: _______%

Proposed Increases:

Card 1 increase: $_______ (from $_______ to $_______)

Card 2 increase: $_______ (from $_______ to $_______)

Card 3 increase: $_______ (from $_______ to $_______)

New totals:

New total limits: $_______

Same balances: $_______

New utilization: _______%

Estimated Score Impact:

Utilization improvement: _______ percentage points

Estimated score increase: _______ points

SUCCESS PROBABILITY CALCULATOR

Rate your situation in each area (1-10 scale):

Payment History: _______ /10

(10 = perfect payments, 1 = multiple recent lates)

Utilization Management: _______ /10

(10 = under 5% utilization, 1 = over 90% utilization)

Account Age: _______ /10

(10 = average age 10+ years, 1 = all accounts under 1 year)

Credit Mix: _______ /10

(10 = diverse mix including mortgage, 1 = only credit cards)

Inquiry Management: _______ /10

(10 = no inquiries in 12 months, 1 = 10+ recent inquiries)

Total Score: _______ /50

Credit Health Assessment:

- 40-50: Excellent credit management
- 30-39: Good credit management
- 20-29: Fair credit management (improvement needed)
- 10-19: Poor credit management (major work needed)
- Under 10: Critical credit situation

Your Assessment: _______

Improvement Priority:

Focus on your lowest-scoring area first for maximum impact.

RAPID IMPROVEMENT ESTIMATOR

30-Day Improvement Potential:

Available Actions:

□ Pay down credit cards by $_______

□ Dispute _______ errors on credit report

□ Request _______ credit limit increases

□ Become authorized user on _______ account(s)

□ Pay off collections account for $_______

Estimated 30-Day Impact:

- Credit card paydown: +_______ points
- Error removals: +_______ points
- Limit increases: +_______ points
- Authorized user addition: +_______ points
- Collections payoff: +_______ points

Total Estimated Increase: _______ points

90-Day Improvement Potential:

Additional Available Actions:

□ Open credit builder loan

□ Negotiate pay-for-delete agreements

□ Complete goodwill letter campaign

□ Establish new credit relationships

□ Pay off additional debts

Estimated 90-Day Impact:

Total from 30-day actions: _______ points

Additional 90-day actions: _______ points

Total Estimated Increase: _______ points

SCORE GOAL TRACKER

Starting Information:

- Starting score: _______
- Starting date: _______
- Target score: _______
- Target date: _______

Milestone Tracking:

Month 1:

- Target score: _______
- Actual score: _______
- Variance: _______

Month 2:

- Target score: _______
- Actual score: _______
- Variance: _______

Month 3:

- Target score: _______
- Actual score: _______
- Variance: _______

Month 6:

- Target score: _______
- Actual score: _______
- Variance: _______

Month 12:

- Target score: _______
- Actual score: _______
- Variance: _______

Final Goal:

- Target score: _______
- Actual score: _______
- Goal achieved: Yes / No
- Days to achievement: _______

MAINTENANCE CALCULATOR

Perfect Credit Maintenance Costs:

Monthly Monitoring:

- Credit monitoring service: $______
- Identity theft protection: $______
- Financial planning apps: $______

Annual Costs:

- Credit report fees: $______
- Professional consultation: $______
- Credit building products: $______

Total Annual Investment: $______

Return on Investment:

Annual Savings from Perfect Credit:

- Lower interest rates: $______
- Better insurance rates: $______
- Avoided fees: $______
- Employment advantages: $______

Total Annual Benefit: $______

Net Annual Benefit: $______

(Total benefit minus total investment)

ROI Percentage: ______%

Lifetime Value of Perfect Credit:

Annual net benefit: $______

Years of maintaining perfect credit: ______

Total Lifetime Value: $_______

This represents the monetary value of maintaining perfect credit throughout your lifetime, not including intangible benefits like reduced stress and enhanced opportunities.

Appendix C: Credit Law and Rights Summary

FAIR CREDIT REPORTING ACT (FCRA) - KEY PROVISIONS

Your Rights Under the FCRA:

1. Right to Your Credit Report

- You can obtain one free credit report annually from each credit bureau

- Additional free reports available if you're denied credit, insurance, or employment

- Right to purchase additional reports at reasonable cost

2. Right to Dispute Inaccurate Information

- Credit bureaus must investigate disputes within 30 days (45 days for complex disputes)

- If information cannot be verified, it must be removed

- You must be notified of investigation results in writing

3. Right to Add Consumer Statements

- You can add 100-word explanatory statements to your credit report

- Statements must remain on file and be included with report distributions

- Useful for explaining circumstances behind negative information

4. Information Time Limits

- Most negative information: 7 years maximum

- Bankruptcies: 10 years maximum (7 years for Chapter 13)

- Unpaid tax liens: Until paid plus 7 years

- Criminal convictions: No time limit

- Inquiries: 2 years maximum

5. Consent Requirements

- Employers must get written permission to check credit

- Insurance companies and creditors can check without permission

- Identity theft victims have special protections

6. Accuracy and Investigation Standards

- Credit bureaus must follow reasonable procedures for accuracy
- Must maintain reasonable procedures to limit distribution
- Required to provide information to data furnishers about disputes

FCRA Damages and Remedies:

Willful Violations:

- Actual damages (financial losses)
- Statutory damages: $100 to $1,000 per violation
- Punitive damages (no specific limit)
- Attorney fees and court costs

Negligent Violations:

- Actual damages only
- Attorney fees and court costs

Criminal Penalties:

- Fines up to $5,000
- Imprisonment up to 1 year
- For obtaining credit information under false pretenses

Key FCRA Section References:

- Section 604: Permissible purposes for credit reports
- Section 605: Requirements for reporting obsolete information
- Section 611: Procedure in case of disputed accuracy
- Section 615: Requirements on users of consumer reports
- Section 616: Civil liability for willful noncompliance

- Section 617: Civil liability for negligent noncompliance

FAIR DEBT COLLECTION PRACTICES ACT (FDCPA) - KEY PROVISIONS

Who Is Covered:

- Third-party debt collectors (not original creditors)
- Debt collection agencies
- Attorneys who regularly collect debts
- Companies that buy debts for collection

Prohibited Practices:

Communication Restrictions:

- Cannot contact you before 8 AM or after 9 PM
- Cannot contact you at work if employer prohibits it
- Cannot contact third parties except to locate you
- Must stop calling if you request it in writing
- Cannot contact you if you have an attorney

Harassment and Abuse:

- Cannot use threats of violence
- Cannot use obscene or profane language
- Cannot repeatedly call to harass
- Cannot publish your name as refusing to pay debt
- Cannot call without identifying themselves

False or Misleading Representations:

- Cannot falsely claim to be attorneys or government representatives
- Cannot misrepresent amount owed
- Cannot falsely threaten arrest or legal action
- Cannot claim documents are legal forms when they aren't

- Cannot falsely claim you've committed a crime

Unfair Practices:

- Cannot collect amounts not owed
- Cannot deposit post-dated checks early
- Cannot threaten to take property unless legally able
- Cannot contact you by postcard
- Cannot use deceptive company names

Required Disclosures:

Within 5 days of first contact, collectors must send written notice containing:

- Amount of debt
- Name of original creditor
- Statement of your right to dispute the debt
- Statement that if you don't dispute within 30 days, debt will be assumed valid
- Statement of right to request original creditor information

Your Rights Under FDCPA:

Dispute Rights:

- Right to dispute debt within 30 days of notice
- Collector must stop collection until verification provided
- Right to request information about original creditor

Communication Control:

- Right to request no contact at work
- Right to request all communication cease
- Right to request communication only through attorney

Validation Rights:

- Right to request debt verification
- Right to see proof you owe the debt
- Right to documentation of debt ownership

FDCPA Damages:

- Actual damages (financial losses)
- Statutory damages up to $1,000 per violation
- Attorney fees and court costs
- Class action damages capped at lesser of $500,000 or 1% of collector's net worth

FAIR CREDIT BILLING ACT (FCBA) - KEY PROVISIONS

Billing Error Rights:

What Constitutes a Billing Error:

- Charges not made by you or authorized users
- Charges for goods/services not received
- Charges for incorrect amounts
- Charges for goods/services not delivered as agreed
- Mathematical or computational errors
- Failure to credit payments or returns
- Charges for which you need clarification

Dispute Procedure:

- Must dispute in writing within 60 days of statement
- Include account information and error description
- Send to special billing inquiry address (not payment address)
- Creditor must acknowledge dispute within 30 days
- Must resolve within 90 days (two billing cycles)

Creditor Responsibilities During Dispute:

- Cannot report debt as delinquent to credit bureaus
- Cannot close account or restrict access during dispute
- Cannot charge interest on disputed amount
- Cannot threaten credit rating damage
- Must provide written explanation of investigation results

Your Rights During Investigation:

- Right to withhold payment on disputed amount

- Right to continue using account for undisputed charges
- Right to receive copies of relevant documents
- Protection from credit damage during dispute period

Resolution Requirements:

- If error found: Must correct and credit account
- If no error found: Must provide written explanation and proof
- You have 10 days to respond if you disagree with resolution
- Must report dispute to credit bureaus if you continue to disagree

Electronic Fund Transfer Act (EFTA) Rights:

Error Resolution for Electronic Transfers:

- Must report errors within 60 days of statement
- Bank must investigate within 10 business days
- Provisional credit required if investigation takes longer
- Final resolution within 45 days (90 days for new accounts)

Liability Limits:

- $0 if reported before unauthorized use
- $50 if reported within 2 business days
- $500 if reported within 60 days
- Unlimited if not reported within 60 days

EQUAL CREDIT OPPORTUNITY ACT (ECOA) - KEY PROVISIONS

Prohibited Discrimination:

Creditors cannot discriminate based on:

- Race or color
- Religion
- National origin
- Sex or gender
- Marital status
- Age (if 18 or older)
- Receipt of public assistance
- Good faith exercise of CCPA rights

Specific Protections:

Age Discrimination:

- Cannot discriminate against elderly applicants
- Cannot close accounts solely due to age
- Cannot require cosigners solely due to age
- Cannot refuse to consider retirement income

Marital Status Protections:

- Cannot require information about spouse unless:
  - Spouse will be liable for account
  - You live in community property state
  - You're relying on spouse's income
- Cannot change terms- Cannot change terms due to marital status change
- Cannot require spouse's signature unless spouse is liable

Income Discrimination:

- Must consider all reliable income including:
  - Part-time employment
  - Social Security benefits
  - Disability payments
  - Unemployment compensation
  - Retirement benefits
  - Alimony and child support (if you choose to disclose)

Application Requirements:

- Creditors must notify you of action within 30 days
- If denied, must provide specific reasons or notice of right to request reasons
- Cannot discourage applications based on protected characteristics
- Must evaluate each applicant individually

Credit History Rights:

- Right to have credit history reported in both spouses' names
- Right to maintain separate credit histories
- Right to have accounts reported under maiden name or married name
- Protection against spouse's bad credit affecting individual applications

ECOA Remedies:

- Actual damages (financial losses)
- Punitive damages up to $10,000 (individual cases)
- Equitable relief (requiring creditor to grant credit)
- Attorney fees and court costs
- Class action damages capped at lesser of $500,000 or 1% of creditor's net worth

Required Notices:

- Adverse action notices must include:
  - Specific reasons for denial
  - ECOA notice of rights
  - Name and address of federal agency regulating creditor
  - Right to free credit report if credit report was factor

CREDIT REPAIR ORGANIZATIONS ACT (CROA) - KEY PROVISIONS

Prohibited Practices:

Credit repair companies cannot:

- Charge fees before completing promised services
- Make false claims about their services
- Advise you to make false statements to creditors or credit bureaus
- Fail to inform you of your rights
- Fail to inform you that you can dispute credit information yourself for free

Required Disclosures:

Before signing contract, credit repair companies must give you:

- Written contract detailing services and costs
- Statement of your rights under CROA
- Three-day cancellation notice
- Disclosure that you can perform dispute services yourself

Contract Requirements:

Written contracts must include:

- Description of services to be performed
- Time frame for achieving results
- Total cost of services
- Company's business address
- Right to cancel within 3 business days

Your Rights Under CROA:

- Right to cancel contract within 3 business days
- Right to sue for damages if law is violated

- Right to actual damages, punitive damages, and attorney fees
- Protection from advance fee payment requirements
- Right to receive services before payment

State Law Variations:

Many states have additional protections:

- Licensing requirements for credit repair companies
- Bonding requirements
- Additional prohibited practices
- Extended cancellation periods
- Enhanced damage remedies

Red Flags to Avoid:

- Companies demanding payment upfront
- Guaranteeing specific score improvements
- Advising you to dispute accurate information
- Telling you not to contact credit bureaus directly
- Refusing to explain your legal rights
- Operating without proper licensing

CONSUMER FINANCIAL PROTECTION BUREAU (CFPB) OVERSIGHT

CFPB Authority:

The CFPB supervises and regulates:

- Banks with assets over $10 billion
- Credit unions with assets over $10 billion
- Nonbank mortgage companies
- Private student loan companies
- Payday lenders
- Large debt collectors
- Credit reporting companies

Complaint Process:

1. Submit complaint online at consumerfinance.gov
2. CFPB forwards complaint to company
3. Company has 15 days to respond
4. You review company's response
5. CFPB monitors for patterns and may take enforcement action

Types of Issues CFPB Handles:

- Credit reporting problems
- Debt collection issues
- Mortgage problems
- Credit card disputes
- Student loan complaints
- Bank account issues
- Auto loan problems

- Personal loan disputes

CFPB Enforcement Powers:

- Issue civil investigative demands
- Conduct examinations
- Require corrective action
- Impose civil money penalties
- Issue cease and desist orders
- Seek restitution for consumers

Consumer Education Resources:

- Ask CFPB database of common questions
- Educational guides and tools
- Financial coaching resources
- Regulatory implementation guidance
- Market monitoring reports

STATE CONSUMER PROTECTION LAWS

Variations by State:

Different states provide varying levels of protection:

Enhanced Protections (Examples):

- California: Comprehensive consumer privacy laws
- New York: Strong debt collection regulations
- Texas: Extensive credit services organization regulations
- Florida: Enhanced elderly protection provisions

Key State Law Areas:

Debt Collection:

- Additional restrictions on collector behavior
- Enhanced damages for violations
- Extended statute of limitations for lawsuits
- Special protections for vulnerable populations

Credit Repair:

- Licensing requirements
- Bonding and insurance requirements
- Extended cancellation periods
- Enhanced disclosure requirements

Identity Theft:

- Credit freeze laws
- Identity theft passport programs
- Enhanced law enforcement cooperation
- Victim assistance programs

Privacy Protection:

- Credit report access restrictions
- Social Security number protection
- Data breach notification requirements
- Identity theft prevention measures

How to Find Your State Laws:

- Contact state attorney general's office
- Visit state consumer protection agency website
- Consult with local consumer law attorney
- Check state banking department resources

Interaction with Federal Laws:

- State laws can provide additional protections
- Cannot provide less protection than federal law
- Some federal laws preempt state laws
- Consumers get benefit of strongest applicable law

BANKRUPTCY LAW AND CREDIT RIGHTS

Automatic Stay Protections:

Upon bankruptcy filing, automatic stay immediately stops:

- Debt collection calls and letters
- Foreclosure proceedings
- Repossession attempts
- Wage garnishment
- Utility disconnections
- Most lawsuits against you

Chapter 7 Bankruptcy:

- Liquidation of non-exempt assets
- Discharge of most unsecured debts
- Process typically takes 4-6 months
- Credit report impact: 10 years
- Immediate debt relief for qualifying debts

Chapter 13 Bankruptcy:

- Reorganization with 3-5 year payment plan
- Keep property while catching up on payments
- Discharge remaining debts after plan completion
- Credit report impact: 7 years
- May be better for credit recovery

Debts That Survive Bankruptcy:

- Most student loans
- Recent taxes

- Child support and alimony

- Criminal fines and restitution

- Debts from fraud or willful injury

Post-Bankruptcy Credit Rights:

- Right to rebuild credit immediately after discharge

- Protection from discrimination by government agencies

- Right to honest credit reporting (marked as "discharged in bankruptcy")

- Protection from attempts to collect discharged debts

Reaffirmation Agreements:

- Voluntary agreements to keep paying certain debts

- Must be filed with bankruptcy court

- Can be canceled within 60 days

- Court must approve if not represented by attorney

Credit Report Accuracy After Bankruptcy:

- Individual accounts should show "included in bankruptcy"

- Balances should show zero after discharge

- Cannot show as currently delinquent

- Right to dispute inaccurate post-bankruptcy reporting

MILITARY SERVICE MEMBERS' RIGHTS

Servicemembers Civil Relief Act (SCRA):

Pre-Service Debt Protection:

- Interest rate reduction to 6% maximum on pre-service debts
- Applies to all types of debt incurred before active duty
- Must request protection in writing
- Protection continues throughout active duty period

Court Proceedings Protection:

- Right to stay (postpone) civil court proceedings
- Protection from default judgments
- Right to reopen default judgments under certain conditions
- Protection applies to both plaintiff and defendant roles

Foreclosure Protection:

- Foreclosure proceedings stayed during active duty plus 9 months
- Applies to mortgages originated before military service
- Court approval required for foreclosure during protected period
- Additional state law protections may apply

Lease Termination Rights:

- Right to terminate residential leases for PCS orders or deployment
- Right to terminate auto leases under certain circumstances
- 30-day written notice required
- Protection from early termination penalties

Credit and Financial Protections:

- Protection from adverse credit reporting during deployment

- Right to request payment deferrals
- Protection from repossession without court order
- Special protections for military families

Military Lending Act (MLA):

- 36% interest rate cap on certain loans to military families
- Prohibition on mandatory arbitration clauses
- Prohibition on certain fees and charges
- Protection from vehicle title surrender requirements

Implementation Requirements:

- Creditors must check military status before taking adverse action
- Must honor valid requests for SCRA benefits
- Violations subject to federal penalties and private lawsuits
- State attorneys general can enforce on behalf of service members

IDENTITY THEFT PROTECTION LAWS

Fair and Accurate Credit Transactions Act (FACTA):

Identity Theft Provisions:

- Right to place fraud alerts on credit reports
- Extended fraud alerts last 7 years for identity theft victims
- Business must verify identity before granting credit with fraud alert
- Right to free credit reports when fraud alert is placed

Fraud Alert Types:

- Initial fraud alert: 90 days, renewable
- Extended fraud alert: 7 years for identity theft victims
- Active duty alert: 1 year for deployed military personnel
- All alerts are free and must be honored by all three bureaus

Red Flags Rule:

- Financial institutions must implement identity theft prevention programs
- Must detect warning signs of identity theft
- Must respond appropriately to suspected identity theft
- Applies to any business that extends credit or opens accounts

FTC Identity Theft Resources:

- IdentityTheft.gov for reporting and recovery planning
- Identity Theft Report for enhanced victim rights
- Sample letters and documents for recovery
- Step-by-step recovery guidance

State Identity Theft Laws:

Most states provide additional protections:

- Credit freeze rights (now federally mandated)
- Identity theft passport programs
- Enhanced criminal penalties
- Victim assistance programs
- Police report requirements and procedures

Identity Theft Recovery Rights:

- Right to place security freeze on credit reports
- Right to obtain identity theft report from FTC
- Enhanced dispute rights for fraudulent accounts
- Right to stop debt collection on identity theft accounts
- Protection from being required to pay debts from identity theft

Credit Freeze Rights:

- Right to place security freeze on credit reports
- Freeze prevents new credit accounts from being opened
- Must be lifted temporarily for legitimate credit applications
- Free for all consumers as of September 2018
- Can be placed and lifted online, by phone, or by mail

Documentation Requirements:

For extended fraud alerts and freezes, may need:

- Identity theft report
- Police report
- Affidavit of identity theft
- Proof of identity
- Proof of address

This comprehensive legal framework provides multiple layers of protection for consumers dealing with credit issues, identity theft, debt collection, and financial discrimination. Understanding these rights empowers consumers to take appropriate action when violations occur and to seek proper remedies through legal channels when necessary.

www.ingramcontent.com/pod-product-compliance
Lightning Source LLC
LaVergne TN
LVHW082013200926
848481LV00010B/2852
9798349508127